THE
WORLD
OF
HUMANISM

1453·1517

BY MYRON P. GILMORE

HARVARD UNIVERSITY

HARPER TORCHBOOKS

HARPER & ROW, PUBLISHERS • NEW YORK

THE WORLD OF HUMANISM, 1453-1517

Copyright 1952, by Harper & Row, Publishers, Incorporated
Printed in the United States of America

This book was originally published in 1952 by Harper & Brothers in The Rise of Modern Europe series edited by William L. Langer.

First HARPER TORCHBOOK edition published 1962, by
Harper & Row, Publishers, Incorporated
New York & Evanston.

Library of Congress catalog card number: 52-11685

To
SHEILA

. . . homo solus in entibus tenet medium corruptibilium et in-corruptibilium, propter quod recte a philosophis adsimilatur horizonti qui est medium duorum hemisphaeorum.

. . . man alone among beings occupies the dividing line be-tween the corruptible and the incorruptible on account of which he is rightly compared by philosophers to the horizon which is the dividing line between two hemispheres.

—DANTE, *De monarchia,* III, 16,18

TABLE OF CONTENTS

vii

ILLUSTRATIONS

The illustrations, grouped in a separate section, will be found following page 110

ix

INTRODUCTION

OUR age of specialization produces an almost incredible amount of monographic research in all fields of human knowledge. So great is the mass of this material that even the professional scholar cannot keep abreast of the contributions in anything but a restricted part of his general subject. In all branches of learning the need for intelligent synthesis is now more urgent than ever before, and this need is felt by the layman even more acutely than by the scholar. He cannot hope to read the products of microscopic research or to keep up with the changing interpretations of experts, unless new knowledge and new viewpoints are made accessible to him by those who make it their business to be informed and who are competent to speak with authority.

These volumes, published under the general title of *The Rise of Modern Europe,* are designed primarily to give the general reader and student a reliable survey of European history written by experts in various branches of that vast subject. In consonance with the current broad conception of the scope of history, they attempt to go beyond a merely political-military narrative, and to lay stress upon social, economic, religious, scientific and artistic developments. The minutely detailed, chronological approach is to some extent sacrificed in the effort to emphasize the dominant factors and to set forth their interrelationships. At the same time the division of European history into national histories has been abandoned and wherever possible attention has been focused upon larger forces common to the whole of European civilization. These are the broad lines on which this history as a whole has been laid out. The individual volumes are integral parts of the larger scheme, but they are intended also to stand as independent units, each the work of a scholar well qualified to treat the period covered by his book. Each volume contains about fifty illustrations selected from the mass of contemporary pictorial material. All noncontemporary illustrations have been excluded on principle. The bibliographical note appended to each volume is designed to facilitate further study of special aspects touched upon in the text. In general every effort has been made to give the reader a clear idea of the main movements in European history, to embody the monographic contributions of research workers, and to present the material in a forceful and vivid manner.

Chronologically the present volume covers the period commonly known as the Renaissance, or at least the Italian Renaissance. Professor Gilmore has interpreted the period as that of the flowering of humanism and has examined what that bold and brilliant expression of the European intellect meant in terms not only of the analysis of traditional patterns, but also of the search for ever broader knowledge and understanding. Although this fascinating age was above all else an age of expanding horizons in the world of thought as in the world of action, the forces which molded the past contributed also to the emergent culture of modern Europe. Professor Gilmore has skillfully traced this interplay of the old and the new. Furthermore, in selecting his illustrations he has eschewed the familiar masterpieces of Renaissance painting, sculpture and architecture and has laid the emphasis on less known but highly instructive examples. His volume provides a fresh and altogether admirable survey of a perennially alluring period.

WILLIAM L. LANGER

PREFACE

LORD ACTON's often-quoted advice to study problems not periods has never been more than partially heeded. Analysis and synthesis cannot be kept in entirely separate compartments. Every attempt to solve a problem looks toward a judgment on a period and every description of a period not only incorporates answers to old problems but compels the formulation of new ones. Even though the effort to be comprehensive achieves no more than the putting together of separate portions of constitutional, economic, political or intellectual history, the result must be different from one dominated by the discipline of a particular set of traditional problems. Indeed one of the justifications for attempting to summarize as a whole the characteristics of any epoch in the history of civilization, no matter how arbitrarily defined, is that such an attempt raises more questions than it answers and opens to the student lines of inquiry which might not otherwise have been suggested.

On the other hand we all know that attemps to find unity and meaning in a very large and complex area of human activities may be undertaken too lightly and carried too far. Too easy an appeal to a conceptual scheme becomes a substitute for thought rather than a further stimulus. Histories of the period with which this volume is concerned well illustrate both the good and the bad effects of a formula. Defined with varying chronological limits, the age of the Renaissance has been perhaps more than any other subjected to the search for a single common denominator, the unique and fundamental change whose effects could be perceived in every department of human activity. Burckhardt's famous generalizations opened new horizons and had a measurable effect on the whole subsequent course of historical thinking, but nearly a century and many thousands of pages later we can think of many instances where the well-known formula has been statically applied and where it has obstructed rather than advanced our understanding of particular phenomena.

Partly because of these doubts and partly because of the arbitrary chronological limits of this volume which fit few if any definitions of the Renaissance, I have not been primarily concerned with "the problem of the Renaissance" or the "periodic concept," interesting as these subjects are to historian and philosopher alike. I have rather concentrated on the analysis of certain more specific problems including some attempts to suggest relationships between traditionally distinct subjects of historical investigation. The categories into which we divide the totality of human thought and action like economics, politics, science and art are frequently arbitrary and in some concrete cases of application meaningless. Nevertheless just as we learn more about a period by questioning the arbitrary dates which have been accepted or imposed as its chronological limits, so we may also learn by asking questions about the relationship, for example, between what we call politics and what we call economics, however conventional our definition of these terms may be. Subjects of this kind are not so broad as attempts to contribute a new definition of individualism, yet they may be broad enough to enlarge our understanding of both problems and periods. This particular inquiry has frequently failed to produce answers of the kind it sought, but the course of the investigation has at least been educational for the investigator.

The list of my obligations is long and would be longer if it could include everyone who has contributed to the making of this book. I am first of all indebted to Harvard University for grants for secretarial assistance from the Milton and Clark Funds and from the Harvard Fund for Advanced Research.

The staffs of the Widener and Houghton Libraries and the Fogg Museum of Art have given me unfailing co-operation and assistance.

Colleagues and friends have made many contributions. Crane Brinton, Elting Morison, David Owen and Robert Wolff read the manuscript in whole or in part and made valuable suggestions. John Fairbank acquainted me with the literature on the Chinese voyages in the sixteenth century. Hans Baron gave me an opportunity to read his forthcoming articles on political developments in fifteenth-century Italy. To Felix Gilbert I owe a particular debt of gratitude. He gave to the entire manuscript the benefit of his deep knowledge of all aspects of the period. None of these individuals is of course responsible for the general views expressed or for errors and faults which remain.

For helpful suggestions in assembling illustrations I am indebted to I. Bernard Cohen, Philip Hofer, Jacob Rosenberg, Arnold Weinburger, Robert Wolff and the staff of the Boston Museum of Fine Arts. Mrs. Joan Braverman Pinck performed invaluable services in the work of selecting and preparing the illustrations.

The typing of the first draft of the manuscript and many secretarial and editorial labors as well were undertaken by Miss Helen Boyer. I also wish to thank my students, Miss Elizabeth Salmon, Mrs. Elizabeth Shoemaker Marcus and Mr. Stephen Fischer for research and secretarial assistance, and Mrs. Ada Djiewanowski for typing the final draft of the manuscript.

In seminar and discussion all of my graduate students have contributed to the growth of this book. I must particularly mention Lewis Spitz. In addition to his many contributions of this kind, he undertook with the assistance of his wife Edna Spitz, the completion of certain sections of the bibliography and editorial work thereon. Without their generous and competent help the publication of the book would have been much delayed.

The editor of the series, W. L. Langer, has at all times given to me the patient and helpful criticism and assistance that the contributors to this series have learned to expect.

MYRON P. GILMORE

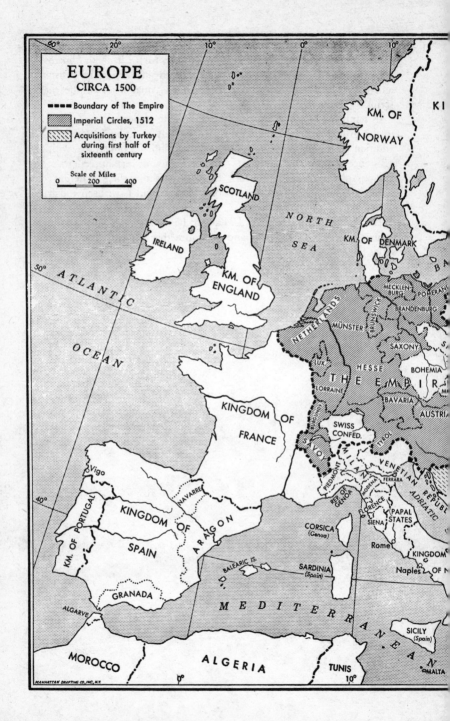

THE WORLD OF HUMANISM
1453—1517

Chapter One

THE FRONTIERS OF LATIN CHRISTENDOM

I. INTRODUCTION

IN THE summer of 1454 Aeneas Sylvius Piccolomini, one of the best-informed men in Europe, was serving as papal legate in Germany. Over a year had passed since the fall of Constantinople to the Ottoman Turks. During that year there had been fruitless negotiations among the European princes on the means of opposing the Turkish advance, and it was by now clear that there was no prospect of united military action. Filled with a deep pessimism, Aeneas Sylvius wrote a long letter to a friend in Rome, in which he described his fears for the future of the Latin Christian world.

"I prefer to be silent," he wrote,

and I could wish that my opinion may prove entirely wrong and that I may be called a liar rather than a true prophet. . . . For I have no hope that what I should like to see will be realized; I cannot persuade myself that there is anything good in prospect. . . . Christianity has no head whom all will obey. Neither the pope nor the emperor is accorded his rights. There is no reverence and no obedience; we look on pope and emperor as figureheads and empty titles. Every city state [*civitas*] has its king and there are as many princes as there are households.[1]

The sources of European strength and vitality were indeed far from obvious to even the most penetrating European observer of the middle of the fifteenth century. It was not merely that there appeared to exist on the eastern borders a threat from an alien society that had just celebrated its most dramatic triumph in the capture of Constantinople. The apparent urgency of the danger only brought out in relief the weaknesses and divisions within the borders of the Christian world. Warfare between states and within states seemed an endemic characteristic of European political and social organization. Who, Aeneas Sylvius asked, could rec-

[1] Pius II, *Opera omnia* (Basle, 1571), 656.

I

oncile the English with the French, the Germans with the Hungarians and Bohemians, the Aragonese with the Genoese? In many places, notably in England and the Iberian peninsula, the monarchy was struggling with the anarchy created by powerful feudal coalitions and complicated by the existence of rival claims to the throne. In Italy the warring city states of the north had only just arranged a precarious peace. It is not surprising that Aeneas Sylvius foresaw an intensification of existing conflicts and feared eventual destruction.

Consideration of the condition of the Christian church could hardly encourage a more hopeful view. The memory of the events of the Schism and the failure of the conciliar movement was still recent. Although the most serious outbreaks of heresy had been suppressed and the Schism ended, the movement for reform had not succeeded and the widespread existence of abuses in ecclesiastical life and organization was admitted. Entirely aside from the question of abuses, however, there were many signs that those attacks on the position and theory of the church which had developed in the late medieval period would grow in scope and intensity. There was a wide gap between the actual jurisdictional position of the papacy and its theoretical claims. Denunciations of the wealth of the church and the prerogatives of the clergy continued. Above all, there had appeared numerous manifestations—of which the *devotio moderna* in the north was only the most significant—of a widely felt need to transcend the formal channels through which the church dispensed the means of salvation, of a need for participation in religious experience that was at once broader, more emotional, and more direct. Medieval religious expression seemed to be dividing into two traditions, one of which preserved the formal, the scholastic, the intellectual elements—Christianity as a system of truth—while the other emphasized the uncomplicated, the mystical, the emotional—Christianity as a way of life. On the one hand were the treatises of Gabriel Biel; on the other the *Imitation of Christ*.

In scholarship, in arts and letters, it might have been supposed a contemporary observer could have discerned an area of promise. Aeneas Sylvius had himself received a humanist education and had participated in the intellectual excitement that had stimulated many of the best minds of his generation. In the Italian centers there was indeed a consciousness of new forms of artistic expression, there was an intensified enthusiasm for classical civilization, there was an increasing knowledge of the Greek language and Greek literature. At the middle of the fifteenth century, however, the earlier manifestations of the Renaissance in Italy had not yet had a considerable effect beyond the Alps. Even in Italy the new learning created new problems. If the classical world was now seen more clearly and more comprehensively, it was also seen at a greater distance. The growing knowledge about Greek and Roman civilization and the awareness of that civilization in time—in a word the new periodization of history—involved a re-evaluation of the relationship between the classic and the Christian traditions. If there were as yet none who doubted the compatibility of the inheritance of antiquity with Christian revelation, the rapidly increasing knowledge about Greece and Rome nevertheless brought with it changes of emphasis and taste, the beginnings of tensions which were to have a profound effect in the period to come. The "modernism" of St. Thomas Aquinas had been successful; Aristotelian philosophy had been incorporated in the Christian tradition. How far could the process be repeated as the intellectual horizon widened?

The perception of a man like Aeneas Sylvius embraced the contemporary political, religious, and intellectual scene. What lay outside his conscious formulation was an analogous general view of the economic condition of European society. Had he attempted to generalize about what we call social and economic conditions, his pessimism would almost certainly have been reinforced. The traditional ethic that had governed economic life was crumbling. The great merchant princes had achieved a position which made them immune from prosecution by the ecclesiastical courts, but the humble village pawnbroker was still subject to the penalties of the canon law.[2] Almost everywhere the various tensions produced by the declining feudal economy overshadowed the potentialities of newer forms of economic organization. The lines of outward expansion beyond Europe were not yet apparent; African and Atlantic voyages had been begun, but their results, although important, were still far from dramatic.

The fears originally expressed by Aeneas Sylvius as a result of the contemporary political disorganization of Christendom might thus have been confirmed by evidence from many other spheres of human activity. Danger from without was matched by weakness within. Altogether the principal basis for hope in the temporal future of European Christian society still depended in the middle of the fifteenth century upon faith in that society as the guardian of Christian revelation. This faith, to be sure, involved a transcendent hope; the belief that the Heavenly City could be realized on earth was the product of an almost cosmic optimism. Yet this

[2] B. N. Nelson, "The Usurer and the Merchant Prince: Italian Business Men and the Ecclesiastical Law of Restitution, 1100–1550," *The Tasks of Economic History, The Journal of Economic History* (Supplement VII, 1947).

faith was not so strong in Aeneas Sylvius as to prevent his taking a dim view of at least the short-run future. He could see nothing good in prospect.

His prediction was nevertheless refuted during the course of the next half-century. What Aeneas could not have foreseen was that the very rivalries and tensions he deplored had creative as well as destructive possibilities. It was not by appeals to the principle of unity, but by the competitive action of individual princes in pursuit of their own aims that the position of Europe in the world was altered. During the last decades of the fifteenth century and the first decades of the sixteenth, energies, which were in part the consequence of the very diversities in the European intellectual and institutional inheritance, found expression to a degree that far surpassed earlier manifestations. The great discoveries, the accumulations of capital, the concentrations of political power, the triumphs of scholarship and art all rested on developments that extended far back into the past, but their effects now began to enter into contemporary consciousness and to create—at least for some minds—a mood of confidence and optimism. This optimism could not yet take the form of a conception of progress, but it centered on the belief that by an effort of intellect and will European civilization could achieve a reformation, indeed a restoration of one of those distant epochs when the secular condition of humanity seemed to have been so superior. Religion could be purified and philosophy attain new syntheses, kings and princes would be advised by the wise, and the benefits of Christianity extended to those new lands and peoples who were entering the horizon of European consciousness. Such hopes rested on the achievements of the age of Columbus, Michelangelo and Erasmus and came to fullest expression in the years when Henry VIII, Francis I, and Charles V were beginning their reigns. The world was full of promise; this first great burst of humanist optimism, however briefly sustained, marks a generation that ever since has seemed like the figures on the Sistine ceiling, of more than human stature, lifted outside the ordinary course of history, symbolic of the great creative development of western culture.

Only a little more than sixty years after Aeneas Sylvius had voiced his fears over the lack of European unity and seen nothing good in prospect, Erasmus was able to feel, although only for a moment and just before the hour of religious revolution struck, that he had lived to see Europe entering a golden age.

This volume is an attempt to summarize the important changes that were taking place in institutions and ideas between the generation of Aeneas Sylvius and the generation of Erasmus: that is, in terms of the dates fixed by great public events, between the fall of Constantinople and the outbreak of the Protestant Revolution.

In this as in other ages of European history the complex mass of events and detailed relationships derive much of their meaning from being considered as parts of a common European civilization. It is true that Columbus was a Genoese in the service of the king and queen of Spain, Michelangelo a Florentine executing commissions for the papacy, and Erasmus a Dutchman by birth, although a European by allegiance; but the dynamic achievements with which their names are connected cannot be fully understood in terms of individual biographies and still less in terms of national histories. Behind the men and behind the countries we must always be conscious of the institutions and ideas that were the common property of western Christendom.

If, however, our understanding of the meaning of the specific events of this period depends in part on our ability to apprehend what was happening to the pattern of European civilization conceived as a whole, it also depends on our knowledge and awareness of the significant variations that existed or developed within that common pattern. These variations were manifold and were conditioned by geographical environment, occupations, social and intellectual traditions. At one level such differences are very obvious. It is clear that there were enormous disparities in the lives, circumstances and opportunities of individuals and groups in all parts of Europe, then as now. The voyages of discovery and the achievements of philosophers, scholars, and creative artists may have given to increasing numbers of men a consciousness of changing horizons in thought as in life, but many more never gazed on a wider horizon than bounded the village in which they were born. The routines of their behavior and the patterns of their thought remained what they had been for centuries past. We must therefore explore not only the evolution of the thought and institutions characteristic of European civilization as a whole, but also the very contrasts in types of organizations and ideals that existed within the common framework.

Of all the complex changes that confront the student of this period it is perhaps most useful as well as most natural to begin with an analysis of the position of Latin Christendom in the world, and an account of what was happening to its boundaries. Such an analysis will not only serve to define more precisely the area of this historical study but also provide a measurable example of revolutionary change. Unfortunately no map exists on which we can plot the fluctuations of ideas and institutions, but the conquest of physical space, the discovery of the world in the literal sense, can be represented on the conventional globe.

In the second half of the fifteenth century the frontiers of Latin Christendom were most radically altered by two great movements, one contracting and the other extending the European horizon and the scope of European activity. In the east the continuing pressure of Ottoman conquest changed the political and economic configuration of the Mediterranean and Balkan regions. To the west and south the succession of great voyages opened ways across the seas that eventually led to empire. Both these movements had their roots in the past, but they came to a climax in the fifteenth century in a series of events that have ever since been regarded as inaugurating a new era. The voyages of discovery and the foundation of overseas empires in particular marked not only a stage in the history of Europe but the beginning of a period in world history characterized by European hegemony, economic, political, and cultural, the end of which has finally come only in our own time in the twentieth century.

II. THE TURKISH THREAT

Although the expansion of Europe was subsequently to be of transcendent importance, those few observers in the middle of the fifteenth century who were able to take a large view of the state of Latin Christendom had their attention fixed not on the Portuguese discoveries but on the eastern Mediterranean. Constantinople fell to the Turks on May 29, 1453. This event undoubtedly has more symbolic than real importance, but its date marks probably better than any other the end of a system of relationships that had prevailed for some seven centuries in the Mediterranean world. Three great societies, Latin Christendom, the Byzantine Empire, and Islam, had existed in a condition of equilibrium often apparently precarious but, in reality, as human affairs run, remarkably stable over a long period. Mutual hostility had erupted from time to time in holy wars and crusades, but had never been strong enough to exclude commercial and cultural exchanges of greatest importance.[3] Now at last the conquests of the Ottoman, representing an invigorated Moslem power, had brought to a close the last age of the Byzantine Empire. Orthodox Christians henceforth survived as Turkish subjects or inde-

---

[3] Grunebaum, *Medieval Islam or a Study in Cultural Orientation* (Chicago, 1946), Introduction.

pendently in Russia, where they were still subject to the Tartar pressure from the east.

The further conquests of the Turks in the period from the capture of Constantinople to the accession of Suleiman the Magnificent in 1520 defined the nature and extent of the danger: it was felt that the fate of Christendom hung in the balance. While the campaigns by which the Turks extended their European dominion can be summarized, and the area of expansion described and charted on the map, the factors that determined the limits of that area, and the varieties of response by the leaders of Christian Europe were more complicated.

On the day after the fall of Constantinople Mohammed II made his formal entrance into the city and ordered the conversion of Hagia Sophia into a mosque. We are told that he paused before the palace of the Caesars to reflect on imperial destiny and to quote lines from a Persian poet about spiders weaving their webs in the palaces of kings. However elegiac his mood, and however objectively he might regard the fate of emperors, there could have been no doubt in his own mind or in those of others about the facts of his position. In celebrating his victory he assumed in the eyes of his subjects the prerogatives that had been enjoyed by the Byzantine emperors, including the role of protector of the Orthodox Christian church.

In many ways Mohammed II was the most remarkable ruler of his age. Great not only as a conqueror but also as an administrator, he developed the institutions he had inherited into an extraordinarily successful political and social organization. Furthermore, his intellectual interests, and his real sense of tolerance where those interests were involved, created a court that has had few parallels in the extent and range of its cultivation.

As a result of the innovations introduced by Mohammed II, the structure of the Ottoman state almost conformed to Plato's ideal republic. A class of guardians, both military and administrative, was created by a rigid educational system that taught from the earliest age an ideal of service to the Ottoman state and to the sultan who was its visible symbol. The subjects of this education were in part recruited from the conquered populations, some of whose children were carried off, converted to Mohammedanism, and trained as a special corps. Originally this practice may have been devised as a means of making use of favored prisoners captured in war. It was later developed, however, into a regular institution by which levies of children from the conquered Christian population were received as tribute every five years.

The majority of these tribute boys, together with recruits, were trained to become members of a military establishment, the famous janizaries, who were the principal striking force of the Turkish armies in the fifteenth and sixteenth centuries. As long as the Turks were able to extend the boundaries of their control, and indeed for a considerable time thereafter, there was an adequate reservoir of human material from which to supply constant replacements for this highly trained infantry.

In addition to the provision for military needs, the system of recruitment was also used to build the ruling class of the empire. A very small number of children who showed promise of extraordinary capacity were set apart in the palace school, where they were subjected to a comprehensive education designed to make them eligible for the highest positions in the state. Although the origin of this remarkable school for civil servants has been traced back to his father, Murad II, its real founder was Mohammed II himself, who may have been impelled to regularize and develop the institution in the period after the conquest of Constantinople, when there was increasing need for high military and civilian officials of ability. In any case, he added to previous practice many features that were dictated by the needs of his own administration. The palace school was thus organized on a formal basis.

The purpose of this school, not unlike that of contemporary Renaissance educators in Italy, was to subject the ablest young men to a common discipline producing a small class with a high *esprit de corps,* destined to occupy positions of leadership. The paradoxical effect of such an institution in the Ottoman Empire, however, was that a vast Moslem state was in fact governed by men who had been born the sons of Christian slaves, while native Osmanlis found themselves excluded from their own government. This is not to be thought of as the same kind of deprivation it would be to a modern western man, because the fundamental character of Turkish government, derived from nomadic origins and carried over into the imperial period, was built on the administration of conquered territory without any sense of identification between rulers and ruled. From this point of view, of course, the whole population, Moslem and Christian alike, were treated as slaves.

Side by side with these institutions designed to produce the guardians and the auxiliaries—that is, the rulers and the janizaries—there was another set of institutions whose purpose was the training of the learned classes—the scholars, priests, educators, and jurisconsults of the empire. Recruits for these professions were received only from free Moslem families, and the sociological basis of this educational system was thus in direct contrast to that which produced the administrative officials and the military forces. Together these two different sets of fundamental educational institutions, not quite equivalent to church and state in western society, composed the structural framework of the Ottoman Empire and were in fact at the basis of its strength and its success.[4]

These institutions were in process of development toward their ultimate form at the time the Turks took possession of the remains of the Byzantine inheritance. Mohammed II therefore already enjoyed the advantages of an educated bureaucracy and a trained military force, fanatical in its zeal and devotion. Once established in the city that had been the capital of an empire for a thousand years, the new sultan was free to resume the campaigns against the Balkan states that had been initiated by his predecessors a century before. During that hundred years the Turks had conquered important portions of the Balkan peninsula: Adrianople had been their European capital since 1361, Serbia and Bulgaria had been overrun after the famous defeat of Kossovo in 1389. Of the few centers of resistance that continued Montenegro was the most effective and Ragusa on the Adriatic was able to maintain itself as a Christian port.

Within a comparatively few years most of the remaining lands south of the Danube were subdued. There was intermittent resistance, successful locally for short periods. John Hunyadi, the Hungarian hero, assisted by the Franciscan, John of Capistrano, held Belgrade against the attacks of Mohammed II in 1456. Upon his death, immediately after his victory, his young son, Mathias Corvinus, was elected king of Hungary in spite of the claims of the Hapsburg. This ambitious and able figure devoted himself to the effort to create a large central European state on the Danube. His position enabled him to represent himself as the champion of Christendom, although his aggression was directed as much against Christian Austria and Bohemia as against the infidel Turks. Mathias played a central role in the papal diplomacy on the eastern question and on more than one occasion had the advantage of subsidies engineered by the papacy in the interest of further repulsing the Turkish advance. Actually, however, aside from the fact that a strong ruler in Hungary was a deterrent to Mohammed's further advance, those victories of Corvinus that had any effect on the frontier were minor. When he died in 1490 Hungary relapsed into a condition of weakness and the way was

[4] Above account summarized from A. Lybyer, *The Government of the Ottoman Empire in the Time of Suleiman the Magnificent* (Cambridge, 1913), and B. Miller, *The Palace School of Mohammed the Conqueror* (Cambridge, 1941).

prepared for the great Turkish victory over the Hungarians at Mohacs in 1526.[5]

In Albania the local leader, Skanderbeg, the "athlete of Christendom," continued to his death in 1467 the struggle for the independence of his native land. He received a certain measure of support from Venice and the papacy, but by no means the continuous assistance that might have been offered to take advantage of his situation.[6]

Beyond the line of the Danube the Turks early achieved effective control of the province of Wallachia, but they were checked in Moldavia throughout the reign of Stephen the Great, 1457–1504. The resistance of this prince was indeed one of the important factors slowing the Ottoman advance up the Danube.[7]

In sum, therefore, while Mohammed II was able during the remainder of his life to round out his Balkan conquests, local and sporadic resistance succeeded in holding substantially the line of the Danube until the renewal of the Turkish attack under Suleiman the Magnificent in the following century.

In the meantime Mohammed II turned to the problem of the Mediterranean and Venice. During the first long war with Venice, from 1463 to 1479, the Turkish position was consolidated and materially improved, chiefly by the capture of Negroponte, the Greek island of Euboea, in 1470, by the reduction of the last Genoese settlements in the east, and by the attainment of final control over Albania and the Adriatic coast. In the peace of 1479 Venice was nevertheless allowed notable concessions, including the retention of the Venetian quarter in Constantinople with commercial privileges and extraterritorial rights.

As soon as the Venetian peace had been arranged, the main Turkish attack was directed against the island of Rhodes, then the principal outpost of Latin Christians in the eastern Mediterranean and long in the possession of the Knights Hospitalers of St. John. At the same time an expeditionary force of the Turkish army sailed from Valona to attack Otranto at the southern end of the Italian peninsula.

These ventures represented the climax of the Turkish threat against the Christian west in the fifteenth century. Otranto fell after a siege of only a month; with great barbarity half the inhabitants were put to death, and the Italian peninsula appeared open to the invaders. At this

---

[5] V. Franknoi, *Mathias Corvinus, König von Ungarn 1458–1490* (Freiburg in B., 1891).
[6] Fan S. Noli, *George Castrioti Scanderbeg 1405–1468* (New York, 1947).
[7] R. Rosetti, "Stephen the Great of Moldavia and the Turkish Invasions, 1457–1507," *Slavonic Review*, VI (1927), 87–103.

crisis and just as he was preparing to lead in person a stronger expedition against Rhodes, Mohammed II died. His death resulted in the abandonment of both the siege of Rhodes and the position already won at Otranto.

After these advances Europe enjoyed a relaxation of the Turkish pressure until the time of Suleiman the Magnificent. This interval was first of all due to the civil war for the succession between the sons of Mohammed, Bayazid and Djem. Djem was defeated and fled in 1482, first to Cairo and then to Rhodes, where he became prisoner of the Knights and subsequently of the pope and the king of France, until his death in 1495. During the years of his captivity he remained a powerful potential weapon in the hands of the Christians and a threat to the security of his brother Bayazid; but the weapon and the threat remained unused, except for the exaction of money payments from Constantinople. Through the rest of Bayazid's reign there were intermittent Turkish attacks in Hungary and Transylvania, but the only serious military effort in the west was directed against Venice in the period from 1489 to 1503.

The comparative cessation of Turkish pressure on Latin Christendom at the turn of the sixteenth century was due only in part, however, to the disputed succession in the reign of Bayazid. A far more fundamental factor was the orientation of Turkish conquest eastward, in part at least because of the strength the western Christians had already displayed, in part to the inducements offered by the weakness of the eastern powers. From 1512, when Bayazid was deposed and Selim I came to the throne, a series of great campaigns expanded the Ottoman territory in Asia Minor and Africa. The short reign of Selim saw the defeat of Shah Ismail of Persia and the addition of large parts of northern Mesopotamia to the Ottoman dominion. Even more significant were the conquests of Syria and Egypt, which were completed by 1517 with the transfer of the caliphate to Constantinople. This was an event of the greatest importance in the development of the Ottoman Empire. The assumption of the religious leadership of the Moslem world provided a basis for further pretensions in the Ottoman expansion across North Africa and in the Near East. At the accession of Suleiman the Magnificent in 1520 there was therefore a new basis for conquest: the eastern frontiers of the Ottoman empire had been secured, and the sultan could again turn west for a renewal of the Turkish drive in central Europe.

Such in brief outline is the history of the Turkish conquest from the fall of Constantinople to the accession of Suleiman the Magnificent. In sum, in spite of impressive Turkish expansion, the European Christians had held a line symbolized by the retention of Belgrade in the Balkans and the fortress of Rhodes in the Mediterranean.

The principal question that emerges from a consideration of the Turkish conquest in this period centers on the relative strength of the invaders and their opponents. To what extent was the fluctuating but relatively stable line between the Ottoman Empire and the Christian west determined by limiting factors of policy or resources on the Turkish side, and to what extent was it a product of the actual resistance of the western powers? In other words, how serious was the Turkish threat? Was European Christendom really in danger of being wiped out? Was the position less precarious or more so than it had been at other times of great crisis like the Arab conquest in the eighth century or the Mongol invasion in the thirteenth?

Questions like these can never be answered with precision. It is necessary, however, to attempt some estimate of the seriousness of the Turkish threat before we can consider in its proper light the fifteenth-century European reaction to the Turks.

The Ottoman sultans have generally been represented as aspiring to world conquest and, in particular, as intent on the destruction of Christian civilization. Gibbon, in a characteristic phrase, described Mohammed II after the conquest of Otranto as eager to adorn the new Rome with the spoils of the old. It was of course a tenet of the Mohammedan religion that the unbeliever must be destroyed, just as the Christian religion taught the extirpation of the heretic and the infidel. Yet the more we consider the personality and position of Mohammed II, the more we may doubt the extent to which he seriously entertained a policy of world conquest. It may certainly be argued that religious conviction no more determined his policies than it did those of most of his Christian contemporaries.

Mohammed II was a statesman as well as a conqueror. Once established in Constantinople, it was entirely natural that he should continue on his frontiers the program of conquest that he had inherited and had brought at once to so dramatic and successful a climax. He had not only to strengthen the institutions of government and society within, but also to enlarge and improve the defense of the empire against foes from without. For this task there were ready his armies, inspired by a dynamic and conquering faith. As a practical consideration the recruitment of both the bureaucracy and the armies depended, in part at least, on additions to the numbers of the subject populations. Economically, also, the strength of the empire would in part be proportional to its control of areas that could furnish grain and other basic foods.

Although the Ottoman state had enemies in both Europe and Asia, the Balkan peninsula was from almost every point of view the most logical place for the concentration of attack. Here the Turks had already been established for more than a century. Here the Christians were weak and divided, and there was an opportunity to add to the subject populations of the empire. Here, also, was one of the granaries of Europe. Finally, in addition to these general considerations, Mohammed II had a personal claim to Serbia through his mother, who had been a Christian Serbian princess; and it was from Serbia's neighbor, Hungary, that it appeared likely the greatest opposition would be offered. Accordingly, the first campaigns of the new sultan after the conquest of Constantinople were directed against the Balkan states.

Thus we have in Mohammed II no Genghis Khan loosing his hordes indiscriminately to conquer as much territory as they could. Inheriting the position of the Caesars, Mohammed II directed his conquests largely to reassembling territories that had once been subject to the Eastern Empire. The famous portrait of the sultan by Giovanni Bellini shows us a face cultivated, cruel and ambitious, but perhaps above all the face of a realist. Much as this man had achieved, he was not without a sense of the limits of the possible. Neither he nor his immediate successors pressed conquests beyond their capacity to absorb and govern vanquished territories. All this is not to deny that whenever there was an opportunity to advance, it was seized upon and made the most of; but these were the advances of a stable state in a world that included and would continue to include other powers. The ambitious design of conquering Christian Europe may be described as ideologically rather than practically important in the formation of the policy of the Ottoman rulers.

Regardless of the intentions of the sultans, limitations were imposed on Ottoman conquest by the facts of Turkish power and resources. In spite of the wealth the sultan had at his disposal, dramatically greater than that of his European counterparts, and in spite of the efficiency of the janizaries as a fighting machine, the Turkish military effort was not clearly superior to that of the European powers.[8] In technological achievements, such as artillery and engineering, the Turks were behind and, although their

[8] E. Fueter, *Geschichte des europäischen Staatensystems von 1492–1559* (Munich, 1919), 182–85.

own lack of knowledge and ability on these lines was to a large extent
made good by Christian renegades or subject Greeks, they were never
able to compete with the progress of western Europe. Even as fighting
soldiers the Turkish infantry was not on the same level as the best
European. The fact that major Turkish expeditions were defeated in the
fifteenth century by the hastily assembled, ill-equipped armies of Hunyadi, Skanderbeg, and Stephen of Moldavia indicates that the great
powers of Europe had, at least on their own frontiers, little to fear. In the
case of the Venetian Empire there were exposed positions which the
Turks could cut off, but, though they could thus accumulate what
amounted to colonial territory, their threats to the metropolis itself did
not succeed.

   In other words, the situation between the Turks and the states of
Christian Europe appears to have been materially different from that
which obtained between the Turks and the Byzantine Empire, Egypt or
Persia. It has been frequently represented that Europe was saved by the
death of Mohammed II and the diversion of Turkish energies eastward
until the time of Suleiman the Magnificent. It is, of course, impossible
to divine what would have happened if the full weight of Turkish military strength had been continuously directed against Europe; but there
were clearly elements of Turkish weakness and European strength that
make it doubtful whether the Turks could have advanced much farther
than they in fact did by the beginning of the sixteenth century. It is
easy to speak after the event, and we must be careful not to minimize a
danger because it was surmounted; but there is a great deal of evidence
to support the conclusion that Christian civilization was not in serious
danger of being annihilated at the hands of the Turks.

   The news of the fall of Constantinople did not reach Rome until July
8, 1453, over a month after the event, although it had been known in
Venice a week earlier.[9] From the Italian centers the news spread through
Europe, but it was August before the fate of the Greek emperor was
known to every court and capital. From the courts it took still longer to
reach the people at large. When we consider the situation of Europe in
the fifteenth century, we have to make an effort to appreciate not only
the comparative slowness with which news spread, but also its lack of
penetration downward into the lower classes of the population. We read
that the fall of Constantinople was announced at Rome by a celebrated
preacher to the people, who burst into loud lamentations, and we know

   [9] L. V. Pastor, *History of the Popes* (Eng. trans.: London, 1891), II, 272–73.

that the pope's summons to a crusade was carried far and wide in the northern countries as well as in Italy. These preachings in urban centers must, however, have reached many elements of the population only indirectly or not at all. The number of people who had any reliable account of Mohammed's conquest and any real conception of the Turkish peril was therefore small, and of this number a still smaller minority was capable of attaching any significance to the event. The thirty to forty million peasants, who by their constant labors supported the structure of European society, had a vision of the world that hardly extended beyond the confines of their villages. Those who, by education, travel, or social position, took a wider view were in some cases hardly better informed on the institutions of the Ottoman government or the tenets of the Mohammedan religion. The literature on the Turks was limited to the accounts of a few travelers or pilgrims; there was as yet nothing like the abundance of pamphlets, descriptions, and histories that appeared in the following period and were widely disseminated through the printing press. There existed in the fifteenth century no account such as that supplied in the sixteenth by Busbecq, the great ambassador of Charles V to Constantinople. Thus, even the decisions of governments were often based on very little real knowledge, and appeals to a larger public were couched in terms that had been traditional for centuries.

The first and most articulate response to the fall of Constantinople was the appeal for a crusade led by the papacy. In this appeal Christian and classical traditions were mingled. From the humanist secretaries of the papal court came a series of letters and treatises indicting the powers of Europe for having permitted the fall of Constantinople and bemoaning the loss of manuscripts and libraries enshrining the inheritance of Greek antiquity. On September 30, 1453, Nicholas V, appealing to Christian duty, issued the bull for a crusade. This exhortation, however, remained entirely without effect. Although everyone paid lip service to the idea of a crusade, there were few who meant their professions to be taken seriously.

In part this attitude must be regarded as a product of the cumulative disillusionment created by the failure of recent crusading efforts. At the end of the fourteenth century Sigismund of Hungary and John the Fearless, heir of Burgundy, had led an expedition against the Turks in the Balkans only to be completely defeated and cut to pieces at Nicopolis in 1396. An even more recent Christian disaster had been suffered at Varna in 1444 when Pope Eugenius IV persuaded Ladislas of Hungary to renew the war against the invaders. The memory of these events contributed to the lack of faith in the traditional methods and dampened the enthusiasm of the Christian rulers for any new appeals from the papacy.

Reluctance to support the papal appeal had also a more realistic basis. None of the great European powers regarded the Turkish threat as sufficiently pressing to require a reorientation of their policies. The response of the great duke of Burgundy, Philip the Good, the richest prince in Europe, was indicative. Olivier de la Marche has given us the account of the famous Feast of the Pheasant held at Lille in 1454. The Knights of the Golden Fleece had been assembled for a tourney and at its conclusion sat down to a banquet of unparalleled magnificence at which the succession of courses was diversified by a series of charades and "entremets" illustrating mythological scenes and proverbs. As the climax of the feast there appeared a representation which rightly impressed de la Marche as *"le plus espécial des aultres."* A huge man appeared dressed as a Saracen of Granada, leading an elephant on whose back was installed in a little castellated structure a lady representing the church in captivity to the heretics. Upon seeing the noble company the lady appealed to their chivalrous ideals and declaimed in verse an elaborate account of the plight of the church since the fall of Constantinople. At the conclusion of her recital the herald of the Golden Fleece brought in a pheasant richly adorned with a collar of gold and pearls, a bird particularly cherished by the Order of the Golden Fleece because of its supposed introduction into Europe by the Argonauts. Presented with the pheasant, Philip the Good rose and, while the company applauded, with his knights took an oath to go on a crusade.[10] The intention thus elaborately and symbolically celebrated was of course never realized in fact. The European crusading tradition had undergone a long evolution since the days of Peter the Hermit.

While few manifestations were as dramatic as this one, the sentiments of other courts were equally ineffective. England was torn by the Wars of the Roses; the Empire was precariously governed by Frederick III, who was threatened by the Burgundians in the west and by the Hungarians and Bohemians in the east; France was still recovering, under Louis XI, from the long struggle with England; and the kingdoms of the Iberian peninsula, although they manifested a traditional interest, had in northern Africa an object for their crusading zeal which was nearer home. The Italian powers were absorbed in a struggle between Venice and Milan.

[10] Olivier de la Marche, *Mémoires,* ed. Société de l'histoire de France (Paris, 1884), II, 340–80.

Initial discouragement did not prevent the papacy and others from continuing their efforts to effect a successful union of European powers. From Nicholas V to Leo X all the popes paid at least lip service to the idea of a crusade. Calixtus II devoted important papal revenues to the assembling of a fleet. Pius II, the former Aeneas Sylvius Piccolomini, whose pessimistic view of the situation has been quoted, when he reached the papal throne himself directed all his efforts to the organization of a crusade. He summoned a European congress at Mantua and when that failed fixed his final hopes on the assumption of military initiative by himself. He died disappointed, after vainly awaiting at Ancona the Venetian galleys on which he was to embark—a scene immortalized in the frescoes of Pinturicchio at Siena, which in its way makes as vivid as the memoirs of Olivier de la Marche the decline of the fifteenth-century crusading spirit.

Paul II, who succeeded Pius II, subsidized the Venetians, the Hungarians, and Skanderbeg. He received the latter at Rome in 1466 and supported his enterprise with grants until the death of Skanderbeg in 1468. The great crisis of his pontificate was the fall of Negroponte in 1470, by which the island of Euboea was lost to the Venetians. Again the pope made efforts to unite Italy for action. He even allied himself diplomatically with Moslem rivals of the Ottomans in Asia Minor against the common enemy. These plans were interrupted by his death in 1471. His successor, Sixtus IV, called for a European congress to form a league against the Turk and sent legates to all the principal European countries to concert plans for common European action. At the crisis of 1480, when the Turks had landed at Otranto, Sixtus again deployed a considerable activity, which lost its object when the Turks retired on the death of Mohammed. Innocent VIII, at the beginning of his pontificate, renewed the conventional appeals to the European powers, but the conflict between Rome and Naples prevented him from taking as active a part in the Turkish question as some of his predecessors. In 1489 he succeeded, in long-drawn negotiations with the Knights of Rhodes, in securing custody of Prince Djem, the younger brother of Bayazid, who had taken refuge at Rhodes after his unsuccessful struggle. This prize the papacy lost to France under Alexander VI, without having used its advantage except for negotiations with Constantinople designed to increase the subsidy paid to keep Djem in captivity.

Even Alexander VI, however, gave some formal attention to the Turkish question and summoned representatives of the great powers to

Rome to consider what steps might be taken to initiate a crusade. The preoccupation of Julius II with the political role of the papacy in Italy coincided with the period of peace with the Ottoman Empire after 1503, and Julius, therefore, of all the popes of the period, gave least attention to the eastern question. During the pontificate of Leo X, however, the vast conquests of the Turks in the east gave grounds for fearing that a mightier power might be directed against Europe, while the absence of the sultan from Constantinople encouraged hope that some advantage might be taken of Selim's involvement in the east. Leo X continued the tradition of his predecessors. Grants for a crusading tax were made; appeals for action were directed to the European sovereigns; the subject was discussed at the Lateran council; and finally, in the year 1517, a congregation was established to consider the Turkish question. This produced one of the most comprehensive memoranda on the subject that had yet been seen, but one which, like others, remained without effect.[11]

Thus, in the whole period from the fall of Constantinople to the eve of the Reformation, the project of common European action against the Turks was constantly discussed, and the ideal of a crusade was kept before the European governments by the papacy. In reality, however, there was at no moment a serious possibility that such common action would be undertaken by the powers of Christendom, and the discussion of the Turkish question in the traditional manner served to conceal the conflicting designs of the European powers, which, it was hoped, could be realized under cover of supporting the crusade. Side by side with a policy of resistance to an alien religion and an alien society we have the development of a policy of accommodation and appeasement, which had, ultimately, the effect of admitting the Turkish Empire as one of the components of the European state system.

The papacy itself pursued a double policy. As early as 1461 Pius II had addressed an extraordinary letter to Mohammed II, in which he urged his conversion to Christianity and promised him, upon such conversion taking place, the title to the Eastern Empire. Innocent VIII entered into negotiations with the sultan on the question of Djem. At the threat of the French invasion in 1494 Alexander VI corresponded with Bayazid and sought an alliance against the French to save both Naples and ultimately Turkey. The discovery of these negotiations was one of the reasons for

[11] Pastor, *op. cit.*, IV, Bk. I, ch. 3; Bk. II, ch. 8; V, Bk. I, ch. 4; VI, Bk. I, ch. 4; and Hans Pfeffermann, *Die Zusammenarbeit der Renaissance Päpste mit den Türken* (Winterthür, 1946).

the insistence of Charles VIII that Djem be delivered into his hands, after the conquest of Rome. As a matter of fact, other Christian powers had preceded the papacy in dealing directly with the Ottoman Empire. As soon as Constantinople fell, the Venetians, who controlled the greatest maritime power of the Christian west, in April, 1454, concluded a treaty of alliance by which they assured, as much as they could, their continuing existence as a Levantine power. Peace and friendship were decreed between the Sultan Mohammed and the signory of Venice. Among the articles was one in which Venice undertook not to support by ships, weapons, provisions, or money the sultan's enemies in their undertakings against the Turkish kingdom.

At various times Genoa, Naples, the Empire, Hungary, and France also entered into negotiations or concluded arrangements with the Turks. Such arrangements were not considered more seriously by the Christians than by the Turks. In 1517, for example, Francis I made a secret proposal to conquer the Turkish dominions and partition them among the three great European powers, France, Spain and the Empire, to the exclusion of the papacy and the other European princes. Thus treaties and arrangements were concluded against a background of mutual distrust and in the expectation that they would be broken. No European publicist or theorist could yet maintain that the Turks had as much right, by natural law, to their dominion as did the Christian princes to theirs, although the subject of infidel dominion had been widely discussed in medieval philosophical and political speculations. This position was not to be taken for another century; but the conditions that made it possible were already developing.

Between the idealistic appeals for a crusade and the realistic attempts to come to an accommodation with the Turks European resistance was, in fact, divided and sporadic.

Seen in this light the fears of those who took an alarmist view appear exaggerated. Many listened to the lamentations of Aeneas Sylvius and the other humanists. It was represented that Christian society had suffered a blow such as had not been known for centuries. For, as Aeneas Sylvius proclaimed in one of his orations,

In times past we have been wounded in Asia and in Africa, that is, in alien lands, but now we are struck in Europe, that is, in our fatherland, our own home. And although someone may object that many years ago Turks crossed from Asia into Greece and that the Mongols established themselves in Europe and that the Arabs occupied a portion of Spain after crossing the straits of Gibraltar, yet never have we lost a city or a place in Europe which can be compared to Constantinople.[12]

These historical parallels are interesting. In the history of Christendom, from the time when the stable institutions of a new society first emerged from the wreck of the ancient world, there had indeed twice before been a threat of annihilation, first by the wave of Arab conquest in the eighth century, when an effective concept of Latin Christendom had scarcely begun to exist, and second by the Mongols in the thirteenth century. The modern historian would be inclined to maintain that on these occasions, too, Europe was saved less by decisive military action on the part of Europeans than by developments on the enemy home fronts that played a large part in determining the limits of their geographical expansion. The twentieth-century historian may agree with the fifteenth-century observer that the Turkish threat was the most serious of the three. Nevertheless it is true that Europe, in spite of its political disorganization, was in a far better position economically and militarily to meet such a threat than it had been in the eighth century or the thirteenth. Such estimates are clearly not susceptible of proof and it is not surprising that to the men of the mid-fifteenth century the Turkish peril, which was after all the one they had to meet, seemed more dangerous than earlier examples. Obviously no one in the fifteenth century could consider the European situation from the perspective on world history achieved by the twentieth. Battles with the Arabs in the eighth century or the fears inspired even in England by the approach of the Mongols were now remembered dimly if at all. No European in effect knew enough of the history of either Islam or the Mongols to make even an approximate judgment whether dangers long past had been real or illusory. Hence it was natural that some members of the generation that saw the fall of Constantinople and the subsequent success of the Turks believed they faced an unprecedented peril.

It is important to remind ourselves, however, how small was the minority that shared this sense of danger. Most of the works containing information about the Turks in this period were addressed to a learned audience. Among the mass of the population a hostility based on the precepts of Christianity was hardly qualified by any real knowledge of the Mohammedan religion or of Turkish institutions. The stereotype

[12] Pius II, *op. cit.*, 678.

Turk, sensual and cruel, flaying the Christian population, was really a product of the pamphlet literature of the sixteenth century, when rulers hoped to increase the contribution of their subjects toward a Turkish crusade by vivid presentations of the atrocities committed by the enemy. In cases where there was real knowledge there was already a disposition to temper the conventional description with praise for some aspects of the Turkish government. There is evidence of considerable migration of peasants into the Turkish dominions in the Balkans, where apparently the immigrants felt their lot would be at any rate no less hard than it was under their Christian rulers. Although Erasmus at the beginning of the sixteenth century believed the worst of the Turkish rule, the question was already being raised whether the stability of the Turkish government and the incidence of taxation did not compare favorably with what prevailed in western Europe. In sum, the populace appears to have been generally indifferent to the Turkish peril except where they were exposed to direct attack, as at Otranto and later in Hungary after Mohacs in 1526, and in Austria at the first siege of Vienna in 1529.

Even among those who were most pessimistic and most vocal there were many whose sincerity was at least questionable. Too many humanists found in the fall of Constantinople a golden opportunity for rhetorical exercises. Many of the laments for the loss of Greek learning and the destruction of manuscripts were inspired more by the authors' desire to display their sensitivity to the cause of literature and their stylistic capabilities than by a deep sense of danger to the whole civilization to which they belonged. Even those whose awareness of the situation was most real, like Aeneas Sylvius, had their pessimism tempered by the promises of the Christian faith. Latin Christendom preserved a unique and priceless treasure, of which the guardian in the first instance was the church, still in spite of recent shocks militant and triumphant. The Turks were a scourge of God. The Christian church, and the society that continued to be in important ways coextensive with it, might be subjected to an almost infinite series of tribulations, for man was wicked and social institutions were imperfect, but it was unthinkable that the hand of God should allow the one society that cherished the fullness of His revelation to be utterly destroyed and swept from the face of the earth. Accordingly, to those few to whom it came at all, despair was relative, not absolute. Meanwhile, in the same years in which the Turkish peril loomed, the voyages of expansion were preparing in the west more compelling secular evidence for hope in the future.

III. THE PROGRESS OF EUROPEAN DISCOVERY

The success of the great voyages of the fifteenth century is the more startling as it seemed suddenly to reverse the previous shrinkage of the area of Latin Christian civilization. For in the middle of the century the horizon had appeared to be generally contracting. The growth of the Ottoman Empire had removed portions of Europe from Christian control long before the fall of Constantinople. Attempts to unite the surviving Orthodox church in Russia with the Roman communion had failed. And in the west no conspicuous gains had been made to balance these losses. In the Iberian peninsula a Mohammedan power was able to maintain itself in Granada until 1492, and the African and Atlantic conquests of Portugal, although of the very greatest consequence for subsequent European history, could not be regarded, at the time of Prince Henry's death in 1460, as a very material addition to the lands and peoples in communion with the Church of Rome.

Above all, the scope of the missionary efforts of western Christianity had diminished. In the middle of the fifteenth century its position in this respect was far worse than it had been a hundred and fifty years before. At that time the accident of the great Mongol Empire had permitted Christian traders and missionaries to cross the plains of Asia and penetrate China and India. Relations had been established with the remains of widely separated Nestorian Christian communities in the east, and archbishoprics and bishoprics of the Latin church had been instituted in several of the principal cities of China and Persia. To those few in a position to make an estimate of the situation it had seemed for a brief period as if western Christianity were on the verge of triumphs beside which the earlier conquests of the peoples of northern Europe would pale into insignificance. Christianity had made much of its progress by the conversion of rulers whose subjects followed their example: Clovis had been baptized with his Franks; if the Mongol emperor of China could only be persuaded to the truth, how many millions of souls would be brought into the fold!

All these bright hopes had disappeared in the course of the fourteenth century. The adoption of Mohammedanism by important branches of the Mongol peoples, the dynastic change in China and the emergence of the Ottoman power in Asia Minor and the Balkans had combined to cut off these promising relations between the civilizations of the east and west. Europe had been thrown back upon itself. A Christian embassy was sent to the court of Tamerlane; European travelers still visited Persia and

India and occasionally in the fifteenth century reached southern China; but the old land routes to Asia were closed. The knowledge of the east acquired in the earlier period had never been wholly lost, and a few first-hand accounts remained describing societies older, richer and more populous than anything in European experience; but the vision had faded. Marco Polo had become a legend.

By the middle of the fifteenth century the learned tradition of geography as derived from antiquity was more generally accepted as the basis for accounts of the world than the practical knowledge provided by the traveler and missionary of the earlier period. Cosmographies and descriptions of Europe and Asia might incorporate some material from Marco Polo and even from accounts of later travelers to the east, but the geographical picture of the lands beyond immediate experience was based primarily on the ancient geographers Strabo and Ptolemy of the first and second centuries B.C. The revival of Ptolemy was in itself an event of the greatest consequence, but his authority would not have been so comprehensive nor so unquestioned had not the wider and more practical knowledge of the east of the late thirteenth and early fourteenth centuries been all but lost.

In spite of this apparent retrogression in the course of European expansion, the conditions already existed that produced the succession of great voyages in the latter part of the fifteenth century. These voyages were the culmination of a process never continuously channeled in one direction and frequently interrupted, but dating back at least to the eleventh century. In the long history of this outward movement two great periods may be distinguished. The first began roughly with the crusades in the eleventh century and reached its climax in the thirteenth and early fourteenth centuries in the great land expeditions to the Orient. During this period the European outward thrust was directed first to the eastern Mediterranean and subsequently overland to distant Asia. This expansion was brought to a close by the great changes in China and in Asia Minor already noticed. It was succeeded by a new age in which Europeans developed the possibilities of communication by sea to the west and south. Any account of the earlier exploration of these possibilities must center on the work of Prince Henry and the Portuguese.

The true significance of the work of Prince Henry lay in the fact that under his auspices the learned tradition of geographical and astronomical theory was brought into relationship with the practical knowledge of mariners. Engaging in no expeditions himself, he established a center in which geographical information was brought together, studied and co-ordinated, instruments developed and an active interest kept alive in the task of enlarging the knowledge of the seas beyond the European horizon. Single-mindedly Henry devoted his talents and resources to this aim during the first half of the fifteenth century. By the time he died, in 1460, the most difficult period, which consisted in making the first advances down the African coast, was over.

Whatever view we take of the incentives that moved Prince Henry—scientific interest, imperial and economic plans, or missionary zeal—there is no doubt that the dynamic which carried on the general process of exploration was largely dependent on the hope of gain. Indeed, in the last years of his life there had already begun a considerable exploitation of the African and Atlantic discoveries made earlier in the fifteenth century. As long as Prince Henry lived, however, the temptation to develop the commercial possibilities of the Guinea Coast and the Azores and Cape Verde Islands at the expense of further discovery was resisted. Commercial exploitation was accompanied by efforts to increase by however little the knowledge of the lands and sea beyond the farthest point that had been reached.

Among the figures associated with Prince Henry in the enterprises of his later years was the Venetian, Alvise da Cadamosto, who came into the prince's service in 1455. Cadamosto's account of the incentives that led him to African adventure indicates the increasingly wider appeal generated by the process of overseas expansion. He tells us that he had sailed on the Flanders galleys of Venice, bound on their usual trip to northern ports. The galleys, forced by contrary winds, put in at Cape St. Vincent in Portugal, where Cadamosto had an opportunity to interview first Prince Henry's men and subsequently the prince himself, "who," he relates,

had caused seas to be navigated which had never before been sailed, and had discovered the lands of many strange races, where marvels abounded. Those who had been in these parts had wrought great gain among these new peoples, turning one soldo into six or ten.

They related so much in this strain that I with the others marvelled greatly. They thus aroused in me a growing desire to go thither.[13]

Accordingly, Cadamosto quit his Venetian galleys and entered the Portuguese service.

[13] *Voyages of Cadamosto,* translated and edited by G. R. Crone, Hakluyt Society, Series 2, Vol. LXXX (London, 1937), 5.

After Prince Henry's death there was for a time a halt in the progress of discovery. The government was committed to military adventures in North Africa and Spain, and it was felt that the lands already discovered provided sufficient scope for commercial activity. In 1469, however, progress was resumed under a new and interesting arrangement between the crown and private capital. Rights to the Guinea trade were in that year leased to the wealthy Lisbon merchant, Fernando Gomes, for five years, in exchange for the obligation to explore annually at least one hundred leagues of territory beyond the last known point. There were certain other stipulations, chiefly on the nature of the payments to be made by Gomes to the crown; but in fact the contract conferred on the merchant rights of monopoly that turned out to be very lucrative indeed. Beyond the immediate interest as to what Gomes accomplished in the way of further exploration, this contract provides a significant illustration of the relation between the roles of governmental authority and private capital in the exploitation of discovery. The first grant was for five years, and under its terms Gomes grew rich, particularly in the traffic in gold dust. The arrangement with him was renewed in 1474. After that date the government apparently felt that Spanish competition and the opportunity of great profit for the public power warranted the resumption of direct action. This activity by the government became particularly important after 1481, when John II came to the throne. The king now took a greater interest in the tradition of exploration he had inherited than had his immediate predecessors, and it was during his reign that the long effort of the Portuguese to reach the east was brought within sight of realization.

Exploration was pushed in two different directions, the old and the new. In 1487 King John dispatched two envoys, Covilham and Paiva, eastward by the route of the Mediterranean and the Red Sea "to discover and learn about Prester John and where cinnamon is to be found and the other spices which from those parts went to Venice through the countries of the Moors." [14] Eventually information came to the royal court from this expedition, but probably not in time to be of use to Da Gama on his voyage to India. In the meantime a series of expeditions, supported by the government, extended the knowledge of Africa. In 1484 Diego Cam discovered the Congo. And at the same time, while Covilham and Paiva were beginning their search for India and Ethiopia by the old route,

---

[14] Father Francisco Alvarez, *Narrative of the Portuguese Embassy to Abyssinia, 1520–1527*, translated by Lord Stanley of Alderley, Hakluyt Society. Series 1, Vol. LXIV, 266.

Bartholomew Diaz made his famous voyage southward and in 1488 rounded the Cape of Good Hope in a storm.

In spite of this great achievement, it was ten years before the results attained by Diaz were further utilized to bring the search for a way to the Indies to a successful conclusion. The death of the heir to the throne in 1491 and the succession problem to which it gave rise, the voyage of Columbus and the negotiations with Spain that followed from it, combined to delay the king's project to send another major expedition. John II died in 1495 and was succeeded by Emmanuel the Fortunate, who never rose to the level of his opportunities, but who got all the rewards of the efforts of his predecessors.

In 1497 Vasco da Gama was sent out with the express purpose of reaching India by rounding the African coast. His expedition consisted of four ships. In sailing south he followed a course far to the west of that of Diaz, rounded the Cape of Good Hope, followed the eastern coast of Africa to a point where he picked up an Arabian pilot and finally reached Calicut in India in the following year.

This port was one of the centers of the eastern trade in southern India. Among its commodities were not only pepper and ginger, derived from its own hinterland, but also cinnamon from Ceylon, cloves from Malacca, and tin from the Malay peninsula. Da Gama's expedition obtained all the goods it could carry, and returned to Europe in the late summer of 1499 with only two vessels of the original four. These two, however, carried a cargo worth sixty times the cost of the whole expedition. It was at once apparent that the hopes of a century had been realized. The king of Portugal assumed the title of Lord of the Conquest, Navigation and Commerce of Ethiopia, Arabia, Persia, and India, and prepared to realize the immense opportunities now opened before him and his people.

The orbit of Portuguese voyages in the east was rapidly expanded. Malacca was reached by 1511, Canton by 1516, and the Liu Chiu Islands by 1518. In the meantime bases within this area were seized and developed, and the Portuguese Empire organized.

In India, Da Gama and Cabral and their successors had found a collection of small Hindu states, which had little interest in sea power and the possibility of exchanges with other civilizations. The trade of the Indian Ocean was in fact a Mohammedan monopoly, and in many cases the Hindu rulers were not unfavorable to admitting competition. The voyage of Cabral in 1500 was the first to leave a Portuguese factor in India. Attacks on this agent in the period between voyages confronted the Portuguese with the necessity of entering the political life of southern

India. In 1503, when Albuquerque on his first voyage defeated the native ruler of Calicut, there dawned on the European mind the possibility that a mere handful of men, equipped with western military power, could decide the fate of a populous eastern kingdom. In these circumstances the king of Portugal determined to strike a blow at the Mohammedan power in the Indian Ocean. Francisco de Almeida was sent out to India in 1505 with the title of viceroy and a considerable naval expedition. His policy was based on the conception of establishing naval dominance of the Indian Ocean, maintained by the creation of sufficient and secure shore establishments. In the prosecution of this policy he fought a number of important naval actions with Mohammedan fleets. It was not difficult to defeat the forces of the Hindu kingdoms of southern India, but when the power of Egypt and the Mohammedan kingdoms of the north had been united, an impressive war fleet was launched. The critical battle was the battle of Diu in 1509, when the viceroy defeated the combined Egyptian and Indian fleets and, in effect, secured the victory of the Portuguese in the whole region of the Indian Ocean.

Almeida was replaced by Albuquerque in 1509. The apostle of sea power gave way to the representative of still more grandiose ideas for the Portuguese domination of Asia. Albuquerque was convinced not only that it was necessary to maintain the control of the sea but also that a large land empire could be established by his people in India and other lands of the Far East. In pursuance of this objective Albuquerque wore himself out in a career of heroic effort, misunderstood and unappreciated at home. In the space of a few years Goa was captured, a base was secured at Malacca, Ormuz in the Persian Gulf was seized, and expeditions had successfully penetrated into the heart of the Mohammedan territory in the Red Sea. When Albuquerque died in 1515, disillusioned and disappointed in the service of the king who had removed him from office at the request of his enemies, the Portuguese dominion in Asia was assured and the bulk of the rich spice trade now followed the route around the Cape of Good Hope to Lisbon.

Meanwhile, during the years when the Portuguese were bringing to so successful a conclusion their effort to find the southern route to India, the continents of the western hemisphere were discovered and exploration and conquest begun. There had been westward voyages in the Atlantic throughout the fifteenth century, but so far as we know they were without significant result until the time of Columbus.[15]

---

[15] S. E. Morison, *Portuguese Voyages to America in the Fifteenth Century* (Cambridge, 1940), 141–43.

A tradition going far back into the Middle Ages supported the belief that there were lands in the Atlantic, whether entirely mythical, never before discovered, or once known and lost to the European view. This tradition was enriched by several actual medieval discoveries, and was stimulated and renewed by the earliest Portuguese successes. The exploitation of Madeira and the Canaries, and the discovery or rediscovery of the Azores and Cape Verde Islands in the first half of the fifteenth century naturally gave an impetus to Atlantic expeditions. The search for new islands was persistent and continuous. The range of Portuguese expeditions alone extended from the latitudes of Labrador to those of Brazil; and there were other attempts made by the Germans, the Scandinavians, and the English. Yet, in spite of many claims, there is no evidence that any of these fifteenth-century voyages, before Columbus, reached the new world.

Behind Columbus' project lay not only the traditional search for new lands in the Atlantic, but also the learned tradition of geography in the fifteenth century. Aided by the revival of Ptolemy, geographers and cosmographers were in substantial agreement on the theoretical possibility of reaching Asia by sailing west. However, even the extraordinary extension Ptolemy had given to his Asia did not sufficiently diminish the length of the sea voyage westward to make such a route seem within the realm of practical realization. The belief of Columbus that he could actually reach the Indies and Cipango by sailing west depended on a further manipulation and interpretation of the Ptolemaic tradition, shortening the western sea and stretching out the length of the European and Asiatic land mass. Arguments for such an interpretation were available to Columbus in the work of Pierre d'Ailly, in Marco Polo's *Travels,* and in parts of the *Cosmography* of Aeneas Sylvius. His theories were perhaps further bolstered by the letters of the Florentine mathematician, Toscanelli.

In spite of such authorities as he was able to muster, the arguments of Columbus in favor of his attempt were insufficient to convince the advisers of the Portuguese sovereign, to whom he first applied for assistance. It was only after a series of rebuffs and disappointments, dominated by Columbus' own persistent belief, that the rivals of the Portuguese, Ferdinand and Isabella of Aragon and Castile, were induced to support his expedition. Whatever his much debated intentions, whatever the relative weight in his own mind of the search for new islands in the Atlantic and the attainment of the way to the east, the success of his first voyage in 1492 convinced him that he had in fact discovered the Indies. This conviction he maintained during the remaining voyages and even to the end of his life.

The exploitation of Columbus' success was even more rapid than that which followed the Portuguese voyages to the east. Indeed, the latter seems an affair of gradual and prepared stages compared with the process in the west, where a long period of tentative effort in the Atlantic was suddenly replaced by the opportunities disclosed by a single dramatic achievement. The voyages of the Cabots in 1497 and 1498 reached Cape Breton Island, Newfoundland, Nova Scotia, and New England. The Portuguese, Cortereal, in 1500 also reached Newfoundland, and in the same year his compatriot, Cabral, discovered Brazil as he was leading an expedition on the southern route to India. The important voyages of Vespucci in 1499 and 1501 revealed the existence of a new continent, to which the name of America had been given by 1507. From the turn of the century, exploration in the west was rapidly pushed. By 1512 Florida had been discovered, and by 1513 the Pacific Ocean. Between 1519 and 1520 Cortes conquered Mexico, and a little more than ten years later Pizarro and his handful of men overthrew the Inca Empire in Peru.

The organization of the Spanish Empire began to take shape in the west as the Portuguese was being built in the east. Juan de Fonseca, who was appointed to supervise the preparations for the second voyage of Columbus, presently became the leading figure in the government of the Indies. Under his direction the lines of the colonial administration were established. He appointed the personnel and developed the procedure of that body which afterward became the Council of the Indies, the supreme authority in colonial affairs under the Spanish crown.

The control of economic affairs was similarly institutionalized. It was not possible to maintain the original concessions to Columbus; nor on the other hand was the imposition of a complete royal monopoly feasible. To guard the royal rights, however, a single port was authorized, first Cadiz and afterward Seville, to receive the traffic from America. In the latter port rigid supervision maintained controls through which the rights of the crown to license trade were administered, and at the same time assured the collection of those revenues that were considered the crown's share in the products of the New World.

In the New World itself, as distinct from the mother country, the institutions established by the crown were at first fairly limited. After the removal of Columbus in 1500, a royal governor was appointed to

serve at the will of the crown. This office was held from 1509 by Diego
Columbus, the son of the admiral. At the same time that this executive
authority was evolving, a royal court of appeal was created in Santo
Domingo whose jurisdiction served as a check on the acts of the governor.

The increasing territory brought under Spanish control on the mainland was ordinarily in the early period governed by the regime of capitulations. Contracts made between the crown and private individuals stipulated that, in return for the labor and expense of conquest, hereditary
privileges and governmental authority would be granted to successful
conquistadores. When at a later date these *adelantados* and captains-
general had served their purpose and vast territories had been acquired
in the name of the Spanish government, it was realized that this system
might eventually undermine the position of the crown by permitting the
development of overmighty subjects. Direct royal control was then extended by the institution of the viceroyalties of New Spain and Peru.

The Spanish were thus able to establish a great territorial government
in the New World, to an extent impossible for the Portuguese, who confronted the populous kingdoms of Asia.

These two great European movements of discovery at the end of the
fifteenth century—the Portuguese to the east, and the Spanish to the
west—were in a sense united by the successful circumnavigation of the
globe. In 1519 Magellan, a Portuguese captain in the service of Spain,
was sent out to find a westward passage to the Spice Islands. Magellan
himself died in the Philippines, but three years after his expedition had
left Europe one of its ships returned to Lisbon from the east, thus sealing
the connection between the achievement of Columbus and that of Da
Gama.

Seen in the perspective of world history, Latin Christendom occupied
in the fifteenth century a territory relatively small and insignificant in
comparison with the habitable areas of the earth's surface. It amounted
in fact to no more than a western peninsula jutting out from the great
Asiatic land mass. From time to time, and especially in the thirteenth and
early fourteenth centuries, vistas had been opened toward the east. These
vistas provided glimpses of societies whose territorial extent, population,
material wealth, and political stability were superior to anything in recent
European experience, and whose achievements in arts and letters bore at
the very least a favorable comparison with the Latin west. This knowledge had never been shared by many and was now in the fifteenth

century blurred and overlaid with a mass of legend. The most optimistic calculation taken in the middle of that century might have concluded that a society that had occupied western Europe for so long a time, with occasional if ephemeral bursts of outward expansion, might continue to survive and hold its own.

No one, however, in this general situation could have foreseen that before the fifteenth century was finished western Europeans would have discovered the vast lands of the western hemisphere that now lay open to exploitation, or would have established the new sea routes to the civilizations of the east, which this time were to be regular and permanent. By 1500 the greatest steps in this unique and dramatic expansion had been taken, and within two more decades—by the time the religious revolution was beginning in Germany—the Portuguese Empire had been established in India and southeast Asia; European Christians traded in Malacca and Canton, and in the New World the Aztec Empire was about to fall to a small band of Spanish adventurers. A man who remembered the fall of Constantinople as a boy could easily have lived to hear the news of the circumnavigation of the globe. Within the space of hardly more than a generation the horizon of Latin Christendom had lifted; Europe was in a position to take a view of the world, and this perspective was not again to be closed.

It is natural that history should have endowed the men and events associated with this achievement with a transcendent significance. Adam Smith in the eighteenth century declared that the discovery of America and of a passage to the East Indies by the Cape of Good Hope were the two greatest and most important events recorded in the history of mankind, and at least half of this judgment is enshrined in the memory of every American schoolboy. Succeeding generations, recalling these names and dates, have celebrated not only the triumphs of individual genius and persistence; they have also and more importantly registered a conviction that here began a new epoch in the history of Europe and the world. We are dealing here with the kind of events that become symbolic of dramatic and revolutionary change. What is often minimized or forgotten is the extent to which the voyages of Columbus and Da Gama rested upon the labors of countless predecessors in the European past, but what is never forgotten is the fact that they were succeeded by increasing numbers of followers who finally carried the civilization of Europe to the remotest parts of the earth. In this sense their historical significance depends upon the belief that they mark the beginning of a continuous process. It may seem unnecessarily obvious to suggest that if Columbus had returned from his first voyage and reported his results to a society absolutely indifferent whether the east was reached or not—if in other words there had been no encouragement, no response, no imitation—then the date 1492 would hardly occupy its present sacred place in the historical calendar. When we celebrate this date the emotional focus is on Columbus with all the drama justified by history and enriched by legend. We forget the extent to which we presuppose or imply the existence in fifteenth-century Europe of a society ready and eager to follow the paths which had been opened. So strongly do we feel that it was natural, indeed inevitable, to seize all the advantages that followed from the great voyages of the fifteenth century that we cannot imagine a condition of affairs in which the achievements of a Columbus or a Da Gama would have remained without consequences. Yet there have been other societies and other times in the history of Europe itself in which comparable achievements appear as isolated phenomena, irrelevant happenings, promising beginnings that led to nothing. The voyages of the Norsemen to North America left no perceptible mark except in literature either on the lands which they reached or on the society from which they came. The successes of the Polos inaugurated no permanent routes between Europe and the east.

If examples from the history of Europe are not convincing on this point, consider the case of China. The same fifteenth century in which the western Europeans began their successful expansion by sea to the east was the century in which the tribute fleets of the Chinese emperors accomplished their most remarkable voyages in the south and west. In the years between 1405 and 1433 seven great expeditions ordered by the Ming emperors sailed to the western seas under the command of the eunuch, Cheng Ho. Their purpose seems to have been the establishment of diplomatic relations and the collection of tribute from the barbarian kingdoms. They were official undertakings of formidable size. Typically each expedition consisted of over 27,000 men embarked in fifty or more huge ocean-going junks. These great fleets visited the East Indies, Malacca, Siam, Ceylon, India, Ormuz in the Persian Gulf, the Red Sea and the eastern coast of Africa. Aden and other Red Sea ports were reached several times and a delegation from at least one of the expeditions was sent to Mecca. The fleets touched at various places on the African coast at least as far south as Melinda and perhaps beyond.[16]

[16] P. Pelliot, "*Les grands voyages maritimes chinois au début du XVe siècle,*" *T'oung Pao*, Series II, Vol. 30 (1933), 237–452.

During the years when the China Sea, the Indian Ocean, the Red Sea and the Persian Gulf were thus being swept by Chinese fleets, the Portuguese were inching along the western coast of Africa and, in 1434, the year after the last great recorded expedition of the Ming, Gil Eannes in the service of Prince Henry rounded Cape Bojeador, only a little more than eight hundred miles from Lisbon. In the long history of the relations between east and west there are few contrasts more dramatic than that presented by these two voyages, the Portuguese with its *barca* of twenty-five tons carrying a handful of men, and the Chinese fleet manned by thousands. Yet the Chinese voyages had no revolutionary consequences in the society from which they came, and in the end it was the west that conquered. Cheng Ho's ships visited over twenty countries and brought back many rare and costly things, but these results failed to stimulate in China the same aggressive impulse to expansion that was produced in the west by a handful of gold dust and a few slaves brought back from the Guinea coast.

The contrast between the achievements and attitudes of the Chinese and those of the Europeans in the fifteenth century is one of the striking coincidences of history, but the Chinese were of course not alone in failing to exploit possibilities of cultural and commercial expansion in the way that became characteristic of Europeans after the fifteenth century. Throughout the medieval and early modern period the civilization of Islam was in some ways in a uniquely favored position to undertake a program of further military, political or cultural conquests until its influence should circle the globe. The far-flung commerce of the Arabs stretched from China to western Europe. Their geographers knew more about the world than those of any other society. Their merchants were in direct contact with the greatest number and variety of religious and political systems. Yet with all this the Arab civilization failed to produce the same kind of thinking and action that developed in Europe. So it has been with others. The expansion of Latin Christendom, with all its fateful consequences, has been a unique phenomenon in the history of the world.

The question that forces itself upon us is: Why was this expansion successful in Europe and not elsewhere? Why did the voyages of discovery "take" in Europe and not in China? Mr. Toynbee has drawn us a picture of a "pre-Da Gaman belt" of civilizations stretching from Europe through the Ottoman Empire and the Mongol states of India to China and Japan. He points out that all these civilizations had certain common social and cultural characteristics. All were essentially peasant societies in which a large mass of agricultural laborers supported a minority of rulers. In each case the ruling class was maintained by religious sanctions as well as by secular political controls. Each of these societies believed it had received the revealed truth and that its way of life was uniquely civilized. Mr. Toynbee considers that of all these particular parochial societies Latin Christendom was the most unlikely candidate to undertake expansion on a world-wide scale and to carry that expansion through to a successful conclusion.

There are many features of the situation that appear to support this view. We might agree with Mr. Toynbee that both the Arabs and the Chinese seem to have been more favorably situated in the fifteenth century than the Europeans. Even in the field of technology the European superiority was far from clear. For, if the Europeans had developed the technical skills to make possible the voyages of Prince Henry, the Chinese, as we have seen, were able to perform navigational feats of incomparably greater magnitude. Clearly, also, the mere existence and availability of any particular technology is less important than what is done with it. Professor Panofsky has reminded us that although Roger Bacon had an optic tube which anticipated the telescope, it was used to see whether names could be read on a gravestone from a distance, whereas Galileo's telescope was directed to the exploration of the secrets of the universe. The particular technological revolution in fifteenth-century Europe that permitted the development of sea communications must therefore be understood in relation to the total complex of ideas and institutions in which it appeared.

Seen from this point of view, Latin Christendom, far from being the least likely candidate for expansion, emerges as the candidate most likely to succeed. Behind those appearances on which Mr. Toynbee dwells we can discern specific characteristics in the European intellectual inheritance and in the European institutional structure that help us to understand the energies behind the voyages of discovery and the overseas conquests. In one sense the remaining chapters of this book may be regarded as an exploration of those characteristics and their manifestations in various kinds of human activity. However, it is necessary to consider here, if only briefly, some of those which were most closely related to the process of expansion.

In the first place, although the western world was indeed assured of its possession of Christian revelation, it was never completely convinced that its own institutions were the most perfect embodiment of that revelation.

A golden age lay in the past; the kingdom of Prester John existed in the east; the lost isles of Atlantis and Saint Brendan were to be discovered in the west. The vision of a mythical "better place," a Utopia that existed somewhere else, fitfully haunted the mind of Latin Christendom and was a spur to curiosity. Perfection was not here, not now; it had existed long ago in time; it might be found again surviving far away in space. Thus the attitude of the European world toward the barbarians and the infidel beyond its horizons was never so completely closed and assured as that which appears to have been characteristic of the Chinese.

In the long run this curiosity was closely connected with Christian missionary zeal. Yet the impulse to proselytize was as intense among the Moslems as among the Christians; in this respect the Christian religion was not unique. What was shared, however, by no other society of the "pre-Da Gaman belt" was the complex of traditions, doubts and hopes that seemed to promise the existence of a center of civilization outside and beyond the horizon with which the Christian world might eventually hope to be in contact. Intertwined with the persistent drive for conversion, this other inheritance of curiosity is of critical importance in the intellectual background that prepared the way for European expansion.

Turning from ideas to institutions it is equally clear that there were fundamental characteristics in the organization of western society that favored the success of expansion. This was nowhere more apparent than in the structure of property relationships and in the provision of financial support for the voyages of discovery.

The contrast between the Chinese and the Portuguese expeditions of the fifteenth century is as striking in this respect as it is in others. The emperor of China, ruling all things, had only to command in order that the wealth of the imperial treasury might be expended on the magnificent expeditions he had ordered. In the west, however, the sovereigns, who could never find sufficient revenue for their ordinary expenses and whose chancellors exhausted themselves in pleading with estates and diets for grants of money, had little capital to put into the financing of hazardous adventures overseas. On the whole, therefore, there were many cases in Europe in which the governments contributed the authority and private individuals the property that made possible these voyages.

The sharp separation between the rights of authority and the rights of property was a fundamental part of the western inheritance. Medieval theory, and to a large extent medieval practice, had insisted that the king should "live of his own"; that is, his expenses should be met by the revenues of his own domain. Only emergencies of a recognized kind justified a demand for a wider levy, and in such circumstances the consent of the estates was requested. The widening scope of action by government conflicted with these ideas, with the result that, almost universally, early modern governments in Europe found themselves hard up. The "ordinary" revenues had ceased to be in any degree sufficient to meet the needs of government, and there was everywhere a resort to those "extraordinary" revenues that had originally been the recourse of emergency, but were now needed all the time as the regular basis of the government's support. In this situation it is understandable that governments had little available capital to invest in exploring expeditions.

Isabella did not have to pawn her jewels to finance Columbus, but the money was secured partly by borrowing on the authority of a royal official and partly by contributions from what we call "private" sources. Columbus himself raised about an eighth of the required capital. There were many examples of authorizations by governments where no funds at all were supplied. In England the charter of Henry VII to Cabot conferred authority to establish in the name of the king of England dominion over such territories as might be discovered, but it explicitly left to Cabot himself and to the faithful merchants of Bristol the provision of the necessary capital. In an earlier period, as we have seen, individuals like Cadamosto had been attracted to the service of Prince Henry by the prospect of turning "one soldo into six or ten." Later, when the kings of Portugal found it impossible to continue as a government what Prince Henry had achieved as a private individual, the rights to the Guinea trade, with the obligation to continue exploration, were leased out to a Lisbon merchant in return for an annual payment. Although there are certainly examples of expeditions in which the governments concerned footed the entire bill, it is clear that the incentives created by the structure of property relationships were already of decisive importance in this early period.

In the conquest of the Spanish Empire in the New World the most important of all the early acquired territories were obtained at no direct cost to the crown. Individual leaders from many walks of life were allowed to participate in the process of conquest on their own initiative. In the name of the sovereign, or by virtue of royal patents, they conquered territory at their own expense, hoping they would be assigned rights that would make their fortune when they had finished. Mexico, Peru, Yucatan, and Guatemala are all examples of territories brought to the Spanish crown in this way.

Similar incentives were largely absent in the case of the Chinese. The great expeditions of the Ming in the fifteenth century were characteristically enterprises financed by the government and staffed by the bureaucracy. Even where merchants were permitted to participate for their own gain, institutional guarantees for private property did not exist on the same scale as in Europe. The opportunity for expansion occurred for both China and Europe; indeed, from the point of view of technological achievement as measured by the size and range of expeditions, the opportunity presented to China was far greater. Yet the European society whose rulers were far less wealthy than the Chinese emperor was in reality in a much better position to seize that opportunity. In the absence of comprehensive monolithic government control the European system allowed for a greater measure of individual incentive and broader basis of participation.

The success of the expansion of Latin Christendom must thus be viewed against the general background of the pluralism of the European intellectual inheritance and institutional structure. Competing ideas and competing interests sustained a great creative effort. At the same time expansion had its price. The altered situation of Europe in the world, the very opportunities that were increasingly opened by the voyages of exploration and discovery accentuated the divergences within the Christian community. In concluding an analysis of the boundaries of European civilization in the period with which we are concerned, we must therefore turn finally to the relationships between changes on the frontiers and the weakening of the historic sense of community within Christendom. In fact, such unity as had existed had begun to be seriously disrupted long before the ideological split in the sixteenth century.

IV. THE TITLE TO DOMINION AND THE UNITY OF CHRISTENDOM

During the years when the Turkish pressure was acutely constricting the southeastern boundaries of Europe and the great voyages were lifting the horizon in the west and south, the effectiveness of the conception of the Christian community became progressively weaker. The consciousness of belonging to a *respublica christiana* had never been universal among the inhabitants of Europe; but its intensity had been greatest in those periods when the geographical area of its allegiance had been most stable. Now that the geographical boundaries were altering with great rapidity, there appeared new opportunties for the development of fundamental rivalries within the Christian commonwealth.

The sense of community had been built on the existence of a common religion. It implied the existence of a geographical area within which this religion was universally accepted. More than the sharing of a common belief, however, was involved in the idea of Christendom. The visible signs of the unity of the various bodies that made up the *respublica christiana* were the existence of the canon law as a universally enforceable body of regulations and the jurisdictional power of the papacy. There was thus a legal and institutional as well as a moral basis for the unity of the European peoples.

The canon law applied in all cases to a numerous and important group of the population—the clergy—and in certain kinds of cases to all classes of the population. More than the Roman law on which it was modeled, it was the common law of the European world. In spite of the long history of conflicts between the canon law and the legislation of the various secular political units, the existence of the canonical courts with their claims and procedures remained an effective reality until their revolutionary rejection in the sixteenth century.

Similarly the jurisdiction of the papacy, although often repudiated in theory and practice and far less comprehensive than it had been in the thirteenth century, was the institutional symbol of such sense of community as existed in the European world. Still in the middle of the fifteenth century the Roman curia received financial support from nearly all European countries. Peter's pence was paid from England, Scandinavia, Poland, Hungary, Aragon, and the two Sicilies. Other types of revenue were derived from Germany and France. The extent to which the papal claims to exact various forms of taxation were admitted may be taken as a rough measure of the actual effectiveness of the international jurisdiction exercised by the papacy. Certainly, the extreme theories of the *plenitudo potestatis* elaborated by the canonists were almost everywhere rejected, yet there was a sense in which the papacy was regarded as a real international arbitral authority. Treaties were sanctioned by oaths, violation of which implied a right of interference and of judgment by the church. In 1468, for example, Louis XI and Charles the Bold made a treaty in which they swore on a piece of the true cross and invoked all the ecclesiastical penalties that might follow the violation of the oath. The fact that neither Louis XI nor Charles the Bold was disposed to pay much attention to such penalties does not affect the persistence of the idea of the papacy as an arbitral authority. The efficacy of this idea was demonstrated most concretely in the papal jurisdiction over questions of marriage, and most vaguely in the disputes over the status of the church and the clergy and the general direction of society toward a spiritual end.

This conception of an international authority presiding over that Christian society which was the Church Visible had received many shocks since the age of Innocent III. The effectiveness of the sense of Christendom had never been more seriously tested than it was in the last years of the fifteenth century when confronted by the changes in the frontiers of Christendom. The sense of community as expressed in the conception of the papal responsibilities was not strong enough to survive the problems created by the Turkish seizure of Christian dominions and by the extension of European dominion overseas.

In confronting the Turkish problem, the papacy suffered from its dual position. It was on the one hand a temporal political power in Italy, with interests and responsibilities like those of other Italian political powers. On the other hand, it was an institution that inherited a long tradition of responsibility for the direction of Christendom. As we have seen, the popes took a leading part in efforts to set on foot a crusade against the Turkish invaders, but at the same time, and almost from the date of the fall of Constantinople, the papacy initiated negotiations with the Turks that could not but have a deeply divisive effect on the European sense of community. The most celebrated example of such negotiations was the history of Djem Sultan.

When Djem had been originally defeated he had sought asylum among the Knights of St. John at Rhodes and concluded a treaty with the Knights whereby he agreed to confide his interests to the grand master. In this document he bound himself to protect the Christians in return for aid in the effort to regain the throne he considered to be rightfully his. Shortly thereafter, however, the grand master entered into direct negotiations with Sultan Bayazid and obtained from him a treaty recognizing the position of the order at Rhodes and stipulating that, in return for keeping Djem in captivity where he could not trouble his brother, the Knights would receive an annual payment. This action of the grand master, in violation of the promise made to Djem, was condoned by the papacy, although in moderately veiled language, when Sixtus IV assured the grand master that it was not necessary to keep a promise made to an infidel.

Djem was subsequently sent to France, where he was imprisoned in various chateaux for seven years and was finally delivered to Pope

Innocent VIII in 1489. For some time thereafter both the papacy and the Knights of St. John received an annual payment from the sultan, until the bad faith of the grand master was discovered.

During the period of Djem's captivity in Rome discussions were entered into involving the payment by the Turks for killing Djem, and also the possible price of aid to the papacy by the sultan against the projected invasion of Italy by Charles VIII. In these circumstances it is not surprising that, when Charles VIII took Rome, he made it one of his conditions that Djem should be delivered to him.[17]

Insofar as these negotiations became known, it is obvious that they must have had an effect upon thinking about the unity of Christian Europe. As early as 1460, when Pius II had written his *Cosmography,* he had included the Turks among the nations of Europe, but it is clear that by this he meant no more than the fact that the Turks had occupied territory that had always been regarded from a geographical point of view as European. By the time his successors were carrying on direct diplomatic negotiations with the sultan, the foundations were being laid for a very different conception of a European community of nations, a conception in which dominion might be justified regardless of religious belief. The Ottoman Empire was on the way to becoming a member of the European state system.

The authority of the papacy and the sense of the common interests of Christendom were likewise weakened in the attempt to establish the legal title to territories discovered overseas. While the dominion of the Turks in Europe, established by right of conquest, was increasingly accepted, the title of European countries to dominion overseas was increasingly asserted without reference to the theoretical jurisdiction of the head of the Christian church.

A series of papal bulls, exemplifying the traditional attitude of the Christian toward the infidel, had conferred on the Portuguese sovereigns the legal right to acquire and govern territories outside the bounds of Christendom. Nicholas V in 1452 had granted to the king of Portugal a bull entitling him to subjugate all the countries of the infidel, seize their property and govern their peoples. Two years later, in response to Prince Henry's intentions, another bull was issued in favor of Alfonso V, giving to Portugal all the regions discovered and to be discovered as far as the Indies (*usque ad Indos*) south of Capes Bojeador and Nun and toward

---

[17] L. Thuasne, *Djem Sultan fils de Mohammed II* (Paris, 1892) is the most complete account.

Guinea. Similar bulls in 1481 and 1484 confirmed the Portuguese in their discoveries. All these documents purported to be grants of title by an authority able to speak in the name of the whole Christian community.[18]

When Columbus returned from his first voyage in 1493, he landed at Lisbon and hence first visited the Portuguese court and described his discoveries to King John. The latter, convinced that some of the domains conferred on him by the papal bulls had been invaded, wrote to Ferdinand and Isabella advancing his historic claims. These negotiations led to an appeal to Rome, and in May and again in September, 1493, Alexander VI issued the celebrated bulls that granted half the world to the Spanish crown and proposed the demarcation line between the Spanish and Portuguese dominions. Subsequent to these bulls, however, direct diplomatic negotiations between Spain and Portugal settled the differences between the two countries by moving the proposed line of demarcation between their respective spheres 270 leagues farther to the west. This Treaty of Tordesillas in June, 1494, contained a clause asking for papal confirmation, but also expressly provided that no papal act *motu proprio* could change its terms. The confirmation was not granted until 1506.[19]

It appears clear that even in the case of the bulls of 1493 the very terms emanated from the chancery of Ferdinand and Isabella. The line of demarcation was probably proposed by Columbus himself. In other words, the papacy was here acting as an instrument of Spanish diplomacy rather than as an arbitral authority settling conflicting claims between two nations. So far as it can be said to have existed at all, the international law that dealt with the acquisition of overseas possessions thus became one of unregulated competition. Spain and Portugal were willing to use, but paid no more than lip service to, the authority of the papacy. Other countries did not consider it necessary to have any regard for the claims of the papal jurisdiction. Henry VII conferred upon Cabot the right to establish in the name of the king of England authority over such territories as might be discovered. Increasingly, public opinion in all the European countries regarded the governments as the sole judges of the conditions in which they might undertake expansion; and the final test was the right of conquest and the ability to maintain such dominion as had been acquired. In much of the writing of the period there is a sense of destiny, the his-

---

[18] Text of the bulls in *Alguns Documentos do Archivo Nacional da Torre do Tombo ácerca das navegacoes e conquistas portuguezas,* edited by Jose Ramos Coelho (Lisbon, 1892).

[19] H. Vanderlinden, "Alexander VI and the Demarcation of the Maritime and Colonial Domains of Spain and Portugal, 1493-1494," *American Historical Review,* 22 (1916), 1-20.

toric mission of the particular group that is to be asserted and fulfilled regardless of the more ecumenical tradition. As the Turkish dominion in Europe was accepted, so the European dominion overseas was justified.

Under this double pressure the meaning of *respublica christiana* began to be transformed. The emphasis shifted from a society whose unity was founded on religious belief to one bound together by sharing in a common civilization. The notion of a Christian community persisted and even those jurists later in the sixteenth century who admitted that the Turks had just as much right as Christians to their dominion by a natural law distinguished within the *societas gentium* ruled by natural law a special society of Christian nations who had unique responsibilities toward each other and toward the infidel.[20] The unity of the medieval world had been strong enough to make indelible the heritage of belonging to a common civilization, but not strong enough to create effective political action transcending the framework of the interests of particular states. Such forms of common political action as the Middle Ages had created in the effort to organize society on Christian principles gradually gave way to the appearance of the European states system. At the end of the fifteenth century there were many signs of the acceleration of this transition. The *Memoirs* of Commines present us with a picture of a society in which the old arbitral appeals were no longer considered, but which showed as yet only the faint signs of the structure of permanent states on which the European states system was to be built. Religious unity still remained formally intact, but its sanctions were increasingly ineffective. It is only later, when that unity had in turn begun to be threatened in the era of religious revolution, that we have in such men as Erasmus and More a strong if despairing assertion of the importance of maintaining a broader sense of community and accepting the "Council of Christendom" against the "council of one realm." Long before the ideological split, however, the forces that divided the interests of one realm from those of another were becoming apparent. They were perhaps most clearly manifest in the problems and opportunities created by the Turkish threat and the European expansion. Yet these divisions cannot be understood solely in terms of the occasions that permitted them to develop, and we must turn from a consideration of the frontiers to the analysis of the economic and political changes that lay behind the internal rivalries and shaped the institutional development of Christendom.

[20] F. L. Baumer, "England, the Turk, and the Common Corps of Christendom," *American Historical Review*, Vol. 50 (1944), 30.

Chapter Two

THE DIRECTION OF ECONOMIC AND SOCIAL CHANGE

I. THE COMMERCIAL REVOLUTION

OF ALL the economic changes which coincided with the age of the great discoveries the expansion of commercial activity claims attention first because it was the most revolutionary alteration, the one of which contemporaries were most aware and of which they could measure most directly the effects. Ultimately, as everyone knows, the new orientation of commerce involved nothing less than the transfer of initiative from the Mediterranean to the northwest countries of Europe. It may, however, be argued that the very obviousness of the long-run effects of a worldwide sea trade has promoted an exaggerated estimate of its immediate impact on the economy of the Christian community. Any attempt to describe the limits of the commercial prosperity created in Europe in the first decades after Da Gama's voyage must begin with a consideration of the nature and organization of the eastern trade before the successes of the Portuguese had opened the direct route to the Indies.

The great traders of the east had been the Arabs, established all the way from China to the Mediterranean as middlemen controlling the movement of spices and other eastern commodities to the west. For the most part the objects of this commerce were materials of small bulk and great intrinsic value, easily transshipped; such items as pepper, ginger, cinnamon, clove, tin, and jewels made up the greater part of a trade that did so much to enrich all those through whose hands it passed.

From southern India, which was the entrepôt of commerce with the farther east, there were in the middle of the fifteenth century two main routes by which this traffic reached western Europe. The first route went to Ormuz in the Persian Gulf, whence goods were shipped up the Shatt-el-Arab River to Basra, where they were transferred to caravans. At Basra the route divided again; the caravans either went across the desert to Damascus or Aleppo and on to the Mediterranean, or they went north to Trebizond on the Black Sea. At all these ports the Venetians as well as other Italians were established and took over from the Arab middlemen the goods that had been brought from such a distance. In the case of the Black Sea commerce it was not only the Italians who supported thriving factories in this region but also the Muscovites and representatives of other northern and central European countries who carried the traffic to the northern orbit of European commerce.

The second principal route to Europe led through the Red Sea. This was a route filled with complications. Ships went from southern India to Jiddah or Aden, where the cargo was transshipped into small boats that worked up the Red Sea to Suez. Here the goods were unloaded again and carried by caravan across to Cairo, where they were finally again loaded on small boats to go down the Nile to Alexandria. At this depot they were bought by Venice.

All these routes were encumbered with a variety of tolls and tariffs, by which the various powers whose territory they crossed hoped to enrich themselves. For example, the sultan of Egypt imposed a requirement that one third of all the imports of merchants living in Jiddah should consist of pepper. This third was to be the sultan's share, and it was stipulated that it should be sold to the government in Jiddah at the prices that had obtained in Calicut in India. In other words, the sultan's pepper arrived free of shipping charges. In effect, this convenient arrangement made the sultan a partner by a third share in every merchant's voyage—at no risk whatever to himself. Furthermore, there were other duties both at Suez and at Cairo, some of them exacted in the name of registration and other straight *ad valorem*. Altogether the exchequer of the sultan was largely supported by the profits of this trade. Similarly, the other great powers through whose territories any of these routes passed had a stake in the maintenance of this commerce. Thus, in spite of differences in religious orthodoxy, the shah of Persia, the Mameluke sultan of Egypt, and the Ottoman emperor were united in resisting the innovations of the Portuguese.[1]

As soon as the latter had, by military action, possessed themselves of the monopoly of the trade with India and the Far East, an attempt was made to organize the transport and distribution of the products of this trade in Europe. The king of Portugal became the fortunate heir of all the Near Eastern monarchs who had previously enjoyed the profits of the pepper trade. He now established a system in which royal rights to a very considerable share of this trade were ensured. In effect, the system amounted to a royal monopoly. The Casa da India was established in Lisbon as the

[1] Whiteway, *Rise of Portuguese Power in India, 1497–1550* (London, 1897).

central organization through which all trade with the Indies was licensed or controlled. Private merchants were required to bring their wares to this state establishment, and were forbidden to sell spices in Europe except upon license granted by the Casa da India, and then only after taxes as high as thirty to sixty per cent had been taken by the crown. The pepper and other spices that in this way came under direct royal control were sold in European markets by royal agents. This commercial activity was the foundation of the prosperity of the house of Portugal in the sixteenth century. It was in pepper that the dowry of the wife of Charles V was paid, and even the great Erasmus of Rotterdam, because he protested against the royal monopoly, lost his favor at the court of Lisbon.[2]

A similar development was taking place in Spain, where the western trade of the new empire had to be organized. Here the principal component, although at first available only in small amounts, consisted of the precious metals. Gold and silver had diminished in supply in western Europe over a long period before the renewal of mining activity and the successes of the voyages of discovery at the end of the fifteenth century. This decline had been due to a variety of causes, among which were the drain of precious metals to the east, where they had been used to buy the luxury products of the eastern trade; the manufacture of ecclesiastical monstrances and jewels; and finally, the exhaustion of some mines continuously worked in Europe since the time of the Romans. This short supply of the precious metals had created monetary problems for nearly every European country. Attempts to depreciate the coinage had been frequently direct or secretly approved by the governments themselves. This situation in part explains the role of the search for gold in the Age of Discovery.

The Spanish followed very much the same pattern as the Portuguese in organizing their trade within the new empire. The Casa da Contracción, established at Seville in 1503, directed the trade with the Indies. It combined the functions of a board of trade, a commercial court and a clearing house for American traffic. Among the other functions of this establishment was the duty to ensure that the crown should receive a fifth of all the goods produced by America. Gold, silver, and precious stones were regarded as a regalian right, and came in any case to the crown. This organization grew and continued to function as the mani-

[2] M. Bataillon, "Erasme et la cour du Portugal," Arquivo de historia e bibliografia, II (1927), 258–91.

festation of a royal monopoly interest in American economic enterprise.[3]

In spite of the fact that great wealth, upon which the successful exercise of political power ultimately depended, was thus poured into the Iberian peninsula, Spain and Portugal failed to take economic leadership, and the center of international trade• became not Seville or Lisbon but Antwerp. For this there were many reasons. The Low Countries had long been one of the most advanced centers of economic development in Europe. From the time of the medieval fairs this territory had been important as the meeting place between the trade of the Hanseatic League and that flowing from the Italian system of commerce. Among the Flemish cities Antwerp was replacing Bruges and Ghent because it was freer of the complicated network of medieval restrictions. The overstrained credit of the Iberian kingdoms, their need to buy manufactured goods and even grain abroad, what we should today call their unfavorable balance of trade, meant that their new riches were drained off to pay both public and private debts. The German bankers, many of whom had made their start by being on the receiving end of the eastern trade when it flowed through Venice, were able to adapt themselves to the changed circumstances and now took a leading part in the disposition of the products of the Spanish and Portuguese monopolies. As the Low Countries had been the medieval intermediary between north and south, so now Antwerp became the center for dealings between the Spanish and Portuguese royal monopolies and German capital, exemplified by houses like the Fugger and the Welser. In this way Antwerp grew to be the great international money market of the sixteenth century, and its bourse was perhaps the best symbol of that closer connection and sensitivity in the European economy as a whole which was manifest in the fact that the late arrival of the Portuguese or Spanish ships in the Iberian harbors could cause a panic in Antwerp and the failure of a distant bank in Augsburg or Ulm.[4]

Besides enriching the Spanish and Portuguese royal families and increasing the prosperity of Antwerp, the influx of spices and precious metals at the beginning of the sixteenth century had another far more fundamental effect. It was an important factor accounting for the enormous price rise which was so striking a characteristic of sixteenth-century

[3] C. H. Haring, *The Spanish Empire in America* (Oxford, 1947), chaps. IV–VIII.

[4] R. Ehrenberg, *Das Zeitalter der Fugger* (Jena, 1896) has a good account of the bourse at Antwerp.

economic history. How far the change in the price level was the result of the import of precious metals as opposed to the financial manipulations of the Spanish government is still debated, but in the long run and on a European scale there can be no doubt of the importance of the former factor.

The price rise began to be noticed in Castile as early as the first decade of the sixteenth century. Although it did not reach those inflationary proportions which caused so much complaint by the middle of the century, it was yet sufficient to have a depressing effect on Castilian industry, since it became cheaper to buy manufactured goods in regions where costs had not yet begun to rise. From Castile the spread of the price rise over the continent can be traced. As might have been predicted because of their political connection, the Low Countries felt its effects soon after they had become evident in Spain, whereas in France and England prices began to rise materially only at the very end of the period we are considering.[5]

On the whole, in those areas that were most severely and earliest affected, prices appear to have gone up faster than wages and rents. This development was followed by important social consequences, the character of which will be considered elsewhere; but there were direct economic consequences as well. The differential between wages and prices permitted certain entrepreneurs to accumulate large amounts of capital which in turn were an important factor in the expansion of industrial enterprise. The capital investments that lay behind printing plants, mining industries, and the expansion of textile industries were thus in part a creation of the changes in the scope of commercial activity. With the increase in capital accumulation there also appeared new incentives for investment and an environment more receptive to inventions and technological innovations. Of course these various aspects of economic activity were mutually interrelated. If the commercial ventures created capital that developed industry, it was equally true that the increase in the productive capacity of Europe was a stimulus to the extension of the lines of commerce and the search for new markets.

Spectacular as were the changes caused in the long run by the enlargement of the scope of commerce, it must again be emphasized that the discovery of America and the sea route to the Indies did not all at once revolutionize the economic organization of Europe. The items of commerce which came from India and the New World in the first decades

[5] Hamilton, *American Treasure and the Price Revolution in Spain, 1501–1660* (Cambridge, 1934).

of the sixteenth century were exotic and small in bulk. They enriched the few royal families, merchants, and banking houses through whose hands they passed and they contributed to the vast expansion of the productive capacity of the European continent that was to come later. They had an immediate effect on prices. But the main lines of the organization of European trade as developed during the medieval period continued. Baltic lumber, Swedish iron, English wool, Flemish and Italian textiles, and French wines were exchanged in the ways which had been traditional for centuries.

It has sometimes been represented that by the establishment of the new route to the Indies the prosperity of Venice was dealt a blow from which it never recovered. While in the long run this may be true, it is nevertheless important to recognize that the decline of Venice was neither sudden nor complete. Anyone who rides down the Grand Canal can observe for himself the number of palaces and other buildings dating from the sixteenth century, after the decline of the city is said to have set in. The spice trade, in fact, had accounted for only a part of the economic activity and the prosperous position of Venice. There was the local Mediterranean-carrying trade, of which Venice inherited much more when Spain and Portugal were fully occupied in more distant ventures.[6]

In the north the Hanseatic League had entered its period of final decline, but this decline was not synonymous with a falling-off in the Baltic trade. In spite of some conspicuous successes, an organization of cities welded together solely for the pursuit of an economic interest had proved, over the years, that it was not able to hold its own against the emergent national monarchies. The kingdom of Denmark and the Dutch in the west and the grand duchy of Moscow and Poland in the east had made serious inroads on the privileged position of the Hanseatic merchants. In all these countries there were signs of the familiar relationship between a growing class of native merchants and the authority of the crown. This relationship was reinforced by the progress of national sentiment and usually operated to the disadvantage of the international merchant of the earlier period. Privileges which had been freely granted to the Hanse in previous decades were now retracted or withdrawn altogether in favor of governmental efforts in behalf of local merchant organizations. In addition, within the Hanseatic League itself there was a growing tension between the eastern and western cities which destroyed

[6] F. C. Lane, "Venetian Shipping during the Commercial Revolution," *American Historical Review*, Vol. 28 (January, 1933), 19–39.

the possibility of the kind of unified action by the Hanse diet which had been feasible at the height of its success. In the west factors deriving both from the physical environment and from economic policy began to undermine the position of Bruges, which had been one of the staple towns of the League. Its pre-eminence in economic activity passed to Antwerp, where the type of economic organization was more susceptible of innovation.

Large-scale changes of this kind were, however, slow. The old forms of commercial activity persisted, although sometimes in new adaptations. For many years they were more important in the European economy than the changes precipitated by the discovery of a new world and the finding of a sea route to the Indies.

II. THE DEVELOPMENT OF INDUSTRY

Enlargement of the scope of European commercial activity was accompanied by an expansion of industrial productivity. This expansion proceeded unevenly and its stages were marked by no dates as dramatic as those of the great voyages. For this reason its treatment within an established period presents particular difficulty. More than most areas of historical study, economic history has been encumbered by a conventional periodization derived originally from other criteria. Modern students have increasingly emphasized fundamental continuities in the growth of the European economy from the eleventh century to the industrial revolution.

Within this evolution few subjects have been more discussed than the origins of capitalism. The triumphs of capitalism in the nineteenth century as well as the subsequent attack upon it have stimulated analysis of the unique character of the economic development of the western world. The most comprehensive question turns on the determination of those factors in European civilization, absent or differently combined in other societies, which permitted and fostered the development of capitalistic organization. A great deal of research has been expended on the location of what are presumed to be decisive turning points both in thought and in economic institutions in the long transition from a feudal to a capitalistic world. While such research has produced a valuable enlargement of our understanding of particular sequences, much of it has been dominated by an attempt to be more concrete than the nature of the subject warrants. The individual innovation must not be lifted from its context and it is clearly important at every stage to try to compare how much of the old continued to exist side by side with the new.

If capitalism is understood as a system in which the ownership or control of the means of production is separated from those who contribute physical labor to the process of production, then it is clear that there were examples of such a type of organization at a very early date. It is sufficient to mention Flemish and Italian textiles, the Venetian ship-building industry and English wool-growing. Throughout the medieval period there were also examples of production for a very distant market. It is thus possible to speak of the existence of industrial capitalism in Europe on the eve of the Reformation and indeed for many centuries before, but it is not possible to speak of a capitalistic Europe at that time.

In the variety of forms of industrial organization discoverable in late medieval Europe, those which in any way anticipate the characteristic factory enterprises of the modern world existed in small proportion. In a society still largely agricultural, most of what was manufactured in the literal sense was produced by the individual craftsman, whether located in a town where he specialized in shoemaking, or in his own hut on a manor where his time was divided between agricultural labor and the supplying of his own needs in clothes and tools. In certain areas and industries a larger scale of activity had been developed, on a basis which still remained domestic. In the textile industry, for example, particularly in Flanders and Italy, raw material was supplied by a merchant entrepreneur to a considerable number of workers in their homes, who were then paid on the basis of piece work. Of establishments where workers assembled in numbers in one place and where the control of the means of production centered in one person or a small group, there were a very few. The famous ship-building industry in Venice may be cited as a familiar example.

One of the most significant facts about the development of the industrial economy of Europe in the decades before the Reformation—a fact less striking but perhaps of greater immediate importance than the discoveries—was the steady increase in the proportion of these large-scale types of enterprise and the growth of an industrial activity prefiguring the later development of capitalism. The European economy as a whole entered a period of renewed prosperity in the second half of the fifteenth and the early part of the sixteenth century, contrasting with the decline of the preceding period.[7] Changes were both qualitative and quantitative.

---

[7] J. U. Nef, "Industrial Europe on the Eve of the Reformation," *Journal of Political Economy*, Vol. 49 (1941), 1–40; 183–224.

Inventions such as printing, innovations in the process of extracting and finishing metals, the casting of artillery, and the provision of Renaissance luxuries on a wider scale were the bases of new industries. At the same time older industries like various forms of textile production achieved a more extended scope. The character of European society at the beginning of the great age of exploration and the relationships between the various types of change occurring in that society cannot be understood without taking into account the concrete ways in which this new productivity was manifested.

Consider, for example, printing as a type of capitalist organization. The establishment of a press obviously required a considerable investment. There was the press itself, the metal for type, the molds or matrices to be cast or punched, the supply of paper to be manufactured and procured; altogether, the investment in what we should call the machinery of the plant was on a larger scale than that of most medieval enterprises. Hence it offers a clear illustration of the separation between the ownership and the operation of the means of production. The production of books called for a large number of specialized laborers, printers, typesetters, typecasters, proofreaders, binders. These were for the most part paid at a wage rate. Their whole situation therefore differed from that of a cobbler's apprentice, for instance, who labored in payment for the technical education he had received and who might hope for advancement through the stages of journeyman to master.

The cobbler's apprentice had of course been far from universally characteristic of the earlier period. Workers in textiles, in mines, and in shipyards had found themselves in a situation anticipating that of printing employees. Yet their numbers were now greater, and the very novelty of the industry and the rapidity with which it developed made their situation clearer. By the middle of the fifteenth century the regular course of advancement in the older crafts was often blocked. Masters associated to resist an increase in their numbers that might diminish their profits; the articles of apprenticeship were made more complicated, and the performance of the chef d'oeuvre often impossibly difficult and comprehensive. But if this general constriction was characteristic of older industries, it was still more true of the new printing establishments. Very few of those who worked in a printing plant had any hope of becoming master printers. It is therefore not surprising that one of the earliest associations of workmen, anticipating the modern union, was the organization of journeymen printers to preserve their interests and better their lot. Some of the earliest examples of sixteenth-century strikes occurred in printing centers like Lyons and Basle, and represented an effort on the part of the workmen to improve their working conditions or raise their wages.

In other respects, too, the printing industry anticipated the later forms of capitalistic organization. Books were actually among the earliest examples of mass production. The press may be viewed as a machine with interchangeable parts that turns out a standardized product consisting of identical units, namely the number of printed pages necessary for a given edition. Furthermore, the management of a press implied extensive planning. A printer in Venice or Seville had to arrange that his books should be ready for the spring book fair in Leipzig, halfway across Europe. In all these ways, therefore—the investment of capital, the organization of the means of production, the standardization of the product, and the conditions of marketing—the book industry illustrates the advances made by industrial capitalism.

Another type of change was to be noticed in industries which had been long established but now found new opportunities for expansion. The old centers of the medieval textile industries in Flanders and Italy encountered rivalries in the programs sponsored by national monarchs and faced the challenge of novel types of organization as well as technical innovation. This expansion was particularly obvious in the case of the silk industry.

The manufacture of silk had been early introduced into Europe from the east by way of the Arabs. The commercial activity and wealth of the Italian towns provided a favorable market and by the twelfth century a flourishing silk manufactory had been established at Lucca. This was followed by the development of similar enterprises in Venice, Florence, Genoa and other places. The rich and elaborate stuffs which were the product of these looms dominated the silk market for some centuries and found an ever increasing demand as the taste for luxury and the ability to satisfy it spread. The profits to be made from the silk industry were one of the incentives prompting attempts at imitation of Italian examples by the national monarchies of the fifteenth century.

In the reign of Louis XI the French government, stimulated by the interest of the king himself, undertook the establishment of the manufacture of silk within the French kingdom. In 1466 workers were imported from Italy and southern France, where there was already a flourishing silk industry in the papal territory of Avignon. The workers were settled in Lyons, where the local authorities were commanded to give them special privileges. The stated object of the royal decree was mercantilistic—to prevent the drain of gold and silver from the kingdom annually spent on the purchase of Italian silks. Here the royal intervention clashed with the interests of the local authorities, providing an illuminating illustration of the social implications of industry sponsored by a monarchical government as contrasted with that which had grown up within the framework of city organization.

The bourgeois of Lyons objected to the extra taxes assessed on them to pay some of the expenses of the new establishment. They resented the intrusion of the foreigner, and in these sentiments were supported by the clergy. Tired of efforts to overcome these difficulties, Louis XI finally abandoned his effort at Lyons and in 1470 transported the workmen and master craftsmen to Tours, which was more amenable to royal control. Here he was successful and the industry began to flourish. From the small beginnings of the first colony of about sixteen members the establishment grew until at the beginning of the sixteenth century there were some eight hundred masters and four thousand workmen involved in various processes of the manufacture of silk, numbers which again doubled by the middle of the sixteenth century. As in the printing industry, the journeymen and apprentices had a smaller chance of rising to the status of masters. The silk manufactories therefore showed, in the agglomerations of workmen involved and in the comparative rigidity of their status as well as in the active intervention of government, signs of change from the pattern of medieval industries.[8]

Another area in which similar changes took place was that of the mining industries. One of the most dramatic examples was the production of alum, which achieved the status of a major enterprise in western Europe in the period after the fall of Constantinople.

Alum was extensively used in the dyeing industry. In the medieval period it had been produced chiefly in Asia Minor and around the Black Sea, where it was mined and refined under western supervision. With the collapse of the Byzantine Empire the Turks became the possessors of the chief sources of alum, and the threat of losing access to an essential raw material, on which so much of the western European textile industry depended, stimulated the search for alum in Europe. In the years following the fall of Constantinople extensive deposits were discovered or

---

[8] For details on the silk industry in France: L. Bosseboeuf, *Histoire de la fabrique de soieries de Tours des origines au XIXe siècle* (Tours, 1900), 1–44, and Henri Clouzot, *Le métier de la soie en France 1466–1815* (Paris, 1914), 15–27.

rediscovered in Italy. Elaborate organizations were developed to work these deposits, and they became the object of diplomatic activity and political struggles in the second half of the fifteenth century.

One of the richest deposits was at Volterra, where mining began in 1458. A partnership to develop the industry was formed, consisting of representatives from Florence and Siena as well as citizens of Volterra. The interests of Florentine finance capital ultimately prevailed over those of the other investors, and Florence declared war and seized Volterra in 1472, appropriating the alum mines as an indemnity and subsequently leasing them to the wool trade for exploitation.

A still more celebrated deposit of alum was that discovered at Tolfa in the papal states in 1460 or 1461. At the very time when Pius II was seeking funds to support a crusade against the Turks, one of the papal servants, who had been an agent for textile firms in Constantinople and had there learned the technical aspects of alum mining, discovered within the papal jurisdiction itself a rich source of this chemical upon which fortunes were founded. The discovery could hardly have come at a more fortunate moment for the papacy. It made possible the enforcement of prohibitions against trading with the infidel and at the same time provided the papacy with an independent source of revenue that enabled it to support the military efforts of Skanderbeg and others who were opposing the Turks. Mining was begun at once and by 1463 operations had reached a considerable scale, involving four mines and as many as eight thousand employees. As in the case of Volterra, the enterprise was run by a *societas* or partnership under contract with the papacy. For many years this partnership was controlled by the Roman branch of the Medici bank and subsequently, at the beginning of the sixteenth century, by the Chigi, the bankers of Leo X. Under this method of administration the papacy sought the creation of an alum syndicate or cartel that would control the whole industry, to the papal advantage. The scale of operations, the numbers of people employed, and the complexities of the organization were again indicative of the degree of progress in the development of industrial capitalism.[9]

A more familiar example of the same phenomenon was provided by the Fugger mining enterprises in the Tyrol and Hungary. Here were located the famous copper, iron, and silver mines that had, by the beginning of the sixteenth century, come largely into the control of the house

[9] Charles Singer, *The Earliest Chemical Industry* (London, 1948), 139–65. Also, Enrico Fiumi, *L'Impresa di Lorenzo de Medici contro Volterra* (Florence, 1948).

of Fugger. Most of these mines had been turned over to the Fugger in return for their loans to the Hapsburg during the period of Maximilian I. In some cases the Fugger company operated the mines directly; in others it processed and marketed the ore that had been mined by smaller organizations. Its subsidiary company in Hungary was particularly noteworthy in developing processes of smelting and rolling that were important technical innovations. The products of these mines were shipped all over Europe and beyond, and the organization that controlled them was certainly one of the most advanced forms of industrial enterprise to be found in the early sixteenth century.

Many enterprises, such as those controlled by the Fugger, and many textile industries were increasingly located outside the towns, sometimes in order to escape from the framework of urban guild restriction, more often to provide the Renaissance prince with a broader control over the most productive forces in the economy. It was in this period that texts of the Roman law provided the ruler with claims to the ownership of metal in his domains as a regalian right. The papal control of alum, the assertion of Hapsburg rights to the mines of the Tyrol and Hungary and the many government attempts to establish a monopoly over the extraction and manufacture of salt indicate the increasing extent to which heavy industry was regulated by political powers. To this general pattern coal-mining was an exception. The coal mines of England as well as those of the continent, chiefly located in Flemish territory, were usually worked by small local partnerships. This was also true of the English tin mines. Where larger amounts of capital were required, a more complicated relationship with political authority was implied. Hence in the copper, iron, and silver mines of Saxony, Bohemia, Silesia, Hungary, and the Tyrol, as well as in the iron mines of Sweden and Spain, the regalian rights became important sources of the prince's revenues, as these mines were developed by firms like the Welser and the Fugger.[10]

It must not be forgotten that these examples of industrial advance, impressive as they were, must be viewed and understood in their relation to the whole traditional economy of Europe. Professor Nef has estimated that not more than two or three millions of workpeople out of a population of perhaps seventy millions were occupied in industrial labor for a larger market. Of these two million, more than two-thirds probably labored in the home either as independent craftsmen with journeymen

[10] J. U. Nef, *op. cit.*, 205.

and apprentices or as wage workers in a putting-out system. The remainder, who worked in building operations, mills, forges, furnaces, and mines, were the early representatives of that industrial proletariat whose eventual growth was to bring about a total transformation of the conditions of European life. In terms of the proportion between innovation and tradition, it can hardly be maintained, as it so often is, that Europe was undergoing a great economic revolution in this period. Yet the steady increase in the number and size of industrial ventures and the rise by small stages in the productivity of the European economy, though it transcends the limits of the period we are considering and though it cannot be followed in all its ramifications and details, was clearly of the greatest consequence for most other aspects of human activity. In the simplest terms the needs and interests of men who worked as wool-carders in Florence, as miners in Tolfa or the Tyrol, or as journeymen printers in Lyons were obviously very different not only from those of peasants, whose labors in the fields were governed by traditional routines, but also from those of the urban small-scale craftsmen.

III. BANKS AND BANKERS

With the growth of commercial and industrial activity mechanisms of credit were established and improved so as to permit financial transactions on a large scale and over long distances. The institutions that handled these credit transactions were the great banks that dominated the financial life of Europe. This was the age of the Medici, the Chigi, the Fugger, and the Welser.

These great houses dealt in merchandise and exchange on a considerable scale, supplied the needs of the political powers, and undertook major financial operations. The character of their activity was exemplified in the fifteenth century by the Medici bank in Italy. The term "Medici bank" is in itself almost a misnomer because, unlike the earlier Florentine houses, this firm was organized on decentralized principles. In the case of the Bardi and the Peruzzi of the fourteenth century there had been a single partnership, controlling not only the home office but also all the branch offices of the organization. With the failure of these companies a less centralized type of organization with more insurance against failures was developed, and this was adopted and perfected by the Medici company.

The principal characteristic of this form of organization was the negotiation of a series of partnership agreements. Each branch of the firm abroad was really a separate legal entity, with its own capital and its own books. The only way in which they were united was by the participation in all these organizations of the members of the Medici family. We have a documentary basis for determining, in the case of the Medici bank at Bruges during the fifteenth century, the relative shares of the Medici partners and of the agents who actually operated the enterprise. In the years from 1455 to 1471 the share of the senior partners—that is, the Medici in Florence—ranged from fifty per cent to almost seventy per cent of the profits. The remainder was divided into three parts, of which one went to the investing partner and the other two to the manager and assistant manager in Bruges. According to the testimony of Commines, the Medici bank was the largest banking house in existence in his day. It had seven or eight branches and employed somewhere between forty and fifty factors. Nevertheless, by the end of the fifteenth century this bank had entered a period of serious decline. This decline has been attributed in part to Lorenzo de' Medici's lack of business ability and his interest in other matters. But there were certainly other factors, possibly connected with its overgrown size, and perhaps even more directly connected with its loan policy. Loans to princes were frequently highly rewarding, but they also led very often to bankruptcy. This had been the case with the Peruzzi in the fourteenth century. In the sixteenth the Fugger repeated the pattern developed by the Medici.[11]

The financial undertakings of the Fugger were the most famous of the whole period. The fortunes of this family had been founded in the fourteenth century by a weaver who used his textile business as a basis for mercantile activity. Capital originally amassed from the cotton trade was invested in other ventures and gradually a vast network of undertakings in the world of industry, commerce, and banking was developed. All these activities were run as a single family enterprise, and there was in the Fugger family a remarkable succession of able men who insured the continuous direction of the firm. The most famous of the whole dynasty was Jacob Fugger the Rich (1459–1525). First intended for a monastic career, he was recalled after his father's death to assist his mother and brothers in the management and expansion of the business. In the partnership agreement of 1494 the share of Jacob was not less than that of his elder brothers, an indication of the extent to which he had made his ability and energy felt in the conduct of the firm. The contracts of that

[11] R. de Roover, *The Medici Bank, Its Organization, Management, Operations, and Decline* (New York, 1948).

year and those of 1502 made arrangements to secure the permanence of the capital investments. It was stipulated that the heirs of any one brother, in the event of his death, were not to draw out their capital for a period of three years. Finally, in 1502, preferred shares, especially based on the holdings in the Hungarian mines, were put aside for the exclusive control of those male heirs who were to succeed to the management of the Fugger enterprises. By 1510, on the death of the last of his elder brothers, Jacob became the sole heir. Although he gave no immediate power to his nephews, he so arranged the succession that one of them came into possession of all the preferred shares.

One of the principal interests of the Fugger firm was banking, and under Jacob Fugger the firm became one of the main agencies for supplying the chronic needs of the governments of Europe. At an early date the Fugger established the closest relations with the house of Hapsburg, and little by little they became involved in the political fortunes of their debtors. During the reign of Maximilian the Fugger made many loans to assist in royal marriages and to support Maximilian's ambitions in Hungary. As security for these loans Jacob Fugger received jewels and plate and, ultimately much more important, royal rights such as the mines of the Tyrol and Hungary.[12]

The imperial election of 1519 was the event that illustrated most dramatically the power of the merchant bankers. The Hapsburg arranged with the Fugger bank for almost unlimited funds to be used to bribe the electors. In this way the Archduke Charles was put in a better position than Francis I of France, who could expend only a limited amount of cash compared to the vast credit engineered for the Hapsburg by the Fugger. The election of Charles V represented the apogee of the Fugger influence, and Jacob Fugger did not hesitate in later years to remind His Imperial Majesty that he would never have gained the crown without the aid of the bankers of Augsburg.

The political role of the great banking houses raises interesting problems. In view of the fact that on so many different occasions men like the Fugger and the Chigi held the purse strings, why did they not have a greater part in the determination of policy? For it is true that the bankers made very little use of their financial power as a lever to influence political decisions. Although an establishment like the house of Fugger

---

[12] On the Fugger, see Striedel, J., *Jacob Fugger der Reiche* (Leipzig, 1926) and the various special studies issued at Munich under the title of *Studien zur Fuggergeschichte*. The most recent biography is that of Goetz Freiherr von Pölnitz, *Jacob Fugger*, 2 vols. (Tübingen, 1949 and 1951).

presided over an unprecedented accumulation of capital which made possible the activities of Maximilian and many other contemporary rulers, it did not control those activities. Jacob Fugger rightly believed that his services had been indispensable to the attainment of the position held by the house of Hapsburg at the beginning of the sixteenth century. Yet the Hapsburg could eventually dispense with the Fugger as decisively, if not as dramatically, as the French monarchy had dispensed with Jacques Coeur in the middle of the fifteenth century.

The failure of the great merchant princes to establish their political position more securely is a measure of the limits of the early economic revolution. The acceleration of commercial and industrial activity and the enlargement of its scope had produced capital accumulations on a scale unknown to an earlier period. Yet these great fortunes were adjusted to an older social order and did not produce those revolutionary effects which might have been expected. To the modern mind there is something puzzling in the fact that while men like these great bankers so obviously held the keys to power, they failed to use them to full advantage. It has been maintained that the Fugger and the Chigi, who amassed the greatest fortunes of their age, carried out neither the real nor the putative interests of the class they represented.[13]

Such a judgment, however plausible in the case of the Fugger, neglects the complexities of the interaction between political and economic forms of power in the early modern period. Variations in this interaction were determined more by the character of the government than by that of the economic enterprise. It would be too simple a generalization to say that in the city states, and especially in Italy, economic power dominated the political, while in the national monarchies and great feudal principalities the political power was able to manipulate the economic. Yet this statement contains more than a half-truth. The size and character of the city-state population fostered a high degree of consciousness of class interests. Indeed, the lines of class division on an economic basis may be described as too nakedly apparent in the structure of city-state political life, and one of the reasons why political organization on a national and monarchical scale was more stable was that loyalty to a monarchy and participation in representative assemblies transcended the lines of purely economic interests. The national state was able to solve a political problem which in the fifteenth century was becoming chronically unmanageable in the life of the city state.

[13] Schumpeter, *Capitalism, Socialism, and Democracy* (2nd ed., Cambridge, 1947), 125.

The greater fluidity of the city-state organization thus permitted the representatives of economic power to attain direct political influence. The Medici provide perhaps the most outstanding example of the transition from banking to political control. The amassing of a fortune was the prelude to political office and finally to the papacy and a hereditary duchy. The Venetian oligarchy for many years illustrated a similar process. And in many of the Hanseatic and south German cities the patriciate who directed the political life of the community consisted of the rich burghers who had attained control of its economic life.

In the monarchies, however, there was more frequently a separation between the personalities and institutions of politics on the one hand and those which represented economic accumulation on the other. Hence, although the French king depended on the activities of Jacques Coeur and the Hapsburgs could not have carried out their policies without the Fugger, we do not find that either Coeur or Fugger controlled the political life of France or the Empire in the same way in which the Medici controlled the political life of Florence. Yet men like Jacob Fugger, swearing to continue to make money as long as there was breath in his body, and Agostino Chigi, the banker of Leo X, certainly followed what they conceived to be their interests as individuals; many of them lived like princes, patronized the arts and left great private fortunes. Where the rewards were so high for activities which were still hard to square with the traditional ethics, those who profited were not yet inclined to go further and question the established hierarchy of power, even when that power was responsible for bankruptcy and confiscation. The great bankers made their highest profits supplying the needs of the traditional authorities. As the source of their wealth was conservative sanction, so they themselves remained politically conservative. To expect them to have played a more revolutionary role would be to carry back into the sixteenth-century conceptions about the behavior of social classes which have been derived from the experience of the nineteenth and twentieth.

IV. THE WORKING OF THE LAND

European society in the middle of the fifteenth century was still, as it long continued to be, based on agricultural labor, which underlay all other forms of economic activity. There was, of course, a great diversity in types of cultivation and in the organizations that had been developed and maintained for centuries for working the land. This diversity was the product not only of obvious differences in geography and climate and kinds of crops but also of variations in political and social conditions.

Yet in the second half of the fifteenth century there still remained many uniformities in the agricultural organization of western Europe. Most of western Europe contained elements of a common pattern. Within the areas of greatest uniformity, in spite of the existence of two types of plow and variations in the system of cultivation, there was a sufficiently common basis to permit charting some of the most significant deviations.

In general, changes that affected the cultivation of the land occurred more gradually than those that marked other types of economic activity. There were no "events" in agriculture comparable to the establishment of new routes in commerce or the development of new industries like printing. The system that governed production from the land had been changing at varying rates of speed, but always slowly, during the centuries of the medieval period. The growth of the number of cities and the increase in the urban population were clearly not the sole factors affecting agricultural conditions, but these developments did entail important changes in the rural economy. Production of foodstuffs had to be increased in order to provide for the needs of the urban inhabitants. This, in turn, required increasing specialization and an adjustment of the characteristic organization of the medieval seigneury or manor. Depending to some extent on the relation between the land and the labor supply, commutation of work services into money rents had allowed the peasant more time for cultivation of his own land and created more incentives for increasing production. Clearly, however, the largest increases had been accomplished by the conversion of whole areas to a single type of cultivation. Frequently the intensification of crop-raising in some places was accompanied by its decline or total abandonment in other localities. In particular, the profits to be derived from the wool trade, together with local shortages in labor supply and changes in population, combined to cause many fields to be converted from tillage to pasture.[14]

Modifications such as these were far from new in the middle of the fifteenth century, nor did they apply universally. Nevertheless there were some areas where the pattern of change could be particularly sharply discerned in the ensuing decades, and its character indicated.

One such area that is particularly well-known was England, where the

[14] *Cambridge Economic History of Europe*, edited by J. H. Clapham and Eileen Power, Vol. I, ch. VIII, "Medieval Agrarian Society in Transition," by Hans Nabholz.

enclosure movement became accelerated after the middle of the fifteenth century. Enclosure was of several kinds and comprised the enclosing of both common arable fields and of common pastures and meadows, whether for grazing or for increasing the tillage. It was the conversions for grazing that created a social problem and that were most vividly reflected in the literature of the time, for they deprived numbers of people of their livelihood and their rights. Among many other famous complaints we have the testimony of Sir Thomas More, written in 1516:

For one shepherd or herdsman is enough to eat up that ground with cattle, to the occupying whereof about husbandry many hands were requisite. And this is also the cause that victuals be now in many places dearer. Yea, besides this the price of wool is so risen, that poor folks, which were wont to work it and make cloth of it, be now able to buy none at all. And by this means very many be fain to forsake work, and to give themselves to idleness. For after that so much ground was inclosed for pasture, an infinite multitude of sheep died of the rot, such vengeance God took of their inordinate and insatiable covetousness, sending among the sheep that pestiferous murrain, which much more justly should have fallen on the sheepmasters' own heads. And though the number of sheep increase never so fast, yet the price falleth not one mite, because there be so few sellers. For they be almost all come into a few rich men's hands, whom no need driveth to sell before they lust, and they lust not before they may sell as dear as they lust.[15]

We can readily understand that the incentive of the huge profits to be derived from the wool trade must have tempted many landlords to convert both open fields and commons into pasturage in the fashion described by Sir Thomas More. There is an abundance of testimony to the prevalence of these changes in the literature of the first half of the sixteenth century. Actually, however, modern statistical investigations have indicated that the impression derived from the contemporary literature is much exaggerated. Most modern authorities would agree that in England, in the area where the enclosure movement for pasturage was supposedly most widespread, not more than three per cent of the arable land was affected.[16] It is understandable that the process produced social dislocations of such a kind as to make those affected peculiarly vocal about the hardships they had suffered. But on the whole, as in so many other cases, if we rely entirely on the testimony of the most articulate classes in the

[15] More, *Utopia,* edited by J. C. Collins (Oxford, 1927), 15.
[16] E. F. Gay, "Enclosures in England in the Sixteenth Century," *Quarterly Journal of Economics,* XVII (August, 1903), 576–97.

population, we run the risk of being seriously deceived. Even though small in extent, however, the enclosure movement was indicative of one type of solution to the problem of the relation between the organization of agriculture and the developing commercial economy.

A somewhat similar situation, with much more serious effects, was to be noticed in Spain in the organization of the Mesta. This guild of the sheep-growers of Castile had been organized in the medieval period for the protection of migratory sheep-growers, who were responsible for producing the famous merino wool, eventually one of the most lucrative of Spanish exports. In the reign of Ferdinand and Isabella the monarchy found that it could establish a very profitable relationship with the Mesta. The more wool produced, the more export taxes could be imposed to the profit of the monarchy. Hence Ferdinand and Isabella granted an important series of privileges to the sheep-growers' organization, which in turn stimulated the process whereby increasingly large tracts of land in Castile were removed from cultivation and turned over to pasturage. In the short run these changes did supply important revenues to the monarchy and likewise enriched the members of the Mesta; but in the long run this system had a most disastrous effect not only upon agriculture, but upon the whole Spanish social structure.[17]

The enclosure movement in England and the position of the Mesta in Spain were two examples of the adaptation of regional agrarian economy to the new economic conditions. One of the effects of these displacements was to provide workers for urban industries as well as recruits for armies and overseas adventures. An available labor supply was one of the necessary preconditions of a capitalist organization of production, and the creation of this condition was much more a product of the pressures controlling the working of the land than it was a result of the technical innovations in mining and manufacturing.

Elsewhere in Europe agricultural changes were less dramatic and more continuous. In France and in western Germany the procedure of evicting tenants and turning whole estates to a special type of cultivation or into pasturage was hardly practiced. The older type of seigneur or manorial lord tended to operate his estates so as to receive rents for the whole instead of partly cultivating his demesne himself and partly receiving services from his tenants. In other words, heritable and alienable tenures were granted either in return for rents or in return for servitudes, now

[17] J. Klein, *The Mesta, a Study in Spanish Economic History, 1273–1836* (Cambridge, 1920).

attached to the soil rather than to the condition of the persons who worked or owned it.[18] These changes were of great social importance, but they did not affect either the areas under cultivation or the way in which they were worked any more than did the relationship of the burghers of the Italian cities to the peasants of the countryside.

On the whole, therefore, the agricultural situation, if it showed in some areas like England and Spain a decisive response to the new economic needs and opportunities, in most parts of Europe remained slowly changing in accordance with already determined lines of development. Yet these changes, small as they were when measured by a later standard, had in the early sixteenth century social repercussions which far outweighed their quantitative aspect.

V. THE SOCIAL CLASSES

The sixteenth century inherited from the medieval period a hierarchic and organic conception of society, firmly fixed in the European tradition in the centuries that followed the breakup of the Roman Empire. The outlines of this conception were simple and familiar. If it was never literally true that society was roughly divided into those who prayed, those who fought, and those who worked, yet these three main functions had an assigned status, and thus the groups who fulfilled them occupied definite places in a hierarchic order. First in dignity were, of course, the clergy, because society was directed to a spiritual end. This class, not hereditary, had been recruited in theory and to some extent in fact from all levels of the population. By the later Middle Ages the nobility had become, in most European countries, a hereditary caste whose privileged position rested upon the theory that it was responsible for supplying protection and justice to individuals lower in the social scale. Below the two upper classes, the first and second estates, were the masses of the people, still largely agricultural and still, for the most part, living on a subsistence level without much capacity either to choose their occupation or to move very far from the area in which they were born. By the end of the fifteenth century there had appeared a more dynamic interaction between this inherited form of social order and the newer forms of economic power.

One key to the understanding of the process by which old forms of social prestige made new adaptations is to be found in the analysis of the pressures created by a money economy and a condition of rising prices.

[18] Hans Nabholz, *op. cit.,* footnote 14.

The most serious rise in prices did not take place until after the beginning of the sixteenth century, but even in the fifteenth it was difficult for those whose income was fixed, and especially for those whose income was derived from the land, to maintain the position to which they had been accustomed.

This situation was particularly noticeable in the case of the higher clergy. Two important changes were to be observed in the social character of the higher ranks of the clergy in this period. In the first place, the higher positions tended to be reserved to those fortunately placed by reason of birth or money, whereas formerly there had been a greater degree of social mobility in clerical recruitment. It had not been unusual in the earlier period that the highest dignities in Christendom were attained by sons of peasants, but a mere reading of the names of the college of cardinals in the pontificates between those of Nicholas V and Leo X indicates to what an extent the greatest benefices in the church were reserved for the sons of royal or noble families. There were still some popes and cardinals who had been born the sons of peasants, but the great majority represented the highest social and economic level. This was in part a consequence of the economic pressures to which the nobility were increasingly subjected. It was entirely natural that a family which found its income diminished, while the luxurious expenditure demanded by its position had increased, should wish to place some of its younger members in respectable positions in the church. Furthermore, once in the church it was frequently found that the same benefices which a hundred years earlier had sufficed to maintain a bishop or an abbot were now inadequate to maintain the standard of living expected of a prince of the church. Hence we see an age of enormous accumulation of ecclesiastical benefices by the highly placed clergy. Such figures as Wolsey in England, Cardinal Estouteville in France and Albert of Brandenburg in Germany illustrate this process of accumulation.

Albert of Brandenburg was perhaps the most conspicuous example. Before becoming archbishop of Mainz he had held two bishoprics and a large number of rich abbeys. His case was the most famous because his expenditures in connection with attaining the archbishopric of Mainz had so close a connection with the indulgence controversy and the announcement of Luther's protest. But, although thus more memorable in history, the practice of this Hohenzollern prince was no different from that in many other countries. Cardinals, bishops, abbots, archdeacons, and canons of cathedrals vied with one another in appealing both to lay patrons and to the Roman curia to have benefices conferred upon them. The irregularities that permitted simony and plurality of benefices had been attacked for many decades, but it seemed increasingly impossible that in this matter the higher ranks of the clergy should resist their economic interests and reform themselves from within.

A corollary of this situation was the increasing separation between the higher and the lower clergy. In many parishes the lower clergy led a meager existence hardly distinguishable from that of the neighboring peasants. Many others, whose economic situation was somewhat more tolerable, were filled with social discontent, since they felt they were men of ability and saw their way to higher positions blocked by the preferment of those more fortunately placed. In these circumstances the level of ability of the lower members of the clergy seriously declined. Many parishes were abandoned altogether, and in the vacuum thus created in the religious life of Europe there was eventually an opportunity for new and revolutionary religious views to spread.

The situation of the nobility had important and interesting relations to the political as well as the social history of these decades. Almost everywhere in western Europe the feudality, deriving its revenues from lands, was increasingly handicapped in comparison with the fortunes now created by trade and mercantile enterprise. Some noble families, who had at an earlier date commuted into monetary payment the services owed them, now bitterly repented of the bargains made by their ancestors and attempted to reimpose feudal obligations. Others found salvation in attaching themselves to the service of the court, and frankly reposed their hopes on the bounty of the prince. Another group was willing and even eager to make a marriage with the richly dowered daughter of a merchant, even though she might lack any claim to distinction of lineage and have no right to the quarterings of nobility. Finally, there was also a considerable number who sank to the level of impoverished gentlemen. Sixteenth-century literature, especially in the northern countries of Europe, was filled with references to chateaux and castles of misery, in which the remnants of a once noble and prosperous family existed on a level not very different from that of the commoners who surrounded them. We have, indeed, in France some striking legal cases in which a country nobleman begs to have his condition of nobility formally removed so that he may enjoy the privileges of gathering wood in the forest, shared by the commoners of his village.

The straitened circumstances of the nobility obviously made them ready as a class to engage in any kind of political adventure that might improve their situation. In this way we can understand the alliances between the princely courts and the nobility as a class, and we can also understand the readiness of the nobility to participate in foreign adventure. The Italian wars that began in 1494 would hardly have continued so long and so uninterruptedly if they had not provided an outlet for the energies and aspirations of a nobility whose functional position at home was disappearing while at the same time its economic situation was being undermined. It may be suggested that in those countries where there was no possibility of keeping the nobility occupied in foreign war, there was much more predisposition to revolution at home. Thus the position of the nobility was a critical one, both for the development of national monarchy and for the international political stability of Europe.

Below the two older classes was the great mass of the population, ranged in a complicated hierarchy determined by the prestige of particular occupations. This hierarchy was constantly being modified by the rise of those families whose fortunes were a product of the new commercial and industrial activity. In these involved gradations it is perhaps useless to seek for any exact analogue to the modern middle class, especially in the sense of finding an equivalent political or cultural influence. The term "middle class" or *"état moyen"* covered in the sixteenth century a multitude of types, as it still does in the twentieth. Yet it is clear that in no country of western Europe of this period was there anything like the number who today consider themselves to belong to this class.

The really significant division was that between what may be called the urban patriciate and the petty burghers. The latter were the product of the growth of a town civilization. They had long flourished in Germany, Italy, southern France, Flanders and the towns of the Hanseatic League. In the earliest stage of communal development they had been the revolutionaries, but their role had long since crystallized into a static conservatism. They stood for the regime of guild restrictions, and for the political forms which accompanied that regime. Their wealth was on a relatively small scale, and the power which had once been theirs was rapidly slipping into the hands of the newer large-scale operators, the international merchant financiers, like the Medici, Welser, Fugger, Chigi. These now appeared as the new revolutionaries destined in their turn to see their methods and achievements outmoded and to become as conservative as the class whose influence they were superseding.

The antagonism between these two groups was one of the most dynamic features of the period.[19] It had repercussions in the political relations between monarchies and communes and it had a perhaps even more important bearing on the coming of religious revolution. The search for new religious certitudes was widespread and many-sided, but it is hardly an exaggeration to say that it particularly appealed to those whose security in a comfortable and well-known communal world was being undermined by political and economic developments which seemed to them unnatural and unjust.

Not only the merchant politicians but also the lesser merchant capitalists had found their ultimate security by clothing their wealth in the sanction of older forms of social and economic power. In other words, they bought land. Almost everywhere in Europe there was a constant attempt by those who had amassed some capital in urban enterprise to buy themselves a property in the country, which in the space of a few generations would convey that title to respectability, if not to nobility, to which they aspired. There were, of course, other ways of rising in the social scale, some of them more direct. A rich bourgeois might marry his daughter into a noble family. He might send his son into the royal service, where increasingly nonnoble persons of capacity were being employed. He might also send his son into the church, as the son of Briconnet, the financier of Charles VIII, became archbishop of Meaux. In all these ways it was possible to attain a position in those upper reaches of society where prestige was traditionally determined by birth or by a particular kind of service.

In this fashion the men who were at different periods the most active in creating new wealth gave their entire allegiance to the values of an older social order. Something of this phenomenon is always present in the rise of new groups to power, but the political conservatism of the merchant capitalist at the beginning of the sixteenth century was an extreme example. The relation which has already been described between the Fugger and the Hapsburg is a measure of the strength of the institutional framework inherited from the medieval period.

Below the classes that had acquired some commercial or industrial wealth were the largest groups in the population, which were of course lowest in the social hierarchy. By the beginning of the sixteenth century there was in many towns the nucleus of an urban proletariat. No longer

---

[19] H. Pirenne, "The Stages in the Social History of Capitalism," *American Historical Review*, XIX (1914), 494–516.

was it possible to go from apprentice through the state of journeyman to master, as it had been in the earlier medieval period. In many cases the guilds were now in the hands of the masters alone, and large groups of journeymen organized themselves like modern workers for an improvement in wages and conditions. This was particularly the case in such industries as printing and textiles. In addition to those who were connected with organized industry there was in the major urban centers an increasing group of casual wage-earners and simple poor, whose existence was obviously closely related to the character assumed by social, political, and even religious agitation in the sixteenth century.

Side by side with this group was the great body of the peasantry, about whose condition it is very difficult indeed to generalize. It has already been pointed out that the effects of such developments as the enclosure movement in England are easy to exaggerate. On the whole it seems reasonable to conclude that in most parts of Europe west of the Elbe the material condition of the peasantry was actually better than it had been in preceding centuries; but, as is not uncommonly the case, their social dissatisfaction was greater. In other words, the background of sixteenth-century peasant revolution appears to be not unlike what we know of revolution at other times. Peasants who had been freed and whose general condition had been bettered by the impact of commerce on the feudal economy were now threatened again from two directions. There were, in the first place, the old nobility, whose desperate condition made them anxious to reverse the process of social evolution and get as much more out of the peasantry as they could; and in the second place, there were the new bourgeois landlords who had bought land in the country wherever they could, and who tended to conduct their farming by much more rational and business-like methods. Between these two types of landlord, the peasantry saw themselves increasingly endangered, and it is not surprising that they were prepared in many sections to give their support to new religious doctrines that promised a new basis of hope here on earth as well as in the next world.

The shocks administered to the traditional social organization, especially by the new forms of economic power, were naturally reflected in contemporary literature. Many documents attest the fact that the actual changes in social groups and levels were accompanied by increasing questioning of the bases of the old order. Such testimony is perhaps more frequently to be found in Italy than elsewhere, as might be expected from the region that saw the earlier and more complete triumphs of an urban civilization. In the middle of the fifteenth century Aeneas Sylvius complained that the old grades were now so completely upset that every servant wanted to be a master; and the debate on nobility in the celebrated *Courtier* of Castiglione may be cited as perhaps even more indicative. This work became so universally the handbook for gentlemen in the sixteenth century that its implications for thinking about social classes are particularly important. After the opinion had been advanced that noble birth is like a bright lamp making visible both good and evil deeds and that thus the humbly born lack an important stimulus to creative activity, Pallavicino replies:

> I say that his nobility of birth does not appear to me so essential to the Courtier. . . . I could cite instances of many men born of the noblest blood who have been full of vices and on the other hand many men among the humbly born who by their virtue have made their posterity illustrious.[20]

The relationship between virtue and nobility had often been discussed in the Middle Ages, notably by Dante, but it became a still more common theme of Renaissance speculation and the view that virtue could triumph over nobility tended to flourish in a social situation which was in significant ways becoming more fluid than in the previous centuries. Such a triumph, however, referred usually only to the achievement of the same ends by a different route. The prestige of the way of life of the nobility remained unimpaired and was usually adopted by those whose "virtue" had permitted them to rise in the social scale. Like the Chinese, who are said to have assimilated all their conquerors, the nobility for many centuries impressed their social ideals on the classes who were replacing them. *Condottieri* who had been born the sons of peasants, scholars whose parents had earned a living as notaries, merchant princes and learned judges all engaged in tournaments and games glorifying courtly love and the traditions of chivalry. In spite of these adaptations, which provide us with some of the most brilliant spectacles and some of the most attractive literature of the Renaissance, the fact remains that the environment was becoming one in which it was increasingly possible to improve one's condition and to rise in the social scale. There were contrary currents and areas of life where new rigidities were imposed, but the general loosening of the old bonds was one of those fundamental changes felt directly or indirectly in every form of human activity.

[20] Castiglione, *The Book of the Courtier*, translated by L. E. Opdycke (New York, 1903), 23.

Chapter Three

DYNASTIC CONSOLIDATION

I. TYPES OF POLITICAL AUTHORITY

To THE mind of the fifteenth and sixteenth centuries affairs of state and the problems of politics had an importance and a majesty transcending the sphere of the economic activities and changes discussed in the preceding chapter. The function of the ruler had long been the subject of intense and elaborate speculation; it was conceived as an eternal problem on which universal judgments could be made. The legitimate ruler belonged in a traditional hierarchy in which there was no place for the great figures of economic life. And these attitudes were actually mirrored, as we have seen, in the relationship between Jacques Cœur and the French monarch, and between the Fugger and the Hapsburg. The bankers might indeed be in many senses rulers of men, but in the formally delimited sphere of government they had no place. The state was endlessly compared with the individual on the one hand and with the universe on the other. The same principle of order was to be discerned at all three levels, and disorganization in one was followed or accompanied by disorganization in another. The planets in their courses, the rulers in the state, and the passions in the individual were clearly related. Indeed, thinking in terms of the body politic, always traditional in the European inheritance, became increasingly popular in the age of Francis I, Henry VIII, and Charles V.

Yet, although the state and its problems thus occupied a large place in men's minds, in considering fifteenth- and sixteenth-century politics we must guard particularly against the danger of being dominated by modern preoccupations. We have become so accustomed to a world of mutually exclusive sovereign states, organized for the most part on a national basis, that it is extremely difficult to put ourselves back into a situation in which neither the external boundaries of states nor the scope of their political power was so precisely defined. The entities we now know as France and England, Italy and Spain, insofar as they existed at all in the fifteenth century, had meaning and connotation very different from those we attach to them.

71

The whole European political system was still enmeshed with feudalism. Political authority and private property, although theoretically and in some important respects practically distinct, nevertheless were in other ways closely identified. Throughout the territory of Latin Christendom a host of authorities, lordships, jurisdictions ecclesiatistical and lay, city states, and larger territorial governments exercised some form of political power and overlapped in their responsibilities. The duke of Brittany, for example, within his territory, exercised functions of government that were not very different from those exercised by the king of France in his. The authority of the prince-bishops of Mainz, Trier and Cologne was equal to that of secular princes. Frontiers can hardly be said to have existed at all in the sense in which we have come to know them. In this situation it is profitless to attempt to determine which political units fit the modern classification of state. The necessary preliminary to the analysis of the dynamic developments of the period is a general indication of the more important types of political organization.

The old ecumenical institutions, the Empire and the papacy, had clearly lost much of their former authority by the middle of the fifteenth century. The papacy had emerged from the conciliar period confronted by the necessity of making compromises with various secular governments and regional churches. The pope, deriving his authority ultimately from his religious functions, still presided over a government that touched the lives of more people in Europe than that of any other ruler; but in the coming period the papacy would be increasingly preoccupied with its Italian possessions and with its position as a territorial power in Italy. The emperor had now for many years ceased to have any real authority outside the Germanic territories. Within these territories he was titular ruler over a confused network of jurisdictions and principalities, although his actual control was largely theoretical. There were the great electorates, the territories of the independent princes and knights, and the free cities. In order to assert any authority at all against this combination, the emperor was increasingly thrown back upon attempts to build up and extend the territories belonging directly to the imperial house. Thus, during the next half-century the imperial policy of both Frederick III and Maximilian was concentrated on the effort to acquire real political power over a nucleus of lands that would become the hereditary basis of the Hapsburgs.

At the other end of the scale from the old universal institutions of western Christendom were the small, compact lordships such as the

Italian despotisms and the city states, some few of which, like Venice which possessed a Mediterranean empire, could be considered among the great powers of Europe. This type of political organization reached its culmination in northern Italy in the duchy of Milan and the republics of Florence and Venice, but even in the north of Europe there were still illustrious examples of the exercise of large political powers by independent communes or leagues of city states. The Swiss cantons and the cities of the Hanseatic League were illustrations of government extended from a communal to a federal basis.

Somewhere between the large, weak universal institutions and the small compact territories are to be ranged most of the governments of fifteenth-century Europe. The nucleus of government was commonly allegiance to the person of the individual ruler or dynasty. Such allegiance often provided the basis for a political organization entirely unconnected with any existing national or state consciousness. Consider, for example, the position of the duke of Burgundy, who in the middle of the fifteenth century undoubtedly represented the most considerable political power in western Europe. With a position achieved more by personal effort than by institutional growth, the dukes of Burgundy had developed effective control over an extraordinary agglomeration of territories bound together solely by the tie of allegiance to a common suzerain. Of the same order of importance territorially, although in most cases much smaller in actual power, were the political authorities that were to evolve as the great national monarchies of modern times. But it must again be emphasized that at this point, in the mid-fifteenth century, although the foundations of national monarchy had been laid in the course of a long evolution, it was still by no means clear that state and nation would become increasingly identified.

The Iberian peninsula was divided into the independent kingdoms of Portugal, Castile and Leon, Navarre, and Aragon, to say nothing of the continued existence of the emirate of Granada. France was emerging from the long struggle of the Hundred Years' War, and the territory that Louis XI could claim to govern when he came to the throne in 1461 bore little resemblance to the France that later dominated the European continent. In the west the dukes of Brittany exercised a practically independent authority, while in the east and north the great power of Burgundy overshadowed the monarchy. Provence in the south, with all the other territories of the Angevin inheritance, remained outside the French king's control. England in 1450 was still in the midst of civil war, and it was to be another thirty-five years before the new dynasty of the Tudors was securely established. In northern and eastern Europe large kingdoms existed, some of them ephemeral creations produced by the attempt of a momentarily effective royal power to achieve a larger territorial basis. The Scandinavian kingdoms had thus been ostensibly united since the Union of Kalmar at the end of the fourteenth century; Poland and Lithuania were under the common rule of the Jagellon dynasty. Hungary and Bohemia, which had been brought within the orbit of the Hapsburg territories, were now again detached and were on the verge of the great period of independence achieved in the second half of the fifteenth century under Mathias Corvinus.

For purposes of analysis the complex changes in the political organization of Europe in the period between the middle of the fifteenth century and the beginning of the Reformation may be considered under three general headings. The first is concerned with the territorial basis of government. How were previously separate and particular entities brought together under one ruler? The second deals with the function of government in practice and theory. What were the actual and theoretical responsibilities of rulers? Finally there is the question of the relationship between states and the evolution of the European state system as it was substituted for the medieval ideals of universalism. Each of these topics will be the subject of one of the following chapters.

In 1458, when Pius II summoned the European nations to a congress at Mantua, the greatest powers with whom he had to deal were Venice and the duchy of Burgundy. Sixty years later, when faced with the problem of organizing European peace, Leo X had to negotiate with a complex of powers that could not possibly have been foreseen by an observer of the generation of Pius II. Every age has its historical miracles, and the historian's vision must be fixed on what actually happened rather than on what could have been or what could be predicted. The enormous and in many ways entirely fortuitous and accidental growth in the power of the Hapsburg, the union of the kingdoms of Spain, the expansion and consolidation of the French monarchy, the stabilization of the dynasty in England, and the failure of the various ambitious plans to unite the kingdoms of eastern Europe under a Slavic dynasty were all new factors in the European political situation. These fundamental changes had come about primarily in the course of prosecuting personal or dynastic ambitions. In politics more than in any other area of activity the pluralism of European culture was manifest. Powerful as were the forces making for integration and combination, they were yet never able to transcend the framework of a system of competing states.

II. WESTERN EUROPE

The process of territorial expansion and consolidation was best exemplified by the French and Spanish monarchies, and their successes on the continent coincided with the secure establishment of the Tudor dynasty in England. Louis XI, Ferdinand of Aragon, and Henry VII, hailed by Bacon as the three magi among the kings of that age, have always seemed to occupy a special place in the long transition from feudal to national monarchy and their reigns have often been regarded as the beginning of modern political history, marking the effective emergence of those great powers whose successive attempts to dominate the European scene were to be the characteristic feature of international relations for the next four centuries. The modern religion of nationalism has given to these events, viewed in retrospect, an appearance of inevitability, as if irresistible forces were working toward an identification of nation and state. This appearance may reflect reality; yet it must not be forgotten that at the turn of the fifteenth century this evolution was far from seeming so inexorable as to exclude other possibilities. The dramatic successes of Louis XI and Ferdinand of Aragon were matched by equally dramatic failures. Dynastic consolidation within the framework of national monarchy existed side by side with a dynastic imperialism which paid no attention at all to "national" boundaries. The territorial "unification" of France and Spain must not be lifted out of its European setting. Comparative study of such phenomena illuminates the factors which conditioned their success or failure and reveals how much that was accidental and arbitrary entered into even the most victorious combinations.

During this whole period the Italian peninsula provided the most extreme example of the limits imposed on individual aggression in any attempt to create a political unit with a larger territorial base or greater conformity with national boundaries. Actually, the territorial lines of the Italian powers had been determined well before the peace of Lodi in 1454. Earlier efforts to create a state that should dominate the Italian peninsula had all failed, and by the middle of the fifteenth century the areas occupied by the greater powers within Italy were roughly established and a condition of equilibrium was accepted. Although Naples, Milan and Florence were to change rulers many times and were to fall successively into the possession of dynasties outside the Italian peninsula, the important changes in the political boundaries of the Italian states were few. There were alterations in the line between the states of the church and the kingdom of Naples; there were extensions of the territory of the larger powers, such as the seizure of Volterra by Florence in 1472. Venice maintained, notably in the Ferrarese wars, the course of expansion on the mainland, which had been begun several generations before and was ultimately to bring the other powers, even those of Europe, into union against her. But the chief attempts to change the lines of political organization in Italy centered on the Romagna, where a number of small principalities professed allegiance to the states of the church but in fact exercised a practical independence which they had in part achieved during the absence of the papacy in Avignon. These territories ultimately became an area of conflict between the expansion of Venice and the ambitions of the papacy, whether the latter was directed to the aggrandizement of a single family, as in the case of the Borgia, or to the enlargement of the states of the church, as in the case of Julius II.

Of the various attempts to found a state by conquest in central Italy that of Caesar Borgia has enjoyed a special celebrity. He renounced his ecclesiastical career in 1498 and began his conquests after the conclusion of the French alliance in the next year. He was married to a French princess in 1499, and returned to Italy with a French title and with the support of French arms. The ambition of Alexander VI was directed not only to the strengthening of the Italian position of the papacy but still more to providing a permanent state for his family. Between 1499 and 1501 Caesar Borgia conquered most of the Romagna and was created its duke. From these initial conquests he advanced to a larger plan and was about to proceed against Bologna and Florence when the conspiracy of his associates interrupted the work of conquest and he was forced to postpone his program until he had dealt with the conspirators by the famous treachery of Sinigaglia. After disposing of his enemies, he seemed to be in a position to go forward with the realization of his plans when he and his father were both struck down by a serious illness, to which his father succumbed in August, 1503.

Machiavelli's famous remark has often been quoted, that Caesar Borgia had foreseen and provided for every contingency except that he might himself fall ill of a deadly disease at the moment of his father's death. Actually it is difficult to agree that, even without this coincidence, Caesar would have succeeded in creating a permanent monarchical position in Italy. In spite of Machiavelli's eloquent appeal to the adoration with which the liberator of Italy would be everywhere received, the strength of the existing divisions is clear. Caesar's conquests did in fact end the independence of a group of small principalities in the Romagna and prepared the way for their incorporation in the states of the church. At no time, however, was there any real possibility that he would be able to create an Italian monarchy; nor, in all probability, did his ambitions reach so far.[1] His dramatic attempt fascinated Machiavelli, because the combination of a Borgia pope and a Borgia secular prince seemed to supply the sole conditions on which Italy could generate a force sufficient to repel the foreign invasions. The same conditions were repeated in 1513, when the election of a Medici pope followed the restoration of the Medici in Florence; this situation was then made the basis for the program of Machiavelli's *Prince*. In both cases the hopes resting on these combinations were deceived. At this period no power or grouping of powers within Italy had the capacity to create, against the forces of division, a political entity broad enough to realize the aspirations inherited from Dante and Petrarch. The most that could be accomplished in the historic conditions was a very partial consolidation—a reduction in the number of petty principalities and city states in favor of somewhat larger groupings.

With the death of Alexander VI and the election of Julius II, who, as the Cardinal della Rovere, had been for many years a great enemy of the Borgia family, the fortune of Caesar was at an end. Julius II was determined that the Romagna should be captured for the papacy and not for the interests of a particular family. At the same time Venice, which was continuing to build up its mainland empire, took the opportunity to seize a share of the spoils of the Borgia inheritance. The territories of the Romagna were accordingly divided between Julius II, who acquired most of them for the church, and Venice, which took Rimini, Cesena, and Faenza. From this time onward Julius II directed an aggressive campaign to consolidate the papal states and oppose the advance of Venice. Perugia and Bologna were conquered by Julius in 1506, when he made the triumphal entry into Bologna which was witnessed by Erasmus. In 1508 the League of Cambrai was organized between the papacy and the northern powers for the despoilment of Venice. By 1510 Julius was satisfied with the territories gained from Venice and, arranging a separate peace with the republic, organized a new combination with the object of driving the French from Italy. In this aim Julius was ulti-

[1] G. Pepe, *La politica dei Borgia* (Naples, 1945), 291–94.

mately successful, but so heavily had he had to rely on Spanish aid that he found himself in the position of having exchanged a French master for a Spanish one. When Julius II died in 1513 it was clear that the papal monarchy was firmly established on an Italian territorial basis. Julius had reaped the harvest of the work of his predecessors, and down to the nineteenth century the states of the church existed as a permanent political entity in Europe. It was also clear, however, that the Spanish were established in the peninsula, and the policy of combination that Julius II had adopted with a view to driving the foreigner out of Italy had in fact brought about the opposite. From the middle of the fifteenth century onward all the efforts toward political consolidation in Italy had therefore resulted only in the enlargement of the territories directly ruled by the pope. In the meantime the failure to transcend the inherited political framework had left Italy at the mercy of those northern powers who had successfully expanded the territorial basis of their existence.

Even in the north, however, the process of consolidation, which appears in retrospect so natural, was far from clear in the middle of the fifteenth century. The fate of the duchy of Burgundy and of the ambitions of Charles the Bold provides an example, in many ways more instructive than that of Caesar Borgia, of the working of those combinations of circumstances that make possible the welding together of permanent political units.

At the time of the fall of Constantinople the greatest power in western Europe was the duchy of Burgundy. The territories acquired by the Burgundian dukes constituted a large agglomeration even before the additions made by Charles the Bold. By marriage, by negotiation and purchase, and occasionally by conquest, the lands under the control of the dukes had grown until they included most of the provinces of the Low Countries as well as the original nucleus of ducal and imperial Burgundy. Connecting these two main bodies of territory were many jurisdictions and fiefs along the valley of the Rhine. Thus had been formed between the French monarchy and the Germanic empire a considerable state. It was entirely made up of territories welded together by personal allegiance to the dukes. The legal position of the dukes themselves had an additional peculiarity: for some of their territories they were vassals of the king of France, whereas for others they were dependent on the Empire. In actual fact, they had come to pursue the course of an independent power. The events of the Hundred Years' War had at a critical moment produced a decisive change in the political orientation of the duchy, and, although the dukes continued to regard themselves and their court as representatives of French culture, they had in fact created the possibility of forming a new state. Thus we have the phenomenon of a group of territories held together by a purely personal tie and lacking a common economic framework, a national homogeneity or even a common political interest, but able to act as a great power because of the political circumstances of the moment.

The consciousness of belonging to the same political body that had developed in the Netherlands, insofar as we can speak of such a consciousness in these territories at all, was entirely dependent on the monarchy of the Burgundian duke. Basing himself on this strong position, it was the ambition of Charles the Bold to create a great middle kingdom between France and the Empire. Many elements were present which seemed to indicate that this enterprise might be successful, and in the eyes of all observers the position of Charles the Bold was far more brilliant than that of Louis XI, who succeeded to the French crown in 1461.

In the pursuit of his ambition, Charles attempted to form a compact block of territories stretching all the way from Switzerland to the North Sea. Those territories already under his control would be rounded out by the acquisition of further territories in Alsace and Lorraine. In 1469 he purchased Upper Alsace from Sigismund of Austria, and in 1475 he conquered Lorraine. In the meantime he renewed efforts, which had been begun by his father, to have himself granted a royal crown by the emperor. When in 1447 this had first been discussed between Philip the Good and the Emperor Frederick III, it had been proposed that Brabant be made a kingdom. Subsequent suggestions had included Lotharingia or Lorraine as a reminiscence of the old kingdom of Lothair, and later Friesland as well as Burgundy were put forward as possible bases of royal titles. All these negotiations failed, however, and after his final interview with Frederick III, when the emperor escaped without granting the royal title, Charles had to accept the fact that he had lost the title that had seemed to be within his grasp, and that might have made all the difference to his position.

However disappointing this failure had been, it did nothing to stop Charles' aggressive designs. His attacks on the Swiss, and his attempt to enlarge his Alsatian territory and recapture Lorraine led directly to the formation of a coalition against him. In the course of the ensuing struggle he was killed at the battle of Nancy in 1477. The great duke of Burgundy had failed to create a permanent state, and on his death his dominions were divided.

If we ask why Burgundy did not become one of the great modern national states, we have perhaps to consider in the first place the fact that the political loyalties developed in the Burgundian territories had been to such a degree purely personal. The Burgundian dukes never succeeded in institutionalizing their personal power. In an age when in other countries there were increasing indications of a growth of loyalty to the crown and to the principle of monarchy, a loyalty that transcended the person of any particular incumbent, there was in Burgundy, of all the many titles held by the dukes, no office that could be thus abstracted. All kinds of symbols and names were used for the Burgundian power, but the very fact that there was no unambiguous name that could be applied to all the territories ruled by the dukes is indicative. In this connection the failure of the duke's efforts to be granted a royal title must be regarded as particularly important. Then there was the accident of Charles' having no male heirs. It is, of course, impossible to say definitely that if Charles had been king of Burgundy, and if the Burgundian monarchs had been as fortunate as their Capetian and Valois neighbors in the succession, there would have been a great Burgundian state lasting as one of the permanent political factors in modern European history. Certainly geography and economics were to some extent against it; but the role of the latter is particularly ambiguous, and it could easily be maintained that these territories would have constituted a more viable economic unity than many other political creations, even though the economic interests were hardly such as to foster a feeling of national consciousness.

We have, then, in Burgundy an example of what might be called an arrested nationalism, a development that reached as far as pride in a house, pride in a race of dukes, but stopped short of becoming a comprehensive national consciousness because the conditions did not permit it so to develop.[2] What remained of such political self-consciousness as did develop became the national sentiment of the provinces of the Low Countries. But even here the residue was not strong enough to prevent a further split in the course of the sixteenth century, when the outlines of modern Belgium and Holland emerged as perhaps the final product of the Burgundian inheritance. The work of the Burgundian dukes is responsible, therefore, for the fact that these two small states exist between the great states of France and Germany, a fact that has been of the greatest consequence for the modern history of Europe. On the other

[2] J. Huizinga, *"Aus der Vorgeschichte des niederländischen Nationalbewusstseins,"* *Wege der Kulturgeschichte* (Munich, 1930), 208–80.

hand, this achievement represents but a symbol of what might have been, a lasting indication of the lines upon which a great Burgundian power might have developed.

In the years when the policy of expansion of the Burgundian dukes was brought to a climax and to final defeat, and in the years when desperate efforts were being made in Italy to create a more comprehensive political power, the kingdom of France was continuing a territorial consolidation that achieved permanence and has remained the classic example in western Europe of the evolution of national monarchy. In this evolution the reign of Louis XI occupies a significant place. The process of growth was by no means steady. Not all the territories acquired by the crown remained continuously in its possession, but by the end of the century the shape of the French state more clearly approximated that which has been familiar in modern times.

The beginnings were slow. Careful diplomacy succeeded in acquiring, if only temporarily, the small provinces on the border of the Spanish kingdoms. Bargaining with the duke of Burgundy brought rights to some of the towns on the Somme whose economic and strategic importance was great. But these early territorial gains were imperiled by feudal reaction at home. For many years the position of Louis XI seemed far less promising than that of his magnificent and ambitious rival in Burgundy. It was the struggle with the latter which gave Louis his greatest opportunity for territorial expansion, and provided historians a specious example of dramatic contrast between the past and the future, between Charles, the representative of a dying chivalric and feudal order, and Louis, the representative of modern politics, a practicing Machiavellian before Machiavelli. Different as were in fact the characters of the king of France and the duke of Burgundy, they worked within a set of historic conditions of which feudalism was still the basis. Both pursued a policy of territorial aggrandizement and there is small justification for awarding the title of "modern" to the one who succeeded.

The death of Charles without male heirs in 1477 brought the whole Burgundian inheritance into question. Legally many of the towns and territories of that inheritance, including the duchy of Burgundy itself, reverted to the French crown. In addition Louis profited by the desperate situation of Charles' daughter, Mary of Burgundy, and the powerlessness of the Emperor Maximilian to the extent of annexing the county of Artois and imperial Burgundy or Franche-Comté. The latter, however, he did not succeed in keeping. Their reunion with the French crown was left for a later successor and a very different set of circumstances. Even without these additions, however, the acquisition of so large a part of the Burgundian inheritance was a major victory.

A second important increase of territory came from the Angevin inheritance. René of Anjou, titular king of Jerusalem, had made a will leaving the provinces of Provence and Anjou as well as his various Mediterranean claims to his nephew, Charles of Maine. The old king died in 1480 and his nephew's death in the following year in turn left the whole of this enormous inheritance to the crown of France, thus returning as it were with interest the appanage created in the thirteenth century by St. Louis in favor of his younger brother. At the end of his reign Louis XI had therefore, by a fortunate combination of accident and policy, nearly doubled the domain of the crown, consolidated the territorial basis of the monarchy and created a position from which the power of the great vassals could be more easily overthrown.

This achievement was far from permanent, and its basis was threatened more than once during the succeeding reigns. Various minor concessions were made to feudal and particular interests, but the most serious territorial question confronting the immediate successors of Louis XI was that of Brittany. This duchy enjoyed practical independence until the death of the last male duke in 1488. At that time his heiress, the Duchess Anne, hoping to maintain her position, concluded a marriage agreement with Maximilian, whose first wife, Mary of Burgundy, had died in 1481. The marriage was celebrated by procurator and the parlement of Brittany registered acts in the name of Anne and Maximilian. This alliance presented the possibility of practical encirclement of the territories of the French crown and at least on this occasion Charles VIII and his advisers felt it essential to pursue the policy of territorial consolidation. By negotiations and threats the Duchess Anne was persuaded, at a meeting of the Breton estates, to repudiate as illegal her marriage to Maximilian and consent to a marriage with Charles VIII. This decision naturally resulted in immediate war with the Empire. Maximilian was joined by Ferdinand of Aragon and Henry VII of England in a coalition against the French, but the war was not prosecuted seriously. It was brought to an end by the determination of Charles VIII to capitalize on his Italian claims and his consequent willingness to make territorial adjustments in the north to leave him a free hand in Italy. Dynastic imperialism thus succeeded the policy of dynastic consolidation at home.

Such fluctuations make it impossible to maintain that the goal of territorial centralization around the historic nucleus of the lands of the French crown was pursued consciously or consistently. French kings of the fifteenth and sixteenth centuries simply did not think like French historians of the nineteenth century. If in the case of Louis XI there was a steady and successful effort to increase and consolidate the royal domain, this policy was subsequently interrupted by so many instances of a contrary course that it is difficult to make out a case for the inevitable growth of the French state toward its natural frontiers. The willingness of Charles VIII to make sacrifices at home in order to prosecute a claim to the distant kingdom of Naples was the reflection of a dynastic and chivalric ideal directly contrary to the policy of national unification.

Clearly, it was not so apparent to Charles and his advisers as it has been to many later historians, that the interest of France required extension toward its natural frontiers rather than distant adventure in Italy. Indeed, we hear nothing as yet of the very idea of natural frontiers. The Italian expedition of Charles VIII in 1494-1495, ephemeral though it was, may be taken as an obvious indication that the ideal of a homogeneous political unit in which the state increasingly approximated the nation was not a conscious ambition.

The same divergent policies, the same lack of clearness and concentration on a single end, the simultaneous existence of several mutually incompatible aims and lines of direction, were still more apparent in the reign of Charles' successor, Louis XII. At the beginning of his reign he arranged the annulment of his previous marriage and contracted a new marriage with Anne of Brittany in order to save the inheritance of Brittany for the crown of France. But at the same time he did not scruple to alienate the duchy of Bourbon as an appanage, abandoning the royal rights over this important territory in the heart of what later became the French state, solely in order to placate the elder daughter of Louis XI and her husband. Such a concession to the claims of the high feudality might be explained as a necessary measure to assure political support. But what can be said of the proposal made in 1501 to betroth the infant daughter of Louis and Anne to Charles of Hapsburg and to give her for dowry the duchies of Brittany and Burgundy as well as all the Italian possessions acquired by the invasion of 1499—that is, the duchy of Milan as well as Genoa and the county of Asti? This astonishing arrangement, if carried out, would have completely undone the results of the reign of Louis XI. It is a further indication of how difficult it is to discern, even among the possessors of the French crown, a steady realization of what is called the true French national interest. This alliance was, however, abandoned by Louis XII four years later in favor of a more "French" solution, the marriage of his daughter with the count of Angoulême, first prince of the blood and destined to be, as Francis I, the successor of Louis XII on the throne.

In spite of this belated recognition of the importance of maintaining intact a solid bloc of territories as the basis of the French monarchy, Louis was not diverted from his Italian claims. His initial successes in northern Italy seemed to promise the realization of even wider ambitions, and between 1501 and 1503 the attempt was made to acquire at least a part of the Neapolitan inheritance. Although the French were forced to leave Naples to the Spanish in 1503, Milan, Genoa, and Asti still remained in French hands until the expulsion of the French from Italy in 1512 by the victorious forces of the league headed by Julius II.

The inheritance of the Italian claims descended in 1515 to Francis I, and a new and again successful expedition, culminating in the battle of Marignano, was undertaken to enforce the claims of the French king to Milan. Thus the pattern of the previous reigns was repeated, and the initial successes of the new monarch created an atmosphere of optimism and vitality. In the end the attraction of the smoke and glory of Italy was to prove a deception, yet the French intervention in Italy could hardly have been undertaken at all had it not been based on the successes of the policy of territorial consolidation at home.

In contrast with that of Burgundy, the French expansion was accomplished under the aegis of an institution with centuries of historic tradition behind it. Where the dukes of Burgundy had had to operate on the basis of a personal appeal, the French kings could invoke their royal power. Furthermore, those lands that were annexed by the crown of France and remained a permanent part of the French monarchy were more homogeneous than those associated under the leadership of Burgundy. While it is far from true that a national French sentiment yet existed in Cerdagne, Rousillon, Provence, or Brittany—and while, as we have seen, the Bretons could entertain with equanimity, or at least without resorting to revolution, the idea that they should be governed from Hapsburg Germany—yet there was a historic bond of community the outward expression of which was the French language. Political association together in loyalty to a common institution fostered the slow growth of a sentiment of belonging to a national group.

In the case of Spain the consolidation of the various medieval kingdoms of the Iberian peninsula, insofar as it was achieved in the fifteenth century, followed a pattern very different from that of France. Instead of expansion from a center or nucleus which represented a single historic tradition, the Spanish kingdom was finally created by the coalescence of more or less equal powers within the peninsula. The creation of a stable political unit by this process has some resemblance to the biological phenomenon whereby unicellular organisms brought together under certain conditions are transformed into an entirely new organism in which the principles of division of labor and specialization have been realized. So, after the union of a number of small political bodies, there eventually emerge a number of common institutions to serve the needs of the whole new body politic. Clearly the organic analogy, a favorite one in sixteenth-century political theory, cannot be pressed too far, but in both cases it may be noted that the conditions which determine successful and permanent combinations are very imperfectly understood.

Both Aragon and Castile had passed through a difficult and depressing period in the first half of the fifteenth century. In Castile the twenty-year reign of Henry IV (1454-1474) had brought the position of the monarchy to a new low. The customary feudal coalitions were given an additional impetus by the incompetence of the king and the existence of a complicated and disputed succession question. Among the claimants to the succession Isabella, the king's half-sister, was the ablest, and gradually her cause became the rallying point for those who hoped to revive and extend the influence of the crown. Like the establishment of the Tudor dynasty in England and the reign of Louis XI in France, the eventual triumph of Isabella marked an important stage in the transition from feudal to monarchical state, but the outcome in Spain was for a long time in doubt and depended principally on the establishment of the dynastic connection with Aragon.

The latter kingdom had also passed through a mid-fifteenth century stage of misrule and disaffection. The reign of John II (1458–1479) was marked by a long struggle over the kingdom of Navarre, which led in turn to a rebellion in Catalonia. By intrigue, desperation, and sheer staying power John finally emerged victorious and was able to bequeath to Ferdinand the Catholic, born in 1452, the whole of the Aragonese inheritance except the kingdom of Navarre and the provinces of the Pyrenees ceded to Louis XI.

Long before the final satisfactory settlement of the difficulties in his own realm John had negotiated the marriage between Ferdinand and

Isabella. Although opposed by the diplomacy of Louis XI and the king of Portugal, and resisted by various disaffected groups in both Aragon and Castile, the treaty was drawn up and signed and the marriage took place in 1469. Henry IV of Castile died five years later and Isabella, with Ferdinand's support, was able to make good her claim to the crown in spite of efforts made on behalf of the supposed daughter of the late king. Neither the attempts of France and Portugal from the outside nor those of rebellious groups within the kingdom were able to create an effective opposition. Although there were some years of hostilities, interspersed by negotiations, treaties were finally signed with Portugal and with the rebellious nobles and Isabella's title henceforth remained undisputed.

Although Ferdinand and Isabella were proclaimed king and queen of Castile together and used a joint seal, Isabella never gave up her authority. The union between the two kingdoms remained purely dynastic. In both Aragon and Castile all the older offices and the inherited pattern of administration were continued. For many years the only institution common to both countries was the Inquisition, established in 1481.

In the past centuries of association between the kingdoms of the Spanish peninsula, Portugal had been even more closely connected with Castile than the latter with Aragon. It might be maintained that, if there were to have been any merger at all between these kingdoms, the most logical union would have been that of Castile and Portugal, rather than that of Castile and Aragon. The orientation of Castilian and Portuguese policy was the same, while Aragon had long been closely involved with Italian and Mediterranean politics. As for language, Catalan, Italian, and Valencian were spoken in Aragon, and the differences between these languages and Castilian were perhaps not appreciably less significant than those between Castilian and Portuguese. The actual outcome, by which a permanent connection was established between the Castilian and Aragonese realms, whereas Portugal persisted as an independent kingdom, seems to have been in large part the result of a series of dynastic accidents.

Undoubtedly there were general conditions in the second half of the fifteenth century which permitted and even fostered the formation of more comprehensive political units. Undoubtedly also, in those cases where there existed large communities of people with a common linguistic and historical tradition, the new large-scale political units were more apt to be formed on the basis of such a sense of community. But there were striking exceptions, and the union of Aragon and Castile with the exclusion of Portugal was one of them. It was at various times proposed that Isabella make a Portuguese marriage. Had she done so, it is possible to imagine that Castile and Portugal together would have formed a mighty Iberian kingdom, presiding together over the great initial effort of European discovery and exploration. In such a situation the whole colonial empire of Asia and the New World together would have been united under one power; and what is still more important, that power might have been uninvolved in the Italian question or in the political fate of the German Empire. Since the Spanish involvement in these questions was largely derived from the past orientation of Aragonese politics and from the activity of Ferdinand the Catholic, Castile and Portugal might have escaped. As it turned out, the union of Castile and Aragon, brought about by the marriage of Ferdinand and Isabella, and for many years personal and precarious, remained permanent with all its fateful consequences for the history of Europe and the world.[3]

With the kingdoms of Aragon and Castile united, it was possible to make a final assault on the emirate of Granada, the last stronghold of Mohammedanism in western Europe. A first expedition was sent against the Moors in 1482, and from this date the war was vigorously prosecuted and was furthered by the development of dynastic quarrels within Granada. The association of the forces of Castile and Aragon in this enterprise was indicative of the sense of community that was to develop between these two kingdoms. It might be said that the conquest of Granada was entirely to the advantage of Castile, as the boundaries of Aragon at no point touched those of Granada. Nevertheless, the soldiers of Ferdinand were engaged equally with those of Isabella, and both sovereigns triumphed when the long campaign was brought to a victorious conclusion in 1492 with the surrender of Boabdil, the last of the emirs of Granada. Thus, with the exception of Portugal and the kingdom of Navarre, which had been lost by John II of Aragon, the whole Iberian peninsula had achieved a limited kind of unification, although in fact there did not yet exist, except in the Inquisition, any community of institutions.

The capture of Granada introduced a further period of expansion. The crusade against the Moors was carried to North Africa in a series of expeditions during the first decades of the sixteenth century. As in the case of France, dynastic imperialism followed dynastic successes at home. By 1510 Algiers had been taken, but the effort to acquire a considerable territory in North Africa never attained what had been originally

[3] R. B. Merriman, *The Rise of the Spanish Empire*, Vol. II (New York, 1918), 55–56.

planned. The energies of the government were engaged in other directions, especially in the great expansionist foreign policy in Italy as well as the new colonial empire.

The most brilliant military and political successes of Ferdinand were achieved in Italy. In the decade which followed the French invasion of 1494 the Spanish king found an opportunity for a series of well-timed interventions in the affairs of Naples and Milan. These maneuvers were executed with a cynical disregard, unusual even in that age, for previous commitments. At all events they appeared to be justified by the results, for by 1504 Ferdinand's manipulations left him in complete possession of the kingdom of Naples, which remained from this time forward a Spanish possession. The political control of the newly strengthened monarchy was thus definitively extended beyond the bounds of the Iberian peninsula.

Ferdinand's final conquests served to consolidate territories on the northern frontier of Spain. The provinces of Cerdagne and Roussillon had been reacquired from France as part of one of the deals over French ambitions in Italy. The kingdom of Navarre was a particular object of Ferdinand's ambition because of its strategic situation and because of the historic struggle for its control which had disrupted the history of Aragon for a generation. By a series of treaties negotiated between 1476 and 1500 the Spanish sovereigns had succeeded in reducing Navarre to the status of a vassal kingdom. In 1512 came the climax. Ferdinand, in his last and most blatant piece of duplicity, published a false treaty purporting to show that the French and the Navarrese had made an aggressive alliance against Aragon. With this as an excuse, and with the pope's blessing, the troops of Ferdinand invaded and conquered the kingdom of Navarre. This victory was regularized by Julius II, whose bull excommunicating the former king absolved his subjects of the oath of allegiance and conferred the title on Ferdinand.

The ambition and ability of Ferdinand and Isabella had been furthered by fortunate dynastic accidents and had brought about the successful welding together of the various kingdoms and provinces of the Iberian peninsula. The result was not yet a centralized monarchy such as existed in France and England. Local autonomy for the kingdoms of Spain continued to prevail for many years. But the dynasty had established a sufficient territorial control with a corresponding increase of resources to enable it to play a dominant role on the European scene as a whole.

In the far north the Scandinavian kingdoms followed a line of development opposite to that which had brought the medieval Spanish kingdoms together. Here consolidation through a dynastic connection never proved strong enough to achieve a permanent state. Norway, which was a hereditary monarchy, and Sweden and Denmark, which were formally elective monarchies, had been ostensibly united at Kalmar in 1397 under the direction of Margaret of Norway, who was regent of the other two kingdoms. The whole evolution in the early fifteenth century seemed to point in the direction of a single state. The population of the three kingdoms was certainly as homogeneous as that of France and was far smaller in numbers.

Yet the dynasty never proved strong enough to impose permanent unity, and the political and social struggles of the fifteenth century produced an eventual separation of the three Scandinavian kingdoms. In Sweden the party favoring union was composed largely of the nobility, many of whom had estates or family connections in the other Scandinavian countries. Opposed to this party were the peasants, who from time to time found leaders who could capitalize on the grievances arising from the imposition of taxes by an alien administration.

The pattern of revolt was established in the early part of the fifteenth century when a series of minor rebellions provided a tradition for the cause of Swedish independence from the Danish king. These rebellions grew into a major struggle of which the climax was the heroic effort of Karl Knudson and his nephew, Sten Sture, against the continuance of Danish rule in Sweden. The preliminary successes achieved under their inspiration were replaced by a series of precarious attempts to maintain the Danish union at the end of the fifteenth century. Danish policy was aided by a division of parties in Sweden and when a strong king, Christian II, succeeded in Denmark in 1513 he was able to intervene again and attempt to establish the Danish rule permanently by the exercise of a policy of extreme repression. Given the historic background, his tyrannical policy aroused such opposition that when the outbreak of civil war in Denmark itself gave an opportunity, Gustavus Vasa was able to begin a revolt in Sweden and sweep the whole country with him in repudiating the Danish connection and establishing the Swedish national monarchy on a permament basis.[4]

During the long and confusing struggle it is clear that something like

[4] R. Svanström and C. F. Palmstierna, *A Short History of Sweden,* translated by Joan Bulman (Oxford, 1934), 56–72, and K. Larsen, *A History of Norway* (Princeton, 1948), 218–26.

a national sentiment, which hardly existed in Sweden at the time of the Union of Kalmar at the end of the fourteenth century, grew in intensity during the whole fifteenth century with the repeated attempts to resist the encroachment of the Danish monarchy. On the other hand the same monarchy was successful in maintaining the union with Norway. If we ask why a dynastic political tie worked in one case whereas in the other the way was prepared for a permanent separation, the answer is far from clear. Personal and contingent factors certainly cannot be neglected. Although there were differences of historic tradition and social circumstances between Norway and Sweden, it is difficult to resist the conclusion that a more politic handling by the kings of Denmark of all the populations subject to their control might have created a permanently unified state. In this case, unlike that of the Spanish monarchy, dynastic union was not followed by the growth of a larger national sentiment.

The age of Louis XI and Ferdinand and Isabella saw great changes in the territorial basis of political organization among the states of western Europe. These changes were the result of the welding together under the auspices of the crown of older and smaller units of government. The process, however, was far from universally manifest or productive of similar results. England, Scotland and Portugal remained within their historic boundaries and the changes within the Italian peninsula were slight. Although the kingdom of France more than doubled the royal domain and the beginnings of a common government were established between Aragon and Castile, the Scandinavian monarchies moved away from union and toward the realization of separate identities. The grouping of feudal territories and even kingdoms under one ruler was not inspired by the conscious purpose of creating anything like a modern "national" state. The nature of the attempts made with varying degrees of success in the countries bordering the Atlantic was more truly revealed in central and eastern Europe, where the Hapsburg Empire through a series of more strictly dynastic accidents attained the proportions of a universal state and threatened to re-create the imperial traditions of the middle ages.

III. CENTRAL AND EASTERN EUROPE

During the years which were marked in the west by the territorial successes of the French and Spanish monarchies the dynasties of eastern Europe made analogous attempts to consolidate and enlarge the lands subject to their control. Outside the frontiers of Latin Christendom the principality of Moscow absorbed neighboring powers and prepared the way for the great future of the Russian state. In Hungary Mathias Corvinus sought to restore his kingdom to a leading position and to construct an imperial state based on the Danubian region. In Poland and Lithuania the Jagellon dynasty successfully followed a policy which for a brief period brought most of the states of eastern Europe into its control. Finally the Hapsburgs, by their series of matrimonial alliances, accumulated the unprecedented collection of territories that became the inheritance of Charles V in the sixteenth century. These attempts, accompanied by varying degrees of success, were all dominated by what might be called feudal or dynastic imperialism. An emergent consciousness of belonging to a national group increased the power of the ruler without as yet defining in national terms the limits of his policy.

Of these four histories of territorial expansion the Russian presents certain unique features. The principality of Moscow in the middle of the fifteenth century consisted of only fifteen thousand square miles. Its slow growth had been repeatedly threatened by Tartar pressure from the east and by rivalry with Novgorod and other neighboring powers. The very precariousness of its existence had stimulated in the inhabitants a sense of identification with the cause of political independence and expansion. The reign of Ivan III (1462–1505), like that of Louis XI in France, was the period when the process of gathering in new lands was accelerated and the most dramatic gains were made.

The territory of Novgorod the Great was absorbed by stages between 1465 and 1488. The great commercial city had come to depend on mercenaries who had no incentive to fight for its independence, and the Moscovites besides controlled the hinterland which furnished food and supplies to the inhabitants. If it came to a choice between being dominated by Orthodox Moscow or Roman Catholic Lithuania, Novgorod preferred Moscow. There was therefore always a party within the city itself ready to make an accommodation with Ivan. A series of interventions established the supremacy of Moscow which was manifested in 1486 and 1487 by the wholesale transplantation of those merchant families of Novgorod who had been a center of opposition.

The fall of Novgorod was accompanied or followed by the absorption of most of the principalities of central and north Russia which had hitherto kept their independence. Tver, Perm, Yaroslavl, Verea and Ryazan were either inherited or annexed.

With this great territorial expansion there developed an ideology center-

ing on a belief in the destiny of Moscow. In 1472 Ivan III married Sophia
Paleologus, niece of the last Byzantine emperor. This princess had been
a refugee at Rome since the fall of Constantinople and the Russian
marriage was arranged for her with the aid of the pope, who hoped that
this alliance would further the cause of union between the Greek and
Latin churches which had been proclaimed at the council of Florence in
1439. Actually the marriage had the opposite effect: the Russian church
repudiated the union even more decisively and Sophia encouraged her
husband in the introduction of the elaborate Byzantine court ceremonial
which exalted the position of the ruler. The doctrine was put forward that
Moscow was the third Rome, now about to assume its sway after the fall
of Constantinople, which had been the second. This doctrine was accompanied by the emergence of fantastic historical legends designed to bolster
among the people of Moscow the sense of an imperial mission. It was
maintained that the regalia of the Greek Empire had been bestowed on
the grand prince of Kiev and that the princes of Russia traced their
descent directly from the Emperor Augustus. These fabulous appeals to
history were also characteristic of western dynasties during the same
period. In France, for example, a whole literature of destiny, embodying
genealogies which went back to Troy and claims to a divine mission for
the descendants of the Franks, had been inherited from the Middle Ages
and flowered particularly in the period of the Italian invasion of Charles
VIII. The process of expansion was generally accompanied by such
ideological justifications. In the Russian case, however, the elaboration
and intensification of the legend of the third Rome was in direct proportion to the threats which Moscow felt it had surmounted. The isolation
of Russians from the religious tradition of the west, the dramatic suddenness of their expansion, the long continued threat of Tartar domination,
which was only now lifted, all contributed to the heightened tone of
their appeals to history.[5]

Thus, although the consolidation of the Russian lands occurred during
roughly the same span of years when the same process was going on in
the west, it had a different basis and was accompanied by a different
ideology. The Byzantine inheritance and the Tartar threat had combined
to make the course of Russian history, in spite of superficial resemblances,
incommensurable with that of the states of Latin Christian Europe.

In Hungary the national sentiment had not the advantage of an
attachment to a historic tradition of the same kind. The fortunes of this

[5] Sir Bernard Pares, *A History of Russia* (New York, 1947), 84–93.

kingdom had been closely united to those of Bohemia and Austria in the first half of the fifteenth century, when the Emperor Sigismund had also been king of both Bohemia and Hungary. This dynastic connection, which foreshadowed the Hapsburg rule in the sixteenth century, was not long maintained after Sigismund's death. His son-in-law, Albert of Hapsburg, ruled for only two years and was in turn succeeded by a posthumously born son, Ladislas, crowned king of Hungary at the age of six weeks. The nominal rule of a child, complicated by various claims to exercise authority in his name, was an encouragement to local and national interests which triumphed when Ladislas died in 1457.

Austria reverted to the Hapsburgs; Bohemia elected a native ruler, George Podiebrad; Hungary bestowed the crown on Mathias Corvinus, son of the hero of the siege of Belgrade. The new kings of Bohemia and Hungary, who both represented to some extent the strength of a native tradition and feeling in those countries, made an alliance as a result of which Corvinus married the daughter of Podiebrad.

This alliance, however, failed to bring about a closer union between the two kingdoms. Both rulers were able and ambitious and quick to seize an opportunity for their own advancement. When Podiebrad supported the Utraquists in Bohemia, Mathias Corvinus conveniently made himself a champion of the church, with a view to acquiring the kingdom of Bohemia for himself. Although he was supported by the Catholic faction and the rebellious elements within Bohemia—and was even declared the elected king of Bohemia—he was eventually defeated. When Podiebrad died in 1471, Ladislas Jagellon of Poland was elected to the Bohemian throne and succeeded in confirming his position by defeating Mathias.

Even before Mathias had tried and failed to annex the kingdom of Bohemia, he had made an attempt, in 1463, to expand his territories at the expense of the Hapsburg, whom he had defeated in that year. After the failure of the Bohemian venture he returned to the attack against the Hapsburg and, taking advantage of a revolt of the Austrian nobility in the year 1485, invaded Austria and conquered Vienna. The emperor was forced to become a refugee from his own territories, and it appeared that Mathias was on the point of realizing his plans for a great central European state based on Hungary as a nucleus. These ambitions were the natural outcome of the king's domestic success. Within a very short time he had made Hungary the leading power of central Europe. A program of military reform had provided an army less dependent on the

old feudal levies; the political opposition of the magnates had been temporarily suppressed, and the creation of a strong monarchy had been
accompanied by legal reforms and an effort to develop the towns as allies
of the crown. The dominion of Mathias was a purely personal creation,
but for a time it was extraordinarily successful and reached its zenith in
the period after the conquest of Vienna. Mathias aspired to the title of
emperor and intrigued with the electors to attain this end. All these
ambitions were brought to a sudden end by his death in 1490 and, as he
left no legitimate heirs, his crown passed to that very member of the
Jagellon dynasty who had been his successful opponent in Bohemia.[6]

The work of Mathias Corvinus was thus entirely ephemeral. It was
founded on the ambition and ability of an individual who had not the
benefit of a historic dynastic connection nor a series of fortunate inheritances. The thirty-six years between the death of Mathias and the battle
of Mohacs present a picture of rapid disintegration which left the Hungarian state no real strength to resist the Turkish advance. The contrast
between the great abilities of Corvinus and the limits of his fortune is a
measure of the advantages enjoyed by those ambitious rulers whose
attempts at expansion were backed by a more solid institutional basis.

A far more considerable success rewarded the efforts of the Jagellon
dynasty in Poland. After the death of the elder Ladislas Jagellon at
Varna in 1444, Casimir IV succeeded his brother as elected king of Poland
and as grand prince of Lithuania. Under his rule the long struggle with
the Teutonic knights was brought to a successful conclusion. The knights
had made a first peace with the Polish power at Thorn in 1416 and a
second in 1435, the effect of which was finally to ruin their prestige as
rulers. In 1453 their subjects, now chronically in revolt, appealed to
Poland for aid against their masters. Casimir IV immediately replied by
promulgating a decree uniting all the Prussian lands with the state of
Poland and granting to the subjects of the Teutonic knights all the
liberties and privileges that belonged to his own subjects. In the initial
stages of the war that followed Casimir was handicapped by the recal-
citrant nobility, who used the occasion to extract as many concessions as
they could, and also by the Lithuanians, who resisted the political connection with Poland. As soon as the king had succeeded in conciliating
the nobility, regulating the Lithuanian question, and strengthening his
military power, victories against the Prussian knights replaced the initial

[6] O. Zarek, *History of Hungary,* translated by Prince P. Wolkonskz (London, 1939), ch.
VII.

defeats. Numerous early attempts at mediation by the pope, the emperor, and other western powers were rejected by Casimir. As the Polish victories continued, however, the king finally accepted an offer of mediation from the pope, and in 1466 a new Treaty of Thorn was signed. By this treaty the Teutonic order ceded to Poland all the western territories it had had under its rule. The Teutonic knights were left with only East Prussia, which was established as a fief of Poland with an obligation undertaken by the grand masters to go in person, six months after their election, to take an oath of fidelity to the king. Although by this treaty the problem of the Teutonic knights was not finally settled, Poland had at least received the territories at the mouth of the Vistula and an outlet to the sea.

This victory left the Polish king in position to pursue a policy of further dynastic expansion, and the situation in the kingdom of Bohemia offered an opportunity. The rule of George Podiebrad, the native Czech elected to the Bohemian crown in 1457, had not achieved political stability. In spite of his energy and activity and his dreams for a European community, outlined in proposals to Louis XI, Podiebrad had encountered the hostility of the Roman Church when he supported the Utraquists. In 1465 he was excommunicated by the pope and his subjects absolved from their oath of allegiance. The break with Rome provided Mathias Corvinus with an excuse for intervention in Bohemia, where he was declared king by those in revolt against Podiebrad. The latter died in 1471 still unreconciled with Rome, and Corvinus, who might then have hoped to have the field to himself, had instead to face the powerful opposition of Poland and the Jagellon dynasty. Casimir IV installed his son Ladislas as king of Bohemia and, by fomenting a revolution in Hungary and sending a Polish army there, forced Corvinus to retreat. Thus the Polish king was left in the position of having practically direct control, through his son, of the whole of Bohemia as well as his own kingdom.

This dynastic expansion was subsequently continued to include Hungary when Mathias Corvinus died without heirs in 1490. The Hungarian magnates, suspicious of a strong native prince, proposed the election of Ladislas Jagellon, in spite of the fact that he already ruled in Bohemia. Although the king of Poland would have preferred to have one of his younger sons elected in Hungary, rather than the one who already possessed a kingdom, he did not offer serious opposition, and Ladislas added the crown of Hungary to that of Bohemia. Thus for a brief period most of the political units of eastern Europe—Poland, Lithuania, Pomerania,

Bohemia, and Hungary—were united under the control of the Jagellon dynasty.[7]

But this empire was destined to be almost as brief as the ambitions of Mathias Corvinus. Casimir IV died in 1492 and his sons disputed the succession. John Albert, the younger son who had been his father's preferred candidate for the Hungarian crown, was declared king of Poland. During his short reign and that of his brother, the influence of the Hapsburgs increased in Hungary and Bohemia. By 1516, when the Emperor Maximilian arranged his famous marriage treaty with Ladislas of Hungary, it could already be predicted that the ultimate political consolidation of central Europe would take place under the auspices of the Hapsburg and not of the Jagellon dynasty.

Of all the efforts to combine independent territories by establishing a common dynastic connection, that of the Hapsburgs was by far the most spectacular and successful. The fortunes of this family were dramatically changed in the space of two generations. Frederick III, whose long reign extended from 1440 to 1493, was one of the weakest and most ineffectual of all the Hapsburg rulers. He was a dilettante, fond of collecting jewelry, interested in astronomy, astrology, and palmistry, but never able to cope successfully with any of the many problems with which he was faced. He was the last of the German emperors to be crowned by the pope at Rome, although his grandson, Charles V, received the crown from Clement VII at Bologna in 1530.

Chief among the problems of Frederick's empire was the development of strong peripheral powers that threatened the integrity and existence of the old complex of the German Empire. In the west the expansion of Burgundy, until the death of Charles the Bold, took more and more territory away from imperial control, and in the face of this threat the emperor had no practical policy. In the east the Hapsburgs had been ousted from both Bohemia and Hungary, and national rulers had been installed there. Both George Podiebrad and Mathias Corvinus offered continued opposition to the Hapsburg interest. Finally, there was the still more powerful threat from the Jagellon dynasty of Poland. Frederick III met a first defeat at the hands of Corvinus in 1463, and subsequently, in 1485, was driven from his old Austrian territories under the threat of losing his imperial authority altogether. The future of the Hapsburg dynasty was finally saved principally by the results of the marriage be-

---

[7] O. Halecki, *The History of Poland; an Essay in Historical Synthesis,* translated by M. M. Gardner and M. Cambridge-Patkaniowska (London, 1942), ch. X.

tween Frederick's son Maximilian and Mary of Burgundy, daughter of Charles the Bold.

This marriage, long the subject of negotiations between the emperor and the duke of Burgundy, had been finally concluded in 1477, the year of Burgundy's disastrous defeat. It appeared for a time after the death of Charles the Bold that the whole Burgundian inheritance would fall to pieces and the position of Mary of Burgundy was consequently precarious, but the situation was stabilized by 1482 when she and Maximilian had recovered Franche-Comté and the county of Artois from the aggression of Louis XI and had succeeded also in securing their position in the Low Countries. Shortly thereafter Maximilian's prospects were further improved by the acquisition, upon his cousin's death, of Hapsburg lands in the Tyrol and Austria. Thus, in spite of Frederick III's weaknesses, his son was presented with opportunities provided by the title to a greater number of territories than had been enjoyed by any emperor since the time of the Hohenstaufen. By 1491, Austria, the Tyrol, Styria, Carinthia, and Carniola, together with claims to Bohemia and Hungary, had all come into Maximilian's hands.

Brilliant as were the prospects which resulted from Maximilian's own marriage and inheritance, they were eclipsed by the further successions which came to the Hapsburgs through the marriages arranged for Maximilian's children and grandchildren.

The first of these alliances and the most important in its consequences was the marriage between his son Philip and Joanna, second daughter of Ferdinand and Isabella. The Spanish sovereigns, like other contemporary European rulers, had made full use of marriage alliances as an instrument of policy. Since much of their own power and success had been the result of the connection between Castile and Aragon established by their own marriage, it was natural to expect that further successes could be achieved by similar means. Their elder daughter, Isabella, had been married to the king of Portugal in the hope that this union might bring Portugal within their family succession. This marriage was concluded in 1490 and, although Isabella's husband died a few months later, she was hopefully remarried in 1497 to Emmanuel the Fortunate, cousin of her first husband.

During the same years negotiations had been initiated with other European powers for the marriage of the remaining children of Ferdinand and Isabella. In 1495 there was concluded between Ferdinand's envoys and those of the Emperor Maximilian the celebrated treaty for the double marriage connecting the Hapsburgs and the Spanish rulers. Maximilian's daughter Margaret was married to John, only son of Ferdinand and Isabella, at the same time that Philip married John's sister Joanna. By these alliances the Catholic sovereigns were able to hope that they had laid the foundations for continuing the work of unification already accomplished in Spain, at the same time enormously increasing the prestige of their dynastic connections and their political influence throughout Europe. Unfortunately the accidents of birth and death failed to conform to the hopes of state policy. The plans of Ferdinand and Isabella were blasted by an extraordinary series of deaths that ultimately brought the whole Spanish inheritance to the Hapsburgs. Their son John died in 1497 without heirs and in the following year he was followed by their eldest daughter, Isabella, queen of Portugal. Her only child, to whom it was hoped would descend the crowns of Aragon, Castile and Portugal, died in 1500 before he was two years old. The whole Spanish inheritance thus fell to the next in line, Joanna, wife of the Archduke Philip. Their children, of whom the future Emperor Charles V was the eldest, in this way ultimately received the tremendous accumulation of territories involved in the combination of Burgundian, Hapsburg and Spanish possessions.

The results of these marriage alliances in the west were still further enhanced by Maximilian's eastern policy. There, although he had inherited claims to the kingdoms of Hungary and Bohemia, he found it necessary to deal with Ladislas Jagellon, actually the occupant of both thrones. By the Treaty of Pressburg in 1491 he extracted from Ladislas a promise of the Hapsburg succession in both Hungary and Bohemia, in the event there should be no direct heirs.

As the Turkish pressure upon Hungary increased, Ladislas became even more desirous of making an alliance with Maximilian, and in 1502 suggested the possibility of a marriage contract. The negotiations dragged out for some time, but Maximilian naturally received these proposals favorably and in 1506, in spite of the opposition of the Hungarian magnates, Maximilian was able to conclude a second double betrothal between his granddaughter Mary and Ladislas' infant son Louis on the one hand, and one of Maximilian's grandsons, Charles or Ferdinand, with Louis's sister Anna on the other. Thus by the same diplomatic means which had assured his family's brilliant inheritance in the west, Maximilian acquired in the east the succession to Hungary and Bohemia, and these arrangements were finally confirmed at the congress of Vienna in 1515. In the following year Maximilian's grandson Charles succeeded Ferdinand the Catholic in Spain, and in the same year the Hungarian marriages of his grandchildren, Ferdinand and Mary, were concluded. The Hapsburg holdings thus stretched across all Europe and seemed to promise a recrudescence of the ideals of the Carolingian Empire.

The Hapsburg Empire was the culmination of the process of dynastic consolidation. Its creation was made possible because no one questioned the idea that crowns and titles to dominion were subject to the same laws as private inheritance. The chief variation in such laws concerned the rights of women to inherit title. It is interesting to speculate on what would have happened to the Spanish monarchies if there had been applied to them a Salic law like that of the French excluding the succession of women. The possibility was at least discussed in Aragon where the estates were reluctant to recognize the rights of Joanna after her father's death. If such a law had been applied, the probability is that the Spanish kingdoms would again have reverted to independent positions and the work of unification would have been a brief episode. As it was, the national interest of the Spanish people insofar as it had been fostered by the work of Ferdinand and Isabella was now destroyed by binding Spain to the ambitions of the Hapsburg in central and eastern Europe.

In part because of the very accidents by which it was created, the Hapsburg Empire could not offer a permanent pattern for the organization of the political life of the European world. Dynastic connections between states created by a series of unexpected deaths in a single family might prove surprisingly lasting; but in the long run the resources of governments backed by more homogeneous populations and more compact territories were more effective. The empire of Charles V looked backward to a fading ecumenical ideal. Governments were assuming increasing responsibility and the real direction of all the kingdoms which came into Hapsburg control was beyond the capacity of any individual. It may well be that the motives and aspirations of the Hapsburg rulers were not very different from those of most other contemporary monarchs. Compared with the cause of dynastic aggrandizement the interest of people counted for very little. Yet those kings whose territories had expanded along more national lines were not only in some concrete ways in a more favorable position, but seem in retrospect to have had history on their side. At the beginning of the sixteenth century the effects of dynastic consolidation were visible in both national monarchies and supranational empires, but the strength of the former was already sufficient to establish the direction in which the European state system was to evolve.

Chapter Four

THE STRUCTURE AND FUNCTION OF GOVERNMENT

ALMOST everywhere in Europe in the middle of the fifteenth century the form of government was monarchical. The tradition of kingship had been derived from the Germanic tribes and was nourished by classical political theory. With the exception of the Italian signories, the Swiss cantons, the cities of the Hanseatic League and some few free cities of the Empire, men lived under a monarchy whether hereditary, as in most countries of western Europe, or elective, as was the case of many of the states of eastern and northern Europe, including Hungary, Bohemia, Poland, Sweden and Denmark. Elective or hereditary, these monarchies were organized upon a basis which defined in specific terms the rights and duties of a king.

Territorially the kingdom was usually composed of an agglomeration of feudal principalities, seigneuries and towns, each with its own local history and particular privileges, brought together by the results of war, the ambition of a dynasty or the divisions of inheritances, and having a common bond in their allegiance to the person and office of the monarch. Politically and socially the subjects were divided into a complicated hierarchy of individuals, groups and orders, determined in theory by the functions performed for the group as a whole and endowed with certain privileges reflecting the political and juridical recognition of those functions. The highest expression of such privileges was to be found in the assemblies of estates; not only the estates, however, but other groups and individuals within the body politic were regarded in theory as endowed with rights which the monarchy had to respect. The structure of government in fifteenth-century Europe therefore commonly presented a dualism. On the one hand were the defined powers of the crown, which enabled it to fulfill its function of government; on the other hand were the privileges of subjects, the guarantee of which was regarded as one of the chief purposes of monarchical rule. In practice the chief theme of the internal history of government in this period therefore followed the

fluctuations between the advance of the monarch's power and the successful assertion of privileges against the monarch.[1]

In its commonest form this struggle centered on the relations between
the crown and the nobility. The latter saw their functional position in
the state and their real power being undermined, and attempted by a
variety of means to recoup their losses. The monarchy on its side discovered that one of the secrets of greater popular strength was the
application of its expanding powers to cutting down the privileges of the
feudal baronage. The emergence of strong monarchies was accompanied
by the suppression of the political role of the nobility. To this extent a
common pattern can be perceived in most of the great states of western
Europe, although it appeared with variations in methods and time. To
the anarchy of the first part of the fifteenth century—the Hundred Years'
War in France, the Wars of the Roses in England, the troubles in Spain—
succeeded the relative order of the final decades of the century, wherein
the growth of the internal powers of government paralleled the course
of territorial expansion.

The Spanish monarchs were perhaps the first to realize lasting success
in the regulation of the feudal class. They began by appealing to the
towns. In the Middle Ages there had existed an organization known as
the *Hermandad,* a league of municipalities which provided mutual assistance and protection to its members. This organization was now utilized by the crown and transformed into something like a national militia
for the preservation of order. As the public peace was primarily threatened by the feudal nobility this development amounted to an alliance
between the crown and the burghers against the magnates. The reorganization of the *Hermandad* was begun by Isabella in Castile. After it
had proved its usefulness in providing a militia paid for by the municipalities it was extended to the kingdom of Aragon in 1488.

The creation of a police force primarily directed against the nobility
was accompanied and followed by other measures. In Castile Isabella
ordered the destruction of baronial castles and strong places. Lands that
had been alienated to favorites in the disorderly period early in the century were now resumed. Perhaps most important of all, the crown took
over direct control of the three great orders of Spanish chivalry. This was
accomplished by having the king made hereditary grand master of each

---

[1] For the interpretation of the evolution of early modern governments, see in general the
studies published by the Commission on the History of Assemblies of Estates, established
by the International Historical Congress of 1933 at Warsaw. The work of this commission
has been edited and published under the direction of E. Lousse at the University of Louvain.

of the orders. In this way the monarchy received the great financial benefit resulting from the revenues of the orders as well as the political
advantage of eliminating a series of offices that might have been a focus
of rivalry and disaffection.

The result of all these measures was that the Spanish nobility came
increasingly to identify its political fortunes with those of the monarchy.
This submission, which was already so largely prepared by Ferdinand
and Isabella, was furthered by their grandson Charles when he came to
the throne. The traditions of the Burgundian court which he had inherited and in which he was brought up had created a ceremonial or
symbolic substitute for the functional position of the nobility. Gorgeous
banquets and elaborate rituals became ends in themselves; a court etiquette
began to evolve; the ritual that surrounded the chapters of the Order of
the Golden Fleece led in a direct line through the Spanish monarchy to
the courtiers at Versailles. Hence when Charles received his Spanish inheritance in 1516 he brought with him to his new kingdoms lessons from
his Burgundian experience which reinforced the work of Ferdinand and
Isabella.

One of the corollaries of the suppression of the political role of the
nobility was the increasing importance of professionally trained lawyers
in the king's councils. The alliance between the monarchy and the towns
was productive of other organs of administration. Educated administrators of bourgeois origin took the place of nobles whose position had been
determined by birth. The identification of interest between the monarchy
and the towns gave the crown an increasing control over the municipalities. In these circumstances the representative assemblies like the cortes
ceased to have the importance they had enjoyed in the medieval period
as a makeweight to the crown. With appointments to the higher clergy
increasingly in the royal control, with the nobility more subservient to
the policy of the court and with a third estate whose representatives were
nominated under royal influence, the independence of the historic assemblies was rapidly disappearing. For long periods during the reign of
Ferdinand and Isabella the cortes did not meet with any regularity and
when they did, it was to confirm plans for the succession or to aid the
crown in pressing financial necessity. This last purpose remained the
greatest bulwark of the privileges of the cortes and was the ground for
their opposition to Charles V at the beginning of his reign, when efforts
were made to recover the medieval liberties. In reality, however, it was
already too late. The battle had really been lost in the reign of Ferdinand

and Isabella and the decisive superiority of the crown had destroyed the medieval balance.[2]

In England, by an institutional development which offers in many ways striking parallels with that of Spain, the Tudors furnished another example of the aims and methods of the new monarchy. The founder of the Tudor dynasty, Henry VII, confirmed his questionable genealogical claim by conquest at the battle of Bosworth in 1485. Behind him lay twenty-five years of civil war and intermittent bloodshed. The great need was for the establishment of order, which could only be undertaken by the crown. Henry VII was able to meet this need although not without having to deal with repeated conspiracies from disaffected elements and with attempts to install pretenders to the succession in the early years of his reign. As in Spain, the Tudor program included a direct attack on the abuses of privilege among the high nobility and the strengthening of the administrative and judicial machinery available to the crown.

The capacity of the English nobility to disturb the peace rested principally on the practices of livery and maintenance. The higher nobles had supported bands of retainers equipped with the badge or livery of their patron, who were often in fact no more than groups of desperadoes whose services could be used for any reckless purpose. Although these armed bands had been the subject of much complaint and there had been attempts to remedy the situation, Henry VII was the first to achieve any substantial measure of success. This he did by using the judicial powers of the council, giving in 1487 to a part of the council jurisdiction over cases involving livery and maintenance and disturbance of the peace. This court which became the Court of Star Chamber functioned under the direct control of the king and without the procedure of the common law. It was thus a powerful instrument for suppressing what the gentry and the bourgeoisie looked upon as the tyranny of the nobility and not for many years was it regarded as an instrument of tyranny on the part of the crown itself.

The establishment of the Court of Star Chamber was accompanied by other measures designed to extend the scope of royal authority. Illegitimate castles and fortifications were destroyed; royal domain which had been alienated was recovered; lands and fortunes of overmighty subjects were confiscated. In this way the king's revenue was augmented and it became unnecessary for him to call on parliament for financial support,

[2] R. B. Merriman, *op. cit.*, Vol. II, ch. 15, and Mariejol, *L'Espagne sous Ferdinand et Isabelle* (Paris, 1892).

a call which was bound to alienate the sympathies of the class upon which the Tudors most relied for political support. Thus it happened that Henry VII used parliament as little as possible, yet when he died in 1509 he left one of the largest treasuries of any Christian monarch. His internal policies were substantially continued in the first period of the reign of Henry VIII, though the accumulated treasure was rapidly spent in support of an extravagant and pretentious foreign policy. On the eve of the Reformation the English monarchy had acquired an extraordinary degree of political and social control and parliament was not again to play an important role against the monarchy until the seventeenth century.[3]

France was slower than either of the two great neighboring monarchies to adapt the position of the nobility to the new authority of the crown. The consequences of this delayed reaction are to be observed in the history of the civil strife in France during the sixteenth century. A promising beginning was made under Louis XI. The internal history of his reign was punctuated with the recurrent warfare between the crown and the greater vassals, of which the War of the League of the Public Weal in 1466 was the most notorious example. By skillful manipulation Louis was on the whole able to prevail over his enemies and to secure the same kind of advantages for the crown that his contemporaries in Spain and England were winning. Yet at the end of his reign the whole position was brought again into question. His successor was a minor and a weakling. The great nobles became rivals for the control of the government and medieval privileges of all kinds were reasserted.

The high point of this reaction was the meeting of the estates-general summoned at Tours in 1484 to debate the question of the regency and to present the grievances of the kingdom.[4] This assembly produced the most significant assertions of the privileges of the subject in the whole late medieval history of France. In one speech it was maintained that the kingship was a dignity which could not be expected to follow the ordinary rules of private property and that no taxes could be levied without the consent of the estates. Actually these fine statements seem to have been inspired by the attempt of the high nobility to retrieve their own position. By proclaiming constitutional doctrines which had a certain breadth of popular appeal the feudal interests attempted to strengthen their own

---

[3] Conyers Read, *The Tudors* (New York, 1936), ch. 1.

[4] On the estates of Tours, J. C. S. Bridge, *A History of France from the Death of Louis XI* (Oxford, 1921–1936), Vol. I.

case for privilege against a strong monarchy. In actual fact, however, the crucial battle over the power to tax had been fought many years before and the French assemblies had during the Hundred Years' War lost that control over supply which their English counterpart was later able to recapture. To this extent the French king had a position envied by his contemporary monarchs; yet in spite of his better control of the purse, he had to confront a feudal nobility still able to offer a greater degree of effective political opposition. During the reigns of Charles VIII and Louis XII and during the early part of the reign of Francis I, the energies of that nobility were drained off in the campaigns of the Italian wars, yet the problem remained to become one of the principal factors complicating the history of the kingdom during the wars of religion.

What the monarchy accomplished in varying degree in the three great national states of western Europe was repeated on a different scale in the smaller countries. Most of them showed the same pattern: increase in the scope of the crown's authority, attack on the feudal nobility, restriction of the meetings of the medieval assemblies and alliance between the king and the middle-class servants who entered the bureaucracy. In Portugal, during the reign of John II, the powers and property of the nobility were much curtailed, and the royal power more strongly established under the reigns of his successors. In Denmark, Christian II accomplished much the same results in the period from 1513 to 1523. Even in the eastern countries there were brief periods, such as the reign of Mathias Corvinus in Hungary, when a similar pattern of development seemed to be assured. Wherever a strong monarch appeared, he had to meet the threat of the higher nobility, and in the ensuing struggle relied chiefly on the lesser gentry or the town burghers. On the whole the political and social evolution of Europe was on the side of the new monarchies. Their cause was so popular that they were able to minimize or in some cases dispense altogether with the traditional representative institutions of the Middle Ages.[5]

Yet there were important areas which illustrated an opposite current. The Empire could not be expected to follow the pattern of development of the national kingdoms. Throughout the fifteenth century there was a continuing struggle between the electors and the imperial authority for control of the emerging organs of administration. As early as 1455 a reform party in the electoral college put forth a program for the attain-

[5] On Christian II, E. H. Dunkley, *The Reformation in Denmark* (London, 1948), ch. I. On Mathias Corvinus, Franknoi, *op. cit.* On John II of Portugal, H. V. Livermore, *A History of Portugal* (Cambridge, 1947), ch. XIV.

ment of a greater degree of order in government. This program was backed by the desire of certain of the electors to secure a larger share of participation in the actual process of governing the Empire. Thus the struggle in Germany was not so much a difference of ends as it was in the contests between monarchy and nobility elsewhere. It was rather a conflict to see who would get possession of instruments of government that all were agreed were indispensable. In spite of his precarious position, Frederick III consistently refused to accept the electoral demand for a supreme council in which it was proposed the emperor and electors would have a joint responsibility. This struggle reached a crisis in the last decades of the fifteenth century, when the reform party was led by the archbishop of Mainz, Berthold von Henneberg. Maximilian's needs for subsidies to meet the Turkish threat and support his dynastic program gave an opportunity to the electoral party to put pressure on the emperor to agree to a series of constitutional changes. At the diet of Worms, in 1495, subsidies were granted in return for certain reforms. An eternal *Landfriede* was proclaimed, that is, a ban on private warfare without limit of time, so as to ensure the maintenance of elementary order. Still more important in its effects, a new court of justice, the *Reichskammergericht* was established. This was to consist of members nominated by the diet and of a president appointed by the emperor. It was to be a court of first instance for disputes among the princes and also a court of appeal for certain kinds of cases. In a series of further reform diets the struggle between monarchy and electors was continued. In 1500 there was set up the *Reichsregiment,* virtually a regency council created for six years. This move amounted to putting the imperial authority in commission. If the council had continued to exist it would have represented a great victory for the electors and the estates. Maximilian therefore made every effort to sabotage the council and extend imperial control over the judicial system. In the course of this contest the first imperial circles were established. In the end Maximilian triumphed over the more extreme demands of the reform party and was able to dispense with the regency council and the estates' control of the judicial system. There remained some very real gains from the reform effort, principally the *Landfriede* and the organization of the imperial circles, but the result was a compromise. Maximilian was never able to make against the estates of his German realm the same progress that had been achieved by his contemporaries in France and Spain. The Empire remained a political unit dominated by the uneasy balance between the great feudal element, now become the princes of states, and the imperial authority.[6]

Farther east, Poland provided the classic example of a country that followed the extreme opposite of the pattern of development of a strong monarchy. During the fifteenth century the whole body of the gentry secured privileges of immunity and the right to participation in authority at the expense of the crown and the great nobles. The competence of the general assembly, which was composed of deputies of the lower nobility, was defined and confirmed. Assurance was given that district and provincial assemblies would be held prior to the general assembly of the estates, so that delegates might be instructed on the agenda and the opinions of the class might be formed. Thus the gentry as a class enlarged its gains at the expense of other classes in the state and came finally to wield an authority greater than that of the monarchy itself. The aristocratic Polish republic of the eighteenth century had an elected king as a figurehead and a diet whose *liberum veto* had become a famous symbol of parliamentary inefficiency. In these circumstances Poland became an easy mark for more aggressive and better organized neighboring states. Although three hundred years separated the triumphs of Casimir Jagellon from the first partition in 1772, the foundations of Polish weakness were laid at the beginning of the sixteenth century in the social and political changes which gave the gentry so much power at the expense of the monarchy on the one hand and of the commercial middle classes on the other.[7]

Poland remained the extreme case in which elements of the medieval assembly of estates acquired political power beyond that of the king. For most of the European monarchies the same period showed an increase in the prestige and power of the crown. In those countries where the political evolution moved away from feudalism the scope of governmental activity broadened. The function of the medieval king had been defined in terms of the concepts of justice and peace. The former implied in practice the preservation of existing rights and privileges, and the latter the maintenance of order. Operating with these concepts, royal government superior to other kinds of feudal government, but not supreme, was in fact often very limited. The natural corollary of increasing power was a redefinition of the objectives of government, giving to the crown a wider sphere of action and a more comprehensive control over subjects which

[6] F. Hartung, *"Die Reichsreform von 1485 bis 1495, ihr Verlauf und ihr Wesen,"* Historische Vierteljahrschrift, XVI (1913), 24–53; 181–209.

[7] *Cambridge History of Poland,* Vol. I (Cambridge, 1950), chs. XIII and XX.

would never even have been considered in a medieval court. Victory—at least partial victory over the nobility—control of more sources of revenue, a greater degree of political independence of the estates: all these were reflected in a more aggressive foreign policy, the support of larger armies and innovations in the character of government at home. The techniques of administration were still far from sufficiently developed to permit the regulation of all departments of life in the state by a central administration. Compared to the experience of even nontotalitarian governments today, early sixteenth-century royal governments would seem very limited and inefficient. But the trend of evolution toward greater centralization was already producing decisive results. The growth of an army and a bureaucracy, the twin pillars of the absolute state, accompanied the increase in the power and resources of the monarch. The states in which this process had been most effective were now in a position to undertake external expansion and to overwhelm the older, smaller governments, whose whole organization was on a different scale and who were unable to compete with the national monarchies.

II. CITY STATES AND FEDERAL LEAGUES

The major unit in western Europe where the government was not organized on the basis of monarchy and estates was Italy. For a number of historic reasons Italy showed the greatest deviations from the common European pattern. Even there, however, were governments where the structure of politics centered on the system of estates as in the larger monarchies.

In the duchy of Savoy, for example, the estates met and functioned very much as they did in France. Clergy, nobility and bourgeoisie were assembled from the several provinces to negotiate with the ducal power the assessment of financial aid. The dukes also showed the same tendency as contemporary kings to find means for dispensing with meetings of the representative assemblies and in fulfilling this aim they were largely successful. The government of the papal territories also made use of assemblies of estates. In the various provinces of the papal states all who had seigneuries and all ecclesiastics who were bishops and abbots appeared in person and were accompanied by representatives of the cities and countryside. The chief occasions for such assemblies were no different under the papal administration from what they were under secular states. Money was needed to support the troops who were the chief instrument of papal policy in Italy. Finally in the kingdom of Naples, the only really territorial state in Italy, the parliament had a long and historic tradition dating back to medieval times. Already in the thirteenth century the Hohenstaufen emperors had summoned representatives of the third estate to their assemblies. The Neapolitan and Sardinian parliaments were like those of England in acting as courts in which judgments were decided and laws published. The greater ecclesiastics and barons were required to attend in person at the provincial estates, together with representatives of the larger towns. Some of the powers of these bodies remained effective in the fifteenth century even while the Aragonese kings were trying to build up a system of absolutism, supported by humanists whose ideal was derived from imperial Rome. After the Spanish occupation Ferdinand began to introduce some of the practices which had been successfully developed at home. The estates became less important, but the political structure of the kingdom of Naples remained more like that of the northern monarchies than most of the other states of the Italian peninsula.

Savoy, the papacy and Naples were, then, the exemplars in Italy of the more general European pattern based on a balance between monarchy and estates. Outside this pattern the governments of the Italian city states like Florence, Milan, and Venice, as well as the smaller lordships and principalities, were characterized by a much greater flexibility of political form. The opportunity for political improvisation, the relative independence of traditional institutions, the disregard for "legality," the consciousness of politics as an autonomous area of activity marked off especially from ecclesiastical control—all this led Jacob Burckhardt to see in the Italian scene the birth of the state as a "work of art." Following Burckhardt's interpretation, many historians have emphasized the critical importance of the history of the Italian states in this period, attributing a "political Italianization" to the northern monarchies, from which date the beginnings of modern politics. From the institutional point of view the thesis that the origins of the modern state are to be sought in Italy cannot be sustained. But the political history of Florence, Venice, Milan and the lesser Italian city states did provide an environment in which certain attitudes toward political activity and certain norms of statecraft were for the first time sharply defined. The question of origins apart, it is in a sense not too fanciful to see in the experience of these states, as in the city states of ancient Greece, a microcosm of the issues which confronted the great national states of Europe at a later period, both in their internal development and in their relations with one another. Because, further-

more, the decline and overthrow of the Italian city states mark the beginning of the European state system, it is instructive to consider the reasons
why they were unable to compete with the larger territorial entities,
whose political organization under even the most absolute of monarchies
included some degree of representative institutions.

The commune of Florence stood in the middle of the Tuscan territories
that were subject to it. The rural inhabitants were entirely deprived of
political rights. It was one of the most striking features of the government
of the city states that active participation in citizenship was confined to a
proportion of those who lived within the actual walls of the city. In the
case of Florence in the fifteenth century, out of a population of perhaps
nearly 100,000, no more than 3,000 were active participants in political
life. The failure to develop a technique whereby the subjects and inhabitants of the countryside could be given greater participation in the
process of government was in the long run one of the most serious weaknesses of the Florentine organization. The peasants, who in the early days
of the commune had been willing to join forces with the burghers in the
attack on seigneurial and ecclesiastical jurisdiction, found as time went
on that they had exchanged one master for another. Since their loyalty
was so tenuous, it was natural enough that the citizenry should prefer
to depend upon a body of mercenaries rather than on the fighting capabilities and devotion of their own subjects.

In the series of disasters occurring at the beginning of the sixteenth
century, Machiavelli had to note the evil consequences of this policy, but
by then it was already too late. It was impossible to create a local militia
able to compete with the armies of France and Spain. Thus one of the
chief factors in the ultimate downfall of the Florentine republic was the
failure to achieve a satisfactory organization for the government of the
subject territories. Whereas in France the people, even in remote provinces, felt some sense of participation—even if only the grudging
performance of a duty and not the exercise of a right—when they elected
procurators to represent their interests in the assemblies of the estates, the
peasants subject to the government of Florence could only feel that they
labored for a community which had no interest in their welfare beyond the
continuance of their constant agricultural labor. It may well be charged that
the sense of participation that existed in France or in Spain was a pure
illusion, inasmuch as the effective right to consent to grants had disappeared. But so long as the assemblies were held at all, even if it was felt
that they were not in a position to oppose governmental demands or

1. Erasmus at Fifty, from the diptych painted in May, 1517, by Quentin Metsys, for presentation to Thomas More
Corsini Palace, Rome

P. S. Allen, *Opus Epistolarum Des. Erasmi Roterodami*, Oxford, 1910.

2. Machiavelli: Terracotta bust of 15th
Century
Societa Colombaria, Florence

3. Pico della Mirandola: Italian School, 16th
Century
Uffizi, Florence

4. Pope Julius II: Anonymous portrait
Chigi Palace, Rome
Chledowski, *Rom*, Munich, 1919

5. Pope Alexander VI: Contemporary bust
Kaiser Friedrich Museum, Berlin

6. Pope Leo X: Engraving by Giovanni
Antonio da Brescia
Hind, *Early Italian Engraving*, vol. VI

7. Savonarola: Caricature attributed to
Leonardo da Vinci
Biblioteca Albertina, Vienna

8. Louis XI: French School, 1456-58
National Gallery, London

9. Charles VIII: from a portrait in the
Czartoryski Gallery, Paris

10. Louis XII: Attributed to Gossart
Windsor Castle

11. Henry VII: Flemish School, 15th
Century
National Portrait Gallery, London

12. Ferdinand of Aragon and His Daughter Joanna
Innsbruck Funeral Monument of Emperor Maximilian

ΠΛΑΤΩΝΟΣ, ΔΙΑΛΟΓΟΙ.

ΕΥΘΥΦΡΩΝ, Η ΠΕΡΙ ΟΣΙΟΥ. ΠΕΙΡΑΣΤΙΚΟΣ.

ΤΑ ΤΟΥ ΔΙΑΛΟΓΟΥ ΠΡΟΣΩΠΑ
ΕΥΘΥΦΡΩΝ. ΣΩΚΡΑΤΗΣ.

ΕΥ. ἱ νεώτερον ὦ σώκρατες γέγονεν. ὅτι σὺ τὰς ἐν λυκείῳ καταλιπὼν διατριβὰς, ἐνθάδε νῦν διατρείβεις περὶ τὴν τῇ βασιλέως στοάν· οὐ γάρ που καὶ σοὶ δίκη τις οὖσα τυγχάνει πρὸς τὸν βασιλέα, ὥσπερ ἐμοί. ΣΩ. οὔτοι δὴ ἀθηναῖοί γε ὦ εὐθύφρον δίκην αὐτὴν καλοῦσιν, ἀλλὰ γραφήν. ΕΥ. τί φῄς· γραφήν σε τις ὡς ἔοικε γέγραπται· οὐ γάρ που ἐκεῖνό γε καταγνώσομαι, ὡς σὺ κ ἕτερον. ΣΩ. οὐ γὰρ οὖν.

ΕΥ. ἀλλὰ σε ἄλλος. ΣΩ. πάνυ γε. ΕΥ. τίς οὗτος. ΣΩ. οὐδ' αὐτὸς πάνυ τοι γιγνώσκω ὦ εὐθύφρον τὸν ἄνδρα. νέος γάρ τίς μοι φαίνεται καὶ ἀγνώς. ὀνομάζουσι μὲν ὃι αὐτὸν ὡς ἐγῷμαι μέλιτον. ἔστι δὲ τῶν δήμων πιτθεύς, εἴ τιν' ἐν νῷ ἔχεις πιτθέα μέλιτον. δῖον τετανότριχα, καὶ οὐ πάνυ εὐγένειον, ἐπίγρυπον δέ.

ΕΥ. οὐκ ἐννοῶ ὦ σώκρατες. ἀλλὰ δὴ τίνα γραφήν σε γέγραπται. ΣΩ. ἥντινα; οὐκ ἀγεννῆ ἔμοιγε δοκεῖ· τὸ γὰρ νέον ὄντα τοσοῦτον πρᾶγμα ἐγνωκέναι, οὐ φαῦλόν ἐστιν. ἐκεῖνος γάρ ὥς φησιν, οἶδε τίνα τρόπον οἱ νέοι διαφθείρονται, καὶ τίνες οἱ διαφθείροντες αὐτούς. καὶ κινδυνεύει σοφός τις εἶναι, καὶ τὴν ἐμὴν ἀμαθίαν κατιδὼν, ὡς διαφθείροντος τοὺς ἡλικιώτας αὐτοῦ, ἔρχεται κατηγορήσων ὥσπερ πρὸς μητέρα πρὸς τὴν πόλιν. καὶ φαίνεταί μοι τῶν πολιτικῶν μόνος ἄρχεσθαι ὀρθῶς. ὀρθῶς γὰρ ἐστι τῶν νέων πρῶτον ἐπιμεληθῆναι, ὅπως ἔσονται ὅτι ἄριστοι· ὥσπερ γεωργὸν ἀγαθὸν τῶν νέων φυτῶν εἰκὸς πρῶτον ἐπιμεληθῆναι, μετὰ δὲ τοῦτο καὶ τῶν ἄλλων· καὶ δὴ καὶ μέλιτος ἴσως πρῶτον μὲν ἡμᾶς ἐκκαθαίρει τοὺς τῶν νέων τὰς βλάστας διαφθείροντας, ὡς φησίν. ἔπειτα μετὰ τοῦτο δῆλον ὅτι τῶν πρεσβυτέρων ἐπιμεληθεὶς, πλείστων καὶ μεγίστων ἀγαθῶν αἴτιος τῇ πόλει γενήσεται. ὥς γε τὸ εἰκὸς συμβῆναι, ἐκ τοιαύτης ἀρχῆς ἀρξαμένῳ.

ΕΥ. βουλοίμην ἂν ὦ σώκρατες, ἀλλ' ὀρρωδῶ μὴ τοὐναντίον γένηται. ἀτεχνῶς γάρ μοι δοκεῖ ἀφ' ἑστίας ἄρχεσθαι κακουργεῖν τὴν πόλιν, ἐπιχειρῶν ἀδικεῖν σε. καί μοι λέγε, τί καὶ ποιοῦντά σε φησὶ διαφθείρειν τοὺς νέους. ΣΩ. Ἄτοπα ὦ θαυμάσιε ὡς οὕτω γ' ἀκοῦσαι. φησὶ γάρ με ποιητὴν εἶναι θεῶν. καὶ ὡς καινοὺς ποιοῦντα θεούς. τοὺς δ' ἀρχαίους οὐ νομίζοντα, ἐγράψατο τούτων αὐτῶν ἕνεκα ὥς φησι. ΕΥ. μανθάνω ὦ σώκρατες, ὅτι δὴ σὺ τὸ δαιμόνιον φῂς σαυτῷ ἑκάστοτε γίγνεσθαι. ὡς οὖν καινοτομοῦντός σου περὶ τὰ θεῖα, γέγραπται ταύτην τὴν γραφήν, καὶ ὡς διαβαλῶν δὴ ἔρχεται εἰς τὸ δικαστήριον, εἰδὼς ὅτι εὐδιάβολα τὰ τοιαῦτα πρὸς τοὺς πολλούς. καὶ ἐμοῦ γάρ τοι ὅταν τι λέγω ἐν τῇ ἐκκλησίᾳ περὶ τῶν θείων, προλέγων αὐτοῖς τὰ μέλλοντα, καταγελῶσιν ὡς μαινομένου. καίτοι οὐδὲν ὅτι οὐκ ἀληθὲς εἴρηκα ὧν προεῖπον. ἀλλ' ὅμως φθονοῦσιν ἡμῖν πᾶσι τοῖς τοιούτοις, ἀλλ' οὐδὲν αὐτῶν χρὴ φροντίζειν, ἀλλ' ὁμόσε ἰέναι.

ΣΩ. ὦ φίλε εὐθύφρον ἀλλὰ τὸ μὲν καταγελασθῆναι, ἴσως οὐδὲν πρᾶγμα. ἀθηναίοις γάρ τοι ὡς ἐμοὶ δοκεῖ, οὐ σφόδρα μέλει, ἄν τινα δεινὸν οἴωνται εἶναι· μὴ μέντοι διδασκαλικὸν τῆς αὑτοῦ σοφίας· ὃν δ' ἄν, καὶ ἄλλους οἴωνται ποιεῖν τοιούτους, θυμοῦνται, εἴτ' οὖν φθόνῳ ὡς σὺ λέγεις, εἴτε δι' ἄλλο τι θύτ' ἐν περὶ ὅπως ποτε πρὸς ἐμοί εἰσι· οὐ πάνυ ἐπιθυμῶ πειραθῆναι· ἴσως γάρ οἱ μὲν δοκεῖς σπάνιον σεαυτὸν παρέχειν, καὶ διδάσκειν οὐκ ἐθέλειν τὴν σεαυτοῦ σοφίαν· ἐγὼ δὲ φοβοῦμαι μὴ ὑπὸ φιλανθρωπίας δοκῶ αὐτοῖς ὅ, τι περ ἔχω ἐκκεχυμένως παντὶ ἀνδρὶ λέγειν, οὐ μόνον ἄνευ μισθοῦ, ἀλλὰ καὶ προστιθεὶς ἄν, ἡδέως εἴ τις μου ἐθέλει ἀκούειν. εἰ μὲν οὖν ὃ νῦν

a

Amaurotū vrbs.

fons Anydri.

Oftium anydri

hythlodaeus.

14. Frontispiece of *Utopia* from the Basle edition by John Froben, 1518
Courtesy, Houghton Library

15. Road Map of Europe in 1501

Wolkenhauer, *Erhard Elzlauts Reisekarte durch Deutschland aus dem Jahre 1501,*
Berlin, 1919

16. Panorama of Rome, from Schedel, *Liber Chronicarum*, 1493
Courtesy, Houghton Library

17. Venice: Wood engraving by Jacopo de' Barbari, showing the arsenal
International Chalcographical Society, ed. by Paul Kristeller, Reichdruckerei, Berlin, 1895

18. View of Antwerp at the beginning of the 16th Century
Frontispiece of Wegg, J., *Antwerp 1477-1559* from a print in the British Museum

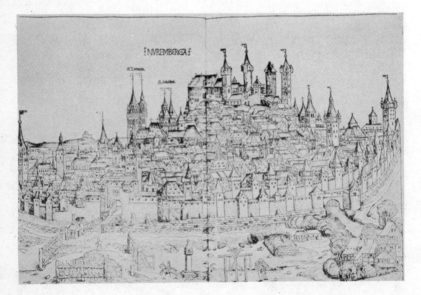

19. Panorama of Nürnberg, from Schedel, *Liber Chronicarum*, 1493
Courtesy, Houghton Library

20. Attack on a Walled Town: Woodcut by Jörg Breu the Younger
Geisberg, *Deutsche Buchillustration*, Munich, 1931

21. Battle of Fornovo, 1495, from *La Mer des Histoires*, 1503
Courtesy, Houghton Library

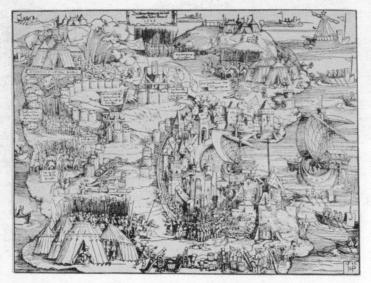

22. Siege of Rhodes, 1522: Sebald Beham
Geisberg, *Deutsche Buchillustration*, Munich, 1931

23. Battle of Ravenna, 1512: Italian engraving, 1530
Hind, *Early Italian Engraving*, vol. VII

25. Meeting of Maximilian and Henry VIII at the Battle of the Spurs: Design by Dürer for the Triumphal Arch of Maximilian
Kurth, *Complete Woodcuts of Dürer*, London, 1927

24. Early 16th-Century Cannon: Woodcut by Hans Burgkmaier
Burkhard, A., *Hans Burgkmaier, Meister der Graphik*, Berlin, 1932

26. Panorama of Constantinople, from Schedel, *Liber Chronicarum*, 1493
Courtesy, Houghton Library

27. Reinforcement of the Fortification of Rhodes by Italian Engineers during the Siege of 1480: Miniature from Caorsin, *De casa regis Zizimi*, Bibliothèque Nationale, Paris

28. Portrait of Prince Djem: from a Turkish manuscript in Vienna

Josef von Karabacek, *Abendländische Künstler zu Konstantinopel im XV und XVI Jahrhundert*, vol. I

29. Italian Engineer Supervising New Building in the Kremlin:
from a contemporary Russian manuscript
V. Snegirev, *Aristotel Fioravanti i perestroika Moskovckogo
Kremlya*, Moscow, 1935

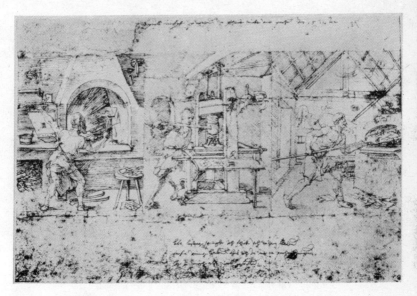

30. Dürer's 1511 Drawing of a Press and Printer. Ray Nash, Department
of Printing and Graphic Arts, Harvard College Library, 1947

31. Occupations of Peasants: Engraving from Ferrara, about 1470
Hind, *Early Italian Engraving*, vol. IV

32. Mining Operations: Woodcut by Sebald Beham, about 1528
Geisberg, *Deutsche Buchillustration*, Munich, 1931

33. Filtration of Saltpetre Lye: Manuscript of 15th Century in H. K. Royal Museum, Vienna

Ferchl and Süssenguth, *Pictorial History of Chemistry*, London, 1939

34. The Building of the Tempio di Malatesta at Rimini: from a contemporary manuscript, *Catalogue of an Exhibition of Italian Illuminated Manuscripts 1400-1550* (Oxford, 1948), Courtesy of the Bodleian Library

35. Mining Copper: Landscape by Met de Bles, Uffizi, Florence

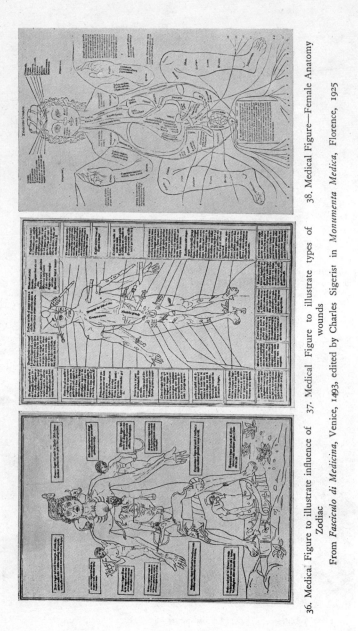

36. Medical Figure to illustrate influence of   37. Medical Figure to illustrate types of   38. Medical Figure—Female Anatomy
Zodiac   wounds

From *Fasciculo di Medicina*, Venice, 1493, edited by Charles Sigerist in *Monumenta Medica*, Florence, 1925

39. The Usurer: Engraving from
Sebastian Brant's Narrenschiff, 1498
Courtesy, Houghton Library

40. Two Men in a Landscape: Anonymous, North Italian engraving, 15th
Century
Courtesy, Museum of Fine Arts, Boston

41. Panorama of Prague, from Schedel, *Liber Chronicarum*, 1493
Courtesy, Houghton Library

42. Florence: Detail from anonymous wood
engraving of 1500
Lippman's *Wood Engraving in Italy in the 15th
Century*, London, 1888

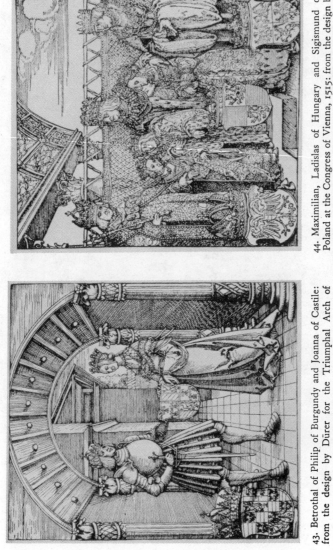

43. Betrothal of Philip of Burgundy and Joanna of Castile: from the design by Dürer for the Triumphal Arch of Maximilian

44. Maximilian, Ladislas of Hungary and Sigismund of Poland at the Congress of Vienna, 1515: from the design by Dürer for the Triumphal Arch of Maximilian

Kurth, *Complete Woodcuts of Dürer*, London, 1927

45. Hieroglyphic Allegory of Maximilian I: Dürer design for the Triumphal Arch
Vienna, Nationalbibliothek

46. Political Allegory on the Meeting of Paul II and Emperor Frederick III: Venetian engraving about 1470
Hind, *Early Italian Engraving*, vol. IV

47. Portrait Group of the Emperor Maximilian and His Family: Bernard Strigel, Kunsthistorisches Museum, Vienna

48. Ferdinand and Isabella with Their Children in Adoration before the Madonna: Unknown Castilian artist, 15th Century, Prado, Madrid

49. Mathias Corvinus: Marble relief, School
of Verrochio

Kaiser Friedrich Museum, Berlin

50. Lodovico Sforza: Beltraffio

51. Albert of Brandenburg: Dürer

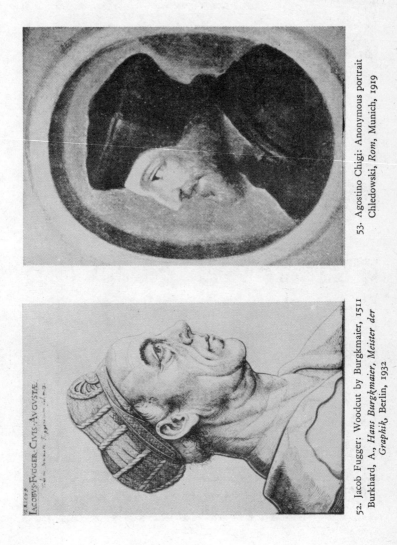

52. Jacob Fugger: Woodcut by Burgkmaier, 1511
Burkhard, A., *Hans Burgkmaier, Meister der
Graphik*, Berlin, 1932

53. Agostino Chigi: Anonymous portrait
Chledowski, *Rom*, Munich, 1919

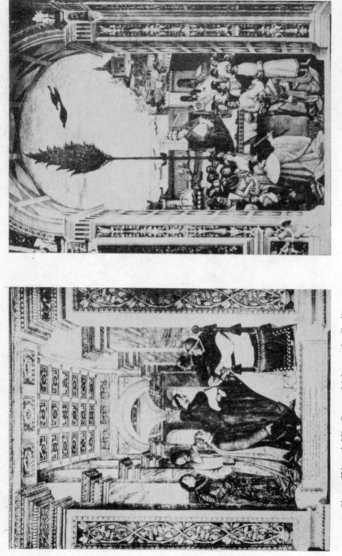

54. Sixtus IV and His Court: Melozzo da Forli
Vatican Gallery, Rome

55. Arrival of Pius II in Ancona to Lead the Crusade:
Pinturicchio fresco in Cathedral Library, Siena

56. Reception of the Venetian Ambassador, Domenico Trevisano, in Cairo, 1512: School of Bellini; Louvre, Paris

57. St. Catharine Disputing with Emperor Maximianus. Contains portraits of the Borgia court including Lucrezia and Djem Sultan: Pinturicchio

Borgia apartments, Vatican, Rome

58. Drunkenness of Noah: Benozzo Gozzoli
Campo Santo, Pisa

59. The Deluge: Michelangelo
From the ceiling of the Sistine Chapel

60. The Drunkenness of Noah: Michelangelo
From the ceiling of the Sistine Chapel

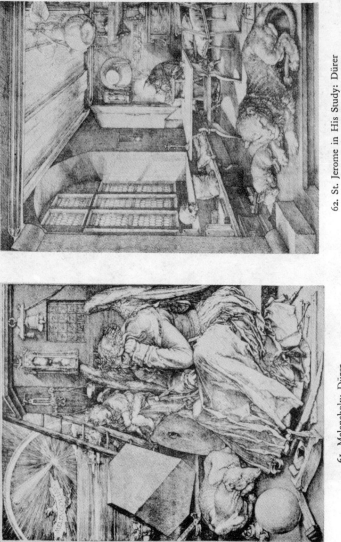

62. St. Jerome in His Study: Dürer

61. Melancholy: Dürer

63. The Hay Wagon, triptych, center panel: Hieronymus Bosch
Prado, Madrid

64. The Crucifixion, center panel of the Eisenheim Altar: Mathias Grünewald
Colmar Museum

governmental requests, there was nevertheless a greater basis for a sense of community than existed in the territories subject to the government of Florence.

Within the city itself, the government was ostensibly democratic; in reality the institutions inherited from an earlier democratic period served in the fifteenth century only to mask a rigid oligarchic control. As in the subject territories, there was a failure to effect a representation of various interest groups such as was achieved on a so much larger territorial scale in many contemporary kingdoms. For purposes of government the city was divided into quarters that dated from the middle of the fourteenth century, and had been preceded by an earlier division into sixths. Each quarter was then further subdivided. The representation of these territorial fractions formed an essential element in the composition of all governing bodies, but it was not a representation based on territorial principle alone. Twenty-one recognized trade guilds constituted what might be called the social basis of representation, which was even more important than the territorial basis. Of these guilds seven were so-called greater and fourteen lesser guilds. The former were represented in the lists of elegible candidates for office at the proportion of four to one. This was the result of the diminution of the power of the lesser guilds after the crisis of 1378–1382, when the revolt of the Ciompi had failed.

Of the bodies elected to govern Florence on this territorial and social basis, the signory was the most important. This was composed of two priors from each quarter and the gonfalonier of justice, making nine in all. These officers were elected by lot from purses filled with the names of the eligible candidates in due proportion to represent the quarters and the guilds. A new signory was installed every two months, with the result that Florence had six principal changes of government annually. The signory was advised by two subordinate colleges, the twelve *boni homines* and the sixteen gonfaloniers of companies. In addition there were the two greater councils: the council of the people and the council of the commune. The latter was the only body of which the membership was not confined to representatives of the guilds. Both councils had the function of approving proposals laid before them by the signory of nine during its two-month term of office. On an extraordinary occasion a *parlamentum* or assembly of all citizens was summoned by the great bell. The result of such a *parlamentum* was generally the appointment of a reform commission, to carry on the functions of government during an emergency. This commission was ordinarily given power to appoint a certain number of its members to revise the lists for the priory and sometimes to designate, instead of electing by lot, the incoming signory. Finally, there were committees appointed by the signory, such as the eight who were responsible for police, the six who constituted a committee on commercial affairs, and the ten who were put in charge of war and peace and whose appointment was generally tantamount to a declaration of war.

It is obvious that this constitution, although democratic in form, was by its very complexity susceptible of manipulation by powerful groups. In effect, from the time of the suppression of the Ciompi, the oligarchic party had been able to realize its policies almost unhampered, without attacking or abolishing any of these basic institutions. In the same way Cosimo de' Medici simply substituted for the oligarchic domination behind the façade of democratic institutions his own personal direction. He and his son and grandson provided a remarkable example of the control of a government. Cosimo took no public office that did not come to him in the ordinary course of events. The only innovation he made was the appointment of a more or less permanent body of inspectors to comb the electoral lists and revise them in the interests of the Medicean party. During a period of thirty years Cosimo served three times as gonfalonier of justice, that is, a term of six months altogether; but without holding any regular office at all he managed to secure control of foreign affairs and succeeded in so confounding the revenues of his family with those of the republic that it was impossible to tell where one left off and another began. The chief source of revenue was a property tax of the same percentage, levied on all citizens and instituted by the oligarchy in 1429. This levy, however, had been supported also by Cosimo de' Medici, and during the period of the Medicean domination graduated taxes were introduced, especially during the forties, when large sums were required to maintain the alliance with Venice against the advances of Filippo Maria Sforza of Milan.

A succession of indirect measures therefore ensured to Cosimo the practical control of the government of Florence. This control was maintained by a policy of encouraging the rise of new men whenever conspicuous ability seemed to demand it. A pretense of democracy was achieved by socially exalting some of the lowly men, and even the former nobility were conciliated by being on occasion admitted to public office. The flattery of all shades of opinion, together with the exercise of a minimum amount of political manipulation, assured to the Medici an enormous popularity during the lifetime of Cosimo and that of his son and grandson. When Cosimo died, no title could be found for him except that of *Pater Patriae,* but he was not the less surely succeeded by his son and grandson than were the Visconti and the Sforza in Milan, who had founded a dynasty. Yet in spite of the fact that the succession descended thus regularly, the Medici government only gradually developed the stability that characterized the despotisms. Piero di Cosimo's brief tenure of power was marked by insecurity and Lorenzo tightened his control after the Pazzi conspiracy had revealed the strength that might rally to an opposition party. At that time (1480), in place of the usual *balia* or five-year commission, he instituted the council of seventy, a self-perpetuating body with wide powers for the conduct of government. As the members of the council were made up of Lorenzo's personal friends and supporters, the Medici position was secured, though at the cost of more obvious manipulation than had been indulged in by Cosimo.

After Lorenzo's death in 1492 the heritage of popularity and the whole carefully built structure of influence were thrown away by the carelessness of Lorenzo's eldest son, Piero. His pretensions, his aristocratic marriage, his withdrawal from the common people, all alienated many of his father's supporters. The crisis was finally precipitated in 1494 by Piero's surrender to the French invaders. After this event the Medici were expelled and a period of constitutional debate ensued about what changes of institutions might be made to improve the Florentine government. Impressed with the stability and success of the Venetian constitution, several citizens put forward proposals to copy some of the principal Venetian institutions in Florence. In particular, it was proposed that there should be a council and a senate. In order to make the council a manageable body it was argued that it should be restricted to those having any ancestor in the last three generations who had occupied one of the major magistracies in Florence. Even with this restriction it was discovered that the council would be unwieldy, and it was therefore suggested that it be divided into three bodies with rotation three times a year in order to assure a more workable assembly. These proposals were vigorously debated and finally adopted owing to the influence of Savonarola, who in his famous series of political sermons really established the new constitution. For the remaining four years of his life Savonarola dominated the political as well as the spiritual activities of the city. He succeeded in keeping down both the partisans of the Medici and the representatives of the older oligarchy until his execution in 1498.

The constitutional debate was renewed after the death of Savonarola, and, in the face of the danger presented by the aggressions of Caesar Borgia, it was proposed that the office of gonfalonier of justice be established for life. Thus for a chief magistrate who had changed every six months was now substituted an executive who had some expectation of continuity. Piero Soderini was elected to this office in 1502 and continued to be the director of the Florentine government for eight years. At the end of this time the fortunes of the Florentine republic were involved with the successful attempt of Julius II to drive the French out of Italy. The persistence of the Florentines in maintaining their French alliance cost them the independence of the republic. At the congress of Mantua in 1512 it was agreed by the victorious league that the Medici should be restored. Within the following months this decision was enforced. Cardinal Giovanni de' Medici entered Florence with a victorious army, Soderini and his supporters were exiled, and the whole constitutional structure built up in the period after 1494 was swept away. A new reform commission was appointed, which proceeded to the restoration of the Medicean constitution, including the appointment of a permanent body of inspectors for the electoral lists. By the time the Cardinal de' Medici was elected to the papacy in 1513, the position of his family was again secure in Florence.[8]

The Medici domination of Florence had begun with the return of Cosimo in 1434 to a stronger political position than he had occupied before his exile. This pattern was repeated in the restoration of 1512. The period of exile had been longer but it ended in the establishment of stricter control. The logical culmination of this process was to be reached in 1527, when the last attempt to create a Florentine republic was followed by the end of independence and the emergence of the Medici as grand dukes of Tuscany. The history of the Medici family thus provides an unusual and direct example of the progress from economic to political power. The basis of the Medici position was the wealth derived from banking and control of the textile industry. But such wealth alone had no political opportunity except in the framework of institutions provided by the city state. In the feudal monarchy, as we have seen, bankers like Jacques Cœur and even the Fuggers, who supplied the necessities of Charles V, had remarkably little influence on policy. Only in a political unit which was outside feudal and monarchic traditions was it possible for a family like the Medici to develop so comprehensive a political power.

[8] F. Schevill, *History of Florence* (New York, 1936), 354–89.

If the political experience of Florence is an outstanding example of the extent to which a family of bankers could acquire almost complete control of the political life of the community, the constitution of Venice demonstrated the vitality and political acumen of an oligarchy whose economic interests resembled those of the Medici, but who were able to govern as a class where the Medici governed as an individual family. Venice provided an unprecedented example of stability. Its constitution continued for centuries to be widely admired, long after the actual power of the city had begun to decline.

In its origin the Venetian constitution revealed the elements that were common to most of the communes of northern Italy. That is, there was an executive element, comparable to the gonfalonier of justice in Florence, who in Venice came to be called the doge. There were, in addition, two councils, one large, which eventually embodied all the noble and patrician elements, and one small, which consisted of the doge and his immediate advisers and which acted as the real ruling body. In the course of its evolution the position of the nobility in both councils grew stronger at the expense of the doge on the one hand, and of the representation of popular elements on the other. From the time when the great council at the end of the thirteenth century had been closed to all except those who could prove that their ancestors had sat in that body, membership became hereditary. Nevertheless, this body still remained so large as to be unwieldy, and, although in theory its function was the control of all public affairs, in practice its principal activity came to be the election of the important officials.

The doge was elected by a most elaborate procedure designed to ensure that there should be no undue influence from any one family or group. Although he presided over the government of Venice and was clothed with all the magnificence of a reigning monarch, he came to be in fact more and more the ceremonial representative of the state and the mouthpiece of the patricians. The real executive authority rested in the senate, a smaller body elected in part for a term by the great council and in part consisting of officials who had a more or less permanent tenure. In all, it consisted of about three hundred persons who managed the finances and the public administration, decided peace and war, and debated treaties. It received the reports of the ambassadors, which were regularly sent from the countries to which they were accredited. The senate worked under an executive committee composed of a select number of its members, which was called the college. Finally, parallel to the senate in power, were the famous ten who had originally been established as a kind of committee of public safety. These men were elected from among the greatest magistrates in the senate, and their principal function was the detection and punishment of any attempted treason in the state. In the end they became an all-powerful body whose precept gave them an excuse for interfering in many departments of Venetian government and life.

In sum, the Venetian constitution reflected the power of a ruling class to maintain its position unquestioned for several centuries. The Venetian oligarchy was remarkably successful in keeping the majority of the people happy in their share of the benefits of the society to which they belonged. This sense of community was however really achieved only in the city of Venice itself, because in the area of their mainland conquests, as well as in many of the islands of the empire, the subject population had no more sense of identification with the government than did the Florentine *contadini* with the magistrates of Florence. The morale of the Venetian aristocracy, combining as it did the qualities of a successful business corporation with those of a ruling caste, was maintained by a severe inculcation of the idea of service to the fatherland. Seldom have political and commercial interests been so successfully intertwined. The young Venetian nobleman was educated to labor for both the profit and the power of the group to which he belonged. For many generations the highest standards of ability and loyalty were preserved.

The attention of political theorists was particularly directed to what was considered to be the classic exposition of mixed monarchy in the Venetian constitution. The doge, the senate, and the great council were assumed to represent the monarchic, the oligarchic, and the democratic principle, and to generations of students in the classical revival, who had read Polybius on the success of the Roman constitution, it seemed as if an ever more brilliant future lay before the Venetians. Actually, although Venice continued to be one of the great powers of the western world until far into the sixteenth century, the voyages of discovery and the revolutionary changes in the routes of trade had begun to undermine the republic's economic position, while at the same time the successful demonstrations of the powers of national monarchy indicated that the political future belonged to those organizations that could command a broader allegiance and could create a more vivid and continuing sense of identification between ruler and ruled.[9]

[9] Ch. Diehl, *Une république patricienne, Venise* (Paris, 1915), 81-120.

The third of the great Italian city states, Milan, had been a medieval duchy. When the last of the Visconti died in 1447 there was proclaimed the Ambrosian republic. This romantic venture was a product of classical reading and nostalgia for the earlier, heroic period of the Lombard communes. Those responsible for the government were not distinguished for political wisdom and the whole episode was based on hopes that bore very little relation to contemporary reality. One of the first acts of the new commune was to hire as the *condottiere* in the war against Venice Francesco Sforza, who had himself been one of the principal claimants to the Visconti succession. Within three years Sforza had turned on his employers, captured the government, settled the war and been recognized by the peace of Lodi as duke of Milan. As a small concession to appearances the government of the Sforza preserved some of the institutions of the Ambrosian republic, but essentially it remained the government of the dictator, the strong man who was able to impose his rule by his capacity rather than his title.[10]

For such a ruler a program of public works and military expenditure was a necessity. In the next generation, when Francesco's original usurpation was compounded by his younger son, Lodovico, who took over the government from the rightful heir, the maintenance of a brilliant court became even more a matter of policy. If the Burckhardtian conception of the state as a work of art means anything it must be understood in terms of freedom from the historic mold of institutions, of the opportunity for improvisation that was enjoyed by such a figure as Ludovico Sforza in comparison with contemporary northern monarchs.

The smaller Italian principalities followed much more closely the Milanese pattern than the Florentine or Venetian. Whether the ruler was hereditary or a usurper, he exercised a direct personal control largely independent of traditional institutions. The Este at Ferrara, Gonzaga at Mantua, Montefeltre at Urbino, Bentivogli at Bologna, sometimes as benevolent despots, sometimes as unbelievably cruel and oppressive tyrants, carried on the functions of government. So strong was the inherited pattern of individualism and particularism that in spite of countless and continuous marriage alliances between the rulers of these city states, political connections never developed beyond the point of military alliances. Far from reaching the kind of unification toward which the monarchy in France was moving, the Italian city states did not even develop those federal leagues which might have served as a substitute and been a bulwark against disaster when the northern invasions began.

[10] C. M. Ady, *A History of Milan under the Sforza* (London, 1907).

Indeed it was not in the advanced civilization of the Italian city states, but in the economically and culturally backward cantons of Switzerland that Europe found the first successful example of federal institutions since antiquity. The nucleus of the Swiss system was originally made up of the three forest cantons of Uri, Schweiz and Unterwalden, which had made a compact of mutual assistance as early as the thirteenth century and had won practical independence from the encroachments of the Hapsburg at the beginning of the fourteenth. In the case of a national state like France the growth of the central power and the assertion of its rights were accompanied by a reciprocal growth of political consciousness on the part of the territories over which the central power was extending its claims until both the central power and its subordinate territories were finally assimilated in one body politic. In the case of Switzerland, on the other hand, although the first phase of the evolution followed the French pattern, the final result was a separation from the control of the central power of the territory in which political consciousness developed. Thus the Hapsburgs, endeavoring to assert their privileges over the forest cantons and having to meet in response the development of a local diet, were in a way comparable to the French crown in its dealings with the provincial estates, let us say, of Brittany; but in the case of Switzerland, geographical considerations as well as the general political weaknesses of the Hapsburg position, in contrast to that of the king of France, made possible the emergence of a new political entity, although its final independence was not assured until the Treaty of Westphalia in the seventeenth century.

The forest cantons grew by the addition of neighboring communes and territories which shared their position and their sentiments. By the middle of the fourteenth century eight small states were grouped in a loose confederation, bound together by a complicated system of allegiances, the terms of which varied from case to case. Further additions were made in the early fifteenth century when Appenzell and St. Gall were brought into the confederation by treaty and part also of French Switzerland was added.

The most brilliant period of Swiss history fell in the second half of the fifteenth century, in the age of Charles the Bold. The growing power of the Swiss had encroached on the Hapsburg territories in the Black Forest, and the current representative of the Hapsburg family, Duke Sigismund of Austria, was forced to make an arrangement with the Swiss, by which he promised to pay a large sum within the year in order to redeem the territories the Swiss had threatened. It was further stipulated that if he did not redeem these territories they would be forfeited to the Swiss. This bargain was completed in 1468, and it is not surprising that the duke soon turned to Charles of Burgundy and borrowed money from him to pay the Swiss, but on terms requiring the cession of a portion of the disputed territories to the Burgundian power. This situation provided Louis XI of France with an opportunity to intrigue to bring together the Austrian and Swiss interests against the aggressive designs of Burgundy. By 1470 this new system of alliances was achieved, and in 1474 the Swiss began their war against Charles. In the years 1476–1477 were fought the famous battles of Grandson, Murten, and Nancy, in the last of which Charles of Burgundy was killed. From this experience the Swiss emerged as a leading military power of western Europe, and Switzerland soon became a celebrated recruiting ground for mercenary soldiery, the need for which was acutely felt by the great powers.

At the end of the fifteenth century, between 1495 and 1499, the Swiss became involved in war in Germany. In spite of the fact that they were still theoretically part of the Empire, they refused to participate in its reorganization or to accept the legal reforms and the imperial circles established by Maximilian in the period between 1495 and 1502. Needless to say, they refused also to pay the taxes imposed in connection with these reforms. Their strategic position enabled them to play a crucial role in the struggle for the partition of Italy and, although they began in alliance with the French, at the time of the invasion by Charles VIII and also during the period of Louis XII's first military adventures, they were eventually brought into opposition to the French by the policy of Julius II in the period from 1510 to 1512. Cardinal Schiner was closely allied with the prosecution of the designs of Julius II, and by his influence the pope was able to recruit a Swiss army that played a critical role in the events leading to the expulsion of the French from Italy in 1512. In this way, by the time the European state system was beginning to emerge along lines familiar in modern times, the Swiss had established a practical independence that was associated with an impressive display of military power.

Their political organization, however, remained very loose. In the age of the Swiss triumphs in Italy the original nucleus of forest cantons had grown to thirteen confederated states. In addition there were four allied territories and three subject or conquered lands. All these territories sent delegates to diets that met at regular intervals. There was, however, no central directing body or executive authority, and decisions of the diet were additionally hampered by the fact that the voting procedure required unanimity. Thus, one state could defeat the intentions of twelve others and prevent the adoption of a common policy. Furthermore, even when a common policy was adopted, the absence of an executive authority meant the possibility of one or more states refusing to put into practice decisions voted by the diet. Very slowly the Swiss federal system evolved in the direction of a more effective control, but it was to be a long time before the federal authority developed to any appreciable extent against the particularist tendencies of the several members. The Swiss confederation remained a unique example in Europe of a league that achieved a successful political organization without being tied to the existence of a central executive power.[11]

While the Swiss league was moving toward the establishment of a permanent political power, a league of city states which had been far more powerful in the medieval period was undergoing decline. The Hanseatic League cannot, of course, be compared to Switzerland except in terms of the development of organizational association between political units having a common interest. From the compact organization of the cantons nothing could be more remote than the far-flung cities of the Hanse; but although it had appeared at one time during its earlier history that the Hanseatic League might provide a basis for a more comprehensive political organization, by the end of the fifteenth century it was clear that other types of organization would prevail. In almost every area of northern Europe in which the Hanse had been dominant in the earlier period it now began to retreat.

In the Netherlands the city of Bruges had been the great capital of the Hanseatic organization and had been privileged by the grant of the staple to maintain a monopoly on many types of commerce. Now a variety of factors undermined the position of Bruges. In the first place, the river Zwyn on which the town was situated began to silt up, and it became increasingly difficult to undertake engineering works on a scale sufficiently comprehensive to keep open from Bruges to the sea a channel adequate to the volume of commerce coming into the Netherlands. From many points of view Antwerp offered more advantages as a harbor, and more and more merchants began to be attracted to Antwerp. Bruges was hidebound by rigid municipal regulations derived from an earlier period

[11] Wm. Martin, *A History of Switzerland; an Essay in the Formation of a Confederation of States,* translated by G. W. Booth (London, 1931), 56–87.

of medieval commerce, which the burghers were reluctant to change, even in those cases where they perceived the possibility of a more liberal arrangement. Gradually, therefore, Bruges sank into decline, frozen in a framework of legal and commercial arrangement designed for an earlier period; Antwerp, manifesting more vigor and initiative, emerged as the economic capital of the future. During this transition period the Dutch and the English increasingly refused to observe the regulations of the Hanseatic staple at Bruges, and the League was not powerful enough to combat these national interests.

In the North Sea, also, the competition the Hanse had to meet from the commercial activity of emergent national groups was a serious factor restricting its power and prestige. From the time when the Dutch came under the protection of the Burgundian dukes in 1433 their commerce had been increasing. They began to seek an ever larger share of the Baltic and Russian trade that previously had been a monopoly of the Hanseatic League. The cities of Danzig and Lübeck continued to oppose the intrusion of the Dutch, but less and less successfully. In addition, the League was increasingly threatened from Scandinavia. The peace of Copenhagen in 1441 was both politically and commercially disadvantageous to the League, and the increasing power of Denmark constantly menaced the position of Lübeck. This threat culminated in open war in the first decade of the sixteenth century and by the time Christian II succeeded to the Danish throne in 1513, with an avowed policy of bringing the whole commerce of the Baltic under Danish leadership, it was clear that the days of the Hanse as a political power were numbered. In spite of the fact that Lübeck was still able to take a decisive part in installing the house of Vasa on the Swedish throne, the city was presently faced by an alliance of Denmark, Holland, and Norway against which it was impossible to prevail.

The Hanseatic diets were, like the Swiss, an interesting variation on the pattern of corporative organization. They represented, naturally, the interests of a single class, and had not therefore the organization of estates, which was the usual characteristic of assemblies on a territorial basis. Their organization was highly informal; every member city was required to send delegates under penalty of being eventually "unhansed." Excuses were accepted only in such cases as a violent visitation of the plague or the involvement in war or domestic revolution. It was considered that the diet could take decisions binding those who were not present. It had no actual regular time of meeting, but met most often at

Whitsuntide, when the weather was fair for traveling, and at the city of Lübeck, in which centered the activity of the League and where its archives and documents were kept.[12]

The fate of the Hanseatic League raises interesting questions as to the extent to which a political organization can be built on economic interest alone. Certainly in the period of its glory the Hanseatic League disposed of more wealth and even more military power than many contemporary monarchies. Yet in the long run the burghers who had in their charge the destinies of the League developed a narrow-minded, oligarchic point of view that put them at an obvious disadvantage in a competitive struggle with territories in which a national political consciousness, with all the power that such a consciousness implied, was beginning to emerge.

III. THE RESOURCES OF GOVERNMENT: PROPERTY AND POWER

Whether kingdoms or city states, all governments of the fifteenth and sixteenth centuries, like governments of other periods, were constantly in need of regular sources of revenue. In some states like Milan, Florence, and Venice, where there were large accumulations of capital and where, as in the case of the Medici, there was a practical obliteration of the line between private capital and public revenue, the problem was not acute. The role of the public authority was well defined and that authority was on the whole able to command revenue sufficient to enable it to perform its assigned functions. In those states organized on a corporative basis, however, and among them especially those whose scope was expanding both territorially and administratively, the situation was different. The ordinary sources of revenue available to medieval governments were no longer sufficient to meet developing political and military needs. European monarchies attempted to solve this problem in different ways and with varying degrees of success. The king of Poland had certainly as much reason for demanding an increase of revenue as the king of France or England, but the Jagellons were never able to establish their claims as securely as the Valois and the Tudors. The solutions of the financial problem that had the most important social and political consequences depended on the complex interaction of the common European political inheritance and the differences in regional and local circumstances. Comparative study of this problem is a most important key to understanding the diversity that developed within the framework of a common culture.

[12] W. Vogel, *Kurze Geschichte der deutschen Hanse* (*Pfingstblätter des hansischen Geschichtsverein*, Blatt XI, 1915).

The great issue of the rights of the monarch over the property of the subject, or, in more general terms, the relation between authority and property, had been one of the central themes in the history of all the states of Latin Christendom. The views inherited from feudal institutions as well as from feudal theory had insisted that a king "should live of his own," and that only certain emergencies justified requests for grants from his subjects. The famous maxim of Seneca—"To kings belongs authority over all; to private persons property"—which Professor McIlwain has declared best embodies the living political conceptions of the later Middle Ages, continued to have vital relevance to political practice as well as to political theory, even though the meaning of both "property" and "authority" was being transformed. In many ways the theoretical separation of the functions of property and those of power paralleled the dichotomy between the privileges and powers of the monarch and those of the individuals, groups, and estates who were the subjects. With the domanial or ordinary revenues failing, governments were confronted with the task of increasing the extraordinary grants from their estates or else finding new sources of revenue.

The appeal to the estates of a realm was the traditional recourse for financial assistance. Such grants might be of several kinds, but were usually limited to the duration of a defined emergency. The estates were almost everywhere in Europe increasingly reluctant to make grants of this sort, even in the most pressing circumstances. There was widespread public opinion in favor of increased governmental action, as of the crown against the nobility, the extension of public order, the prosecution of an aggressive foreign policy and other aims, but when it came to footing the bill, those who had the money were, perhaps not surprisingly, more attracted by the possibilities of further capital accumulation or the necessities of maintaining a position than they were by the needs of contributing to the interests of the wider community to which they belonged. Chancellors exhausted themselves and their audiences in pleading for amounts sufficient to carry on enterprises to which government was committed. In some cases, notably that of the French monarchy, there had been established permanent taxes which had originally been emergency grants but which could now be collected annually without the necessity of recourse to the estates. Such was the celebrated *taille* as well as numerous *aides*. For this achievement the French kings were envied by neighboring monarchs. Maximilian, for example, is reported to have described Louis XII as the king of beasts, because he could get from his subjects what he wanted, Ferdinand of Spain as the king of men because he was granted a reasonable sum, and himself as the king of kings because he was not able to extract anything at all from his subjects. Yet, even on this favorable view, the revenues collected by the French monarchy were entirely insufficient to meet its commitments.

In the absence of an adequate regular revenue established by the consent of the estates, many governments resorted to the kind of borrowing from bankers and private capitalists that we have already discussed in considering the position of Jacques Coeur and the Fugger. Such borrowing was the more necessary, even when the regular taxes brought in a considerable amount, because the way in which the revenue was collected did not permit the accumulation of an immediately available sum of capital. The *taille,* for example, was collected over a period of a year, came in driblets, and was almost invariably spent before it had been received. Hence the resort to tax farmers or bankers, who could advance the estimated sum to be collected, in return for themselves taking over the rights of collection or at least a mortgage on the results. Similarly, custom duties such as those on woolfells and leather were collected over a long period, and did not supply the want of immediate cash. Such cash could usually be secured only by loans from bankers, often at exorbitant rates of interest and at the price of a lien on some source of government revenue.

The relationship between impecunious monarchy and the merchant capitalist has already been considered. It developed during this period with many variations. Loans were secured by the alienation of regalian rights of all kinds, and in some cases, as in France during the reign of Francis I, the beginnings of government bond issues are to be found in the allocation of the revenues of the Hôtel de Ville in Paris to the payment of interest and amortization charges on short-term loans.

In addition to grants from the estates and loans from bankers and private individuals, many other expedients were adopted by early modern governments to increase their revenues without violating too openly the property rights of the subjects. A method much resorted to, especially by Henry VII in England, ably served by Empson and Dudley, was the interpretation of legal precedents so as to justify confiscations of the property of the nobility. These measures served the double purpose of depressing the overmighty subject and improving the economic status of the crown.

Among the methods for increasing governmental revenue none was more interesting and fraught with more consequences than the sale of public office. This was classically developed in France, where it eventually became one of the regular sources of funds for the *ancien régime*. Under Louis XI certain financial and judicial offices were declared irremovable, and from this it was but a short step toward regarding them as the dispensable property of the incumbents. As more and more offices were offered for sale, entrepreneurs who had accumulated some capital found that it could be profitably invested in buying an office. In this way capital, originally derived from commercial or industrial activity, was deflected from further utilization in such activity. The opportunity to improve one's status by association with the royal service was a powerful attraction to many of the bourgeoisie. A life of commercial or industrial adventure was exchanged for security, and the wages paid for fulfillment of the duties of the office could be regarded as a more than reasonable return on an initial investment of capital. From the point of view of the monarchy sums of ready cash were thus acquired, the repayment of which to individuals took the form of disbursements that the monarchy would in any case have had to make. In the long run the whole system became an elaborate mechanism by which new forms of wealth were infused into the old hierarchy of power, and the practice is an illustration of the social and economic consequences of the monarchies' search for revenues. It flourished most completely in France, but it was practiced also in Spain, where it was partially applied to municipal offices, and to a lesser extent in the Netherlands, in Germany, and in Italy. Seen as a European phenomenon, the development of property in office represented a stage between a feudal and a bureaucratic society.[13]

Another source of wealth for the state was the attempted regulation or control of various forms of economic enterprise. The activities of the Portuguese and Spanish governments in the commerce of Asia and the New World have already been mentioned. Needless to say, these activities were among the principal sources of revenue for the Iberian crowns, and it was eventually upon wealth derived from the New World that the Spanish effort to dominate the continent of Europe was based. In addition to the obvious wealth derived from overseas enterprise, the control and encouragement of wool-growing in England, responsible for the enclosure movement, perhaps diminished the average wealth of the community as a whole, but certainly added to the royal exchequer

---

[13] R. Mousnier, *La vénalité des offices sous Henri IV et Louis XIII* (Rouen, 1947) has a discussion of the earlier history of the sale of offices in chapter I.

through the export taxes on wool. Similarly in Spain the organization known as the Mesta was granted a succession of privileges because of its financial importance to the government. In all these ways and many others the economic and social divergences within the system of European states were conditioned by the nature of their solutions to the fiscal problem.

There was a very wide variation in the degree of success achieved by these efforts to increase the resources of government. Henry VII of England left a full treasury to be dissipated by his successor, in contrast to the condition of practical bankruptcy that so constantly frustrated the Emperor Maximilian. Yet it is important to reflect that no state in western Europe, however devious and persistent the methods adopted by its ruler, succeeded in getting the kind of control over the property of the subject that was enjoyed by the Ottoman sultan, so strong was the western tradition that property was one thing and government another. It may indeed be argued that, from the point of view of maintaining institutional limits to state authority, the struggle between government and property was to fill much the same kind of function in the coming period as the struggle between state and church had done in the earlier. As the real wealth of the European world increased in the late medieval period the concept of property changed. What had been the ownership of defined rights tended to be transformed into the ownership of defined things. Roman legal ideas prevailed over medieval. Those rights which came to be thought of as functions of government were still regarded as "owned" by the rulers, while tangible property, which had been the focus of a variety of rights, became the subject of exclusive ownership by single individuals. Medieval dominium was becoming divided into sovereignty on the one hand and property on the other. One of the important effects of this dualism was to create sanctions, moral, legal, and institutional, for the proprietary rights of subjects. It cannot be too strongly emphasized that the existence of these sanctions was one of the conditions providing the most powerful incentives for the dynamic activity of the western European people in this period.

Clearly, the fact that the increasing capital accumulations were not developed under direct control of the state made more difficult the task of finding resources to supply the needs of governments. The solution arrived at in the various ways described above had the merit of maintaining the institution of property with all its sanctions as a makeweight to the authority of the state, and at the same time making available to the government through a series of expedients a share of the generally increasing wealth, in amounts sufficient to make possible territorial consolidation and political and military action on a larger scale. These changes were reflected both in political theory and in the emergence of the European state system.

IV. FORMAL POLITICAL THEORY

Political theory, whether legal or philosophic in form, had necessarily to take into account the institutional changes described in preceding chapters. As the scope of political action increased and its content changed, older ideas about the nature of the state were modified. These modifications centered chiefly on an analysis of the responsibilities of the ruler and on the establishment of an autonomous and secularized realm of political activity. The modern state began to take shape in theory as well as in fact; indeed, many students have considered this the most striking characteristic of the age of Machiavelli.

In spite of significant innovations, however, the older traditions naturally persisted. Fundamental ideas on the nature of political authority and the purpose of political organization had been shaped by the long tradition of classical and Christian thinking on these subjects. In every western European country secular authority was distinguished from ecclesiastical, but society was universally believed to be directed to a spiritual end. The state existed to support justice, and one of the most important aspects of justice was the maintenance of the Christian religion. Another aspect was the maintenance of the rights of the subject, which were, as we have seen, defined in proprietary terms. Thus, both the sphere and the object of the state were interpreted in terms of specific institutions like the church and property, as well as in terms of traditional morality. Views derived from this inheritance were still reiterated; yet side by side with the traditional analyses—and even among those who considered that they were only stating past truths—there appeared significant new descriptions of the powers of government.

Political theory vacillates between the effort to set before mankind an ideal commonwealth and the attempt to describe the general rules governing political behavior as it is. Both realist and idealist may deviate from traditional lines, but those whose business it is to define the actual functions of government cannot depart too far from surrounding fact. Perhaps lawyers are, of all such theorists, the most closely attached both to circumstances and to inherited tradition in an especially rigid form.

For this reason the views of legal theorists are sometimes particularly symptomatic.

Many among fifteenth-century authors whose political writing was cast in legal terms recognized the claims of the new monarchies. In England Sir John Fortescue was the author of a series of important treatises on the government and laws of England. A portion of his work was dedicated to the exposition of a program for strengthening the monarchy. Fortescue considered it essential that the crown be endowed with revenues sufficient to meet the ordinary expenses of government and he emphasized also the importance of a council, selected on the basis of ability, to advise the king in the making of policy. It was also necessary to have a sufficient staff of well-trained administrative servants to carry out the policies determined by the king in council. All this reflected the contemporary need for order, acutely felt during the period of the Wars of the Roses. In spite of his understandable desire to strengthen the monarchy on lines later realized by the Tudors, Fortescue was concerned also to defend the rights of the parliament. Particularly, he reiterated the traditional doctrine that the estates had an inalienable right to consent to grants of money required by the crown for extraordinary expenditures. In this respect Fortescue considered that there was a great contrast between the French and English practice; in his terms England was a *dominium politicum et regale* while France was a *dominium regale*.[14]

Fortescue's analysis of France, however, was far from being accepted by all his continental contemporaries. Philippe de Commines, for example, the famous servant of Louis XI and Charles VIII, asserts in his *Memoirs* —in terms quite as strong as those used by Fortescue himself—that no king in Christian Europe, unless he be a tyrant, has a right to exact monies from his subjects without their consent.[15] The same doctrine was upheld, in fact, at the estates of Tours in 1484, when Philippe Pot made a stirring address in which he maintained that the kingship was a public dignity and that its support concerned the representatives of all the estates of the realm.[16] It is apparent that many men, like Commines and Fortescue, practical men of affairs, were very clear-sighted in perceiving and analyzing the needs of contemporary government. They all agreed that the powers of the monarchy ought to be extended in order to permit

[14] On Fortescue, C. H. McIlwain, *The Growth of Political Thought in the West* (New York, 1932), 354–63.

[15] Commines, *Mémoires*, edited by B. Mandrot (Paris, 1901–1903), I, 443–44.

[16] Jean Masselin, *Journal des états généraux de France tenus à Tours en 1484 sous le règne de Charles VIII*, edited by R. Bernier (Paris, 1835), 487.

the state to preserve a greater degree of order. What they were not will-ing to face was the reluctance of assemblies of estates to grant means to the governments in anything like the amounts, or with anything like the regularity necessary to support the kind of program they wanted govern-ment to undertake. The need for order was deeply and widely felt, but, as is not infrequently the case, people were reluctant to pay the price. Where this reluctance secured the redress of grievances in return for a grant —as in England—it provided a basis for political control. Elsewhere, as the government was frequently driven to resort to measures of getting money that would avoid the control of the estates, a basis for a more absolute and comprehensive state power emerged.

Those who were in favor of a more absolute conception of govern-mental authority found support in the teachings of Roman law. As political power emerged more and more in fact from its connection with feudalism, many theorists discovered that texts of the Roman law were more adaptable to the new situation than the current coin of medieval custom. Such a work as Peter von Andlau's *Monarchy of Caesar* empha-sized the extent to which all power must be regarded as emanating from the state. His work was of the greatest importance in preparing for the reception of Roman law in Germany, and also in developing the concept of the imperial authority that lay behind the reform movement of the great diets at the end of the fifteenth century.[17] Not alone in Germany, how-ever, but everywhere in Europe the Roman law tended to be accepted in lieu of the customary traditional law. This was a process that was realized to the maximum in Germany and to the minimum in England, with a wide range of variation between these two poles.

Side by side with those who hoped to solve the problem of government by an appeal to the Roman legal tradition, and by emphasizing the legal and institutional framework of the state, were those who appealed equally to tradition but emphasized the moral training of the individual rather than the legal basis of the state. *The Institution of a Christian Prince* of Erasmus was perhaps the leading example of this type of litera-ture. Written in 1516 for the instruction of the future Charles V, who was then being prepared to receive his vast political inheritance, Erasmus's treatise belongs to a long line of "Mirror of Prince" literature extending back beyond the writings of St. Thomas and Egidius Romanus. The usual pattern was a description of the duties of the prince, followed by an

---

[17] Joseph Hürbin, *Peter von Andlau, der Verfasser des ersten deutschen Reichstaatrechts* (Strassburg, 1897).

analysis of those qualities that would best enable him to fulfill his responsibilities. Many of the humanists produced pieces of this sort upon commission from contemporary rulers, but in spite of their edifying character these treatises were increasingly unrealistic and had little effect upon the actual conduct of government.

Erasmus' work was the product of the scholar's study and far removed from the experience and insights of such men as Commines and Fortescue. Yet even here the signs of the times were to be found. The comparison between the position of God in the universe and that of the prince in the state was old and familiar, but it was developed by Erasmus with such richness of detail and allusion that we seem to be already on the way to the triumphant cry of Bossuet: "O Kings, you are gods on earth!" Precisely because the position of the ruler is so powerful, every effort must be directed toward providing him with a proper education. Here Erasmus reflected the humanist faith in what could be accomplished by education. If only rulers could be rightly taught, then the age of the philosopher-kings dreamed of by Plato would have arrived. For a brief moment in the second decade of the sixteenth century it seemed as if this age were dawning. Charles V, Henry VIII, and Francis I had among their preceptors and friends the greatest representatives of the new learning. If they controlled more power than their predecessors, they also had more opportunities for enlightenment. Within a short span of years, however, these bright hopes were blasted and it became clear that even the best of educations was not enough. While the hope lasted, however, the homilies and moral treatises directed to the edification of the prince mirrored not only an intensified moral tradition but also the growing importance attached to the position of the ruler.[18]

Thus in different ways the lawyer like Fortescue, the statesman like Commines, and the humanist like Erasmus revealed a consciousness of the growing scope of governmental activity. Yet all these men maintained traditional views about the purpose and limits of governmental authority. In their works the old and the new were balanced, but among their contemporaries was one whose break with the past was far more decisive, and whose name has ever since been associated with the beginning of the theory of modern politics.

Nicolo Machiavelli was born in 1469, the year in which Lorenzo de' Medici came to power in Florence, and the year in which Ferdinand and

[18] Erasmus, *The Institution of a Christian Prince,* translated with an introduction by L. K. Born (New York, 1936).

Isabella were married. His youth was passed in obscurity, and he emerged as a politically active figure only in 1498 when he was appointed secretary to the council of ten of the Florentine republic. He continued in this office, with numerous diplomatic missions and with many opportunities to observe the course of practical politics, until the restoration of the Medici in 1512. He was then forced to leave office and for the remainder of his days, in spite of numerous attempts to re-enter political life and to gain the favor of the Medici, he lived as a private citizen. All his work was produced during this period of retirement and some of it was directed to the immediate end of recapturing a position in politics. He died in the year of the sack of Rome, 1527, disillusioned with the course of affairs in Italy and embittered by his long exclusion from useful political activity.

The latter half of Machiavelli's life fell in the period of the Italian wars. From 1494 until his death, in a span of a little more than thirty years, Machiavelli saw Italy devastated by the invasions of the French, the Spanish, and the Germans. He was able to look back on the age of Lorenzo de' Medici as a golden age of political stability. He had seen governments rise and fall; he had seen great powers league together to destroy smaller powers; he had seen examples of the success that attended bad faith and the violation of treaties. It is natural, therefore, that his greatest concern was to find some formula for retrieving a sense of security, for re-establishing a condition in which at least the minimum requirements of civil order would be met.

In order to find the answer to his questions Machiavelli turned to history. As has frequently happened in time of great crisis, when revolutionary events seem to deny the basis of historical continuity, men adjust themselves by seeking a reinterpretation of the past. More than a century of humanist tradition had concentrated upon glorification of the classical past, and therefore it was to Roman history that Machiavelli directed his analysis. Looking back over the centuries he was profoundly impressed with the long and successful course of the Roman republic and the Roman Empire. If any light could be shed on why the French and Spanish were defeating the Italians, and why Florence was failing in the sixteenth century, it could perhaps be found by asking why Rome succeeded. Could not historical rules, uniformities, be extracted from the history of Rome, and might these not be applicable to political success in all times and in all places? In his approach Machiavelli was following a good humanist example. Argument from classical precedent was decisive.

Among reasons he considered most important in explaining the continuity of Roman political institutions was the ability of the founders—or, in his terms, the *virtù* of the legislators. Men like Romulus and Numa Pompilius, who presided over the foundation of the Roman state, or Moses, the lawgiver of Israel, had exemplified a combination of intelligence and will, thought and action. This quality, the ability to carry out in practice an abstract scheme, was what Machiavelli primarily meant by *virtù*.[19] It was a quality historically possessed by all great leaders and, in Machiavelli's opinion, conspicuously absent in the Italy of his own day, though possessed by the Ottoman Turks, the French, and the Spaniards. From this he concluded that there was a static amount of this kind of ability in the world. When it was concentrated at a single time and in a single place, as it was at the foundation of the Roman republic, it bore fruit in a marvelous set of institutions that endured through centuries.

In addition to the abilities and achievements of the great men of Rome, Machiavelli considered that great importance attached to the maintenance of the Roman religion among the people. Religion was a binding force that kept alive the loyalties of a people living together in a community. When the old Roman religion began to decay, it brought about also the decay of the civilization of the republic.

Another factor, part cause and part symptom of the healthy condition of a republic, was the existence of a citizen army. The devotion of men to the fatherland, and their willingness to die for it, was a measure of the soundness of its institutions. Here again it was obvious how great a contrast existed between the past and the present which Machiavelli saw all around him. Warfare in Italy was then typically conducted by mercenary armies instead of by citizens. This was in part a natural result of the oligarchic constitution of the Italian city state. It was felt to be dangerous to arm the poorer citizens and the inhabitants of the countryside, lest they turn against their rulers and dispossess them. As Machiavelli only too well perceived, it was equally dangerous to entrust the fate of a government to an army of mercenaries. If the mercenaries failed, all was lost anyway; but if they succeeded they were only too likely to dominate the state for which they had fought.

Thus, from his analysis of Roman history Machiavelli concluded that among the principal factors of stability in a political society were leadership, religion, and patriotism. Where these qualities could be realized there would be both a powerful and a peaceful society, one in which the

[19] F. Ercole. *La politica di Machiavelli* (Rome, 1926).

individual might expect a certain degree of liberty and the protection of life and property.

Yet there remained a great question. Rome had possessed all these advantages in the beginning; and yet Rome had fallen. How was the decay of Roman society to be explained? Here Machiavelli drew on a philosophy of historical change. This philosophy was primarily based upon a view of the nature of man that was interestingly related to both Christian and classical traditions. Machiavelli accepted a large measure of the Christian tradition on the nature of man. For him, men were evil and corrupt and had to be coerced to do good. Because of the evilness of man the institutions he creates are always bound to decay, no matter how firmly established they seem to be. Thus, a belief about the nature of man which is essentially Christian was combined with a belief about the course of human affairs which was essentially cyclical and classical. There exists a cycle of human institutions in which fortune plays a considerable part. Those favored moments in history when good institutions have been established and a happy life is possible are bound to wither away.

In his emphasis on inherent evil in the nature of man Machiavelli was appealing to a continuous element of the Christian tradition. His description of good, on the other hand—especially social and political good—was limited to the interest of the community. Thus Machiavelli defined the good solely in terms of whether or not the individual is acting in the interests of the community as a whole. He pointed out that every man has a temptation to serve his own interests, but it is the community he ought to serve, and if necessary should be compelled to serve. Now, it was certainly in the tradition of western Christian political thought to emphasize the general interests of the community, and this teaching can be found in the great writers on political theory from St. Augustine to St. Thomas Aquinas. In addition, however, there is found in this Christian tradition an emphasis on a higher law beyond that of the interest of the community, a law to which the individual can appeal. This part of the Christian tradition of political theory is not found in Machiavelli. In his identification of morality with action in the interests of the community—especially the community defined in terms of a particular state—lies his greatest departure from the Christian tradition.

Because of the existence of a historical cycle, in which good times are bound to deteriorate and bad times are likely to last for a considerable period, it is necessary to act in accordance with the morality that prevails at the particular stage of the cycle that has been reached. Machiavelli found himself living in a bad time. The first necessity was, therefore, to recognize that action was only possible within certain limits. The kind of security Machiavelli would have liked was the kind provided by the Roman republic; but, living in Italy in 1513, he saw that this kind of society would be impossible to create. The only kind of public order that could be achieved in a time when morality was decaying was the public order created by a prince who was feared. It was necessary to act in accordance with the times. It was no good longing for the existence of religious and patriotic feelings that could not, in the nature of things, be attained overnight. Therefore, limiting himself to what was possible under contemporary conditions, Machiavelli tried to point out in *The Prince* what could be accomplished by intelligence and will. Even in the worst of times leadership need not be lacking; and extraordinary leadership might struggle with fortune and improve the situation.

The methods that would have to be used in such a struggle were those suited to the character of the age. Machiavelli had seen Florence defeated and brought nearly to ruin by the perfidy of the French, the papacy, Caesar Borgia and others. In a time when your enemies are using every subterfuge and bad faith against you, you cannot observe traditional morality. Hence, Machiavelli wrote a program for an Italian prince who might take advantage of the favorable conjunction of events existing in 1513.

Shortly after the Medici had been restored in Florence, Leo X, son of Lorenzo the Magnificent, was elected to the papacy. Thus there was created a situation in which a single family controlled both the papacy and one of the most important governments in Italy. A somewhat analogous situation had existed under Alexander VI, when his son Caesar Borgia had been nearly successful in building a large territorial state in the Romagna. Hence, when Machiavelli wrote *The Prince* he recurred to the example of the Borgias, in order to point out how near they had come to success and in the hope that the younger Lorenzo de' Medici, to whom the treatise was dedicated, would succeed where Caesar Borgia had failed.

Machiavelli hoped that, if such a leadership could be found, Italian national feeling would rise to the occasion. The famous last chapter of *The Prince* is an appeal to the national sentiment of the Italians, and an apostrophe to the savior who will deliver Italy from the barbarians. It voices the hope that such a liberator will be welcomed everywhere in

Italy and hailed as the father of his country. Whether or not this chapter was written separately from the rest of the book, it hardly accords with the realism Machiavelli had shown throughout the earlier chapters. In many ways these earlier chapters may be interpreted as a refutation, chapter by chapter and page by page, of the ethical and idealistic treatises on the virtues of the prince, characteristic of humanistic literature. It almost looks as if Machiavelli, when he came to the end, made a desperate appeal to the existence of a patriotic sentiment which his whole observation of the Italian scene must have proved simply was not there. He had bewailed its absence; he had studied its effect in Roman history; he had invoked the dictator in Italy precisely because the sense of community was wanting. Yet he seemed in this last chapter to feel that an Italian national sentiment could be created overnight by the provision of forceful leadership. The great analyst of the methods of political realism yielded here to a romantic view of nationalism, the other great force that was to dominate the modern political scene. *Realpolitik* could use nationalism, and indeed became far more powerful when based on nationalism; but it could not create nationalism. Louis XI and Ferdinand of Aragon could accomplish what they did, not only because of what they were in themselves, but also because of a certain sense of community in their realms. Caesar Borgia was no Romulus. The forceful union of people under a prince who was feared—a dictator—was a substitute for the sense of community and genuine patriotism that might have flourished in other historic conditions. Had Machiavelli been consistent to the end, he would have realized that, where nationalism did not exist, the most skillful efforts of *Realpolitik* to evoke it were, at least in the short run, doomed to failure.[20]

At the very time when Machiavelli was proposing the remedy of the strong man for the evils of his time and country and holding up to admiration an ideal derived from the study of Roman history, a younger contemporary in England was also engaged in examining contemporary politics and society. As in all times of crisis, there was a widening gap between the way things ought to be and the way things were. If Machiavelli applied himself to the latter, Thomas More described the former. The older traditional approach to the problem of government was thus neatly split into a realist and an idealist tradition. In the work of More the traditional materials of political thought were used to con-

[20] F. Gilbert, "The Humanist Concept of the Prince and *The Prince* of Machiavelli," *Journal of Modern History*, XI (December, 1939), 449–83.

struct a frankly unreal Utopia, existing neither in time nor in space, contrasting with the real world of European monarchies, while in the work of Machiavelli the new realistic analysis was used to describe the contemporary scene. Both drew on the inspiration of humanist interests, but Machiavelli remained fundamentally a pessimist about the immediate future of the European situation while More represented the optimistic hopes of the Erasmian circle.

This optimism was not without qualification and there were many aspects of the coming capitalist society that More condemned. In the first book of the *Utopia* what More was against was made very clear. Hythlodaye's long speech, describing what he would do if he were in the council of the French king, was More's great plea against the Italian wars. It was argued that all this activity and expenditure of men and money might in the end be of no effect, and that a king would do better to devote himself to the realm God had given him and the improvement of the condition of his subjects. More and Hythlodaye join in the bitter recognition that if any such advice were given, it would not be heeded. The same book contained the famous indictment of the enclosure movement in England, already noticed in an earlier chapter. There were also complaints against interference with the status of the clergy.

In these cases More was opposing the new politics and the new economics, and expressing fear of their effect upon the church. He made these protests in the name of justice; and the ideal of justice that he cherished was a medieval one. Every estate as well as every smaller group, and even every individual, was regarded as having certain rights. The existence of the civil society of Christian Europe was maintained by the protection of these rights. It was the duty not only of rulers but of all men of good will to resist their infringement. Thus, the More who pleaded in the *Utopia* for restraints against the greedy landlord, and who deplored the wars of Francis I, Henry VIII, and Maximilian, was the same More who ultimately refused to recognize the oath of supremacy and who considered it beyond the competence of parliament to separate England from the corpus of Christian Europe.

But if the *Utopia* was in part an attempt to restate Christian social and political ideals which More felt to be passing away, it was also an attempt to establish rational norms by which the extent of the present evils could be judged. The second book contained the description of the imaginary community described by Hythlodaye. The territory of *Utopia* was divided into fifty-five cities with their surrounding regions, each of which had a large degree of autonomy. It was ruled by an elected prince and senate. Property was held in common, and one of the chief functions of the government was the just regulation of economic affairs. In each city there were also elected priests who were charged with the direction of the spiritual life of the people, a life organized for the worship of a supreme being, with a wide latitude for individual variations in belief. Under these institutions the community led a prosperous, pacific existence.

Now it has often been argued that the characteristics of this Utopian community may be taken as evidence that More believed in toleration, in a communistic distribution of property, in pacifism, and in the whole range of institutions and scale of values there described. It has been maintained that his actions as chancellor in later life were wholly inconsistent with the beliefs stated in this part of the *Utopia,* and that we have here one more example of a young radical gone conservative in old age. Argument of this sort, as Mr. Chambers has shown,[21] misses the point. What More was really trying to do in the second book, aside from some humanistic *jeux d'esprit,* was to show how far a community of men, operating on a basis of natural reason, could proceed to the development of a good society. If the pagan virtues of wisdom, temperance, justice, and fortitude could accomplish so much, then Europeans who had the advantages of Christian revelation ought to be the more ashamed that they had not risen to a higher level than the contemporary scene represented. In the light of reason as well as in that of revelation, in the light of the classic as well as the Christian tradition, the abuses in European institutions were condemned. But the basis of those institutions, their true and proper use as distinct from their abuse, was left untouched by More's excursion into the imaginary realm of natural reason.

It is a remarkable fact that, at the moment when the national state was in fact emerging as the dominant force in the political life of Europe, the greatest theorists of their generation misunderstood, denied, or deplored the current trend in politics. Machiavelli and More both recognized that monarchies like France, Spain, and England disposed of the decisive power in the world of the sixteenth century, and they recognized further that that power was being arbitrarily used, unchecked by the moral laws of the Christian tradition. To this extent they both recorded an existing state of fact. The realm of political behavior was more cleanly

[21] R. W. Chambers, *Thomas More* (Westminster, Md., 1936), 125–44; 256–66. Recent criticism of these views in Russell Ames, *Thomas More and His Utopia* (Princeton, 1949), 12–21.

separated than ever before from the world of ethics, just as economic activity was also achieving a separate compartment, though the latter process had not then gone so far. Machiavelli envied France, but he had his eye fixed on the city state. His *patria* was Florence, and his ideal was the expanding city state of antiquity, the Roman republic. He never really understood the impossibility of an effective national sentiment appearing in the Italy of his time, and his predilections led him to put far too great an emphasis on what could be accomplished by an individual state.

The thinking of Erasmus and More also revealed an admiration for the kind of city state that had been discussed by Plato and Aristotle. The Utopian community was made up of a league of city states and Erasmus praised this form of polity even in the work he wrote for Charles V. All his life he significantly signed himself Erasmus of Rotterdam and shunned the capital cities of the monarchies in order to live in the semi-independent communes of the Netherlands and Switzerland. More of course lived under a national monarchy and served it well but ultimately went to his death rather than yield to the claims of the new nationalism.

The admiration for the institutions of the city state was not entirely nostalgic. The constitution of Venice was widely admired, and the Swiss cantons were considered to have as free and healthy a government as was to be found in Europe. Even the Hanseatic League had not as yet entirely decayed, while Flemish towns continued to be centers of culture that in many ways rivaled their Italian counterparts. There were many indicatons that the day of this city-state civilization, which had had its most brilliant period in the fourteenth and fifteenth centuries, was done. Yet those who perceived this most clearly were still free to regret it; Machiavelli looked with nostalgia on the golden age of Lorenzo de' Medici, which was destroyed by the aggression of the northern barbarians; and More, with a far wider horizon, deplored the growth of the monistic power of the state at the expense of a medieval pluralism in which he found a greater guarantee of the rights of individuals as well as groups. Far apart as were their ethical systems, both realist and idealist were in substantial agreement about the actual forces governing international political action. Their analyses reflected the facts of the relations between the powers, and provided the framework within which evolved the European state system.

Chapter Five

THE PARTICULAR INTERESTS OF THE CHRISTIAN PRINCES

I. THE BALANCE OF POWER IN ITALY, 1454–1494

IN TRACING the internal political history of the European states in the age of the great discoveries we have so far considered the territorial extent of the unit of government and the function of the ruler in practice and in theory. Equally important is the question of the relation between states and the beginnings of what may be called the European state system. Although this problem must be studied over the whole range between city states and national and supranational monarchies, it is convenient to begin with some consideration of the system of alliances among the smaller units in Italy.

Many students have found in the political experience of the Italian states in the second half of the fifteenth century not only a significant contribution to the rationalization of government, but also the real beginnings of systematic international relations as we know them in modern times. Among others Mr. Toynbee has recently given a suggestive analysis of the growth and operation of balance-of-power politics. He has pointed out that in Italy earlier than elsewhere conditions favored the development of a systematic equilibrium. A multiplicity of city states had achieved practical independence of the Empire. In the absence of unification or a federal system these states regulated their relationships by a series of combinations which produced results somewhere between the extremes of anarchy and imperial order. Intense competition for territory and influence had the effect of generating coalitions or alliances against any one state which seemed to be gaining a momentary advantage over the others. Particularly in the forty years preceding the French invasion of 1494 there seemed to prevail an equilibrium during which the diplomatic or military gains by any one power were offset by a combination of other powers. During these forty years of relative peace in Italy, which created the political environment of Italian Renaissance culture, the greatest territorial consolidation of the northern monarchies was taking place.

This situation has led Professor Toynbee to discern a general law governing the workings of the balance of power. He finds that "in any given constellation of states in which the political units are in this dynamic relation with one another the pressure is greatest at the heart of the constellation and relaxes progressively towards the periphery." [1] The unequal distribution of political pressure meant in the Italian fifteenth century that the contending states were unable to make any but the most insignificant territorial gains while the northern monarchies, on what Mr. Toynbee calls the periphery of the system, grew enormously until these new larger powers came into the Italian scene to upset the balance which had been theretofore established. The history of the balance of power in Italy has thus been represented as a prefiguration of the course of modern international relations. The system of alliances in Italy in the fifteenth century can be compared to the system of alliances in Europe in the nineteenth. Just as Florence, Venice, and Milan were overwhelmed by the northern monarchies, so France, Germany, and England are now in the twentieth century overshadowed by the great powers of the United States and Russia.

Such a comparison may well help us to understand the tragedy of Italy in the sixteenth century and of Europe in the twentieth, but we must be careful not to press the parallel too far. The attempt to find a conscious application of the principles of balance of power in the fifteenth century may be as unhistorical as the claims made for modern nationalism in the same period. The relations between the Italian states in the forty years from 1454 to 1494 do have an importance transcending the conflicting and often petty interests of the Italian peninsula, but we may still ask how far these relations were governed by the concept of an equilibrium consciously understood and applied.

It will be remembered that by the middle of the century five great powers had come to dominate the Italian peninsula, although not to the complete exclusion of the smaller principalities and city states. In the south were Naples and Sicily, at the beginning of the period united in the Aragonese Empire, but separated in 1458 when Alfonso the Magnanimous died and was succeeded by his illegitimate son Ferrante in Naples, while Sicily reverted to Aragon. In the center was the papacy, governing the states of the church. The republic of Florence lived during these years under the most brilliant period of the Medici domination. In Milan the Sforza had usurped the dukedom in 1450 and retained it in their family

[1] A. Toynbee, *A Study of History* (Oxford, 1934), Vol. II, 302.

until the fall of Lodovico fifty years later. Thus three of the greater powers entered, in the middle of the fifteenth century, a period of internal stability. The long reign of Ferrante in Naples and the undisturbed succession of the Medici and the Sforza in Florence and Milan respectively were powerful factors in the comparative peace of the period. Venice alone among the secular states was ruled by an oligarchy rather than a single family, but the Venetian constitution had a deserved reputation for its success in preserving internal order.

The Treaty of Lodi (1454) ended the war that had begun over the question of the succession of Francesco Sforza to the duchy of Milan. It was a war fought chiefly between Milan and Venice, as the latter had used every opportunity to enlarge her dominions on the mainland at the expense of the territories controlled by the Milanese. In this struggle Cosimo de' Medici, who had previously found in Venice the most useful ally of the Florentine republic, reversed his position and decided to give his support and friendship to Sforza. This decision, so important for the peace of Italy during the remainder of the century, was taken not only out of conviction that Sforza had high personal capacities but also on the grounds that a continuing rivalry between Milan and Venice would provide too good an opportunity for intervention in Italy by outside powers. By the terms of the treaty, Venice received some territorial compensation, and in return accepted the Sforza succession and joined a league for peace, adhered to also by the other Italian powers. This was not, however, entirely a national manifestation, because some governments outside Italy, like the Swiss cantons, also entered the league. In this way Francesco Sforza came to power in Milan, supported primarily by the diplomatic assistance of Naples and Florence, who together were able to overawe the interests of Venice and the papacy. The pattern established at Lodi remained the fundamental alignment of Italian interstate politics throughout the remaining years of the fifteenth century.

Those who have upheld the theory that this half-century saw the beginnings of balance of power politics have emphasized the maintenance among the major Italian powers of an unstable equilibrium, disturbed by a series of crises but restored by the conscious efforts of statesmen, chiefly Cosimo and Lorenzo de' Medici. Such crises were occasioned periodically by the problem of succession in one or another of the larger states. Only four years after the peace of Lodi, for example, Alfonso the Magnanimous died in Naples. The fact that he left the kingdom to his illegitimate son Ferrante gave an opportunity to the house of Anjou to put forward its historic claims. These claims were supported by the French king and a French army was sent to attack Genoa. In order to resist the threat from the French an alliance was concluded between Francesco Sforza and Ferrante which upheld the latter's claim to the Neapolitan succession. Again, in the middle sixties, after the deaths of the two principal architects of the peace of Lodi, Francesco Sforza and Cosimo de' Medici, the famous *condottiere,* Bartolommeo Colleoni, attempted to carve out a little state for himself in territory which had previously been held by Milan and Florence. Pressure brought by these two states, under the terms of their alliance, and supported by Naples caused this attempt to fail, and a threat of general war was created.

Apart from these relatively minor disturbances, which must be seen against the background of more or less constant pressure from the Turks, the most serious attempts to upset the *status quo* occurred during the pontificate of Sixtus IV (1471–1484) and were occasioned by the aggressive and ambitious plans of the pope himself. Sixtus IV had a large number of relatives for whom to provide, some of them able and all of them grasping. In pursuit of the family interest, to which he was devoted, he succeeded in arranging an alliance with Naples which had the effect of detaching that kingdom from its by now almost traditional alignment with Florence and Milan. With Florence thus in a more isolated position a plot was set on foot in the curia itself, and probably with the knowledge and encouragement of the pope, to overturn the Medici regime and seize additional territory for the papal family in the Romagna, particularly the lordship of Imola. The conspirators in Rome were allied with the Pazzi, the leading rivals and opponents of the Medici in Florence. Assassination of Lorenzo and his younger brother had been planned for Easter Day, 1478, and the attack was actually made in the cathedral of Florence on that date. Giuliano de' Medici was killed but Lorenzo escaped, immediately re-established his position, and took vengeance on the Pazzi. The situation remained threatening, however, because Florence faced the combination of Naples and the papacy in the south and the hostile designs of Venice in the north.

It was in these circumstances that Lorenzo de' Medici undertook his celebrated expedition to Naples to make a personal appeal to Ferrante to maintain the peace. This gesture was widely interpreted as a chivalrous and gallant undertaking and convinced many of his contemporaries of Lorenzo's sincerely peaceful intentions. But this effect was to some extent calculated and it must be mentioned that the risks taken by Lorenzo were actually of the slightest, as the expedition had been prepared by secret diplomatic negotiation and was carried through more as a brave show to influence public opinion than as a stroke of *Realpolitik*. Furthermore, this presumed triumph of Medicean diplomacy was facilitated by the fact that it coincided with an acute phase of the Turkish pressure, for Otranto had fallen and the ultimate intentions of Mohammed II seemed to include the conquest of Italy. The momentary sentiment toward union among the states of Christian Italy in the face of greater threat from outside may well have weighed more heavily with Ferrante than the pleas of Lorenzo. Yet in spite of these considerations Lorenzo's expedition restored the old system by bringing Naples back to the Florentine alliance, and it has therefore been most frequently cited as an example of the operation of an equilibrium within the peninsula.

Only momentarily thwarted by the failure of the Pazzi conspiracy, Sixtus IV renewed his aggressive attempt a few years later. This time, in 1482, he planned in direct alliance with Venice the dismemberment of Ferrara. Again the alliance of Milan, Florence and Naples held and was able to apply sufficient pressure to defeat the pope's plans. Only a little more than a decade later the precarious system of security by which the independence of the Italian states was maintained came to an end with the first large-scale invasion by the armies of Charles VIII. The crisis of 1494 was in part the direct result of the break between Naples and Milan and it can be argued with some plausibility that if this alliance had been maintained, foreign intervention could have been staved off at least for a time.

In this way the history of the relations between the Italian states in the second half of the fifteenth century can be represented as the history of two systems of alliances by which a series of crises were resolved by diplomatic means.[2] There are certainly instances like the intervention of Lorenzo de' Medici in Naples which appear to have preserved the peace by restoring the balance of strength between the two sides. Yet there are many aspects of the Italian scene which make it impossible to find in it merely an anticipatory microcosm of the later diplomatic experience of the European powers.

In the first place, there is very little evidence that Italian statesmen of the fifteenth century were operating with the conscious aim of maintaining a balance of power. The effort, often ruthlessly pursued, to increase

[2] E. W. Nelson, "Origins of Modern Balance of Power Politics," *Medievalia and Humanistica*, I (1943), 124–42. Professor Nelson has distinguished seven crises between the peace of Lodi and the invasion by Charles VIII in 1494.

the power and prestige of the individual state was not connected with any concern for the collective group of states. Those who have sought for the origins of the system of balance of power in the Italian fifteenth century have appealed most often to the testimony of Guicciardini, whose *History of Italy,* written in 1536 after a quarter of a century of disasters, looked back to the golden age of Lorenzo de' Medici as one in which the affairs of Italy were maintained in balance. Even before Guicciardini wrote, the humanist Bernardo Rucellai had used the phrase "balance of power" in his history of the invasion of Charles VIII.[3]

If, as is generally claimed, Rucellai was the first person to use this phrase, then it seems arguable that the theory of a balance of power was first elaborated by Italian publicists and historians in the early decades of the sixteenth century as they looked back and interpreted the political experience of the preceding half-century. Their own preoccupation with ways of maintaining peace led them to seek an explanation for the comparative stability of the decades before the northern invasions. But the whole process of interpretation was governed by the desire to find an applicable lesson of history which might better the increasingly hopeless Italian situation of their own day. Hence the idealization of such a figure as Lorenzo de' Medici; hence also the theory of a systematic equilibrium among the Italian states which could be maintained only by neglecting some of the most important realities of Italian politics.

One of these realities was the inequality in strength and position among even the five greater Italian powers. Venice especially had ranked and continued to rank as one of the first powers of the western world. Her colonial empire gave her resources equal to those of a great territorial monarchy; she was on occasion able to stand alone against the Ottoman Empire, and at the time of the League of Cambrai in 1508 her strength was still such that an opposing coalition of all the great powers of Christendom did not seem entirely unequal. Neither Florence nor Milan nor Naples could pretend to such a position. The total resources therefore available to the two systems of alliance were by no means as equally balanced as is ordinarily implied when the term is used.

Another major factor was the extent of foreign influence in Italian politics even before the invasion of Charles VIII. Under the influence of Guicciardini's interpretation, the relations between the Italian states are often discussed as though they were a closed system isolated from the rest of Christendom. Actually several of the Italian courts and chanceries maintained the closest contacts with powers outside the peninsula. The long connection of Aragon with the kingdom of Naples was only temporarily interrupted during the rule of Ferrante, and provided the background for eventual Spanish domination. The Venetian Empire and commitments in the eastern Mediterranean meant that there was more concern in the grand council over what went on in Constantinople than over the possible maneuvers of the king of Naples. Indeed, the threat of Turkish invasion had been present for all the Italian powers since the capture of Constantinople and at least once seemed an imminent reality. And in addition to the Spanish influence on the one side and the Turkish danger on the other there was French intervention from the north. The dynastic claims to Naples and Milan were pretexts ready to be taken up and prosecuted at any moment. Francesco Sforza and Cosimo de' Medici threatened Venice with an appeal to French intervention and Louis XI, as we have seen, actually sent French troops to Genoa in 1458. If Michelet went too far in claiming that it was the divine mission of France to conquer Italy and so spread the culture of the Renaissance to northern Europe, he was at least right in declaring that Italy was bound to be conquered and that the choice lay between Spain, France and the Ottoman Empire. The existence of these constant threats from the outside makes it clear that the Italian system of states was not so isolated and independent as is often maintained. Consequently it seems improbable that rulers like the Medici and the Sforza could have looked upon their relations with other Italian states as a separate compartment of political activity. It is impossible to deny that there was a feeling for Italy and Italians against the "northern barbarians," but the equilibrium achieved by the Italian powers in the forty years between Lodi and Charles VIII's invasion must be understood and studied in the context of the general European scene.

II. THE PRACTICE OF DIPLOMACY

The theory that Italian statecraft in the fifteenth century was the seedbed of modern politics is one of those comprehensive generalizations which must be analyzed before an attempt is made to judge its validity. We have already seen that the fundamental institutions of the modern national state-monarchy, centralized administration and representative assemblies of the estates—were shaped in the medieval period. The innovations of the sixteenth-century monarchies lay in a direct line of development which extended back to the Germanic invasions. To this development the example of the Italian city states contributed only very indirectly. In this sense the search for the origin of the modern state in Renaissance Italy is doomed to failure.

If the generalization is interpreted to mean that Italy saw the emergence of balance-of-power politics which foreshadowed the subsequent course of the European state system, then this assertion also must be qualified, as set forth in the preceding section.

Yet even if these specific interpretations be repudiated, there remain some areas in which the hypothesis of Italian influence can be substantiated. To speak, as Mr. Toynbee does, of the "political Italianization" of France, England and Spain in the age of Louis XI, Henry VII and Ferdinand and Isabella is an enormous exaggeration, but it nevertheless remains true that the careers of these monarchs do illustrate the theory of politics as a rationalized autonomous activity developed by the school of which Machiavelli was the most celebrated product. While it would also be an overstatement to claim that the divorce of politics and ethics was a novelty, still it cannot be denied that Italian thought and Italian example powerfully contributed to the consciousness of their increasing separation. One way to put it would be to say that Italian terms became fashionable and that traditional modes of behavior were tricked out in a new language. The pattern of politics in northern Europe in the first decades of the sixteenth century might in fact be compared to one of those elaborate chateaux on the Loire constructed by the French monarchy and nobility. Many of these buildings were covered with Italian decorations but their fundamental structure remained French and medieval.

The area where this borrowing from Italy was most apparent was in the practice of diplomacy. There is no doubt that the technique of carrying on relations between states was first developed to a high degree and perfected by the Italian states. By the time of Machiavelli and Guicciardini diplomatic practice had already been institutionalized, and it is obvious that both of these authors owe to their diplomatic experience a great deal of the stimulus and substance of their thought on the nature of statecraft.

The development of techniques of communication and information between governments had been stimulated by the multiplicity of the Italian states and the intensity of the competition between them. A shift of alliances, a betrayal by a paid military leader, a new negotiation for a marriage contract all had a more sudden and serious effect in the life of the city states than was possible in the relations between large territorial governments. Hence from an early date there was a tendency to use every means to acquire knowledge about the possible intentions of one's potential adversaries. Side by side with the regular and formal channels of diplomacy there developed the use of the secret agent, the spy, the paid informer at another court. The secret archives of Venice are filled with records illustrating the extremes to which such practices were carried. Often the council haggled with an individual over the amount of his reward for the successful accomplishment of a mission, including perhaps even an assassination. Merchants and bankers who had to maintain agencies in other capitals were useful contacts for the gathering and transmission of political information. When the Portuguese voyages were opening up the African route to the east, Venice maintained agents in Lisbon as well as in Alexandria to keep the closest touch with the developments which were likely to be so damaging to her commerce. It was the age of the elaboration of codes and ciphers, and geniuses like Alberti contributed to the art of cryptography.

In the field of formal diplomatic relations the Italian powers were the earliest to employ regular envoys, whose term and training were subject to special legislation. The Florentine government had regulations for the training of diplomats and the papacy of course had an elaborate code governing the use of the legatine authority. But it was Venice which played the leading role in the evolution toward modern diplomacy. At a very early date Venetian envoys had been sent to the court of Constantinople and Rome, and the system had become so regularized and extended that by the end of the fifteenth century the republic had its ambassadors in most of the courts of Europe. These envoys were chosen from among the patrician oligarchy, whose sons were educated with emphasis on the ideal of service to the state. Their conduct was governed by a series of minute regulations drawn up by the senate and council. An ambassador was required to send a dispatch weekly containing all information about the court to which he was accredited which might be of interest to his government. The dispatches were read in council, so that the Venetian government had spread before it regularly an up-to-date survey of the international scene. At the height of the system an ambassador was accredited to a foreign government for not more than three years, lest he become too attached to his new environment and lose sight of the honor and advantage of his own government. In addition to the regular dispatches he was required upon his return to deliver a relation to the doge and senate giving a summary account of his mission and describing his journey in some detail. These relations, which are conserved in consecutive series from the beginning of the sixteenth century, are among the most valuable documents for the history of the period. They constitute a mine of information on geography, climate, industry and commerce, intellectual life and the religious situation, as well as shrewd portraits and character sketches of the leading figures in the governments of Europe.

A single example from the first decade of the sixteenth century will illustrate the comprehensive character of the information contained in the relations and serve to explain why they have been found so invaluable by historians of all aspects of the period. In 1506 Vincenzo Quirini gave to the doge and senate an account of his mission to the court of Burgundy occasioned by the succession of Maximilian's son Philip to the kingdom of Castile, which he claimed in right of his wife Joanna, daughter of Isabella, who had died in 1504. Quirini began his recital with a description of Philip and Joanna and their family. He commented on Joanna's jealousy and seclusion, and on the difficulties created by her warped personality. From the royal family he turned to the great officers of the court and gave a summary of their functions and salaries. The expenditure of the court, not only for the maintenance of officials but also for military purposes, was characteristically reported in detail. The description of the court and its principal figures was followed by comment on the lands subject to the Burgundian rule, the number of provinces, the general aspect of the principal cities, estimates of the population, nature of the economy, products of special excellence, among which was included in addition to the cloth of Holland and the tapestry of Brabant, music. There followed an analysis of the characteristics of the Burgundian peoples, their temperament, political sympathies, taste in food, and general style of life. On top of all this there was a fairly detailed account of the judicial and ecclesiastical system, interspersed with penetrating remarks on how well the civil and ecclesiastical bureaucracies were performing their jobs and on those parts of the system that stood in greatest need of reform.[4]

This mass of information, roughly comparable to that provided for a odern government by an intelligence agency, ensured that the Venetian government approached the consideration of any particular problem of foreign policy provided with enough background knowledge to make

[4] *Relazioni degli ambasciatori al Senato,* edited by E. Albèri (Florence, 1939), Series 1, Vol. I, 3–30.

reasonable decisions that took into account a wide range of variables in the situation. As the contest between the various states of the European community became more accelerated and more acute, it became more than ever necessary to have up-to-date information of this kind. An understanding of the dominant personalities at a foreign court and the intrigues which were being carried on there might make it possible to anticipate one of those shifts of alliance which sometimes seemed to come with bewildering suddenness. Knowledge of an enemy's resources and of the details of his ordinary governmental and military expenditure was of the most obvious importance in calculating the probabilities of continued resistance. These necessities were perhaps first experienced in the intensity of competition among the city states and republics of Italy, and it was therefore in this environment that the practice of diplomacy began to be institutionalized. In addition to the Venetian successes, the Roman curia provided a constant object lesson in both the means and ends of diplomatic activity. By the end of the fifteenth century many of the governments in the Italian peninsula maintained a regular and permanent system of envoys at foreign courts. If the northern monarchs still tended to send ambassadors only on special occasions and for special purposes, the pressure of events was rapidly compelling the adoption or development of the techniques which had been so successful in Italy. As soon as most of the great powers of Europe were involved in a struggle which linked them more closely together, diplomacy, like war, was bound to be intensified. This result was brought about by the rivalry for the control of the Italian peninsula.

III. THE INVASION OF ITALY

The Italian question was the first great common preoccupation of European diplomacy. The rivalries among the larger territorial units began to assume a definite pattern and were brought out in sharp relief against the declining sense of community. The French invasion of Italy in 1494, regarded even by contemporaries as opening a new era, has always been advanced as one of the dates dividing medieval from modern times. If the Hundred Years' War may be taken as the last of the great conflicts between feudal monarchies, the Italian wars can be described as the first of these internecine struggles in which the issues were fought out by all means of war and diplomacy on a European scale.

The problems crystallized by the action of Charles VIII were not settled for over half a century. Viewed comprehensively, these problems

were the result of the accumulation of power by the northern monarchies
at a rate surpassing that which could be attained by the states of the
Italian peninsula. The resulting disparity of means was a constant invitation to invasion. The conflicts of French, Aragonese and German ambitions in Italy were in a very real sense the result of the same expansionist
forces that sent Castile and Portugal to the New World and to Asia;
what took the form in the latter of aggressive adventure overseas led in
the former to the conquest of weaker territories within the bounds of
Christian Europe. It is a remarkable fact that the age which saw the discovery of new worlds and the most acute pressure from the Ottoman
Turks should have been most preoccupied with the internal struggle in
Italy. Yet the implications of great events on the periphery of Christendom entered slowly into the consciousness of ruler or peoples, while the
outcome of a Ravenna or a Marignano continued to claim more attention
than the fall of Egypt or Persia to the Turks or the continuing exploration of the American continents. For all these reasons an analysis of the
circumstances surrounding the first invasion of 1494 illuminates more
than the ephemeral adventure of Charles VIII.

The French monarchy had acquired its direct legal claim to the kingdom of Naples at the death of René of Anjou in 1480. This claim derived
ultimately from the thirteenth-century grant by which the papacy had
conferred Naples on Charles of Anjou, younger brother of St. Louis.
During the intervening centuries there had followed the long, complicated history of the rivalries between the Angevin and Aragonese houses
for the Neapolitan inheritance. By the fifteenth century the question of
right had been so confused by a succession of additional grants, retrac-
tions, adoptions, legitimations, and recognitions of conquests that it
could hardly be unraveled by the keenest legal minds of Europe. What
was important was that a historic claim existed which could be asserted
and acted upon at any time. Seen against this background, Charles VIII
and Ferdinand of Aragon may appear to be merely the last protagonists
of an almost "colonial" rivalry, dating back to the thirteenth century but
now prosecuted on a larger scale and with all the resources of monarchies
established on a more truly national basis. But it would be an illusion to
consider that this inheritance determined the Italian wars of 1494 and
the subsequent years. Behind the pretext lay the realities of the moment,
personalities and political and social pressures.

Charles VIII was himself an abnormal weakling whose capacity to
direct the affairs of the French crown was very limited. He was dazzled

by the traditions of chivalry, personal honor, and the ideals of a crusade, and only too willing to entertain grandiose projects in which he saw himself as heir of the crusading tradition, being crowned king of Jerusalem and leading victorious armies against the Turk. Achievement of the position in Naples would be a step on the way to conquest of Constantinople. It appears probable that Charles sincerely believed in the rightness of his claim and viewed his whole Italian expedition as a vindication of justice that would at the same time serve the cause of the Christian religion against the infidel. The crusading tradition in the later Middle Ages had expressed itself not only in such sterile symbolism as the Feast of the Pheasant at the court of Burgundy, but also in many exponents of missionary zeal, from Raymond Lull to Nicolas Clenard. Whatever his motives, it was evident that the French king had but a feeble understanding of the actual situation he would meet in Italy and of the problems his expedition would create. Among his advisers were men whose aims were far more realistic.

Commines, as a survivor of the regime of Louis XI and an opponent of the new direction of French policy, described in terms of great bitterness the "new" men whose influence on Charles VIII was, he felt, so unfortunately decisive. From his point of view the king's favorite advisers, De Vesc and Briconnet, were *arrivistes,* men of no family, who abused their favor with the king for what they could get out of it.[5] However prejudiced this testimony may be, it is clear that their enthusiastic support of the king's Italian policy rested in large part on hopes of personal advancement, both financial and political. They provided the obvious channel through which Italian diplomacy could work to put pressure on the French government.

Individual motives found a wider support in the condition of the country. In many respects France was ahead of her neighbors in the organization of monarchical power. Charles VIII inherited from his predecessors a bureaucracy and an army that gave him the means to implement a more aggressive policy abroad. In addition, however, he had inherited a social problem that was perhaps an even more important determinant. The higher ranks of the feudal nobility had for generations opposed the increases in the power of the crown, and, although they had been successfully suppressed from time to time, particularly during the reign of Louis XI, their disaffection remained one of the principal problems of the kingdom. The functional position of the nobility had been

---

[5] Commines, *Mémoires,* edited by Mandrot (Paris, 1901–1903), Vol. II, 99.

undermined at the same time that the basis of their economic support was contracting. Incomes derived from the land, as we have seen, were less and less adequate to the support of a class whose style of life was becoming ever more expansive. The position of the nobility thus constituted a major political and sociological problem; it was of first importance to find a way to occupy the nobility and to expend their energies. Foreign adventure was the alternative to domestic revolution, as the history of the sixteenth century was to show.

In spite of the existence in France of a monarch bent on conquest, a social class in want of occupation, and a country organized to support military adventure, it is obvious that the timing of the invasion depended on developments in Italy. Here the key figure and principal instigator of the French was Ludovico Sforza, the admired impressario of political intrigue, who ruled in Milan by a double usurpation. His father, Francesco Sforza, had acquired the duchy by conquest, putting an end to the Ambrosian republic which the citizens of Milan had vainly tried to establish after the death of the last Visconti. The inheritance thus acquired descended to Francesco's eldest son, Galeazzo Maria. At the latter's death, however, Ludovico usurped the reality of power although the title of duke was left to his nephew, Galeazzo's son, Gian Galeazzo. Ludovico's position, thus originally insecure, was still further threatened after the death of Lorenzo de' Medici.

The historic alliance between Milan, Naples, and Florence, which dated from the peace of Lodi, began to fall apart in circumstances resulting from Ludovico's ambition and complicated by the relationships between personalities at the three courts. Gian Galeazzo, the rightful duke of Milan, kept in the shade by his uncle, was married to a Neapolitan princess, Isabella of Aragon. This lady, a good deal more strong-willed than her husband, bitterly resented her position at Milan, where Ludovico and his wife, Beatrice d'Este, presided over one of the most brilliant courts in Renaissance Italy. Accordingly she appealed to her grandfather, Ferdinand of Aragon, and stimulated at Naples maneuvers directed against Ludovico. This orientation of Neapolitan policy was discreetly followed by Florence, where Piero de' Medici was much influenced by his wife, whose Orsini relatives held high position at Naples. Behind this interplay of personal attachments and jealousies lay hopes of aggrandizement and a new alignment of powers in Italy.

Ludovico was thus confronted with the possibility of a coalition directed against the territories of Milan. At the very least it appeared that the hereditary enmity of Venice could no longer be kept in check by the system of alliances. In this situation Ludovico directed his diplomacy north of the Alps and appealed to Charles VIII to prosecute his claim to the kingdom of Naples. It was an appeal supported by various kinds of bribery and persuasion, furthered by all the arts that had won Ludovico the reputation of a master politician and diplomat. He was widely admired for a master stroke, by which it was considered he had removed the Neapolitan threat and at the same time diverted the attention of the French from their claims on the duchy of Milan itself. It is entirely possible that he himself intended his manipulations to remain in the realm of threat. After all, there had been earlier examples of appeals to the French and other powers which were merely intended as weapons in the game of Italian diplomacy. If this was the case no one could have been more surprised and alarmed than Ludovico himself when his intrigues produced the reality of the French invasion. Whether he intended it or not his triumph was brief. Five years later the French took up their claim to Milan itself, Ludovico was driven out, and, upon attempting to return, was captured and spent the rest of his life in a French dungeon, with ample opportunity to meditate before he died on that favorite theme of Renaissance speculation, the wheel of fortune.

The success of Ludovico's appeal to Charles VIII was of course furthered by the fact that the ground had been prepared to receive it. The disposition of the French king and his advisers, and the social condition of the nobility have already been noticed. But there was yet another factor that made possible the realization of the plan to intervene in Italy. The monarchy had not available the ready resources to finance the invasion and, in order to supply its needs, turned to the Italian bankers who controlled more ready capital. Commines describes how, before proceeding, it was necessary to borrow, at fourteen per cent interest, 100,000 francs from the bank of the Sauli at Genoa. It was the perennial problem of the relationship between public authority and private property.

The power of the state, although growing, did not extend so far over the property of the subject as to permit the government unlimited freedom of action. Just as the governments of Spain and Portugal were forced to resort to private sources of capital to finance their overseas expeditions, so the government of France had to turn to the bankers. The fact that most of the banks in France were then in Italian hands established a connection that became one of the determinants of French foreign policy for over half a century. The initial loans were followed by others. As the government was more and more committed, the political influence of Italian capital mounted. For it was always possible for those who made the loans to refrain from pressure for repayment, provided the active intervention of the French in Italy was continued. Thus Italian exiles who had an interest in the overturn of a particular regime at home could use their financial power to restore their position under French protection. The wealth of Italy was not only a goal the attainment of which entered into the calculations of the northern powers; it was also a means that in some cases made the invasions possible.

The brief triumph of Charles VIII in 1494 was thus the product of an exceedingly complex set of historical circumstances. Motives ranged from Charles VIII's dreams of a crusade through the insecurity of Ludovico, the cupidity of Charles's advisers, and the hopes of the Italian exiles. Behind these individuals the historian can discover economic and political factors of which contemporaries were only partially aware; yet least of all, perhaps, is this event to be explained in terms of nationalism interpreted in anything like its present sense. Modern French historians have been divided in their judgment. There are those who have condemned the policy of Charles VIII and his successors because it deviated from the "historic" policy of expansion toward the "natural" frontiers. Yet surely neither at this date nor for a long time to come did any one think of a French *state* comprehending all the territory within the boundaries Caesar had defined for Gaul. The dynastic policy of Charles VIII cannot be judged in terms of the aspirations of the Third Republic.

On the other hand, those who have justified the Italian expeditions on the grounds of the historic medieval connection between the French monarchy and the Italian peninsula, and on the grounds of the cultural services performed by France for the rest of the European world, are equally unhistorical in a different way. There had indeed been many French interventions in Italy from the time of the Norman conquest of Sicily onward, but there had also been analogous interventions in other directions that had not had similar consequences. The connection of the French monarchy with Flanders and with England had been at least as close as the connection with Italy, without producing the same kind of expansionist effort in those directions. And to believe that France had a manifest destiny to disseminate Italian culture is to accept Charles VIII's own conception of his mission, with the terms transposed. The new learning had already had its representatives in Paris and other places in the north before 1494. French, German, and English scholars had been in Italy, and Greek had been taught in several of the northern centers. The direct cultural results of the earlier invasions have been much exaggerated, and it is certainly possible to argue that, without military and political conquests, the culture of the Italian Renaissance would have been as widely accepted.

Modern judgments, whether in praise or blame, have thus often been equally wide of the mark. The French expedition of 1494 cannot be understood in terms of nationalism. It took place in an environment still largely conditioned by the medieval inheritance. It was surrounded with prophecies and appeals to a savior, of which Savonarola's are only the most famous. The notion of a decisive role to be played by a particular king or people had many parallels in earlier centuries. In France the tradition extended at least as far back as the *Gesta Dei per Francos* and included many writings of the period of Philip the Fair, especially the *De recuperatione sanctae terrae*. But if the aims of Charles VIII are to be on the whole understood in a medieval context, the methods by which those aims were realized, the concentration of power, the dependence on financial capital, the diplomatic negotiations all looked toward the modern world. And if we are to seek a judgment we can hardly find one more penetrating than that given by a contemporary. Sir Thomas More, writing his *Utopia* some twenty years later, put into the mouth of Hythlodaye in the first book a description of the aims of contemporary international politics.

Hythlodaye imagines himself included in the French king's council, and asks how his advice should be taken on the problem on which:

they beat their brains and search the very bottom of their wits to discuss by what craft and means the king may still keep Milan, and draw to him again fugitive Naples. . . . If I, silly man, should rise up and will them to turn over the leaf, and learn a new lesson; saying that my counsel is not to meddle with Italy, but to tarry still at home, and that the kingdom of France alone is almost greater than that it may well be governed of one man. . . . Furthermore if I should declare unto them that all this busy preparance to war, whereby so many nations for his sake should be brought into a troublesome hurly-burly, when all his coffers were emptied, his treasures wasted, and his people destroyed, should at the length through some mischance be in vain and to none effect; and that therefore it were best for him to content himself with his own kingdom of France as his forefathers and predecessors did before him . . . and with other kingdoms not to meddle seeing that which he hath already is even enough for him, yea, and more than he can well turn him to— this mine advice, Master More, how think you it would be heard and taken?

So God help me, not very thankfully, quoth I.[6]

When More wrote this judgment the struggle for Italy had been going on for twenty years. It was to continue for almost another half-century. More's analysis might have been better applied to 1559 than to 1515. Yet, by the earlier date the pattern was already clear. The consequences of the first French expedition of 1494 revealed themselves in the struggle for Italian territory in the period from Fornovo to Marignano, when the characteristic operation of alliances within the European state system first became apparent.

IV. THE EUROPEAN STATE SYSTEM, 1494–1515

Few periods in the history of European diplomacy were so complicated as the age of the first Italian wars. The years between 1494 and 1515 furnished endless examples of the statecraft of princes. The existence of a common object of ambition in the domination of Italy, the consciousness shared by many rulers of the increased means at their disposal, the search for advantage in the shifting alliances and betrayals provided a framework for the development of a Machiavellian virtuosity. But behind the confusing maneuvers of individuals and the bewildering series of momentary triumphs there can be discerned the beginnings of that pattern of international organization that was to replace the medieval community.

The principle of a coalition formed to resist the swollen power of a single state was invoked as soon as the extent of the first French victory became apparent. The armies of Charles VIII had encountered no serious resistance; at the end of the year 1494 they had already entered Rome, and a few weeks later took possession of the kingdom of Naples. Confronted with the prospect of French rule permanently established in the southern part of the peninsula, the papacy took the initiative in a diplomatic effort to undermine the French position. In spite of the fact that Charles had attempted to secure a free hand by a series of deals with Ferdinand, Maximilian, Henry VII, and Ludovico of Milan, most of his newly won allies were ready to desert him and associate themselves in a coalition powerful enough to force the French to retreat.

The Holy League was formed in 1495. It consisted of Venice, the papacy, Maximilian, the Catholic kings, and Ludovico. Its ostensible purpose was the convenient pretext of the defense of Christianity against the Turks. Commines, then acting as French ambassador in Venice, was not deceived, and as soon as he reported the true situation to his master at Naples it was clear that the French position had become untenable. The

---

[6] More, *Utopia,* edited by J. C. Collins (Oxford, 1927), 31–33.

retreat was even more rapid than the conquest. Charles VIII succeeded in extricating his army almost intact, in spite of the indecisive battle of Fornovo, fought in July, 1495; but the League rightly celebrated its victory, since it had forced the abandonment of the prizes of the conquest. The French returned home, dazzled by the glories of Italy, stricken with the new epidemic of syphilis, and determined to renew an attempt that had held so much promise. The Aragonese were restored in Naples, with the aid of Spanish troops, and Ferdinand remained in power and influence, the real victor of the first of the campaigns.

Charles VIII died before he could fulfill his intention of resuming intervention in Italy, and it was left to his successor, Louis XII, to continue to support the French claims, this time directed initially not against Naples but against the former French ally, Milan. Louis XII inherited from the Visconti marriage of the Orléans family a direct claim to the duchy of Milan and, since Ludovico had betrayed the French cause in deserting the alliance and supporting the Emperor Maximilian, there was additional reason for attempting to dispossess him and conquer his territories. The realization of Louis's aims fell in with those of the Borgia papacy, and there followed a characteristic reversal of alliance in which France, the papacy, and Venice—in spite of the commitments of 1495—now appeared leagued together for the despoilment of Milan.

In July, 1499, the second great French army entered Italy and, with the aid of Swiss mercenaries, swiftly conquered Milan and drove out Ludovico. This initial victory was compromised by the failure of the French king to keep his engagements with the Swiss. Ludovico was able, with their help and that of the Emperor Maximilian, to raise a new army and to return. He was finally defeated, however, at Novara in 1500, where he was captured and taken to France to end his life in the dungeon of the Chateau of Loches. A French administration was installed in Milan and there seemed a prospect that the duchy would be permanently annexed to the crown of France.

The initial success of Louis fed his ambition. The price of the aid given to the Borgia was their assistance in acquiring the kingdom of Naples. In the same summer in which the triumph over Ludovico was achieved, the French king made a deal with Ferdinand by which they agreed to partition the kingdom of Naples. The new system of alliances thus permitted French domination in Milan and a part of Naples, Borgia domination of central Italy, and Spanish acquisition of the southern part of the Neapolitan kingdom.

The French triumph was brief. In 1503 the death of Alexander VI and the illness of Caesar Borgia brought about the end of the Borgia supremacy. Giuliano della Rovere succeeded to the papacy with a program incompatible with the maintenance of the French alliance. At the same time Ferdinand took advantage of every dispute over the new boundary established in Naples to press the Spanish interest. His great captain, Gonsalvo da Cordova, drove the French out of Naples by 1504, and Naples became—and this time remained—an annex of the Spanish crown.

The dynamic of the position of the powers in Italy forced the continuance of attempts to control an ever larger part of the territories in the peninsula. A brief period of equilibrium succeeded the fall of the Borgia and the Spanish conquest of Naples. The interest of European diplomacy centered for a few years on the marriage schemes proposed for Charles of Burgundy, and on the relations between the emperor, Ferdinand, and Louis XII. In 1508, however, under the auspices of the Archduchess Marguerite of the Netherlands, there was concluded the League of Cambrai, of which the ostensible object was the traditional one of a holy war against the Turks while the real purpose was the coalition of the great powers of Europe to reduce Venice.

This famous league was initially concluded between Henry VII of England, Louis XII, Ferdinand, and Maximilian. Julius II adhered to it in spite of the increased Italian territory that was to be given to foreign powers, because it promised the readiest way to enlarge the territories of the church in the Romagna. In 1509 the campaigns began. Venetian territory was invaded by a French army, and the Venetian troops were defeated at Agnadello while papal troops invaded from the south. The fundamental rivalries between members of the coalition, however, prevented the realization of the program of Cambrai. Once his ambition had been attained, Julius II was anxious to make peace with the Venetians and turn to the problem of driving the northern barbarians out of the Italian peninsula altogether.

In 1510 the pope absolved Venice and came to an agreement about the disposition of the territories Venice had taken from the Borgia inheritance. Shortly thereafter Ferdinand was brought into the agreement, and a new "Holy League" was founded with the object of driving the French from Italy. The brilliant victories of the French captain, Gaston de Foix, at first defeated the plans of the coalition. The battle of Ravenna in 1512 was a victory for the French and seemed to promise the conquest of all northern Italy. But it cost the life of Gaston de Foix, and there was no general of his talent in the French service to replace him.

At this critical moment, Maximilian, who had hitherto refused to join the coalition of Julius, deserted the French alliance, signed a peace with Venice, and left Louis and the French to their fate. The pope, supported by the alliance of the Swiss under Cardinal Schiner and by the adherence of Maximilian, triumphed; the French were driven out of Milan and had to translate to Lyons their council, called at Pisa to depose Julius II. In spite of a new defection by Venice and the momentary return of the French into northern Italy, it seemed, by the time Julius died in early 1513, that his aims had been substantially achieved. The new pope, Leo X, peacefully inclined, was willing to accept the dissolution of the council of Pisa as a guarantee of French intentions, and it appeared that a new stage had been reached in the Italian question—marked by the Spanish possession of Naples, the imperial possession of Milan, and the independence of the states of the church, with a close alliance between the papacy and Florence, where the Medici were restored.

Any prospect of settlement along these lines vanished with the change of ruler in France. At the end of 1514 Louis XII died and was succeeded by the ambitious and dynamic Francis I, who was determined to prosecute the Italian claims of France. He immediately assembled an army, in which there were many mercenaries recruited from Switzerland and even from Albania, and crossed the Alpine passes in the spring of 1515. The great battle of Marignano, which made such an impression on contemporaries, was fought in 1515 and, although the issue was long in doubt, the French finally conquered. Once more the Sforza puppet was expelled from his inheritance and a French administration installed in Milan.

The victory of Marignano caused Leo X to desert the policy initiated by Julius II. The pope rushed to meet the conqueror and come to an arrangement with him, excusing himself to Ferdinand and Maximilian because of the imminent danger in which he found himself. In 1516, at a meeting between Francis and Leo X, the French domination of Milan was accepted and the concordat of Bologna concluded. In the year following the death of Ferdinand a general peace was arranged. The Treaty of Cambrai, of March, 1517, was the pact that seemed to Erasmus to promise a golden age of European peace. The definitive settlement of the Italian question seemed to be based on France in the north, Spain in the south, with the papacy dominating the territory in between. Actually this promising arrangement was no more permanent than the earlier truces. On the contrary, the rivalries forged in the Italian conflict were generalized and accentuated within the next two years by the problem of the imperial election and the conflict between the Hapsburg and Valois interests.

Thus it cannot be claimed that the period of a little more than twenty years between the invasion by Charles VIII and the Treaty of Cambrai produced a settlement of the Italian question. The military and diplomatic events of this period, however, did serve to define the interests and capacities of the European powers in relation to each other. In the years just before the Hapsburg threat came into existence the practice of European diplomacy was evolving a means to meet that threat. If there was as yet no conscious appeal to a theoretical principle of balance of power on a European scale, there had nevertheless developed a clearer realization of the interdependence of the European state system and a conviction that the independence of each and perhaps ultimately the security of all depended on common action against any one power which appeared to be acquiring too great a preponderance.

Chapter Six

THE CONDITION OF THE CHRISTIAN CHURCH

THE economic and political changes which have been summarized in the preceding chapters produced serious strains in that most comprehensive of all governmental systems, the Christian church. The growing powers of secular states made compromises inevitable. Economic pressures and an expanding standard of wealth accelerated the scramble for the accumulation of benefices. The resulting decline in moral and institutional standards was felt in all parts of the great ecclesiastical organization, but was most dramatically apparent at the apex of the system in the papacy itself. To the long history of opposition to Roman financial exactions and papal control of appointments was now added an increasing lack of respect for the head of the church and his immediate court. Never had the gap appeared so wide between the pretensions of the incumbents of the see of Peter and their actual performance.

The two humanist popes of the mid-fifteenth century, Nicholas V and Pius II, had maintained a high sense of the responsibilities of their position, and if their patronage of the new learning had created precedents that in the long run might be dangerous, yet their pontificates had been free from serious scandals. Beginning, however, with the pontificate of Sixtus IV in 1471, the decline was rapid.

Sixtus IV, born Francisco della Rovere, was the son of a poor and large family. He had distinguished himself in the Franciscan order and in theological disputes on the currently debated doctrine of the Immaculate Conception. Strong, intelligent, ambitious, he embarked on a career of political activity motivated in part by the desire to provide in a suitably splendid way for his eleven nephews and two nieces. Melozzo da Forli's celebrated picture of the pope receiving Platina, the papal librarian, shows us, symbolically enough, Sixtus attended by his favorite nephews, whose faces reveal their greed, complacency, and ruthlessness. It was a family which had "arrived." During this pontificate significant steps were taken toward enlarging the papal control of the Romagna, where lordships were created for the various nephews. In pursuit of these political aims the pope involved his name and position in the Pazzi conspiracy of 1478. The ensuing war failed to bring him the extensive gains for which he had hoped and when he died in 1484 he left the inheritance of a papacy increasingly dedicated to its position as a princely power in Italy. The tone of his court had become more and more magnificent and an extravagant luxury the common order of high ecclesiastical life in Rome.

His successor, Giovanni Cibo, who took the title of Innocent VIII, was elected at a conclave distinguished for the openly political struggle between the rival candidates. He was weak, compliant, undistinguished, and dominated by the influence of Giuliano della Rovere, who was considered pope in all but name. Innocent's pontificate was notable because of the extent to which the pope's own children were avowed and openly provided for. His death in 1492 fell at a critical turning point in Italian political history, but it can hardly be supposed that if he had continued to live he would have had a very great influence on the evolution of the system of alliances.

Roderigo Borgia came to the throne in 1492 and took the name of Alexander VI. He reigned for eleven years. Although many of the famous scandals associated with his name and pontificate are highly colored versions of the truth, yet he has long since ceased to have any serious defenders. One of the most ambitious and aggressive of all the popes, he centered his hopes on the position of his family rather than on the institution which he presumably served. For over a decade his maneuvers, bargains and shifts of alliance occupied the center of the stage of European diplomacy, but in the end his favorite son, Caesar, failed to hold the position it had cost so much to win. This disastrous pontificate marked the lowest point of corruption and immorality in the Vatican itself.

After the short reign of Pius III, who died less than four weeks after his election, Giuliano della Rovere at last came to the papal throne as Julius II. The most famous of Renaissance popes, the "papa terribile" devoted himself to the enlargement of the states of the church on lines laid down by his predecessors. By a tremendous effort of energy and will he triumphed over a series of crises and lived to see the defeat of the French and the failure of the attempted council of Pisa. He had in a sense delivered the church, but at the price of opening the way to the Spanish domination of the Italian peninsula. One of the greatest patrons in the whole history of the arts, Julius commissioned the work of Michelangelo,

Bramante and Raphael. Indeed, the sudden flowering of the style of the High Renaissance in Rome has been attributed to his personal inspiration. It has been suggested that this style was the appropriate expression of the pontiff's religious ideals, the product of a sincere conversion.[1] Whatever the personal religious beliefs of Julius II and their relationship to the artistic achievements of his age, there were many contemporaries who considered the pope's career and ambitions far removed from Christian example. Perhaps no document better illustrates this aspect of contemporary opinion than the satire, *Julius Exclusus,* attributed to Erasmus. This indictment was written, if Erasmus was the author, after his return from Italy in 1509 when he became a member of the circle of Sir Thomas More. Early in his Italian journey in 1506 Erasmus had been at Bologna and had stood among the crowd to watch the pope's triumphal entry into the city after its fall. In a way the satire may be taken as a measure of the gulf that divided the beliefs of the northern observer, educated in the atmosphere of the *devotio moderna,* from the ideals of the Renaissance papacy. Although the satire was not published until 1514 and was always denied by its author, it had a rapid circulation and must have made a profound impression on all who read it. It is cast in the form of a dialogue between Julius II and Saint Peter, in which the former, contrary to his expectation, finds himself excluded from Heaven. Every resource of the author's irony is directed to making manifest the incompatibility between the aims and achievements of this greatest of Renaissance popes and the ideals of the founder of Christianity. Julius finds that he is equipped only with the keys of his money box and of his political power, not with those of the Kingdom of Heaven. Saint Peter refuses to recognize in the warlike figure with his magnificent tiara and pallium the representative of the apostolic succession he had established. The success of this satire, and of others like it, is an indication of the degree to which the prestige of the papacy was declining among the intellectuals.

Julius's successor, Leo X, the eldest surviving son of Lorenzo de' Medici, brought to their culmination the classical and secular tastes as well as the religious irresponsibility of the Renaissance papacy. Leo had been brought up in the most cultivated circles in Italy and had been tutored by Poliziano and Marsilio Ficino. Surrounded with a brilliant and sophisticated group of humanists and littérateurs, he was sensitive, pleasure-loving and easygoing. The interests of the pope and his circle

[1] F. Hartt, "'Lignum Vitae in Medio Paradisii': The Stanza d'Eliodoro and the Sistine Ceiling," *Art Bulletin,* 32 (1950), 115–45; 181–218.

centered on music and the theater—especially on the comedies of Plautus, on the collection of books, manuscripts and gems, as well as on hunting parties and al fresco lunches accompanied by classical masques. In the midst of all this the serious business of the papacy was neglected and it is not surprising that the court was quite unprepared to meet the great blow that fell at the end of Leo's pontificate. Yet in spite of all this, the "pagan" atmosphere of the papacy on the eve of religious revolution has been much exaggerated. The performance of the comedies of Plautus did not necessarily mean the rejection of the Christian religion. Sarpi's celebrated description of Leo as possessed of all the qualities to make a perfect pope if he had but had the slightest interest in religion is unfair. Leo was a product of the religious thought of the neo-Platonic circle in Florence and within the terms of this tradition it is probably true that he thought of himself as entirely Christian. Yet his was not a type of Christianity which could be understood or even tolerated by most of the members of the church over which he presided. What was needed was a pope who would take a literal and serious interest in the need for reform within the Christian community. This Leo utterly failed to supply.[2]

During the first years of Leo's pontificate the fifth Lateran council, originally summoned by Julius II, continued to sit. It met infrequently and was attended principally by representatives of the Italian clergy. The reform decrees of earlier councils were reaffirmed and solemnly issued by papal bull. Simony and plurality were condemned, and it was insisted that candidates for ecclesiastical office should fulfil the canonical qualifications. But at the very time when these old formulas were being reiterated, some of the most important sees in Christendom were being conferred on princely children and the practice of multiplying great benefices in the hands of a single person had never been more widespread. The council promulgated some interesting decrees on usury, condemned current heresies on immortality and managed to settle some of the long-standing controversies within the Franciscan order.[3] On the whole, however, its work was negligible in the face of the needs which it confronted, and it perhaps chiefly served to demonstrate that the highest organs of the church were so caught in a network of vested interests that only lip service could be paid to the cause of reform. Leo X might congratulate himself in 1517 on the successful conclusion of the council, which was celebrated with ceremonies of characteristic magnificence, but nothing

[2] P. Hughes, *A History of the Church*, Vol. III (New York, 1947), 386–435, for the above survey of the Renaissance popes.

[3] Hefele-Leclerc, *Histoire des conciles* (Paris, 1921), Vol. VIII, Part 2.

had been done to restore the moral prestige of the papacy or to make a
real attack on the whole system of ecclesiastical abuses. The hour when
reform might have met with successful response was slipping away while
Leo enjoyed his pontificate, the last to preside over a united Christian community.

The question how far and in what ways that community was affected
by conditions in Rome is difficult to answer with any precision. The great
majority of the inhabitants of Christendom remained ignorant of the
realities of the situation at the papal court very much as the vast framework of the Roman Empire had been undisturbed by the corruption of a
Nero or a Caligula. The complicated machinery of the curia's business
continued, and those pious communities and individuals who received
dispensations, indulgences, privileges and confirmations from even an
Alexander VI had little or none of the information even then being
recorded by Roman diarists and diplomats which was to fix the character
of these popes in history.

Even a firsthand view of the Renaissance papacy did not always produce a revolutionary impact on the northern beholder. It is extremely
doubtful whether Luther's visit in 1510 and 1511 gave him the impres-
sions he afterward described.[4] If a serious Augustinian monk on the
business of his order could have returned from a winter in Rome in these
years with only so much sense of shock as could be recollected later, when
it served his purposes, rather than registered at once, how much less
affected must those have been who never made the Italian journey at all.
To subsequent historians the papacy of this period has become a symbol
for all the evils that afflicted the church universal. Yet to the minds of
most men, Rome was still remote and the papacy remained an institution
of final appeal. Unhappily the very conditions which led to such appeals
were the same as those which were corrupting the church at the center.
Secularism, extravagance and immorality were not confined to Rome but
appeared at all levels of the hierarchy and in all parts of the Christian
world.

II. SYMPTOMS OF FAILURE

Apart from conditions in Rome, the areas where disintegration was
most seriously felt were in the episcopate, in the institution of monasticism, and in the compromises which it had been necessary to make with
the new monarchies.

[4] L. Febvre, *Martin Luther un destin* (Paris, 1928).

The condition of the episcopate varied from country to country, but in general those states where a strong monarchy was established were the scene of a continuing struggle between the royalty and the papacy for control of the higher ecclesiastical positions. Kings frequently chose their chief ministers from among ecclesiastics of high rank or alternatively wished to reward their most faithful servants with appointment to episcopal station. There were obvious reasons for this relationship. The clergy still provided the most highly educated class, from which the royal administration might select its bureaucrats. The monarchs on their side were frequently not in a position to dip into their secular revenues to find for their most reliable servants rewards commensurate with their status and services. Hence the familiar alliance between the royal governments and the higher clergy of which the period provided so many conspicuous examples.

At the highest level of governmental activity four famous cardinals serve to illustrate the way in which this relationship was worked out. Wolsey in England, Georges d'Amboise in France, Berthold von Henneberg in Germany, and Ximenes in Spain were all principal ministers of their respective monarchs. Some of them served the state for years and derived their main revenue from their accumulation of benefices. It was an arrangement the pope had compounded, because the papacy received a profitable revenue from the dues and dispensations that permitted these departures from canonical rules. Thus both the monarchy and the papacy had a financial interest in the appointment to the higher ecclesiastical positions of men whose first interests and responsibilities were often not ecclesiastical. To this were added the apparent pressures that led many noble families to seek episcopal positions for their younger sons as a means of maintaining their standard of life or supplementing income derived from the land. It was the great age of pluralities among the higher clergy, and of increasing monopoly of the upper clerical ranks by the aristocracy.

In these circumstances it was obvious that there was very little time for even those bishops most serious in intent to apply themselves to the affairs of their dioceses. Others, without any conflict of duty, simply preferred the life of the court or of literature to the obligations of their offices. Hence, episcopal duties were widely neglected in every country of Christendom. Visitations, ordinations, and in many cases the entire administration of dioceses were delegated to men of inferior capacity, whose financial rewards were inadequate and who had not the interest that might have been expected from the original incumbent in the performance of his high office. The tragic culmination of this development may be illustrated in the career of Wolsey, who entered his archdiocese of York for the first time at the close of his life, when he had already been disgraced. An even more striking example is provided by Antoine du Prat, chancellor of France and one of the negotiators of the concordat of Bologna. He was rewarded with the archbishopric of Sens and never entered his cathedral church until he was carried in for his funeral.

The failures of the higher clergy were reflected and matched in all lower ranks. The system of pluralities left many parishes unprovided, and there were very general complaints of the ignorance and incapacity of the parish priests as a class. The question of the state of education among the inferior members of the first estate is one on which it is very difficult to generalize. The impression created by the caricatures of Erasmus is probably exaggerated. Both among the regular and the secular clergy there were men highly educated in the traditional sense, who opposed and feared the program advanced by Erasmus and his followers. Lack of the new learning was not incompatible with a profound training in scholastic philosophy and theology. Yet it is also clear that there were many secular priests whose education was of the most rudimentary kind and who were not even able to get through the necessary offices. The much discussed question of the status of the regular clergy has also probably been somewhat twisted by the emphasis put upon some famous scandals and the satiric attacks of the humanists. There were many kinds and degrees of failure in monastic institutions and in the mendicant orders all over Europe, but it may be questioned whether the abuses were so much worse than they had been in the past as to cause the general stirrings of doubt about the institution of monasticism itself. The failure of an institution to work as well as it is assumed to have done in the past may cause its intellectual rejection, but it is surely often equally true that the institution ceases to work and becomes riddled with abuses because people have stopped believing in it. In many places, notably in France, Spain, and the Low Countries serious reforms in the regular orders had been undertaken and carried through with a considerable measure of success, but these islands of restorative action were too isolated to have a significant effect on the general situation.

If the most characteristic abuses in the ranks of the regular as well as the secular clergy had been recurrent throughout the whole late medieval period, what was really new at the beginning of the sixteenth century was the framework of ecclesiastical organization in which they occurred. Ever since the close of the conciliar period there had been an increasing decentralization in the institutional life of the church corresponding to the growth in the power of national monarchies in western Europe. It is therefore necessary to consider briefly the most characteristic variations in ecclesiastical organization from country to country with their corresponding effects on what may be almost called national churches.

In England the organization of the church was more centralized than across the Channel either in France or in Germany because of the primacy of the archbishop of Canterbury. Furthermore, a legatine authority had often been granted and exercised for the Anglican church as a whole and in the extraordinary powers conferred on Cardinal Wolsey this tradition was carried even further. Assertions about various kinds of independence were backed by a long tradition of resistance to papal financial and jurisdictional claims in which the statutes of provisors and praemunire represented the principal rallying points. At various times of crisis this tradition was revived and emphasized and the most fundamental questions on the position and prerogatives of the clergy were brought into discussion. One such occasion was created by the case of Richard Hunne in the winter of 1514 and 1515.

Richard Hunne was a well-to-do merchant tailor and freeman of the city of London. An altercation begun with a priest over perquisites for serving at Hunne's infant son's funeral led to suit and countersuit in ecclesiastical and civil courts. Hunne was condemned for heresy and put in prison where he was soon afterward found hanged, in all probability a suicide but in the opinion of the London jury the victim of a murder by ecclesiastical authority. The public discussion which followed involved the most prominent persons in the church and the government and raised in the sharpest form most of the issues between clergy and secular authority. It was asked whether a secular court had any authority to summon a cleric and if so under what circumstances; to what extent those who held minor orders could plead benefit of clergy; whether a papal constitution could be binding in a country whose usages were to the contrary and whether a temporal ruler could restrain a bishop.

In the end there was a compromise. Wolsey made a formal disavowal on behalf of the church of any attempt to interfere in the royal prerogative. The cleric who had been under indictment for the murder of Hunne was summoned before a royal court but allowed to plead not guilty and go free. Thus the issue was temporarily settled but alarming depths of disagreement and tension had been revealed. All the great questions of the relationship between church and state had been raised by a dispute begun over a piece of mortuary cloth whose value was insignificant—questions involving a declaration of the royal supremacy, and doubts about the benefit of clergy, appeals to the pope and the validity of canon law in England. Already the ground in England was thoroughly prepared for the step ultimately taken by Henry VIII.[5]

Across the channel the tradition of Gallican independence was certainly as strong if not stronger than the Anglican. Among the fourteen archbishoprics in lands subject to the French king at the beginning of the sixteenth century none enjoyed the primacy which had been established by Canterbury in England. The archbishop of Lyons inherited perhaps the oldest claim to a primacy in Gaul, but he was never able to assert it successfully. The archbishop of Rheims prided himself on the title of born legate of the pope, but, as in the case of Lyons, this was more a title of honor than a real manifestation of authority. Hence from the point of view of relations with the royalty there was no exact equivalent of the English situation where the king could deal with the higher clergy by means of a conference with Canterbury and York. And from the point of view of the internal organization of the French church, there was a lack of directive authority.

Since 1438, with some intermissions, the regime governing the Gallican church had been at least in theory that established by the Pragmatic Sanction of Bourges. This document among many universally accepted propositions also affirmed the supremacy of an ecumenical council over the pope, the necessity for canonical elections in the Gallican church, and finally the inadmissibility of papal reservations and certain other fiscal rights. Although it was not found possible to enforce all these provisions, and although the Pragmatic Sanction was suspended under Louis XI and again under Francis I, it remained the theoretical basis of the liberties of the Gallican church.

Not only did the church in France suffer some disorganization on a national scale because of the lack of a central authority, but within the dioceses, also, there had been a serious decline of the episcopal authority. Many benefices theoretically in the collation of the bishop were in fact at the disposal of a host of other authorities; indeed, it has been calculated that the average French bishop controlled the patronage of not more than

---

[5] This case is discussed in some detail in H. Maynard Smith, *Pre-Reformation England* (London, 1938), 83–90.

half the benefices in his diocese. Many livings were in the gift of mon-
asteries, of cathedral chapters and, in some cases, of lay authorities. There
was also an increasing number of religious communities exempt from the
episcopal jurisdiction and dependent only on Rome. Even in the case of
those corporate groups presumably most closely tied to the jurisdiction of
the bishop, there had developed a tradition of independence, and relations
between bishops and cathedral chapters were embittered by continuing
struggles in which the chapters constantly sought to attain a greater
degree of practical independence. In some cases these efforts were so
successful that the authority of the bishop was severely limited. In these
circumstances one of the few weapons at the disposal of the episcopal
authority was the attempt to obtain benefices *in commendam:* that is to
say, if a rich abbey in the diocese fell vacant, instead of having a canonical
election, which was theoretically assured by the regime of the Pragmatic
Sanction, the bishop might apply to Rome and have the position bestowed upon himself, thus becoming abbot *in commendam.* In this way
many of the secular clergy, especially in the upper ranks, actually controlled more and more positions which in right belonged to regulars. Only
by this means, it was felt, could the bishops repress the inconvenient
movements for independence that might have centered on an abbey or
convent within their jurisdiction. Thus at the end of the fifteenth century,
both on a national and a diocesan scale, the Gallican church presented
serious weakness.[6]

The whole confused situation was to a great extent clarified by the
conclusion in 1516 of the famous concordat of Bologna between Francis I
and Leo X. Many clauses of the Pragmatic Sanction were in this new
document reaffirmed, but there was significant omission of the statement
of the conciliar theory that ecumenical councils were superior to the pope,
and there was a still more significant alteration in the principles governing appointment to consistorial benefices. In fact, by the new arrangement
the monarchy emerged with practical control over the highest positions
in the French church. Henceforth the monarchy nominated, the chapter
or convent elected, and the pope provided; but of these three steps the
royal nomination was by far the most important. In return for the papal
concessions to monarchical control, certain fiscal rights of the papacy,
such as the annates, were reaffirmed and the arrangement was therefore
satisfactory to both crown and papacy, although it was bitterly opposed by
the parliament and by the Gallican church. These bodies felt that ancient

[6] Imbart de la Tour, *Les origines de la Réforme,* Vol. I (Paris, 1905).

liberties were being sacrificed to a business arrangement concluded by the crown and the papacy. In spite of the opposition, however, the concordat was accepted and eventually became the charter under which the Gallican church operated until the French Revolution. Its existence must be regarded as one of the principal factors in explaining the failure of Protestantism to achieve a more definite success in France than it eventually did. The temptation that existed so obviously in Germany and in England for the secularization of ecclesiastical property was removed by the very considerable control already achieved by the French government in 1516.[7]

In Spain also, and at an even earlier date, the government had secured a large measure of control over the ecclesiastical organization. The Spanish church had inherited from the long medieval struggle against the Moors a tradition of militant orthodoxy. During the reigns of Ferdinand and Isabella this tradition was manifested in the creation of the Inquisition, the conquest of Granada and the expulsion of the Jews.

In 1478 Ferdinand and Isabella asked permission of the pope to establish the Inquisition in Castile. Their purpose was primarily to set up a tribunal to deal with the problem of converted Jews who had relapsed. The bull granting their request was promptly issued by Sixtus IV and within a few years the organization had assumed form. Its special power lay in the fact that it combined ecclesiastical and civil authority and served actually as one of the principal means for extending the power of the Spanish kings over the church. Although in theory the Inquisition acted in the name of Rome, in practice it was the instrument of the monarchy, which exercised complete control over the appointment and dismissal of all its officers. Instructions for the use of its judges were drawn up under royal supervision and for many years the only administrative organ common to both the realms of Aragon and Castile was the Inquisition.[8] By this means, therefore, Ferdinand and Isabella were able to accomplish more perfectly what was partially achieved in France at a later date, namely the national control of the church. To a degree unparalleled in any other western European country the Spanish church became independent of administrative control from Rome.

Because of this independence, won at an earlier date and more completely than in the other national monarchies, the Spanish authorities were in a better position to deal with the problem of the reformation of the traditional abuses. The ecclesiastical hierarchy in fifteenth-century

[7] On the concordat of Bologna, J. Thomas, *Le Concordat de 1516,* 3 vols. (Paris, 1910).
[8] R. B. Merriman, *op. cit.,* II, 86–97.

Spain had been no freer than other churches in western Europe from those evils which were the subject of common indictment. The same charges—inflated wealth of the higher clergy, pluralities, simony, immorality, neglect of pastoral duties, ignorance, departure from monastic rules—all were heard as often and probably with as much justification in Castile and Aragon as in France and England. Once a serious effort at reform of these abuses had begun, however, the extent of the administrative control of the Spanish church gave it a better chance of success.

In Italy the lack of any strong centralizing secular power meant that there was no contest for the control of the church such as was carried on in England, France, and Spain. In some important ways the papacy took the place of the national monarchies elsewhere and it was natural that appointees to Italian bishoprics should have a loyalty to the papal cause that could not be expected of an archbishop of Toledo or Canterbury. The ruling families of Italy supplied candidates for the college of cardinals, for the episcopate and for the papacy itself. With the higher clergy so closely attached to Rome, whether by hope of patronage or by interest in the cultural activities of the curia, there was no possibility of developing an effective administrative leadership for reform movements outside Rome. As a consequence appeals for the reformation of abuses remained on an individual basis until the time when there came to be substantial changes in the personnel and interests of the papal court.

If, among the countries outside Italy, Spain represented the maximum of secular control of the church, the German Empire, where the monarchy was weakest, gave most opportunity for the development of ecclesiastical power. In considering the state of the church within the Empire one of the most important facts to be recorded is its enormous relative wealth. Not only had the number of foundations created by German piety always been large and well endowed, but the peculiar constitution of the Empire permitted the phenomenon of the territorial prince-bishop. Thus, in the highest rank the three spiritual electors, the archbishops of Mainz, Trier, and Cologne, functioned not only as metropolitans of the German church, but also as secular princes of great wealth and political importance. Their position at the apex of the hierarchy was paralleled by other ecclesiastical officers, abbots, and bishops, who similarly enjoyed a dual power, derived on the one hand from their ecclesiastical offices and on the other from their status as territorial princes. The closer ties existing between the upper ecclesiastical offices and positions in secular politics made it all the easier and more natural that the nobility should look upon the benefices of the church as a means of provision for their own families. Thus the upper level of the German hierarchy became a private preserve of the noble and princely families, to an extent more extreme than elsewhere in western Europe. Such documents as the *Onus ecclesiae* indicate the amount of complaint created by this situation.

In contrast to the upper clergy, the lower clergy and especially the parish priests were becoming increasingly poorer. There was a superfluity of clerics, especially in some of the towns where many had neither money to live on nor duties to perform. A larger proportion of these were products of educational institutions of very low standards. They eked out a living as vicars for those who had rich benefices or in other ways which only increased the contempt and unpopularity with which they were regarded by the populace.

As elsewhere in Europe, the condition of the regular clergy varied considerably from order to order and from one monastic house to another. But if there were houses and individuals who maintained the old standards, there were many others that were veritable travesties of monasticism and furnished plenty of material to satirists and reformers. The manifesto of the Revolutionary of the Upper Rhine, the *Ship of Fools* of Sebastian Brant and the *Epistolae obscurorum virorum* made familiar the picture of the corrupt, lazy, immoral and unjustifiable monk.

These attacks were the more serious because they were combined with strong sentiments against Rome and the demands of the Roman curia. Precisely because there was no national monarchy in Germany to find a solution comparable to that of the Inquisition in Spain or the concordat of Bologna in France, the papal exactions were greater in amount and more severely felt. The German situation was in sum a good illustration of the point that revolutions often begin not where the old institutions are at their weakest but where they are strongest, so that particular abuses assume a greater prominence and produce a correspondingly greater reaction.

The incident which precipitated revolution was the indulgence controversy. Behind this lay the whole history of princely bargaining for ecclesiastical position and of papal financial exactions. The archbishopric of Mainz fell vacant in 1514 for the second time within a few years. The people subject to the archiepiscopal jurisdiction had already suffered from financial pressure as they had been taxed to pay the usual dues sent to Rome by a new incumbent on receipt of his pallium. When the new vacancy occurred Albert of Hohenzollern, younger brother of the elector of Brandenburg, was put forward as a candidate. What was unusual even in this period of plurality of benefices was that this young prince had already been given the two bishoprics of Halberstadt and Magdeburg. It was clear to all concerned that the new position to which he aspired would require a very particular dispensation obtainable only at an extraordinary outlay of cash. An arrangement was finally concluded by which Albert was confirmed as archbishop of Mainz and the Hohenzollern family assumed the charges for the payment of the dues to Rome both ordinary and extraordinary. To supply the Hohenzollerns with the cash necessary for such a payment, recourse was had to the Fugger bank, which managed most of the large-scale financial transactions of the curia with Germany. When Albert was installed as archbishop, therefore, it was under the burden of a large debt to the house of Fugger.

In the same year in which Albert was elected and confirmed, Pope Leo X announced a renewal of the preaching of indulgences granted by his predecessor in favor of the building of St. Peter's in Rome. Territories in Germany had not been included in this campaign before, but it was now proposed that a special indulgence be granted, to be preached for eight years in the territories of the archbishop of Mainz, the profits to be allocated partly to repayment by the Hohenzollerns of their debt to the Fugger and partly to the Roman court for the building of St. Peter's. This arrangement, which included provision for a share for the emperor, was so complicated that the negotiations dragged and the actual preaching was not begun until early in 1517. Johann Tetzel, who had had long experience as a preacher of indulgences and had frequently conducted such campaigns, had been selected to lead the preaching in the territories of Mainz.

The efforts of Tetzel were so enthusiastic as to exceed contemporary ecclesiastical doctrine on the subject of indulgences. It had already long been maintained that Christ and the saints had accumulated a treasury of good works in Heaven upon which the pope, as head of the church, could draw in order to remit the temporal consequences of sin. It was in theory always maintained that the indulgence, whether plenary or partial, applied only to the remission of ecclesiastical and temporal consequences. Such an indulgence must also in theory be preceded by a genuine contrition and the act of penance, which alone were capable of removing by the operation of the sacrament the true guilt and the eternal consequences of the particular sin. When these doctrines were applied to the dead, numerous difficulties arose as to how far an act of contrition had to be performed.

What Tetzel preached was, in fact, very close to the popular proverb that as soon as a coin tinkled in the money box a soul flew out of purgatory. Tetzel's campaign had proceeded for only a few months when it was challenged by Martin Luther's theses, tacked on the church door at Wittenberg.

The drama of events that began in Germany in 1517 thus has seemed to many the direct outcome of the institutional decay of the Roman Church. This proposition which amounts to saying that the culmination of abuses produced the Reformation is a very partial and inadequate view of one of the greatest revolutions in the history of western thought.

In the first place, it is by no means clear that the abuses we have been discussing in this section were all so much worse than they had been fifty or a hundred years before. Tetzel was a scandal and it is true that the monetary demands of the curia in the age of Julius II reached a new high, but there had been indulgence scandals before and for the past three hundred years there had been many popes who could be and were accused of avarice. On the more general problems, like the condition of the monastic orders, simony and plurality among the higher clergy, neglect of pastoral duties, it is very difficult to generalize. If there were some areas where it is possible to prove a considerable worsening of the situation at the beginning of the sixteenth century, there were others which warranted the conclusion that many of the abuses had been the subject of the same constant complaints for two hundred years. Speaking of Europe as a whole, the picture was certainly not one of unrelieved and progressive decline until the situation became so intolerable that it produced a revolutionary reaction.

Even if it be admitted that the incidence of abuses was greater in the age of the Renaissance papacy, we have to ask again the question how far the phenomenon of conversion on so considerable a scale can be understood in these terms. The failure of belief in the traditional system was not only a reaction against errors and abuses in accepted institutions; it was far more an attempt to accommodate within an inherited framework the results of new thinking, the product of new scholarly interests which developed independently of the institutional defects in the church.[9] In other words it was not only negative but also and far more significantly positive. Men do not cease to believe in so comprehensive a system as was inherited by the sixteenth century entirely or even mainly because of

[9] L. Febvre, "Une question mal posée. Les origines de la Réforme française et le problème général des causes de la Réforme," Revue historique, CLXI (1929), 1–73.

the existence of scandalous monks or usurpations by secular powers or the election of worldly bishops who neglected their duties. Behind the cessation of belief lay new needs and interests, expressed at their highest level in the intellectual history of the time but reflected also in countless changes in daily life. The existence of abuses and the organizational failures of the church were only the negative side of a far more comprehensive change. We can understand this change better if we first consider the limitations of those reform movements that were attempted within the traditional framework and then turn to those conditions that created at least in the minds of some the hope for a reformation of a very different kind than actually came to pass.

III. THE CONDITIONS OF REFORM: SAVONAROLA

The universal demand for the reformation of the church in head and members, which had culminated in the period of the councils, was not silenced by disappointment over the failure of the council of Constance to act on the subject. Again and again throughout the fifteenth century men of good will sought to make effective the traditional hopes for closing the gap between the ideals and the actual institutions of the Christian church. Indeed these attempts, although less organized, were accentuated as the scandals of the Renaissance papacy increased.

The theorists of the conciliar period had produced a body of conclusions on the constitution of the church and the prerogatives of an ecumenical council. The most formal expression of such conclusions had been enshrined in the decrees *sacrosancta* and *frequens* of the council of Constance. In addition to these "legal" statements, which maintained the superiority of a council over the pope and also provided for regular sessions of ecumenical councils, there was a large and varied literature, tracts, treatises and commentaries, which developed and defended the conciliar position. Among the important points in this position were the belief that a council could reform a pope, the subjection of the papal legislative and administrative authority to the canon law, the creation of sanctions against the misuse of papal power and in general the appeal to an older constitution of the church before the *Plenitudo potestatis* of the papacy had developed. This program commonly emphasized, as did Nicholas of Cusa in his *De concordantia catholica,* the active divine headship of the church and minimized the role of the papacy. It was of course opposed and with increasing effectiveness by the defenders of the papal monarchy who depended on Torquemada's *Summa de ecclesia,* according to which a council was only an assembly of prelates under the authority of the pope.

In spite of and in part because of the political victories of the Renaissance papacy the conciliar program was invoked throughout the fifteenth century and the continuity of this tradition was an important element in understanding the appeal to a council in the reformation period. As Jedin has pointed out, the conciliar ideas derived their strength less from their constititional principles than from the increasing need for reform and from the hope that a new council could succeed where those of Constance and Basle had failed. One of the principal centers of opposition to the papacy continued to be the University of Paris, whose theologians maintained the validity of the decrees of Constance. In France there was frequent agitation for summoning a council and the question was discussed also in Germany and Bohemia. Even within the curia itself, in the college of cardinals, there were proposals for a reform council especially on the eve of papal elections. Amid all the multiplicity of proposals there were, however, only two actual attempts, both of which were feeble and ended in failure. The first was the product of individual impulse. In 1482 the Balkan prelate Zamometic appealed in Basle for the opening of a new council which should be a continuation of the old. He supported his appeal by claiming the right of the individual in the event the church fell into grave danger through the sins and errors of the pope. His manifesto received little encouragement and he was easily silenced. A more serious attempt was made in 1511 when a minority of the cardinals, backed by the French king, issued a summons to a council to be held at Pisa against Julius II. The unanswerable reply of the pope was to summon the fifth Lateran council himself and declare the Pisans schismatic.

The history of the attempted council of Pisa illustrates one of the reasons for the failure of such appeals. The idea of a reforming council was a weapon which could be used against the papacy by the secular governments in an effort to achieve purely political aims. This misappropriation of the conciliar purposes, of which the French action in 1511 is an example, did much to discredit the movement for organized reforming activity in the decades before the Reformation. The persistence of these efforts furnished the background for the Tridentine reforms of the Catholic Church and their failures and compromises are among the conditions which determined the success of Protestantism.[10]

To the tradition advocating reform on the basis of rational conviction,

[10] H. Jedin, *Geschichte des Konzils von Trient*, Vol. I (Freiburg im Breisgau, 1949), 1–93.

in the hope of improving the Christian church and society and bringing a little nearer the realization on earth of the Heavenly City, was added an expectation of change derived from more mystical sources. Joachimite prophecies and the predictions of the Spiritual Franciscans had long provided a basis for expecting apocalyptic changes. In the second half of the fifteenth century the very defeat of what might be called the "constitutional" program for reform served to throw more emphasis on hopes that were based entirely on faith. To the moderate reformer there succeeded the spiritual revolutionary, whose strength lay in the identification of his program with the will of God.

The relationship between this medieval current of reforming activity and the conditions that determined its success or failure can perhaps best be illustrated by considering the career of one of the most famous reformers of the period, a man who devoted himself to the cause of purifying the church. Savonarola was excommunicated by the pope and was hanged and burned by his opponents with the connivance of the church. In controlling the religious and political life of the republic of Florence for a period of four years, which began and ended in revolution, he was attempting to realize ideals inherited from the Christian past.

Savonarola was born in Ferrara in 1452, the son of a family who served the Este. From an early age he had a strong religious vocation and a preoccupation with the spiritual life. He had also conceived a distaste for the kind of life represented at a Renaissance court, as he had had opportunity to view it at Ferrara. These impulses finally led to his flight from his family to a Dominican monastery in Bologna. In the strict observance of this establishment Savonarola found a refuge, and there he devoted himself to a career of study and meditation. Not unlike many other prophets and reformers, his active career was preceded by such a period of withdrawal and meditation. When he had completed his studies he appeared as a preacher dedicated to the mission of acting in the name of God to correct the evils he saw around him in the church and in society.

At first his preaching was not a success. In his native city he was unhonored and at Florence, where he went to preach in 1481, his sermons were thought to be too coarse and too lacking in polish. For a time he retired to smaller places, where he developed his own style and appeal, particularly making use of prophetic denunciations. He began to achieve a reputation as a prophet of doom, calling on men to mend their ways. At the same time he distinguished himself as an able administrator in the affairs of his order.

With this reputation he was called to Florence in 1490 by the intervention of Pico della Mirandola, who persuaded Lorenzo de' Medici to offer him the priorate of the Dominican convent of San Marco, which was in the gift of the Medici family. This time his success was immediate. He began his preaching in the cloisters of the monastery, then moved to the monastery church, and finally to the cathedral itself as his fame spread and his audiences grew. The prophetic vein grew stronger and stronger. He proclaimed that the church would be punished and purified at the hands of an avenger, and that the crisis was at hand. His personality and the force of his message combined to give him an extraordinary degree of influence both within the Medicean circle and with the Florentine public at large.

When the army of Charles VIII crossed the Alps in 1494 the prophecies of Savonarola appeared to be vindicated. A time of chaos and confusion was indeed at hand. The French king was hailed by Savonarola as the savior sent to purify the church. The Medici were expelled from Florence, and in the ensuing conflict between democratic and oligarchic ideas of constitutional development, Savonarola emerged as the spokesman of the popular party and the leading political figure. Under his influence was introduced the great council, modeled on the Venetian constitution, which was, as we have seen, widely admired as incarnating the ideal of a mixed constitution and providing for the maximum degree of stability.

Savonarola's practical political dictatorship within the framework of this constitution provided him with the opportunity to realize his religious ideals. The next four years were to show how uncomfortable the rule of a saint could be. The Kingdom of Christ was proclaimed in Florence, but Savonarola's highest aim was directed not only to achievement of the rule of perfection in the Florentine republic, but also in Italy and in Christendom as a whole. The program involved radical reforms of the papacy and the curia, against which increasingly violent denunciations were directed. It was Savonarola's hope that Charles VIII would prove the political savior under whose auspices the work of reform could be carried through. We have the series of letters and appeals directed to the French king, which recall the tone of the letters of Dante to Emperor Henry VII. In the end Charles VIII proved an even more feeble instrument for the salvation of Italy and the church than had the German emperor of two centuries earlier.

Savonarola's ecumenical program was matched by an intensified effort to direct every aspect of Florentine life. His sermons contained bitter denunciations of luxury and vice, in the tradition of medieval preaching. He painted a highly colored picture of the evils of Florentine society. Bands of young people were organized to go about the city collecting the symbols of vanity and evil living, with a view to their destruction. The results of these inquests were committed to the famous bonfires of vanities in 1497 and 1498.

It was inevitable that this powerful but individual movement for reform should collide with the interests and policies of the papacy. Savonarola's appeals naturally had little effect on Alexander VI, who took little notice of him until it appeared that the reform program might be linked with an opposition to the political ambitions of the papacy. In spite of Savonarola's bitter denunciations of Alexander VI, their relations were not at first entirely hostile. After the murder of the pope's son, for example, Savonarola wrote him a letter of condolence, in which he mingled sympathy with an exhortation to reform, based on the hope that the personal blow suffered by the pope would lead to his conversion. The hope was of course disappointed and, as Savonarola persisted both in his inconvenient religious zeal and in his alliance with the French, the pope proceeded to take strong measures to suppress the friar. Attempts to have Savonarola ordered away from Florence were followed by excommunication.

At the same time that papal pressure against him was increasing, Savonarola's political position in Florence became dangerous. Although his whole career as the dictator of the city lasted for only four years, one of the most remarkable things about him was that he was able to maintain even for so long the intensity of his hold over the Florentine populace. The later Middle Ages had seen many occasions when a powerful preacher was able to transform the moral life of a community for a brief period, but no one had been able to sustain such an influence so long as Savonarola and especially over a community of the size and character of Florence. In the end, however, even his hold weakened and factions in the city, hostile to the friar, succeeded in bringing about his ruin. The ancient rivalry between Franciscans and Dominicans was used to provide a test of Savonarola's miraculous powers. The extraordinary scene in 1498, when the city assembled to see re-enacted an attempt to invoke a judgment by God, ended in the discredit of Savonarola and his supporters. He was seized and tried by the municipal court acting in conjunction with the papal legate. During the trial he was tortured, confessed, subsequently retracted, and was finally burnt at the stake.

The period of Savonarola's career as a reformer, thus brought to an end, covered hardly more than four years. His fanatical sermons and letters as well as his religious poetry and treatises remained to have a considerable influence in sixteenth-century Spain and Italy. But as a reform effort, as an attempt to purify the church, this episode had been a failure and nothing was left but the strong impression Savonarola had made upon his contemporaries, to which many of the greatest minds of his generation left testimony.

The failure of Savonarola's reforming effort illuminates the essential conditions surrounding the realization of such ideals at the beginning of the sixteenth century. His appeal was essentially in the medieval tradition. It made no compromise with the new learning and the new philosophy and it made no successful use of the new political forces. His exhortations to Charles VIII harked back to the earlier expectation that a savior would appear armed to reform the church, not looking to the actual use which might be made of the power of secular government within the bounds of a national kingdom.[11]

It seems clear, at least in retrospect, that no reform program was likely to succeed unless it made certain compromises with contemporary ideas and institutions. The extent to which such compromises were possible, whilst still keeping the old framework, was the great question that faced the dawning sixteenth century. Many of those all over Europe who had at heart the reform of church and society, and who were desperately seeking new religious certitudes, were willing to go far in attempting to combine in a new synthesis the new learning and the inherited Christian tradition. There was a moment of great optimism associated with the ideals of the Christian humanists. But before we can understand these ideals and the reasons they in turn were doomed to failure we must attempt to describe the achievements of scholarship and philosophy in the second half of the fifteenth century, achievements that profoundly changed both the intellectual and the spiritual horizon. Where Savonarola's attack was entirely negative in the sense that it was prompted by the attack on traditional abuses, the hopes of the humanists were fixed more positively on the possibility of including in their reforming program the results of the intellectual achievements of the fifteenth century.

[11] G. Schnitzer, *Savonarola*, Ital. Translation (Milan, 1931).

Chapter Seven

SCHOLARSHIP AND PHILOSOPHY

I. MANUSCRIPTS AND LIBRARIES

THE positive religious ideals that were often linked with the protest against abuses in the church were only in part the heritage of the reforming tradition as it was exemplified in programs like that of Savonarola. At the beginning of the sixteenth century such ideals had been far more often shaped by the rapid intellectual changes of the preceding period and especially by the growth in the knowledge of antiquity. Before considering the reform program of humanism we must therefore give some account of the scholarship on which it was based.

The greatest age of discovery of manuscripts in the west had preceded the fall of Constantinople. The generation of Poggio, Niccoli and Nicholas of Cusa had brought to light the most important lost works of Latin antiquity and nothing quite like the experience of this age was to be seen again. But if the most important discoveries were over, the process of research was carried on in a more systematic and organized way and important finds were still made. Nicholas V and his successors subsidized attempts to find the lost decades of Livy in places as remote as Denmark and Crete. Humanists like Decembrio, Valla, Politian, Merula and others made investigations in the various great monastic establishments in Italy and Spain. Particularly rich finds were made at Bobbio at the end of the century. The discovery of the Medicean manuscripts of Tacitus and the printing of the *editio princeps* in 1515 gave increasing popularity to the influence of Tacitus over Livy, who had been so favored by the earlier generation of humanists. Thus Tacitus, the resigned historian of imperial corruption, fittingly attained his greatest influence at the very moment when the Italian states were coming under increasingly despotic foreign control.[1]

Research for manuscripts in the west was matched by continuing efforts to acquire copies of Greek authors from the wreck of the Byzantine

---

[1] R. Sabbadini, *Le scoperte dei codici Latini e Greci*, Vol. II (Florence, 1914). See also G. Toffanin, *Machiavelli e il "Tacitismo"* (Padua, 1921).

world. The enthusiasm for Greek in the world of Italian scholarship had begun long before the fall of Constantinople and it is as certain as anything can be that if the Turks had never taken the remains of the Greek Empire, the cultural exchanges which had begun with the west would have continued and grown. The point had been reached where agents and collectors of manuscripts would have been sent and Greek teachers would have been imported into Italy regardless of who ruled in Constantinople. The fall of the city did stimulate an already developed interchange, and a large number of manuscripts were brought to Italy by refugees and émigrés. Cardinal Bessarion, who had adhered to the Roman Church after the council of Florence, made it one of his principal aims to acquire the largest possible library of Greek manuscripts, and his deputies were sent to many places throughout the Mediterranean world. The famous refugee scholar, John Lascaris, made two expeditions to the east for the Medici, returning from the second in 1492 with over two hundred Greek manuscripts.

Such efforts were sustained by an enthusiasm for the increase in knowledge about classical civilization which for the extent of its appeal has had few parallels in the history of Europe. The new learning was taken up by kings and princes and its findings were communicated to an ever widening circle of the educated public. Had there been newspapers at the beginning of the sixteenth century we can imagine that the achievements of classical scholarship would have been reported on their front pages in much the same way as the advances of contemporary science are noticed today. Some idea of the quality of this enthusiasm was communicated in the letter which a young Italian humanist leader wrote to a friend from Paris, where he had gone to lecture and to spread the gospel of the new enlightenment. On the thirtieth of July, 1511, he wrote:

I began to lecture on Ausonius. You know how impatiently these lectures were awaited. There was such a crowd that the portico and the two courts of the college could not contain it. And what a distinguished audience. Receivers general, counsellors, king's advocates, rectors, theologians, jurists, heads of colleges, professors of every faculty, the number is estimated at more than two thousand. Never before either in Italy or in France have I seen a more august or a more numerous assembly of educated men. As I had more or less foreseen this I had prepared a discourse of some merit. I know this by the fact that though the lecture lasted two hours and a half, and the heat was suffocating, none betrayed the least weariness. Indeed when I had finished my peroration, they remained in their places as if expecting something more.[2]

[2] J. Paquier, *Jerome Aleandre* (Paris, 1900), 50–51.

This account may well be said to reveal more about the humanist than it does about his audience. The complacency and self-assurance were particularly characteristic. Yet there is independent testimony to the excitement created by Aleander's lectures and this incident could be matched by hundreds of others. If there should be matter for surprise in the fact that a discourse of such length on a third-rate ancient author could create such a sensation, we must remember that the popular appeal of humanist scholarship lay less in its content than in its method. Here was a new way of looking at literature, at history and at the world. It seemed to convey to its practititioners a heightened sense of vividness and reality. Absorption in the new ways of studying antiquity was far from monopolizing the contemporary attention of the learned world. The picture would be false if we forgot that side by side with an Aleander lecturing on Ausonius the professors of scholastic philosophy and theology continued their analysis of Aristotle and Aquinas. Yet every age has its intellectual fashions and the learning which captured the attention of the literate public was the kind of humanism Aleander and his like represented. The continuous growth of this enthusiasm for ancient texts stimulated the search for manuscripts and impelled princes and wealthy individuals to become collectors and to establish libraries.

Many of the great libraries of Europe thus came into being in the fifteenth century. Not only scholars like Pico della Mirandola and Cardinal Bessarion and princely patrons like the Medici and the dukes of Urbino, but even the distant kings of Hungary and Poland were affected by the desire to accumulate treasures of literature and learning. In the space of a hundred years the number of considerable libraries in western Europe was at least doubled.[3]

The majority of the new collections were to be found in Italy and among the most celebrated was the Vatican, the pre-eminence of which began to date from the pontificate of Nicholas V. This pope employed a great number of scholars and collectors, with the ambition of making the Vatican collection unique. Despite the fact that many of the volumes assembled during his pontificate were afterward dispersed, the work he subsidized remained the nucleus of the great papal collection.[4]

Other patrons achieved results of almost equal importance. Cardinal Bessarion in 1470 bequeathed his library to the republic of Venice, where

[3] Pearl Kibre, "Intellectual Interests as Reflected in the Libraries of the Fourteenth and Fifteenth Centuries," *Journal of the History of Ideas*, VII (June 1946), 257 ff.

[4] E. Müntz, *La Bibliothèque du Vatican au XVe siècle d'après des documents inédits, contributions pour servir à l'histoire de l'humanisme* (Paris, 1887).

it became the center of the Marcian collection. In Florence the library subsequently named the Laurentian had been built up by the activities of Cosimo de' Medici and his grandson Lorenzo. These famous Italian libraries have remained largely intact, but others equally celebrated both in Italy and north of the Alps were subsequently widely dispersed. Pico della Mirandola, for example, had a library matched by few of his contemporaries, and north of the Alps the Hungarian king, Mathias Corvinus, had made a similarly impressive collection. In France the beginnings of the royal library may be dated from the reign of Francis I, when Fontainebleau was enriched with the spoils of the Visconti-Sforza library from Milan.

Insofar as the catalogues of these libraries remain or can be reconstructed, they give us an interesting index of the intellectual interests of the period. The most noticeable change in late fifteenth-century libraries, as opposed to earlier collections, was of course the increase in the number of Greek texts. The library of Eugenius IV in the first part of the fifteenth century contained 340 books, of which only three were in Greek, but by the time Nicholas V died in 1455 there were in the Vatican Library almost twelve hundred volumes of which between three and four hundred, or roughly a third, were in Greek. This proportion was maintained, and in the pontificate of Sixtus IV, in a catalogue of 1484, we have over a thousand volumes in Greek out of a total of 3,600. The Laurentian Library in Florence and the Marcian in Venice reflected a similar growth in the number of Greek manuscripts. During the fifteenth century, however, this phenomenal increase in the available Greek texts remained largely confined to the Italian peninsula.

Less marked, but in some ways of almost equal significance, was the increase in the number of Hebrew texts in Christian libraries. Pico della Mirandola, the foremost Christian Hebrew scholar of his time, had more than a hundred Hebrew manuscripts in his library, and Federigo, the famous duke of Urbino, had almost as many. The papacy had collected Hebrew manuscripts at a very early period, and there were said to have been 120 in the library of Urban V at Avignon. The northern Hebrew collections, like the Greek, lagged behind the Italian at the beginning of the sixteenth century. Reuchlin, who was a greater Hebraist than his master, Pico, had only thirty-six Hebrew manuscripts in his library.[5]

The new resources represented by the collections of Greek and

[5] Pearl Kibre, *op. cit.;* see also the same author's *The Library of Pico della Mirandola* (New York, 1936).

Hebrew manuscripts did not displace those works which enshrined the traditional culture of the Latin Christian world. The catalogue of the books of Cosimo and Lorenzo de' Medici recently exhibited at Florence, on the occasion of the fifth centenary of the birth of Lorenzo, is in this respect a revealing document.[6] The number of patristic and biblical texts was still greater than the Greek or Roman. Among the oldest and most valuable books in the library we find listed a ninth-century and a tenth-century manuscript of the Evangel in Greek, a Greek Bible, the works of St. John Chrysostom, Eusebius, St. Gregory Nazianzen, Clement of Alexandria, Dionysius the Areopagite, Orosius, Boethius, a Psalter, St. Paul's Epistles, St. Augustine and a collection of the lives of the saints. Such a list, matched with the Aristotles, Plutarchs, Homers, Vergils and Ovids, hardly indicates the sense of a conscious opposition between a "pagan" and a "Christian" past and between sacred and profane studies which has seemed to many a characteristic feature of the period.

It is a noteworthy fact that the libraries of the great age of humanist scholarship were almost entirely formed by princes and private persons and that the great universities took a very small part in collecting the essential documents for the study of antiquity. Whereas the intellectual achievements of the Middle Ages were the product of work within the walls of a university, the center of research now shifted to the patron's library. This enlargement and secularization of the area of scholarly activity was further accelerated by the development of the printing press and the growth of a lay reading public. The aristocratic libraries had to share with the printing establishments the function of laboratories of the most significant research the age was accomplishing.

II. THE DEVELOPMENT OF PRINTING

The invention and development of printing with movable types brought about the most radical transformation in the conditions of intellectual life in the history of western civilization. It opened new horizons in education and in the communication of ideas. Its effects were sooner or later felt in every department of human activity.

There are very few scholarly subjects which have been more debated than the story of the beginnings of this transformation. In an age inclined to emphasize process rather than the single event and the social setting rather than the contribution of the individual, the figure of Gutenberg

[6] Catalogue, *Mostra della Biblioteca di Lorenzo nella Biblioteca medicea Laurenziana* (Florence, 1949).

has diminished in importance. Attention has been rightly turned from the drama and legend of the poor printer of Mainz to the general conditions of the fifteenth century that permitted the development of typography.

Among such conditions one of the first in importance was the growth of a secular reading public. If the ability to read had remained a prerogative of the clergy it is doubtful that any technical innovation would have been adopted, or applied even if it had been made. The very fact that the printing process spread so rapidly poses the same kind of problem already discussed in connection with the process of exploration and discovery. From the point of view of the general historian it has been proved again and again that the individual achievements of technology are far less important than the preparation of the environment in which they occur. Just as the Chinese had performed greater feats of navigation than the Europeans in the fifteenth century and yet their voyages had remained without effect, so also in the case of printing the Chinese had had for centuries paper and the art of printing on it with wooden blocks; yet they had never developed the technique of book-printing for mass production.

The social and economic evolution which made it possible for larger groups of people to be interested in reading also provided accumulations of capital in amount sufficiently large and widely distributed to set up printing establishments. These, as has already been shown, required a considerable investment. Here again the property structure of European civilization, including both the distribution of wealth and the sanctions against government, were of decisive importance. The rapidity with which printing spread over Europe depended upon the incentives to individual initiative.

In addition to these general factors the state of technology too had reached a point where advances were possible. The art of making paper, originally invented in China, had been carried to Europe in the Middle Ages by the Arabs. As early as the thirteenth century paper was produced in Italy and southern France. Printing with inks from wooden blocks, also long known in the east, had developed in Europe with the arrival of paper. From this basic technology, the step to printing with movable types was gradually taken in the fifteenth century.

Block-printing had been used as a device for illustrating devotional books and it had soon become a natural addition to cut a short inscription explaining the illustration. From the short inscription it was again a natural step to cutting a whole page of text which could be reproduced indefinitely. Looking back it seems obvious that the idea of cutting up such blocks into movable type must have occurred to many workmen almost simultaneously. As a block-carver labored over a single letter in his page of type he must have thought with regret of the amount of time it had taken him to cut the same letter on another page the day before. Various experiments with interchangeable letters led to the discovery of metal types.[7] It is here that Gutenberg's innovations were probably of critical importance. Without going into all the controversial detail that has surrounded his career and his achievement, it seems today to be a conclusion accepted by students of the subject that sometime between 1440 and 1450 the critical step was taken in the process of improving the casting of type which made possible the assembling of fonts in sufficient quantity to undertake printing on a large scale.

From the earliest work at Mainz—the fragments of an astronomical calendar, the "Last Judgment" fragment, the indulgences of 1454 and 1455, the Gutenberg Bibles and the Psalter of 1457—the art of printing spread very rapidly across western Europe. Workers from Germany in most cases introduced the process in other countries. By the end of the century there were seventy-three presses in Italy, fifty-one in Germany, thirty-nine in France, twenty-four in Spain, fifteen in the Low Countries and eight in Switzerland. Such a rapid growth in the space of fifty years, in an age when the growth of technological innovation was not nearly so rapid as it is today, is testimony to the prepared state of the general environment.

In spite of the fact that the collectors of manuscripts and the aristo-cratic humanist scholars at first rejected the printed books as vulgar, most of these presses rapidly became workshops of scholarship and some of them were among the greatest centers of the new learning. The press of Aldus Manutius in Venice undertook the printing of the Greek classics and was conducted with a sense of dedication to a mission. "If you have to speak to Aldus be quick about it because time presses," was the motto said to have been installed by Aldus himself. Aided by Greek refugees and by some of the greatest of western scholars—with whom for a time Erasmus was associated—the work of publishing the recovered Greek classics went forward with incredible activity. The Aldine press remained the outstanding example, but other printing offices too united the work of

---

[7] Pierce Butler, *Origins of Printing in Europe* (Chicago, 1940), and D. McMurtie, *The Book* (New York, 1937), 101–96.

the printer and the scholar. The sense of vitality and enthusiasm that had waned in the traditional lecturing of the universities now blossomed over the making of books by the new process, where typesetter and corrector bent over the sheets as they came from the press.

The printed page was the first of those media of mass communication which have finally grown to the point where they dominate our lives. The anonymous appeal directed more to emotion than to reason became possible. The printed broadside became a weapon of political activity and played its first great part in the spread of the Reformation.

Great masses of people were given for the first time an opportunity for vicarious participation in far larger areas of activity. The horizon was potentially widened for all, but the question may also be raised whether some qualities of experience were not also lost in the process. Mr. Mumford has pointed out that what was true in print came to be equated to what was true in reality.[8] Already before the sixteenth century was over there were educators who found it necessary to argue for more pictures in children's primers so that the importance of the visual image should be restored. In all the legal relationships which knit together individuals and groups, public and private concerns, the written and presently the printed document came to be more important than unwritten custom. European society was moving toward a capitalist order and some of its new needs were served directly by the printed word. In print it was easier to keep a strict account of time and money, and the wider dissemination of the clock also paralleled the spread of the written word.

At the beginning of the sixteenth century, however, none of these more general aspects was so important as the effect of the new invention on scholarship. In spite of the fact that the older generation tended to look with scorn on the production of the printed book as a vulgarity and a threat to the artistic and economic value of their manuscripts, scholars of all types soon adjusted themselves to the new possibilities. To apprehend how much this was true we have only to remember that the career of an Erasmus would have been impossible without the standardization and wide dissemination of the printed page. The mere fact that a single emendation by a great scholar could now be circulated in thousands of copies without the danger of a copyist's error signified a complete revolution in the conditions of activity of the learned world.

Thus, although the implications of printing were in the long run of critical importance for propaganda and for educational theory and practice

[8] L. Mumford, *Technics and Civilization* (New York, 1936).

in a capitalist society, its first revolutionary results were felt in the world of scholarship where a great impetus was given to the wide dissemination of accurate knowledge of the sources of western thought, classical and Christian.

One of the principal results of the activity of scholars and printers was the rapid increase in the knowledge of Greek literature and philosophy. In the general expansion of the intellectual horizon Greek studies occupied the most important place. In the several centers of which Rome, Venice and Florence were the most important, the great texts of Greek thought were edited, published, translated and commented.

At the Vatican in the mid-century Nicholas V presided over the great project of translating a large part of the corpus of Greek literature. In this effort the Greek exiles of the second generation played an important part. George Trapezuntios translated a large part of Aristotle and the *Laws* of Plato. Theodore of Gaza and Cardinal Bessarion translated other treatises of Aristotle, and Gregorio of Città de Castello translated the *Nichomachean* and *Eudemean Ethics*. This work was, however, far from limited to the refugees from the east. Italian scholars, who had by now mastered the Greek language, co-operated with the Greeks: Leonardo Bruni translated Aristotle; Lorenzo Valla, Thucydides; Perotti, Polybius; Poggio, Diodorus Siculus; Guarino da Verona, Strabo; and Piero Candido Decembrio, Appian. Well might Nicholas V say of himself: "In all things I have been liberal: in building, in the purchase of books, in the constant transcription of Greek and Latin manuscripts and in the rewarding of learned men." [9]

Many of the works which had been translated at Rome were published in the Greek text for the first time at the Aldine press in Venice. The fundamental labor of printing correct editions of the Greek classics was undertaken by Aldus Manutius and the scholars whom he gathered around him in the Venetian Academy. Nearly half of this group were exiled Greeks, and it was due to their assistance that Aldus was able to accomplish his great work in so short a time. When he died in 1515 not a single major Greek author remained unprinted. In the twenty-one years between 1494 and 1515 no less than twenty-seven *editiones principes* of Greek authors and Greek works of reference had been produced.

[9] L. Pastor, *History of the Popes*, Vol. II, 165–214.

Upon these achievements northern scholars could draw to spread Greek learning in the north.[10]

Of all the aspects of the Greek revival the one which had the greatest influence on contemporary intellectual history was the interest in Plato, which in the fifteenth century centered in Florence. Here the Greek envoy and teacher, Manuel Chrysoloras, had translated the *Republic* at the beginning of the fifteenth century. His work had been continued by the secretary of state, Leonardo Bruni, and others. Here also Giovanni Aurispa in the thirties had brought back among the manuscripts he had collected in Constantinople the Greek texts of the whole Platonic corpus. And most important of all, at the council of Florence the aged scholar, Gemisthos Pletho, had kindled an enthusiasm for the study of the Platonic dialogues and initiated a controversy between the followers of Plato and those of Aristotle which continued throughout the century and served to crystallize the philosophic currents of the age.

It was in this atmosphere that Cosimo de' Medici, following the fashionable interests of the learned world, gave his support to Platonic studies. Marsilio Ficino was a young man in his early twenties when he first came into contact with the ruler of Florence. The son of one of the Medici doctors, he had studied in the grammar schools and at the University of Florence, and perhaps also at Bologna. Like many other young scholars, he had begun the study of Greek, in which there was now no lack of regular instruction, so that he might study the heritage of ancient thought in the original. Cosimo de' Medici was favorably impressed with his promise and in 1462 furnished him with a villa at Careggi, a library, and an income, on the understanding that he would devote his life to the study of Platonic philosophy. Thus began the Florentine Platonic Academy which was to have such a pervasive and subtle influence on the artistic, literary, and spiritual life of the succeeding generations.

Ficino first occupied himself with translations from the Greek to the Latin. Among his earliest significant works was the translation in 1463 of the *Corpus hermeticum,* by which it was assumed the wisdom of ancient Egypt lying behind the Greek tradition was made available. This was followed by concentrated work on the Platonic dialogues. By the time Cosimo died in 1464 ten dialogues were finished and the rest were completed by 1468. Ficino then turned to commentary and to the exposition of his own philosophy. The *Theologia Platonica* was finished in 1474 and was followed by the treatise, *De Christiana religione.* In his later years

[10] J. Sandys, *A History of Classical Scholarship* (3rd ed., Cambridge, 1921), Vol. II.

he resumed translating various neo-Platonic sources such as Porphyry, Proclus and Dionysius the Areopagite. The life work of one man thus provided for Latin civilization a direct knowledge of the texts of some of the most important works in the heritage of classicism and Christianity.[11]

The influence of Ficino's work on the cultivated circles of Florence, Italy, and even Europe, was exercised without the benefit of an institutional setting. The name of "Academy" in fact implies a more formal organization than ever existed. Ficino did no regular teaching or lecturing. He did give discourses from time to time to large audiences in Florence and frequently entertained the intimates of his circle at Careggi with banquets and symposia. The Academy in fact consisted simply of the group who met at Careggi and who were united in their devotion to Plato and his interpreter. By personal influence of this kind, Ficino's doctrines, in spite of the lack of a formal school and the absence of notable successors, were spread to artists, poets, moralists, and religious reformers.

One of the fundamental and most characteristic doctrines of the Platonic Academy at Florence was the emphasis on the traditional hierarchical principle in metaphysics. In Ficino's interpretation of this principle there were of course elements directly derived from Plotinus, but there was an even stronger reassertion of the medieval idea of a hierarchy of species ranging from the lowest order of being up to God. In the great series of creation man occupied a middle position. The human soul imprisoned in the body was condemned to melancholy and to a cloddish existence until impelled by the will; the intellectual had the duty to try to apprehend higher things and so to ascend toward that union with the divine which was the true end of man. In this process love was the operative force, not reason, for Ficino believed that the human intellect was powerless when confronted by subjects which transcended its scope. "We are united," Ficino wrote,

more closely with God through the joy of love, which transforms us into the beloved God, than through knowledge. . . . Furthermore, recognizing God, we contract His amplitude to the capacity and concept of our mind; but loving Him, we enlarge the mind to the immense amplitude of divine goodness. There, so to speak, we lower God to our level; here, we lift ourselves to God. For we know as far as we comprehend; but we love both what we see clearly

[11] P. O. Kristeller, *The Philosophy of Marsilio Ficino,* translated by V. Conant (New York, 1943).

and what we expect as the remainder of the divine goodness beyond our clear sight.[12]

In his general optimism, in his emphasis upon the freedom of the will and the possible glory of man, and in the development of a theory of love Ficino has been regarded as the formulator of a Renaissance philosophy. The earlier humanists had lacked a metaphysic. Their interests had been primarily in grammar, rhetoric, ethics and politics.[13] Science and philosophy they left to the Aristotelians and the despised scholastics. Through the work of Ficino the Platonic revival now provided humanism with a philosophy in terms of which many of its developing interests and activities could be justified and understood.

Yet it is a mistake to regard Ficino as marking a sharp break with the previous philosophic tradition. In recent years his true position has been much more appreciated and it has been pointed out that Ficino cannot properly be understood as simply reviving a Platonic and neo-Platonic philosophy which had lain dormant for centuries in the heritage of the west. In the first place, there is a direct continuity between the medieval Platonic tradition and the work of Ficino. His perceptions of Plato were quite as much conditioned by the interpretations of St. Augustine, Dionysius the Areopagite, the German mystics, and Nicholas of Cusa as by his direct study of new texts. In the second place, there was a considerable influence of Aristotle and the great scholastic tradition from St. Thomas. There is indeed a story that in his youth the figure who most influenced Ficino was St. Antoninus of Florence—who might be taken as the opposite of the archetype of the Renaissance man.

Thus the Platonic revival when it came gave a new emphasis and a new tone to religious thought and provided a wider horizon, but it did not represent a conspicuous change of direction. Ficino thought of Plato as belonging to a series of interpreters of the divine, beginning with Zoroaster and stretching on through Hermes Trismegistus and Pythagoras. All this ancient wisdom, of which Plato represented the culmination, only anticipated and confirmed Christianity. In various ways, indeed in more ways than could have been imagined a hundred years earlier—it was still believed that a single truth could be discerned by those who were sufficiently learned. The Platonic tradition was the major part of the Greek revival which reinforced men's understanding of the divine plan

---

[12] Ficino, *Opera omnia,* 663, cited in Kristeller, *op. cit.*
[13] P. O. Kristeller, "Humanism and Scholasticism in the Italian Renaissance," *Byzantion,* XVII, 1944–45, 346–74.

for the universe. And that understanding was at the same time further deepened by the exploration of the other great source of western thought, the Hebraic, equally an achievement of the scholarship of the fifteenth century.

IV. THE HEBREW REVIVAL

The knowledge of Hebrew among Latin Christians during the Middle Ages had been even slighter than the knowledge of Greek. Only a very few individuals ever attained mastery of the language and theirs were unique achievements without important cultural consequences. Nothing testifies more strongly to the isolation of Jewish culture in the midst of the European community than the fact that the whole Hebrew learned tradition remained a closed book to the Christians, the sources of whose own religion were nevertheless so closely connected with that tradition. The Jewish settlements in various European centers maintained an unbroken written and oral inheritance in spite of persecution and attempts at conversion. But this inheritance began to penetrate Christian thought only in the period before the Reformation, and the same fifteenth century that saw the revival of Greek studies saw also the development and expansion of Hebrew scholarship among Christians. In a sense there were interesting parallels between the two phenomena. The opportunity in both cases had existed all along. For centuries European merchants and travelers had been in touch with the Byzantine Empire, and colonies of Italian traders and administrators had been established in Constantinople and on the Black Sea. Yet all this intercourse resulted in no impetus to the study of the Greek language in Europe. Similarly in the case of Hebrew studies learned Jews had lived and taught in Frankfort, Toledo, Prague, and many other cities of the European world without European scholars being stimulated to learn Hebrew. Distances in space and time are far from being the only factors that prevent communication between cultural systems; the direction of intellectual interests is determined by conditions affecting the whole of society, which are often far beyond the consciousness of the scholar. The expanding intellectual horizon of the fifteenth century brought both Hebraism and Hellenism into clearer relationship with the contemporary European world.

The beginnings of Hebrew studies in this period were centered in Italy and Spain. In Rome, again at the court of Nicholas V, Gianozzo Manetti, who died in 1459, was distinguished for his knowledge of both Greek and Hebrew and for his zeal in the collection of Hebrew manuscripts. The famous monk, Ambrogio Traversari, also devoted himself to Hebrew studies among his other scholarly labors. Mention has already been made of the collections of Hebrew manuscripts assembled in the Vatican Library.

Spain had been a great medieval center of Jewish studies not only because of the Jewish community living there until the expulsion of 1492, but also because of the direct influence of Arabic philosophy on Hebrew exegetical and mystical works. Jewish Cabala as well as the Talmud became influential on Christian thinking in the latter half of the fifteenth century. The most famous element in the former, the Zohar, had been elaborated in Spain by Moses de Leon in the thirteenth century. Written in the form of a commentary on the Pentateuch, it was in reality a compilation of cabalistic theosophy. It included some portions of great antiquity and some of fairly recent addition. Central to its doctrine was the theory of emanations, by which was explained the relationship of a transcendent god to the world. The importance of love as against the intellect and the will was also emphasized. In all these doctrines there was a strong current of neo-Platonism which had entered them by means of the Arabic tradition. Hence there were remarkable similarities between the metaphysical and theological doctrines expounded by the Florentine neo-Platonists and those of the cabalistic literature, and the appeal of the latter to Christian thinkers when it began to be made available is partially explained by the extent to which it seemed to confirm presuppositions already held.[14]

Among the Christian Hebraists of the Renaissance none was more important nor more influential than Pico, the prince of Mirandola. This dazzling and enigmatic figure has seemed to many to summarize in his life and work the intellectual interests and enthusiasms of his age. Born in 1463, the heir of the princes of the little feudal principality of Mirandola, Pico was connected with half the ruling families of Italy. In addition to the advantages of his birth, fortune and good looks, he showed from his earliest years a precocious mind. The contemporary system of abuses allowed him to receive his first ecclesiastical appointment at the age of ten. The charge of lack of capacity at that early age was promptly refuted by the extent of the course of formal education upon which he embarked. Of all his contemporaries there were few who were exposed to quite so many educational influences. He attended many of the celebrated universities of Italy, especially Padua and Bologna, as well as Paris,

---

[14] J. Blau, *The Christian Interpretation of Cabala in the Renaissance* (New York, 1944).

which was still the capital of the scholastic world. At each center he stayed long enough to feel that he had exhausted what his masters had to give him, and then moved on in search of new truths and new methods. His curiosity was apparently insatiable, but it was matched by his ambition and assurance. When he was hardly twenty he conceived in Paris the idea of summarizing all human knowledge in a compendious *summa* in the medieval tradition, and decided to go to Rome to defend publicly the nine hundred theses into which he had compressed the philosophic wisdom of the ages. There he announced that he would dispute with all comers and generously issued an invitation to scholars to attend the disputation, promising to pay the expenses of those who came from a distance. The *Oration on the Dignity of Man* was written in Rome as an introduction to the nine hundred theses.

Unfortunately the ecclesiastical authorities were not impressed with his capacity as an encyclopedist. Pope Innocent VIII was disgusted with his presumption and caused an inquiry to be made into Pico's work to see whether it was heretical. At the end of this inquiry a small number of Pico's propositions were indeed declared heretical and others suspect. The number of those involved was no more than thirteen out of nine hundred. Nevertheless this was sufficient to interrupt the projected disputation. Pico wrote a hasty apology, but in order to avoid arrest and condemnation left Rome and took refuge in France. There he was eventually arrested at the instigation of the papal legate and put in the prison of Vincennes, just outside Paris. Influential friends arranged his escape and from Paris he went to Florence, where he was enthusiastically welcomed by Lorenzo de' Medici and the circle of the Platonic Academy.

The rest of Pico's short life was spent in Florence, where he quickly became the most celebrated member of the Academy. He devoted himself feverishly to scholarly activity. The exploration of the Greek and Hebrew philosophical traditions and their concordance with the Christian particularly engaged his attention. Under the direction of Savonarola, whom he had been instrumental in summoning to Florence, he began to lead a regular and devout Christian life. He was only thirty-two when he died of a fever in 1494 at the moment when Charles VIII and his invading army were about to enter the gates of Florence. His dramatic career was thus brought to an almost symbolic close.

Considering the shortness of Pico's life he left a remarkably large and varied body of work. All of it was written within a comparatively short space of time, which disposes of the argument that a series of "periods" is to be traced in his intellectual evolution. There is the commentary explaining the doctrines of the neo-Platonic cosmology, which was written in 1486, and there are the nine hundred theses or conclusions written for the dispute in Rome. Of these a large number were taken from medieval philosophers like St. Thomas and Albertus Magnus and many others from the Jewish Cabala, from Arabic writings and from the Hermetic corpus. In connection with these theses the *Dignity of Man* and the *Apology* were written. From the Florentine period there is the *Heptaplus*, an esoteric and learned commentary on the Book of Genesis with a sevenfold interpretation of the text. At the same time Pico wrote in Florence his metaphysical treatise on *The Being and the One*, which dealt with the relation of God to the created world. Finally, just before he died, he wrote a treatise on astrology.

Through all these works runs the great influence of Pico's Hebrew studies. He had acquired the beginnings of his interest in this language from Johann Alemanno and Elia del Medigo. Both these Jewish scholars had migrated from the Levant—Alemanno from Constantinople and Del Medigo from Crete. The latter taught at the University of Padua and supported Aristotelianism against the current fashionable Platonism. He was widely read in Arabic philosophy as well as being an authority on the Cabala. From such sources Pico derived his interest in Hebrew and his very eclecticism permitted the development of these interests side by side with the Christian, Platonic, and Arabic. In a sense he was only building on the methods developed by medieval scholasticism, but it was through him that a consciousness of Hebrew and particularly cabalistic thinking entered the western world. The other philosophic traditions had been familiar before or were being developed in the neo-Platonic school at Florence.

Pico's most celebrated pupil and the greatest Christian Hebraist of his generation was Johann Reuchlin. Reuchlin had already acquired a humanist education as well as a training in the law before his first Italian journey. This was undertaken in 1481 when he was at Rome and studied at the papal court. Nine years later he returned to Italy, this time to Florence, and it was then that he met Pico at Florence and became interested in Hebrew studies. He engaged Hebrew teachers and made rapid progress, the results of which were apparent in a work on the Cabala published in 1494. By the time he published the first Christian-Hebrew grammar in 1506 he had become the foremost authority in Europe on Jewish literature. His reputation had hardly been established when the whole subject of the relation of Hebrew thought to the Christian tradition came under violent discussion in Germany.

A converted Jew named Pfefferkorn had succeeded in acquiring from the Emperor Maximilian a mandate empowering him to supervise the destruction of such Jewish literature as was dangerous to Christianity. As he carried out his task Pfefferkorn had aroused some scandal by the violence of his proceedings and also by the suspicion that he was compounding with wealthy Jews and synagogues to make a fortune by exacting bribes to buy immunity from his persecution. Protests to the emperor brought about an appeal and the opinion of Reuchlin was sought as an authority on Hebrew. Reuchlin submitted a temperate argument in which he proposed that some few Hebrew books particularly condemnatory of Christianity be destroyed, but at the same time he pled for increasing the understanding of both the Talmud and the Cabala, and maintained that such understanding could only result in benefit to the Christian religion.

Reuchlin's recommendation, intended to be confidential, was released by Pfefferkorn, who argued against it in a violent pamphlet. Reuchlin of course replied and the controversy presently became one of great violence, as each of the protagonists found supporters. Pfefferkorn was defended especially by the Dominicans of Cologne, who felt they had a vested interest in the maintenance of his program. On the other hand, the representatives of the new learning flocked to the aid of Reuchlin. As a result the issue became a *cause célèbre* dividing the intellectual life of Germany and to some extent of all Europe. The most celebrated document produced by the controversy was the famous satire, *The Letters of Obscure Men,* which did so much to discredit the church and the older system of university instruction in Germany.[15]

The Reuchlin controversy was an extreme example of the disintegrating effect upon traditional modes of thought of a heightened consciousness of the Hebrew tradition. Although outbursts of anti-Semitism had been recurrent throughout the medieval period, Pfefferkorn's particular attempt to destroy Jewish literature was stimulated by the extent to which knowledge of Hebrew sacred books was penetrating Christian thinking. Against such reactions, however, must be put the positive contributions brought about by this knowledge. Like the revival of Greek, Hebrew scholarship introduced changes of decisive importance in the evolution of the Christian tradition. The sources of that tradition were now available

---

[15] F. G. Stokes, ed., *Epistolae obscurorum virorum* (London, 1909).

to an increasing number of trained scholars for textual examination in the original languages. The sense of revivification which accompanied the effort to interpret the original sources can hardly be overemphasized. Men felt that a new light had dawned. In spite of the fact that the sense of history was more acutely developed by philology and that the history of Christianity was therefore seen in greater perspective, the scholars who worked with the new tools felt themselves to be nearer the revealed word. At the same time an impulse was given toward a theory of natural religion. Ficino, Pico, Reuchlin and other explorers of diverse philosophical and religious experiences were convinced that behind apparent diversity lay unity and that the single truth was most perfectly expressed in Christianity. The assimilation of Greek and Hebrew learning could then in the long run only redound to the purification of Christianity. Scholarship had thus its practical uses in the service of the church. It was this conviction that underlay the hopes of the early sixteenth-century reformers and it was these ideals which inspired the Christian humanists.

V. BIBLICAL SCHOLARSHIP

The first landmark in the application of philological techniques to the understanding of biblical texts dates from the middle of the fifteenth century. The *Annotationes* of Lorenzo Valla were notes on the language of the Vulgate pointing out various errors, misunderstandings and doubtful translations from the Greek of the New Testament. This work was an attempt to apply to the fundamental texts of the Christian religion the same method for understanding which was already proving so succesful in eliciting the meaning of legal documents of the ancient world. Valla's work remained in manuscript but was found and published by Erasmus in 1505. Erasmus regarded himself as overwhelmingly indebted to the ideas and the method outlined in Valla's work and from it came the major inspiration for his own work on the New Testament, which he regarded as a continuation of his humanist predecessor's.

The first decade of the sixteenth century saw, besides the dedication of Erasmus to the task of producing an edition of the New Testament in the original Greek, a great effort of biblical scholarship in Spain under the direction of Cardinal Ximenes. The great scholarly achievement of the University of Alcala, founded by the cardinal in the first decades of the sixteenth century, was the Complutensian Polyglot. The Old and New Testaments were both printed with the original languages and the Vulgate in parallel columns, in order that difficulties in the interpretation of the Vulgate might be cleared up and errors corrected. A learned staff labored on this great work for many years. Manuscripts were sent from the Vatican and were acquired from many other sources. The New Testament was actually printed in 1514, two years before the *Novum instrumentum* of Erasmus, but its publication was delayed. To Erasmus the honor therefore remains of having given to the western world the first edition of the New Testament in Greek. The Complutensian Old Testament followed the New, and the whole was complete in 1522. It is one of the great monuments of scholarship and of printing skill in the first half of the sixteenth century.

It must be remembered, however, that the purpose of Ximenes was much more in line with the medieval tradition than it was with modern criticism. It is true that the preface to the first volume, outlining the scope and purpose of the work, stated that no translation can ever fully and exactly represent the original, and that it is necessary to go back to the sources of sacred writings. But it is clear that the whole work was designed to reinforce the authority of the Vulgate rather than to correct it. In the Old Testament the versions were arranged in parallel columns, with the Vulgate occupying the middle place between the Hebrew and the Septuagint. This arrangement was introduced with the remark made by Ximenes that it had been adopted because it symbolized the middle place occupied by the Church of Rome between the synagogue and the Greek church, like the position of Christ on the cross between two thieves. This reveals the spirit in which the critical work was approached. Far more scholarship in the sense of searching of manuscripts was bestowed on the Complutensian Polyglot than Erasmus was able to put on his edition of the Greek New Testament, but the Erasmian edition, although almost exactly contemporary, represents far more nearly the ideals of modern scholarship. Just as Ximenes intended his university to be a nursery of great men for the Spanish episcopate, so his Polyglot Bible was intended to strengthen the Roman tradition.

The *Novum instrumentum* of Erasmus, containing the introduction and text of the New Testament in Greek together with Erasmus' new Latin translation, was published in 1516. Erasmus had neither a perfect mastery of Greek nor a sufficient number of manuscripts to make this famous edition a critical one by modern standards. Nevertheless, it represents a landmark in the history of scholarship and a greater one than the Complutensian Polyglot because it raised questions about the authenticity of the Vulgate text.

By the eve of the Reformation, therefore, the European learned world had been supplied with editions and commentaries on the Old and New Testaments which represented the application to scripture of the humanist techniques. Upon this achievement rested the hopes of a whole generation for a purification and restoration of the Christian church.

VI. THE SENSE OF HISTORY

The common denominator between Greek and Hebrew scholarship was a new understanding of history. The development of a sense of perspective on the past, the ability to place oneself in time with respect to an age as a whole, the awareness of historic distance, all this was a contribution essentially of humanist thought. It was of course a contribution built on the Christian inheritance, which stressed the linear evolution in which the Incarnation was the most important event and the Last Judgment was the goal toward which society was tending. But in spite of this historic element in Christian thought the Middle Ages had singularly lacked a sense of the reality of time. Countless representations of biblical and classical scenes on manuscripts and portals testify to the fact that these distant events were thought to have happened only yesterday. The Flight into Egypt is the peasant family in the next village on their mule.

This tradition had a powerful hold on men's minds and indeed in many ways was not completely shaken off until the triumph of historicism in the nineteenth century. No popular representation today of imperial Rome or of Old Testament Judea such as Hollywood has from time to time given us would be attempted without all the apparatus that archeology and history, fake or real, could supply. But down through the eighteenth century popular audiences were not bothered by the fact that Greeks of the Age of Pericles appeared in the costumes of Versailles. Yet the attainment of a sense of distance in time and space which is one kind of reality has been accomplished at the sacrifice of another kind of reality. Today the process has gone so far that we feel self-conscious about trotting out characters dressed in historical costumes as if for a fancy-dress ball. Shakespeare in modern dress or St. Joan in modern talk may come with a greater shock of recognition.

At the beginning of the sixteenth century this sense of history, which was subsequently to triumph, was only beginning to be manifest in humanist thought. The tradition of the medieval chronicle continued in many forms. Whether such chronicles purported to give the history of a national group, a political entity, a city or a monastery, they began with the history of creation and pretended to universal scope. Among the most famous examples of this genre was the *Nürnberg Chronicle* of Hartmann von Schedel, published in 1493 and illustrated with woodcuts by Wohlgemut, the father-in-law of Dürer. Mixed with the realistic portrayal of German cities were representations of biblical events and wonderful prodigies. A work of this kind, still essentially medieval, exemplified the philosophy of history shared by the greatest number of the contemporaries of Columbus.

Side by side with these interpretations of the past, however, there appeared increasing numbers of direct personal accounts of contemporary episodes and experiences. The *Memoirs* of Commines remains perhaps the most famous example, but diaries such as those of Burchard, Infessura and Marino Sanudo belong in the same category. Personal, secular, limited to the life span of the individual, these accounts are at the opposite extreme from the world chronicle. To those who were concerned with a more remote past they opened possibilities of a more individualistic and realistic treatment.

In still another category was the formal humanist historiography modeled on ancient examples. The tradition which had begun in Italy with Bruni and Poggio was carried on in most of the Italian courts. Rucellai wrote his *History* of the invasion of Charles VIII, which Erasmus thought worthy to be compared with Sallust, and Polydore Vergil had begun as early as 1505 the collection of materials for his history of England which was finally published only in 1533. The chief contribution of the Italian school of humanists was to limit history to past politics and treat it as an autonomous area for study. The emphasis was upon the pedagogic value of history and upon the belief that the record of the past was in reality philosophy teaching by example. In many of the more formal humanist histories the chief figures were described as personifications of abstract and traditional virtues and vices, and this approach was replaced only in the sixteenth century with the more realistic observation of the age of Machiavelli and Guicciardini. Divine intervention and prodigies of all sorts might still be allowed—and even in some cases recommended—but the thread of political action could be followed by the interpretation of human motives.

Works of this kind were bound to raise by implication the question how far man controlled his own history. What areas in the past could be understood in terms of a secular understanding of men's behavior and so what could be learned from history? The question preoccupied the historical work of Machiavelli and Guicciardini and it frequently received a pessimistic answer. Yet in the long run these histories were written in the faith that men would learn from them. In the twenty-fifth chapter of *The Prince* Machiavelli considered how much fortune can do in human affairs and how it may be opposed. He felt that

fortune is the ruler of half our actions, but that she allows the other half or thereabouts to be governed by us. . . .

I would compare her to an impetuous river, that when turbulent, inundates the plains, casts down trees and buildings, removes the earth from this side and places it on the other, everyone flees before it and everything yields to its fury without being able to oppose it, and yet though it is of such a kind, still when it is quiet men can make provision against it by dykes and banks, so that when it rises it will either go into a canal, or its rush will not be so wild and dangerous. So it is with fortune. . . .[16]

If even the pessimistic Machiavelli could see that the study of the past might enable men to make this much provision for the future, the hopes of those who studied the distant classical and Christian pasts were still more comprehensive. Both antiquity and early Christianity were now seen as remote eras, but they could be known through the proper application of historical techniques and the fruit of the knowledge would be the restoration of the piety and learning that lay at the roots of western civilization.

[16] Machiavelli, *The Prince*, ch. 18.

Chapter Eight

THE PROGRAM OF CHRISTIAN HUMANISM

I. THE BASIC ASSUMPTIONS

THE movements for the reform of the church and society at the end of the fifteenth century were diverse in origin and character. Yet, viewed as a whole, they can be conveniently divided into two main types. There was in the first place the pietistic and mystic approach to the problem of ecclesiastical reform, inherited from the Middle Ages. This tradition emphasized the reliance on immediate divine guidance, the role of inspiration and the importance of the sanctified individual, whose extraordinary piety made manifest the operation of grace. In a corrupt society secular remedies were of no avail, only the indirect attack could be successful; the purification of society would be accomplished more by example than by precept, especially where the example was understood as the direct and immediate revelation of the divine plan, though exhortation and the imposition of discipline were not excluded. This conception of the nature of reform drew on the background of Franciscan and Dominican mysticism, on the piety of the Brotherhood of the Common Life, and in its more extreme aspects on the apocalyptic hopes of those heretics and prophets who had appeared outside the framework of orthodoxy in the late medieval church. The tradition was broad enough to include the mystic who withdrew from the world and the activist who applied his inspiration to a direct program for reforming abuses. From the point of view of their essential belief in the nature of man and his relation to God, individuals as various as Thomas à Kempis, Standonck and Savonarola can be grouped together.

The other principal category of reformers was inspired by the new scholarship and the new philosophy. They were above all distinguished by a belief in the power of the human intellect to bring about institutional and moral improvement. The new Greek and Hebrew learning, they held, could be productive only of good, even when it seemed at first glance farthest removed from the Christian tradition. The program of Christian humanism was built on a conviction of the importance of the rational faculties of man and it exalted the role of an intellectual aristocracy. It emphasized nature rather than grace, ethics rather than theology and action rather than contemplation.

The distinction between these two traditions does not imply that the European reform movement was sharply divided into two opposing camps which had no common meeting ground. If the contrast between an Erasmus and a Savonarola seems to reveal in a heightened form the differences between two approaches to the contemporary crisis in church and state, yet there were many in every European country who occupied an intermediate position. The reality behind the term "Christian humanist" covers a wide range of accommodation between Christian and classical ideals, but even the broadest interpretation of the humanist position cannot obscure the basic assumption which distinguished the generation of which Erasmus was the leader.

Among these intellectual reformers the results of assimilating the new learning had not yet reached the point of leading any to a conscious rejection of the Christian tradition. Much of what is commonly written and repeated about the paganism of even the Italian fifteenth-century humanists is misleading. There were some who moved in the direction of a theory of natural religion, and many who made a distinction between the observances of the uneducated and the beliefs of the intellectual aristocracy. But in an atmosphere still saturated with the forms, the thought and the daily ritual of Christianity it was impossible either to revive ancient paganism completely or to anticipate modern agnosticism. In whatever proportions the Christian, the classical and the Hebrew traditions were combined, the humanist of the age of Erasmus had as his most basic hope the more complete realization of the form of Christianity in which he believed.

The philosophical and theological position of this group rested on the acceptance of the natural world. In this respect their thought was not very different from the Thomistic solution of the problem of the relation between nature and grace. But if the compromise was fundamentally the same as that of the scholastics, the philosopher who inspired it was no longer Aristotle but Plato. Neo-Platonism was to the humanists what Aristotelianism had been to St. Thomas and his followers. It provided Christian humanism with a philosophy the influence of which was subtly and pervasively felt in many forms of thought and expression, including those far removed from metaphysical speculation.

Among the important implications of this disposition to come to terms with the natural world outside the boundaries defined by revelation was the more complete acceptance of the corpus of classical literature as containing nothing that was incompatible with Christianity. Greater learning could not corrupt; it would only purify. Erasmus, in a letter to the young Adolph of Veere, justified the study of even the most profane of classical authors, and in his edition of the works of St. Jerome discounted the story of the saint's dream about being beaten before the gates of Heaven for being a Ciceronian and not a Christian. If these arguments contained echoes of patristic and medieval justifications for the study of classical literature, yet they were now given a new emphasis and contained perhaps unconscious admissions of the growth of secular tastes.

All these assumptions found concrete expression in the theories of education of the Christian humanists. The nature of man, fundamentally good although corrupted by original sin, was capable of improvement by an intellectual discipline. Learning, whether sacred or profane, would increase piety. Indeed, this belief in the potentialities of educational reform was perhaps the most distinguishing characteristic of this school of reformers, marking them off most clearly from those whose hopes were committed to more revolutionary and more mystical ways of activity. In the minds of many of the humanists a new program of education was not only necessary; it was all that was necessary. Hence the multiplicity of treatises on the education of children, and the collections of precepts for those who were to occupy important positions in life. Today it may seem naïve to have held that peace, harmony and the fuller realization of a Christian society could be achieved by offering a new system of education. Yet these were the objectives in the mind of Erasmus when he wrote in the preface to the New Testament that he wanted every plowboy to be whistling the Psalms as he plowed his furrow. This was perhaps the first significant appearance of a hope which has recurred again and again in western thought and has remained one of the outstanding characteristics of the evolution of European civilization. It appeared in the early sixteenth century, in the Age of Enlightenment and again among those liberal utilitarians and devotees of progress in the nineteenth century who were the heirs of the Enlightenment. Each of these occasions was marked by an increasing broadening of the educational base; the humanist hopes were successively democratized.

So far these hopes have been disappointed in every age, but earlier deceptions have not prevented their recurrence in a new set of circumstances. For the humanists at the beginning of the sixteenth century there was, however, a particular brightness in the prospect for European civilization because there was no past history of disillusionment. Even a John Stuart Mill did not envisage that when the plowboy had learned to read he was more likely to read the Hearst papers than the Psalms, but the liberals of the nineteenth century had at least historical perspective on the experience of humanism and the enlightenment. The generation of Erasmus, on the other hand, could not have anticipated that their expectations would go down to disappointment in the wars of religion, as those of a later age were doomed by the wars of nationalism. There was thus a kind of innocence in this otherwise sophisticated group who represented an aristocracy of intellect, the first apostles of the salvation of society by the use of human reason.

This mood and these assumptions were shared in different ways and different degrees in all countries of European Christendom at the beginning of the sixteenth century. In spite of great differences in emphasis and divergent theological and philosophical interests, their common bond was an acceptance of the new learning and an attempt to apply it to the reform of church and state. In the short run their very willingness to build on and even to compromise with the results of humanism gave them a greater degree of success than was achieved by a Savonarola, but in the long run the Lutheran revolution was to prove that this kind of rationalism was not enough.

II. REFORM AND THE NEW LEARNING IN SPAIN

The earliest movement of ecclesiastical reform to achieve substantial success occurred in Spain during the reign of the Catholic kings. Its importance lay not only in what it revealed about the vitality of the Spanish religious tradition, springing from centuries of crusade against the Moors, but also in what it meant for the future. The resistance to Protestantism in Spain during the sixteenth century, as well as the character of the Counter Reformation, depended in part on the direction given to religious life and institutions during the reigns of Ferdinand and Isabella. The central figure in this reform movement was one of the most remarkable prelates of the age, Cardinal Ximenes de Cisneros, the confessor of Isabella, who combined the political interests of a Richelieu with the ascetic practices of a Franciscan monk.

Ximenes had been born of a noble family in 1436. After studying law and theology at the University of Salamanca he embarked on his ecclesiastical career by serving for some years at the papal curia in Rome as a consistorial advocate. Returning to Spain in 1465 his work at Rome was rewarded by the bestowal of an expectation to an important benefice. This papal provision was viewed with hostility by the local clergy in Spain, already prone to resist papal appointments to higher clerical positions, and Ximenes' first reward was worth a long legal controversy and a brief period of actual imprisonment. As soon as this matter was settled, however, he appeared to be embarked on the usual career of a Renaissance ecclesiastic. Benefices began to accumulate and he became vicar-general to a bishop.

At this moment one of those religious experiences still not uncommon in an increasingly secularized society changed the whole direction of his life. He decided that a career in the secular hierarchy would not bring him the spiritual reward which now seemed the most important of all goals and he accordingly joined the strict observants of the Franciscan order. Even the practices of this order were not at first sufficient to satisfy his need for asceticism and he presently withdrew into a still more solitary and hermetical existence.

From this isolation, which increased his reputation for sanctity and severity, he was finally recalled in 1492 to become the confessor of Queen Isabella. It was apparently with great and sincere reluctance that he accepted the active role now thrust upon him. His advancement was rapid. By 1494 he had become the provincial of the Franciscan order, and by 1495 archbishop of Toledo and primate of Spain. The cardinalate followed, and for the last two decades of his life Ximenes became the most powerful person in Spain, the chosen adviser of Ferdinand and Isabella, on occasion acting as regent. To his other titles he added that of grand inquisitor in 1508. He outlived both his sovereigns and died in 1517 as he journeyed to meet the young King Charles to give an account of his government.

One of the chief aims of Ximenes, as soon as he attained power, was the reform of the Spanish church. This program was developed in several directions.

In the first place there was the question of the reform of the regular orders. Here Ximenes adopted as a standard the rule of the Franciscan Observants and tried to force the laxer Conventuals to conform. At the same time pressure was exerted to require the regular canons of cathedral chapters to follow the oaths they had taken to lead a life in common, devoted to the service of the church. Among these chapters there had been some particularly wide departures from the original intent of the establishments. Wealthy canons were living lives indistinguishable from those of the upper classes of the laity and in no way fulfilling their responsibilities. In his attempts Ximenes was not entirely successful, but he did undoubtedly improve to a marked degree the standards of the orders and the canons regular. In insisting on the rule of the Franciscan Observants he not only alienated the Franciscan Conventuals but also provided a basis for nourishing the historic rivalry with the Dominicans, who had themselves embarked on a scheme of reform. Also, the extreme severity on which he insisted alienated many cathedral chapters. Nevertheless, this aspect of Ximenes' reforming work was of central importance in preserving the vitality of the Spanish church at a time when in other countries, such as England, very little of the same effort was being exerted, at least from within the hierarchy.

Much more immediately successful was the attempt to raise the level of the Spanish episcopate. This was the aspect of Ximenes' program most affected by the results of the new learning and the Renaissance philosophy of education. The cardinal's chief purpose in the founding of the University of Alcala was the provision of trained candidates for the higher places in the Spanish church. The university consisted of a group of colleges, most of which were limited to a small number of students so that they would have the advantages of more intensive instruction. One college was to concentrate on theology, still the queen of the sciences; another was devoted to law and a third to the teaching of the three languages most important for the fundamental documents of the Christian tradition, Latin, Greek, and Hebrew. Professors were appointed for four-year terms and were paid largely by the students' fees. At the same time Ximenes made provision for retirement pensions, declaring that as long as he had given the professors lunch during their middle years he would like to give them a good dinner in their old age. The scholarship which emerged from this foundation is sufficiently attested by the Complutensian Polyglot, already noticed in an earlier chapter, as one of the landmarks of biblical scholarship which the age produced. The foundation became, as Ximenes intended it to be, the seminary of bishops for the Spanish church, and its training was largely responsible for the steady improvement in the character and standards of the episcopate. It was one of the leading examples in Europe of the way in which the new learning was adapted to the service of the church.

The Inquisition provided Ximenes with another institution through which the work of reform could be carried forward. Since all its tribunals were directly subject through the grand inquisitor to the control of the crown, it was the principal administrative channel through which Ximenes could extend his supervision of the church as a whole. As grand inquisitor, Ximenes issued a series of instructions combining the fervor and piety of a Savonarola with indications in the most minute detail on how the newly converted Moors and Jews were to conduct themselves. Some of the earlier rigidity associated with Torquemada was modified but on the whole Ximenes remained true to the spirit of the institution as it was founded.[1]

The work of Cardinal Ximenes thus embraced the whole range of religious life and ecclesiastical institutions in Spain. It is instructive to consider the basis of his success compared with that of his Italian contemporary, Savonarola. In character, aims, and achievement there was of course a great gulf between the two reformers. The one was excommunicated by the pope and hanged and burned by his opponents with the connivance of the church. The other was a cardinal, primate of Spain, and the closest adviser of the Spanish kings. The one controlled the religious and political destinies of Florence for four years which began and ended in revolution. The other directed the destinies of Spain for over twenty years without ever encountering serious opposition. Yet different as were their situations and their mental horizons, both men shared the same mystic experience and fundamental piety and were motivated by the same desire to purify the church, to make the imperfect institutions of this world correspond a little more closely to the City of God.

The contrast between the successes of Ximenes and the failures of Savonarola illuminates the essential conditions surrounding such reforming ideals at the end of the fifteenth century. Savonarola's appeal for reform was an essentially medieval appeal. It made no compromise either with the new learning or the new political forces. The summons to Charles VIII was couched in the same terms as the letters of Dante to Henry VII, and the emphasis was upon a moral reform rather than on intellectual effort assisted by the developing knowledge of Greek and Hebrew. The program of Ximenes, however, although equally inspired by tradition and mystic experience, and equally based on the framework of inherited dogma, was to a far greater extent adapted to contemporary political and intellectual realities. The new learning was introduced in the University of Alcala for the purpose of serving the old theology. And

---

[1] On Ximenes see Bataillon, *Erasme et l'Espagne* (Paris, 1937), ch. I.

reforms in discipline and morals were introduced by using the authority of the new Spanish monarchy.

It seems clear, at least in retrospect, that no reform program was likely to succeed unless it made with the present order the kind of compromises that were worked out in Spain. The extent to which such compromises were possible, whilst still keeping the old framework of ecclesiastical organization, was the great question that faced the dawning sixteenth century. Already in the case of Spain something of the old ecumenical ideal of European Christendom had been sacrificed. Ximenes may have looked ultimately to the purification of the church throughout its whole body, but in practice his work was confined to what was beginning to look very like a national church. Many of those all over Europe who had at heart the reform of church and society, and who were desperately seeking new religious certitudes, were willing to go even further than Ximenes in attempting to combine in a new synthesis the results of the new learning with the inherited Christian tradition. In those first years of the sixteenth century the range of combinations was more varied and the quality of hope more intense than was to be possible again for many years after the Lutheran revolution had begun.

III. ENGLAND: SIR THOMAS MORE AND HIS FRIENDS

The University of Alcala under the patronage of Cardinal Ximenes represented one of the greatest triumphs of the cause of the new learning in the service of the church. Yet its influence remained curiously isolated, and the educational methods of humanism penetrated but slightly the curricula of the medieval universities or the schools at a lower level. In England, by contrast, although there was no single establishment which embodied like Alcala the aims of the educational reformers, representatives of the new learning established themselves within Oxford and Cambridge and also reformulated the principles of secondary education. And as the movement was more widely diffused in England, so it aroused a greater hostility among the defenders of the scholastic tradition.

Among the earliest and more important of the innovators in education in England was John Colet, dean of St. Paul's and re-founder of St. Paul's School. Son of a family who had won substantial position and wealth in the City of London, he had received a higher education in the medieval tradition. He was particularly well grounded in mathematics and scholastic philosophy and in the rhetorical and grammatical courses, which included an emphasis on Cicero and Seneca. His slightly older contemporaries, Grocyn and Linacre, who had preceded him to Italy, may have taught him some rudimentary Greek and they certainly stimulated his enthusiasm for an Italian journey. When he went to Italy in 1493 he found his spiritual home in Florence and was profoundly influenced by the teaching of Pico and Ficino and the whole neo-Platonic philosophy. He returned to England with a sense of mission which included an emphasis on the importance of the direct study of the sources of Christianity and an enthusiasm for Platonic theology.

Directly after his return he began at Oxford the famous lectures on St. Paul's Epistle to the Romans. In interpreting Scripture Colet seems to have worked with a strange combination of rational criticism and mystic faith. He was not a philological critic and never had those doubts about the validity of the Vulgate text which were already disturbing some of his contemporaries. Nevertheless, he did believe in dealing directly with the text and not with commentaries. In the study of the Word, divine inspiration would illuminate difficulties and from such study there would accordingly emerge greater insight into essential meaning. Without denying the allegorical and other traditional interpretations of scriptural passages, Colet's method nevertheless changed the medieval emphasis by stressing the importance of the literal sense. This method brought to great numbers of people a new sense of immediacy and freshness in confronting the sacred texts. This new kind of knowledge, regarded by Colet and his friends as the product of the operation of divine grace rather than as the achievement of rational man, could only increase the sum of human virtue.[2]

If in his dependence on grace and his disposition to deny the natural world Colet was rather an Augustinian than a humanist, yet in his educational ideals he shared the hopes of many of his more secular-minded contemporaries. So strongly did he believe in education that he sacrificed a large part of his fortune to the founding of the School of St. Paul's and spent most of his life trying to realize the program which he was convinced would increase both Christian piety and humane learning. From the group of which Colet was the center there radiated a whole educational movement. He was able to convince not only many of his friends and followers but many patrons as well of the validity of the new approach. The humanistic foundations at Oxford and Cambridge date from this time. The new learning penetrated the old

[2] On Colet, Eugene Rice, "John Colet and the Denial of Naturalism," to be published in a forthcoming number of the *Harvard Theological Review*, and the works there cited.

universities and its cause was taken up by a whole group of prelates and men of affairs who gave it weighty support. Among the most prominent of these were Warham, the archbishop of Canterbury, and above all Sir Thomas More, who was just then beginning his promising career in the king's service.

Born as he himself said of "no famous family but honest stock" in 1478, More had been educated at St. Anthony's, then the best school in London, and afterward entered the household of Cardinal Morton. The practice of educating children of the gentry and upper bourgeoisie by placing them as clients or pages in the households of people of great position was very common both in France and in England. In these relationships many interesting and almost familial ties were formed which afterward became the basis for parties and influential groups in political and cultural life. More himself paid many tributes to the importance of his association with the cardinal's household. His education was completed at Oxford and at the Inns of Court, where he embarked on a legal career after having considered and rejected the church because he regarded himself as unworthy.

His brilliant qualities and achievements brought him rapid advancement. From the accession of Henry VIII in 1509, More was in a favored position. He was closely associated with most distinguished members of the humanistic circles in England. He had already been host to Erasmus, with whom he had developed a close friendship that was to last until the final tragedy of More's execution. He had been a member of parliament and an undersheriff of London, and the prospect of the highest offices in the land opened before him.

In 1514 he was sent to Antwerp on a royal mission to discuss modification in the *Magnus Intercursus,* the commercial treaty negotiated between the Low Countries and England during the reign of Henry VII. While on this mission, in conversation with Peter Giles of Antwerp, More conceived and wrote, at least in part, the *Utopia,* which was completed in 1516 and subsequently published in Latin on the continent under the supervision of Erasmus.

The *Utopia* was More's most fundamental and comprehensive piece of social criticism, but on the narrower ground of the relationship of the new learning to the Christian tradition, More never expressed himself better than in the letter written to the authorities of the University of Oxford after a demonstration there against the teachers of Greek. The letter was written in March 1518 and still stands as a brilliant defense of

the place of humanistic learning in society and in religion. To the charge
that humanistic learning was inevitably secular and corrosive in its effects
More responded:

No one has ever claimed that a man needed Greek and Latin, or indeed any
education, in order to be saved. Still, this education which he calls secular does
train the soul in virtue. In any event, few will question that humanistic
education is the chief, almost the sole, reason why men come to Oxford;
children can receive a good education at home from their mothers; all except
cultivation and book-learning. Besides, not everyone who comes to you does
so immediately to pursue theological studies. It is proper that some should also
pursue law, in which case the wisdom that comes from the study of humane
things is requisite; and in any case it is something not useless to theologues;
without such study they might possibly preach a sermon acceptable to an
academic group but they would certainly fail to reach the common man. Now,
from whom could they acquire such skill better than from the [classical]
poets, orators, and historians? Moreover, there are some who through
knowledge of things natural [i.e., rational] construct a ladder by which to
rise to the contemplation of things supernatural; they build a path to Theology
through Philosophy and the Liberal Arts, which this man condemns as
secular; they adorn the Queen of Heaven with the spoils of the Egyptians!
This fellow declares that only theology should be studied; but if he admits
even that, I don't see how he can accomplish his aim without some knowledge
of languages, whether Hebrew or Greek or Latin; unless, of course, the
elegant gentleman has convinced himself that there is enough theology
written in English or that all theology can be squeezed into the limits of
those [late scholastic] "questions" which he likes to pose and answer, for
which a modicum of Latin would, I admit, suffice. But really, I cannot admit
that Theology, that august Queen of Heaven, can be thus confined. Does she
not dwell and abide in Holy Scripture? Does she not pursue her pilgrim way
through the cells of the holy Fathers: Augustine and Jerome; Ambrose and
Cyprian; Chrysostom, Gregory, Basil and their like? The study of theology
has been solidly based on these now despised expositors of fundamental truth
during all the Christian centuries until the invention of these petty and
meretricious "questions" which alone are today glibly tossed back and forth.
Anyone who boasts that he can understand the works of the Fathers without
an uncommon acquaintance with the languages of each and all of them will
in his ignorance boast for a long time before the learned trust his judgment.[3]

This statement may stand as one of the most eloquent expressions of
the conviction that there was a positive accord between the aims of the
new learning and those of religion. If the idea that through knowledge

[3] Translation by T.S.A. Scott-Craig in *Renaissance News,* Vol. I, No. 2, 1948.

of things natural a ladder could be constructed to the supernatural was not in the least new, still the range of the new learning had posed the problem more squarely than in the thirteenth century, and the emphasis on direct knowledge of the sources made still more evident the acquisition of the necessary tools of scholarship. Sharing the beliefs of Colet in what could be accomplished by education, More differed from him in his willingness to find less opposition between things natural and things supernatural.

More's whole career was a practical expression of the ideals which he had developed in the course of his youthful studies. The combination of the hair shirt and other practices of traditional and rigid piety with the worldly position of the lord chancellor was in a way another example of the principle of accepting the natural man and the natural world sanctified by the message of Christian revelation. Although this principle had been a commonplace of most thinkers of the later Middle Ages, More's interpretation of it had a distinctive character compounded of his learning, his sense of humor and his interest in the form of Platonism which had been made fashionable in Renaissance Italy. Although many of his qualities appear to be distinctively English, his whole life and thought were a protest against the parochial and the national. He went far beyond both his English and continental contemporaries in the range of his social criticism, but his ideals in education and religion were at the very center of the thinking of the Christian humanists and were shared by many in France and Germany who had never read his works nor even heard his name.

IV. LEFÈVRE D'ETAPLES

In France also during this period scholarship and a concern for the reform of society were characteristically intertwined. Even the most conspicuous representatives of what might be called the purely scholarly tradition, like Guillaume Budé, nevertheless believed that the function of sound studies was the reformation of society. It was only later in the century that the divorce between scholarship and action became so complete that the great student of Roman law, Cujas, could reply to those who questioned him about the issues of the civil wars, *"Nihil hoc ad edictum praetoris."* Even the most abstruse works of Budé, such as the treatise on Roman money, are filled with paragraphs in which the lessons of history are drawn and the way to reform in church and state is pointed. In the *De philologia,* in the interesting dialogue between Budé and

Francis I, the scholar expresses the Erasmian hope that the king might find a place in his council for the wise. And the same conviction was responsible for his urging upon Francis I the founding of the Collège de France.

More important than Budé for the reforming tradition in France was his contemporary, Lefèvre d'Etaples.[4] Lefèvre was born in 1455 and studied first in the University of Paris, where he took his doctor's degree. Like many others of his generation he made the Italian tour in continuation of his scholarly career. In the winter of 1491–1492 he studied at Florence, where he absorbed the work of the Platonic Academy, and also at Padua, where he read Aristotle with Ermalao Barbaro. His interest in Aristotle was the outgrowth of an earlier concern which had produced a brief résumé of the *Organon* in the period before his Italian journey.

When he returned to France Lefèvre's intellectual interests represented an extraordinary mixture of traditions. He had been affected in important ways by the Christian mystics of the later Middle Ages, such as Eckhart and Tauler, and he had also read with great attraction the works of Raymond Lull. Lull's interest in the conversion of the Moslem world to Christianity by means of rational argument had a particular appeal in an age when new lands and peoples were being discovered and there appeared to be a greater opportunity for the spread of the Christian religion. With these traditional interests Lefèvre combined an extensive knowledge of both Platonic and Aristotelian philosophy as it had been developed and increased in the fifteenth century. He began to give lectures on Aristotle at the University of Paris and developed a method for expounding the literal sense of philosophic propositions which was closely parallel to the exegetical method applied to the Scriptures by Colet.

In spite of his apparently brilliant future as a scholar of secular philosophy, Lefèvre soon began to turn his attention more exclusively to the texts of the Christian tradition. He described how a light "so bright now shone in his eyes that human doctrines seemed to him dark in comparison with divine studies." An intense religious experience, the nature of which remains obscure, led him in 1507 to the consideration of a monastic career. This step he did not take, but the effects of the experience remained with him and from this time onward he devoted his energies in a more concentrated way to the exposition of Christian truth. Two years before, in 1505,

---

[4] On Lefèvre, Renaudet, *Preréforme et humanisme à Paris pendant les premières guerres d'Italie, 1494–1517* (Thèse Paris, 1916), and more recently, but written from a somewhat tendentious point of view, F. Herman, *Histoire doctrinale de l'humanisme chrétien*, 4 vols. (Tournai, 1948).

he had published a translation of the theology of John of Damascus in which he substituted for the scholastic formulas a direct knowledge of biblical texts.

In this work he announced as one of the great principles of Christian humanism, "We must affirm nothing of God but what the Scriptures tell us about him."

In 1509 he produced his important Quintuplex Psalter. Five versions of the Psalms were placed side by side in parallel columns in an effort to elucidate the text. This method was directly in the line of biblical criticism inaugurated by Valla. It was everywhere being used by scholars who as yet had no doubt about the possible effects of the application of rational techniques to the understanding of sacred texts. In 1512 Lefèvre published his still more important commentary on the Epistles of St. Paul. Here again appeared the parallel texts of the Vulgate and his own translation corrected by references to the Greek. Even though he seems to have had but one manuscript, his work represented an advance in the purification of the text. This was the work in which Lefèvre developed the doctrine of justification by faith, thus anticipating by some years one of the main principles of Protestantism. He viewed faith as springing only from divine grace, unmerited by human works. As a corollary of this he emphasized the fact that the human will was bound by divine dispensation. In this conviction, in spite of his many close ties with humanistic thought, he parted company from those of his contemporaries who proclaimed the capacity of the human will and the human intelligence to take an active part not only in the construction of a better world here and now but also in the process of salvation.

Other works of criticism, religion and philosophy followed. In 1514 Lefèvre published an edition of the works of Nicholas of Cusa. This great figure of fifteenth-century thought, often described as the last of the scholastic philosophers, had had a complicated and subtle influence on his contemporaries and successors. In science, philosophy and political theory he had made original contributions. His interest in the Augustinian and neo-Platonic tradition was taken up and continued by the Platonic Academy at Florence while his mathematical and physical work stimulated the criticism of Aristotle which was continuing at the University of Padua. Through all his works ran a concern for unity which was the sharper as the actual unity of the European world appeared to be more threatened in his generation. In metaphysics he attempted to reconcile the divergent philosophical traditions of the late medieval world and in the cause of the church he worked to bring together Greek and Latin Christianity. It was perhaps this aspect that appealed most strongly to Lefèvre d'Etaples. If knowledge of the true sources of Christianity could provide a common denominator, then perhaps the whole enlarging world could be organized as the City of God on earth.

In accordance with this aim Lefèvre in his critical works attempted to purify and make available basic documents of Christianity. Three small treatises, of which the first appeared in 1517, demonstrated the falsity of ecclesiastical traditions with respect to Mary Magdalene and St. Anne. His *Commentary on the Four Gospels* and his translation of the New Testament, his two most important works, appeared in 1522 and 1523.

As in his writing he tried to achieve a more solid, profound and scientific knowledge of Christian sources, so in his life Lefèvre tried to disseminate this knowledge to even the illiterate and to realize the implications of it. He became a member of the household of Guillaume Briconnet, Bishop of Meaux, then the leading practical reformer in France. The group at Meaux not only attempted to abolish the usual abuses in the diocese; they also embarked on a program of education designed to raise the general standard of Christian piety and to encourage a more direct participation in religious life. The emphasis was upon the life of the spirit rather than on the maintenance of traditional observances. Printed broadsides were designed to provide simple French translations of selected scriptural passages. The techniques of philology were to find their justification not only in the increased understanding of the intellectual élite, but also in the improved religious education of the masses.

If, however, Lefèvre was an apostle of the application of the new philology, his science was combined in a strange balance with his predilection for mysticism.

Here Lefèvre represented a unique combination of the classical and the Christian elements. The philological tradition as established by Valla and carried on by the great work of Erasmus and others presumed that the exercise of human reason could distinguish the truth in scriptural texts and that by this means man could rise from the knowledge of things human to things divine. For Lefèvre the exercise of reason was accompanied and conditioned by a mystical illumination of the spirit. His characteristic method, before setting himself to the interpretation of a revealed text, was to pray for illumination. It might be charged by a skeptical critic that if he really believed in divine illumination of the intelligence there was no need to emphasize the role of the trained reason and the apparatus of philology. On the other hand, if he were a really scientific critic, what was the need of appealing to the divine illumination? But such a charge would be carrying a twentieth-century view back to a period when the separation between the truths of revelation and the truths of reason had not become familiar. Indeed, in his confidence in the congruence of reason with inspiration Lefèvre anticipated the reformers and we seem to hear the voices of Calvin and Knox declaring that the Scripture speaks plainly and for all to hear. Only perverseness and obstinacy could prevent a man from understanding the work of God.

But if Lefèvre looked forward he also looked back, and for this reason he has become an embarrassing figure in the history of the Reformation. Anticipating many of the most characteristic doctrines of Luther, and condemned by the faculty of theology of the University of Paris, Lefèvre nevertheless eventually repudiated Lutheranism and the reformers at Strassburg and died in communion with Rome. His was the tragedy of one who expected to revivify religious life and reform the abuses in the church by example and education. The group at Meaux, of which he was the central figure, devoted themselves to the circulation of translations of the liturgy and the Psalms with the ideal of putting in every hand the direct sources of Christian inspiration. At the same time they organized an institutional reform within the diocese whereby the characteristic abuses which had grown up in the late medieval church were corrected. All this effort, however, was intended to be accomplished within the church tradition. There was to be no break with the visible unity, however corrupt some elements of the church visible might be. Lefèvre and his colleagues were not the stuff of which revolutionaries are made. They were most of them too reasonable, too intellectual, even too timid to commit themselves to the leadership of a popular movement. Their tragedy was part of the larger tragedy of the whole movement of Christian humanism.

V. GERMAN HUMANISM

In no major country in Europe did there develop so sharp a separation as in Germany between the followers of the new learning and those who upheld the scholastic tradition. Whereas much of the energy behind the humanist program was applied in Spain, France and even in England to the reform of the institutions of ecclesiastical society within an inherited framework, in Germany the same energy was directed along lines more definitely anti-Roman. This result was in part due to the greater relative economic and political strength of the church in Germany and to the absence of an effective central authority.

The golden age of the German medieval universities had come later than those of the other European countries. The great foundations in the Empire dated from the fourteenth and fifteenth centuries and there remained therefore a vigorous and powerful scholastic tradition in the higher intellectual and religious life of Germany. This tradition had not been seriously undermined by the pietistic movement of the *devotio moderna*. The schools of the Brotherhood of the Common Life did indeed emphasize training in morals and their methods centered on the development of the ability to read the Fathers and some of the classics. On the whole, in spite of the claims for a "northern Renaissance" centering on this educational movement, their aims do not appear to have been very different from those of the cathedral schools of the middle ages and their horizon was very little wider.

Although the ground was prepared by the *devotio moderna* and by the traditions which derived from the circle of Charles IV in Bohemia, the real challenge to traditional modes of thought came from Italy. Humanism often found its first support at the courts of princes and bishops, but it also had from the beginning a closer connection with university life than it had ever had in Italy. Little by little scholars trained in Italy in grammar and rhetoric were appointed to professorial chairs and all the great universities became battlegrounds between the scholastic and the humanist ideals. In this struggle it is important to remember that the humanists identified themselves with the reforming tradition; their methods would lead to success where councils and mystics had failed. The contest was not between those who defended the church and those who attacked it in the name of "free-thought" or "paganism," but rather it was a battle on the part of the humanists to have the worth of their educational ideals recognized in the citadels of orthodoxy.[5]

Among the earliest and most famous of the scholars who proclaimed a humanist message was Johann Wessel. He had received his training in Italy and was teaching Greek at Heidelberg shortly after the middle of the fifteenth century. There he was succeeded by his even more famous pupil, Rudolph Agricola, "the father of German humanism," who had studied under Theodore of Gaza. The influence emanating from such

[5] W. Andreas, *Deutschland vor der Reformation* (Stuttgart, 1932), 503–73. Also G. Ritter, *"Die geschichtliche Bedeutung des deutschen Humanismus,"* *Historische Zeitschrift* 127 (1922–23), 393–453, and the same author's *Die Heidelberger Universität. Ein Stück deutscher Geschichte*, Vol. I, *Das Mittelalter* (Heidelberg, 1936), 449–91.

men as these, combined with the educational practice of such great teachers as Conrad Celtis and Jacob Wimpheling, resulted in the establishment of those centers of "poets" and humanists which came to have an increasingly large part to play in the intellectual life of sixteenth-century Germany.

One such center, of particular interest since it existed at Luther's university, was that grouped around the humanist, Mutianus Rufus, at Erfurt. Mutian had studied in Italy and had been profoundly influenced, like so many others, by the neo-Platonism of the Florentine circle. He was a quietist, and developed into a believer in a kind of universalism. It seemed to him above all necessary to direct the church away from the emphasis on the efficacy of the sacraments and the performance of outward acts and toward the cultivation of an inner spirit. Mutian has been represented as a pantheist and there are statements in some of his letters which seem to support this view, but in fact his more consistent position was built on the acceptance of a transcendent God whose existence and truth were testified by the many religions of history, but whose real nature was perhaps best understood by philosophers like the divine Plato.[6]

In spite of the fact that he wrote almost nothing and did no formal teaching, Mutian became the center of an influential circle of younger humanists whose whole attitude toward the ecclesiastical establishment was more critical than that of the older generation of humanist teachers in the Rhine Valley. Among this group were Crotus Rubeanus and Eoban Hess, the poet who wrote Christianized versions of Ovid, and especially the notorious Ulrich von Hutten, whose life and work were in many ways an epitome of the aims of German humanism in the first decades of the sixteenth century.

Hutten was the son of an ancient family of Franconian knights. Such families were suffering from the economic and social changes which made increasingly anachronistic the basis of their position, and, in these circumstances, Ulrich von Hutten was destined originally for the church. He had his early education at the monastery of Fulda. Under the influence of a friend who had returned from Italy, Hutten broke with his family's plan, escaped from the monastery and pursued a career as a wandering scholar and man of letters in various universities in Germany and on an expedition to Italy. He was early connected with Mutian's circle at Erfurt and his poetic and other writing won him a great reputation.

[6] L. Spitz, "Mutianus Rufus," to be published in *Journal of Warburg Institute*, 1952.

From the beginning of his literary career he had a deep interest in contemporary politics and the future development of the Empire. His Italian journey had contributed fuel to his detestation of Rome and the papacy and he deplored the financial exactions which he felt drained the wealth of Germany to the Roman curia. What he desired most for Germany was the better organization of the Empire toward a form of state more resembling what had been achieved in France and Spain. He supported the ambitious plans of the Emperor Maximilian, who in turn recognized his literary talents, crowning him poet laureate in 1517. His political position remained ambiguous, however. He desired a strong state and looked to the action of the emperor; he opposed the territorial princes who, he felt, hampered the exercise of the imperial authority. At the same time he also fought for the free knights, which was natural enough since it was the class to which he belonged, but this allegiance obscured his political clarity, since the progress of western monarchy depended in part on the curbing of this very element.

One of the crises of Hutten's career occurred over the Reuchlin controversy. Hutten was one of the principal authors of the *Epistolae obscurorum virorum,* which heaped ridicule on the scholastic discipline in the universities and sharply increased the gulf between the church and the new learning. His reforming ideas thus took a far more secular direction than had been characteristic of most humanists in other areas and in other national traditions. He would perhaps have been perfectly happy under Henry VIII; he was poles apart from Cardinal Ximenes and the work of the University of Alcala. The strength of his anti-Roman sentiment found expression in the opportunity to republish the demonstration by Valla of the falsity of the Donation of Constantine.

In the meantime, while German humanism had been increasingly concentrating on the reform of political society and the attack on the papacy, there had been preparing under quite different auspices the demand for a reform in religious thought. In his Augustinian monastery and at Wittenberg Luther slowly and in spiritual agony developed his conviction that the assurance of salvation depended on the complete surrender to God, that justification was by faith alone. After Luther's first great manifesto, Hutten, like Leo X, dismissed the whole affair as a quarrel of monks and hoped the Augustinians and the Dominicans would tear themselves to pieces. But as soon as it became apparent that Luther's position would be a basis for an attack on Rome and the papacy Hutten rallied to the cause. A woodcut of the time of the diet of Worms shows a triumphal procession led by Hutten, who holds captive behind his horse a crowd of bishops and monks. There follows the triumphal chariot of the Savior flanked by Luther and Carlstadt. The common people hail their deliverer and eagerly await the restoration of the Gospel in all its purity.[7] German humanism and the religious ideas of Luther thus came together to make a revolution. Significantly enough it was a revolution the leadership for which had not come out of the new learning but out of an Augustinian monastery. The representation of Hutten, mounted, ushering in the new era belied the facts. It was to Luther, not to Hutten, that the people looked. Furthermore, it was a revolution which destroyed the hopes for reform which had been nourished for a whole generation by the man who in a very real sense had been the inspiration of Hutten in Germany, of More and his friends in England, of Lefèvre in France, and even of Ximenes in Spain, a man who had essayed reform within the framework of Christendom rather than of one nation, the greatest humanist of the age, Erasmus of Rotterdam.

VI. ERASMUS

The figure of Erasmus dominated the cultivated world of Europe in the first two decades of the sixteenth century. In the history of European literature perhaps only Voltaire achieved a comparable eminence and influence during his lifetime. His friends and followers spread his influence from England to Poland and Hungary and from the Scandinavian countries to Spain and Italy. He was on familiar terms with the greatest rulers of the age, who competed with each other in honoring him and seeking to tempt him to their service. His enormous correspondence remains the single most valuable source for the intellectual history of the period.

The secret of his pre-eminence and the significance of his achievement have nevertheless remained elusive. Few figures so well known in the history of European thought have been so variously estimated. For some he was above all the precursor of the Reformation, a kind of John the Baptist preceding Luther. There is the old story related in contemporary accounts of the charade performed before the Emperor Charles V in which Erasmus was represented as gathering the fagots, Reuchlin arranging them, and Luther illuminating the blaze. On the other hand, he has been described as a kind of deist, a precursor of the eighteenth-century Enlightenment, who would have been happier born in the later age. On

[7] Bainton, *Here I Stand: A Life of Martin Luther* (N. Y., 1951), 2.

the one hand his tolerance and moderation have been interpreted as the vacillations of a craven neurotic who had not the courage to take a position and who was afraid of the arena of practical life, and on the other hand they have been taken as the finest manifestations of a man of courage with serious religious convictions and a program for the reform of society which was doomed to failure. In the midst of these wide divergences it is important to attempt to distinguish between the aims of Erasmus as they were understood by himself and his contemporaries and his influence as it has been estimated by successive generations of historians.

Born probably in the year 1466, Erasmus was educated in the Schools of the Common Life and at an early age and without a true vocation was persuaded to enter a monastery. Here he continued until he was ordained a priest in the year 1492, a step which he afterward bitterly regretted and which was the occasion of the dispensation sought in later years from the Roman court. Dissatisfied with the opportunities for intellectual life at the monastery, Erasmus sought and received employment with the bishop of Cambrai, who was presently persuaded in 1494 to send him to Paris, where he became a resident of the celebrated College of Montaigu, then under the direction of the reformer, John Standonck.

Erasmus' first residence in Paris was interesting because it revealed the tensions between his interests and his vocation, of which he himself was probably hardly aware. His tastes were secular. He loved a good dinner, a glass of wine, and a companionable discourse in a garden, and these tastes were enhanced and satisfied by his study of classical literature and by his association with some of the early humanists in Paris. Nevertheless, he had not in the least abandoned his devotion to Christian practices and he had not begun to question even the institution of monasticism. During and after an illness we have on the one hand an account which seems to accept, and with sincere emotion, the possibility of a miracle; and, on the other hand, a letter to a friend filled with antique resignation and excluding the possibility of divine intervention. The appeal to the influence of the stars and the action of the antique gods had been a commonplace during the medieval period. It had coexisted with the most sincere and emotional beliefs in the truths of the Christian religion. Nevertheless, in the case of Erasmus one feels the tension between the classical and the Christian becoming more acute. The very self-consciousness and more complete recovery of the classical past added a new element to familiar combinations and raised more insistently the question whether there was an inner contradiction between the classical and the Christian ethic. In the early period, without yet questioning established Christian institutions or the system of dogma, the secular character of Erasmus' tastes and the active direction of his thought were already apparent.[8]

The first work upon which Erasmus' European reputation began to grow was the collection of *Adages,* which was published in 1500. This was a collection of proverbs culled from ancient authors, with short elucidations and comments. At the time when the first collection was made Erasmus knew little Greek and the collection was far from the form which it assumed eight years later, after he had visited Italy and had the benefit of a close association with the workshop of Aldus at Venice. The edition of 1508 more than trebled the number of adages and included many acute comments and discourses inserted on the topical problems of the age. The work became a mine of information and a standard reference work for scholars and writers. It was one of the achievements which most contributed to the fame of Erasmus in a circle wider than that to which his purely scholarly works appealed.

In the meantime, in 1503, Erasmus had published the *Enchiridion militis Christiani,* a homily addressed to the laymen who wished to practice the Christian virtues. Erasmus himself tells us that it was written at the request of a lady who asked him to advise her dissolute husband on the practice of Christianity. More conventional theologians had apparently tried to interest the lady's husband and had failed. The result of Erasmus' acceptance of the lady's request was an outline of what he characteristically called the philosophy of Christ. The homily centered on the description of those Christian virtues which could be realized in an active life. Throughout the emphasis was upon the spirit rather than upon the letter. Penances, fasts, good works, availed nothing if they were done without a genuine spirit of Christian charity and, on the other hand, the omission of pious practices might still be regarded as unimportant in the sight of Heaven if the intention was in accordance with the spirit of the Gospel. A simple and genuine piety was contrasted with the elaborate structure of formalism which shut out the pious seeker.

At first the book had comparatively little influence, but by the second decade of the century it had attained great popularity and was widely read. Its influence may be interestingly traced on both the Reformation and the Counter Reformation. In Germany many of those who accepted

---

[8] E. Rice, "Erasmus and the Religious Tradition," *Journal of the History of Ideas* (1950), XI, pp. 387–411.

the arguments of Luther were influenced by Erasmus' arguments against outward conformity and in Spain the whole movement of the *illuminati,* afterward so bitterly condemned by the Inquisition, was inspired by the Erasmian message. No other book in Spain before the middle of the sixteenth century was so widely printed and circulated as this treatise.

One of the fruits of Erasmus' Italian journey was the *Praise of Folly,* published in 1511 upon his return to England when he was staying in the household of Sir Thomas More. This famous satire, which had perhaps a greater and more direct influence on European literature than any of the other works of Erasmus, was directed against the follies and vices of the age. Following a good classical model, Folly personified speaks and pleads for her reputation, alleging her extreme usefulness to man. Surveying the whole range of human behavior, Folly points out how pervasive is her rule in the affairs of mankind. By this device Erasmus was able to undertake a thorough if gentle and humorous criticism of the aspects of contemporary society which he felt were most in need of reform. He was of course particularly severe on the abuses in the ecclesiastical organization. The institution of monasticism, ignorance and neglect among the higher clergy, formalism instead of obedience to the spirit of Christianity were all a part of the reign of folly.

The same themes were taken up again in the *Colloquies,* which were not published as a collection until 1522. These had been begun by Erasmus when he had pupils in Paris at the beginning of the century. At first they were no more than phrase books intended to facilitate the speaking and writing of Latin. Gradually they became more complicated and assumed dialogue form, so that they gave an opportunity for the dramatic juxtaposition of the characters. They are filled with topical allusions, and again the abuses and shortcomings of the church are a major subject of discussion. The characters and the dialogue of the *Colloquies* not only played their part in the immediate religious crisis but also had a great influence on the literature of more than one European country during the remainder of the century. The giants of Renaissance literature, Rabelais, Shakespeare, and Cervantes, showed in different ways their indebtedness to the *Colloquies* of Erasmus.

In considering the satiric work of Erasmus and especially his attacks on the church, it must be remembered that the whole atmosphere of the discussion of ecclesiastical institutions changed greatly during the course of the sixteenth-century revolutionary struggle. After the Protestant attack and after the council of Trent it became impossible for the supporters of the Roman Church to admit the possibility that some bishops were unworthy, some abbots corrupt, and some priests ignorant. These facts had nevertheless been the most common complaint of generations of the most saintly critics of the church in the period of the waning Middle Ages. The relationship of Erasmus to the Catholic religion ought no more to be deduced from his strictures against current abuses than ought impiety to be charged against all the itinerant priests and authors of gravamina and orators against abuses in the fourteenth and fifteenth centuries.[9] Imperfections were freely admitted in the earlier period which after Luther seemed unallowable, lest they undermine the whole structure further. Hence, although it is true that Erasmus had raised doubts about such institutions as monasticism, his criticisms ought to be evaluated against the background of the frankness of the fifteenth century rather than against the silence of the sixteenth-century churchmen.

In addition to his didactic and satiric works, the greatness of Erasmus was founded upon his scholarly achievement. As early as his first visit to England in 1498—a visit which marked an epoch in his life—Erasmus had determined to devote himself to the provision of the classic sources of Christianity, and this objective was fulfilled in part by the great edition of the New Testament in 1516.

This work was followed by the famous editions of the Fathers, beginning with St. Jerome, with whom Erasmus himself felt a historical sympathy, and after the great Latin Fathers came the Greek Fathers. In spite of gaps in the series of publications, in spite of standards which would not be accepted by modern scholarship, Erasmus could feel that he had accomplished almost singlehandedly the great ambition of a generation of humanist scholarship. The great classics of antiquity had been supplied in original versions by the work in Italy, but it was in the north that the sources of Christianity were restored and made available. With the fulfillment of this program Erasmus hoped there would come an age when the texts of the faith were understood directly by everyone— when, as he said, the housewife at her work and the plowboy at his plow sang Psalms during their labors.

It was a great effort of education which was to make the Christian past live again and was to bring the extension of the philosophy of Christ. This philosophy, as Erasmus depicted it, was one of charity made manifest in action. It embodied the attitudes which Erasmus himself tried to put

---

[9] See the remarks on this subject in P. Hughes, *A History of the Church* (New York, 1947), Vol. III.

into practice when he was confronted with practical questions. When he was asked, for example, to write the *Institution of a Christian Prince* for Charles V, the virtues which he described were those which corresponded to his ideal. In a consultation on the Turkish war he voiced a Christian pacifism. The *Querela pacis* also contained his plea against the destructive wars ravaging the European continent. These ideals owed much to the inheritance of Christianity. Yet it was a Christianity infused also, and perhaps more than Erasmus knew, with the spirit of antique culture. It was a Christianity which recognized the possibility of growth and change in the historic institutions of the church. Erasmus in reality stood for a kind of sixteenth-century modernism. Like the St. Jerome whom he so much admired, he was not interested in theology or in metaphysics. He never seems to have felt the acute sense of sin and unworthiness which was characteristic of a Luther or a Savonarola. But in spite of the secularized character of his interpretation of Christianity he did cling to the unity of Christendom as fundamental. Detesting as he did the fanaticism of extremes, he yet eventually chose to part company with Luther conclusively, not so much over a matter of any particular doctrine—not even free will or justification by faith—but over the indissolubility of the European Christian community. Indeed, when it came to the critical turning point, this was the reason why all the leaders of the great early generation of Christian humanists refused to accept the reform on the conditions posed by Luther. For Reuchlin and Lefèvre, for More and Fisher as well as for Erasmus, it was essential that reform take place within the framework of the organized Christian church. For this ideal More and Fisher ultimately lost their heads upon the block, and Lefèvre, Reuchlin, and ultimately Erasmus, refused to leave the church. If we are to view them as "precursors" at all, they are rather precursors of the Catholic Reformation in the sixteenth century than of Protestantism. In the end they could more easily accept the disappointment of their hopes than the division of the Christian community.

Chapter Nine

ART AND SCIENCE

I. THE ARTIST AND THE PATRON

THE years when many men looked hopefully toward the prospect of an Erasmian reformation synchronized with one of the greatest periods of creative achievement in the plastic arts in the whole history of western culture. The peak was reached in the first decades of the sixteenth century. Leonardo da Vinci died in 1519, Raphael in 1520 and Dürer in 1528. Although Michelangelo lived on past the middle of the century, the Sistine ceiling had been finished in 1512 and the *Moses and Slaves* for the monument of Julius II by 1516. Behind these men of greatest genius lay the brilliant achievements of the Italian *quattrocento* and of the French, Flemish and German schools in the north.

No formula of sociological analysis has ever been evolved which adds much to our understanding of the conditions which favor or determine great periods of artistic creation or intellectual activity. Clearly a certain allegiance to a common set of religious or philosophical beliefs may be desirable. Yet an orthodoxy too weighty and oppressive is as blighting in its effects as a condition of anarchy in which there is an absence of all standards. There is a very broad area between the extremes of uniformity and chaos; historical examples give us no easy guide to the relationship between religious tradition and artistic creation. Whatever one's personal preferences, it is difficult to deny for example that a great art was produced by the "irreligious" nineteenth century in France as well as by the "religious" thirteenth century.

Another variable of great importance, but difficult to measure and ambiguous in its effects, is the factor of stability in the social order. Great artists have been able to work in periods of political and social disturbance, when the threat of war and the danger of the sack of the city were constant. On the other hand, those epochs when political order has been maintained at its maximum have not generally coincided with the emergence of an original, lively and lasting art. These comparisons indicate what is perhaps an obvious truth, that a psychological sense of security is more important than the actual physical security of the individual, however it may be measured. Cellini's *Autobiography* describes a society where physical violence was of ordinary occurrence and a stab in the back a usual way of dealing with an enemy. Yet what we should call the nervous breakdown rate was, so far as we can judge, very small compared to that of a modern American urban community, where movement in the streets is comparatively safe in spite of the occasional gangster. Even the most striking contrasts, however, fail to suggest criteria which can be universally applied; the history of artistic achievement is filled with exceptions and an "ideal" proportion between stability and disorder is as difficult to determine as that between belief and doubt.

At the beginning of his *Siècle de Louis XIV* Voltaire declared that for those who had any taste at all only four ages in the history of civilization counted: Periclean Greece, Augustan Rome, Medicean Italy and the France of Louis XIV. Different as these ages were in many respects, they suggest one common factor of great importance and that is the high degree of public or private support for the artist and his work. Even if the range of inquiry be extended far beyond the periods which appealed to Voltairian taste, it will be found that a close relationship between the artist and his "public," even if the public be limited to a few highly placed and cultivated individuals, always appears to have been one of the most important conditions of creative activity. Such a relationship has assumed a multitude of different forms; the creation of works of art for the enjoyment of a community like the citizens of Athens or the worshipers in a medieval cathedral was obviously very different from the execution of a commission for the court of Louis XIV or for a modern captain of industry. Thus one important kind of periodization in the history of art is established by the social conditions imposed on the artist.

In the later Middle Ages the position of the artist in society was changing in many important ways. From being a craftsman like any other, the artist was becoming a creator of the "fine arts." From working primarily to fulfill the religious and social purposes of the community, he was beginning to work more and more to express his own ideas or those of his patron. The Renaissance thus became the first great modern age of the individual patron. Merchant prince and despot competed for the services of the greatest architects, sculptors, painters and scholars.

In the case of many rulers, especially those of the smaller Italian states, the need for splendor was connected with their precarious political position. Generosity to the arts, a princely style, the provision of magnificence were useful in the struggle for popularity. A defective title could be overcome by proving that its owner was a prince by nature if not by inheritance. It was far more necessary for a Ludovico Sforza than for a king of France to surround himself with a brilliant and luxurious court and to provide bread and circuses for the people. Increases in wealth opened to *condottieri* and usurpers a new means of maintaining their position, and some of the most conspicuous patrons of art and literature displayed their generosity in the service of their political position.

The use of wealth for civic splendor, such as was counselled by an artist like Leon Battista Alberti in his *Della famiglia,* was also justified by appeal to ancient example. If there was no contemporary equivalent of Augustus, there were plenty of examples of merchants and princes whose role could be identified with that of Maecenas. The sanctions of classical and contemporary social theory, however, competed with the traditional medieval ethic based on the prohibition of usury and emphasizing the sins of acquisitiveness, and this conflict produced in certain cases a further impulse to the activity of the patron. Although the canonical enforcement of restitution for ill-gotten fortunes had long since ceased to apply to the merchant prince, there was enough force in the old beliefs to create in the minds of some men a sense if not of guilt, at least of a conscious desire to spend a fortune in ways that would benefit the community. The building of chapels and the commissioning of many public works of art were therefore not only positively the result of a new conception of wealth, which should be spent for civic purposes, but also negatively the product of impulses conditioned by the Christian medieval tradition on the nature of wealth. Once the pattern of patronage was established, the pressure of competition and the prestige of fashionable example led to widespread imitation. The attainment of a certain position in the church, in secular politics, or in the world of merchant capitalism came almost automatically to imply expenditure in aid of scholarship and the arts. The urge to acquisitiveness was balanced by the necessity of applying wealth to purposes which were socially approved.

The Italian city states and princely courts provided the environment in which flourished the most famous exemplars of patronage. Among these the Medici achieved a pre-eminence which raised them to the status of eponymous heroes. Cosimo made little distinction between his private fortunes and the public revenues of the city. He used his wealth to build the palaces and churches and to support the scholars and artists who were the glory of fifteenth-century Florence. This tradition was inherited and furthered by his grandson Lorenzo, whose court was already more aristocratic and further removed than his grandfather's from the center of Florentine public life. The focus of interest shifted from the Medici Riccardi palace to the villas in the country, and from an art whose purposes were more broadly communal to the refined enjoyment of a selected few. The third and climactic stage of Medicean patronage was reached when Lorenzo's son came to the papal throne as Leo X. Here he presided over a court unrivaled in its combination of magnificence and cultivation, where poets, artists and scholars received their rewards in the service of a secularized ecclesiastical order. Leo aspired to create at the papal court the undisputed cultural capital of the western world, and in the eyes of his contemporaries he succeeded. The restoration of piety, learning and peace was attributed to the pope in whose reign fell the beginning of the greatest of religious revolutions, and this ironic contrast was dramatically symbolized in the sack of Rome in 1527. Six years after the death of Leo X the end of the Medicean age saw the widespread dispersal of the scholars, artists and poets whom papal patronage had gathered together.

The pontificate of Leo X had united the traditions of the Medici with those of his papal predecessors over a period of nearly a century. Beginning with Nicholas V most of the popes had been distinguished for their patronage of scholarship or art. The names of Nicholas V and Sixtus IV were associated in the most important steps taken in the creation of the Vatican Library; the same Sixtus embarked on the reorganization of the papal palace and the building and decoration of the Sistine Chapel. Alexander VI was responsible for the adornment of the Borgia apartments in the Vatican. Above all Julius II, the immediate predecessor of Leo, was the archetype of director and organizer of creative activity. For him Bramante, Michelangelo and Raphael began their greatest works, while a host of lesser figures labored to create an environment to correspond with the genius and energy of the pope and with his idea of his position in the church and in the world. In the sheer drive with which he pursued his plans and in the grandeur of the results he obtained, Julius II eclipsed all his contemporaries as a patron of the arts, as he did in so many other respects. In spite of the tensions and difficulties which often characterized the relations between Julius and the artists who served him, he brought to its culmination the princely encouragement of artistic endeavor, and his name remains rightfully associated with the greatest monuments of his age.

The Medici and the popes represented the two most famous and successful traditions of artistic patronage in the Italian scene, but a similar activity was manifest in almost every court and commune in the peninsula. Ferrante of Naples continued the practices begun by Alfonso the Magnanimous, with emphasis upon the support of the humanists grouped around the figure of Pontano. In Milan, Ludovico Sforza and his wife, Beatrice d'Este, presided for a brief period over one of the most splendid and brilliant courts in Italy, of which the chief ornament was Leonardo da Vinci. The smaller courts rivaled and sometimes surpassed the larger. The zeal of the dukes of Urbino for scholarship, literature and art has remained celebrated, and their capital supplied the setting for the *Courtier* of Castiglione, which became the manual of manners for the courts of Europe. In Mantua, the Gonzaga supported the school of Vittorino da Feltre and his successors, and commissioned Mantegna to decorate their palace. Above all the court of the Este at Ferrara became a celebrated center of patronage of all the arts. Here Borso d'Este built his Palazzo Schifanoia, decorated with the allegorical frescoes of Francesco Cossa. Here Boiardo and Ariosto were supported and encouraged to produce works glorifying the Este family. To Ferrara came Lucrezia Borgia as the bride of Alfonso d'Este, and here too Isabella d'Este filled her celebrated grotto with commissions assigned to the leading painters by herself and her humanist advisers. Altogether the court of the Este may be taken as an example which brings into sharpest focus the variety of interests characteristic of self-conscious Renaissance patrons of the arts.

Italian examples were soon being imitated in the courts north of the Alps. In Poland, Hungary and the Empire the marriage of the sovereign with an Italian princess invariably brought in the bride's train a whole troup of artists, scholars and humanists. Libraries were founded, manuscripts collected, palaces designed or remodeled and humanist histories subsidized, all in the Italian manner. Even in distant Moscow the Kremlin was rebuilt under the supervision of a Bolognese architect. In the western monarchies opportunities for direct contact with Italy were of course far more frequent and the higher clergy particularly began to emulate their Italian counterparts. The careers and endowments of such cardinals as Wolsey, Amboise and Du Bellay matched the achievements in patronage of the great ecclesiastics of Renaissance Rome. The monarchs themselves were somewhat slower in developing the possibilities revealed by Italian example, and it was not until the generation of Francis I and Henry VIII that the French and English kings began to practice on a considerable scale the patronage of the man of genius. After the meeting between Francis I and Leo X at Bologna in 1516 Leonardo da Vinci returned to France in the pay of the French king to spend the last two and a half years of his life. He died at Amboise in 1519. This migration was perhaps the most dramatic symbol of the recognition of the "great name" in "fine arts" and of the effort to emulate what had been achieved by the relation between patron and artist in Italy.

The transformation of the position of the artist in society was now complete. In the medieval period he had most often worked for a communal enterprise as an anonymous craftsman, indistinguishable in status from those who labored at other crafts. Now not only had he assumed something of the character of the genius,[1] set apart from others by a special gift of creative ability in the arts, but also his whole activity tended now to be to a large extent determined by the relationship with a patron, whose commissions he had to receive and satisfactorily execute if he was to continue in his profession at all. These changes and these conditions must therefore underlie our understanding of much of the artistic achievement of the age.

II. THE CLASSIC TRADITION IN ITALY: MICHELANGELO

The conviction that the Christian and classical components of the European cultural inheritance could be welded together to create a harmonious and true interpretation of the world and man was far from new in the fifteenth century, but it was certainly now more self-consciously maintained. As the assimilation of Greek and Roman literature became more and more complete and the knowledge of antiquity more historical, it became increasingly impossible to maintain such a synthesis, but the delicate balance, or perhaps better the pretense to such a balance, so long as it lasted, dominated the creative work of the artist and the taste of the patron alike, allowing classical gods, goddesses and heroes to coexist happily with Hebrew prophets and Christian saints and martyrs.

The fact of inspiration from the ancient world is obvious, since the artistic expression of the period was pervaded with antique themes and antique forms, but it is of importance to try to understand more precisely the nature of this classical influence. How for example did it differ from previous exemplifications of classicism, of which there were so many in

[1] Erwin Panofsky, *Albrecht Dürer* (Princeton, 1943), Vol. I, 242–43.

the Middle Ages? To what extent was there a change in the concept of the 'classic between the Italian *quattrocento* and the succeeding generation, the generation of Michelangelo? Are we to regard a classical influence as in itself a creative force or merely as a fashionable decorative form applied to the products of contemporary modes of perception and interpretation? In discussing such questions as these the various meanings which may be assigned to the concept of "influence" inevitably condition the results of the inquiry.

In the early medieval period classical themes and classical motives had survived, but had no active role in the intellectual life. At the court of Charlemagne, for example, we find biography being written in direct imitation of Roman models and the illuminations of manuscripts copied with extraordinary fidelity from Roman painting and Roman sculpture. The vast majority of classical texts which have survived were the work of Carolingian scribes whose understanding of the meaning of what they were copying was nevertheless severely limited. It has in fact been suggested that all the fragments of the classical past which found their way into western Europe in the Carolingian period may be looked upon as if they were in quotation marks—encapsulated survivals into an alien environment, not conveying any sense of their mutual relationship or their place in a great historic tradition.[2]

By the twelfth century elements from the classical past have been much more actively assimilated. In the process of assimilation, however, there had occurred, as Professor Panofsky has pointed out, an interesting divorce between form and content. No sense of history yet intervened between the man of the twelfth century and his appreciation of some text or artistic motif which had descended from Greek or Roman civilization. Texts of Roman law were considered to have a universal validity still applicable to the feudal institutions of Europe. It did not occur to the imagination of the European of this period that the life and civilization of antiquity was incredibly remote and that artifacts and traditions had been inherited from a civilization which had passed away forever. Accordingly, perfectly free use was made of classical forms without any understanding of their classical meaning. At the same time there were many examples of classical literary themes adjusted to the purposes of Christian eschatology. After an artist had seen a classical model his virgins and saints were apt to be carved and painted in antique draperies

[2] Erwin Panofsky, *Studies in Iconology. Humanistic Themes in the Art of the Renaissance* (Oxford, 1939), Introduction.

and antique poses. On the other hand, Pyramus and Thisbe, Dido and Aeneas, and the whole pantheon of classical gods and heroes were represented as contemporary Christians. The moralized Ovid has been instanced as one of the most complete examples of the relationship then existing between the Christian and the classical traditions. In the complete absence of the sense of history, artistic forms and thematic content led separate existences.[3]

By the time of the humanistic movement, roughly beginning with Petrarch and Boccaccio in the middle of the fourteenth century, the growth of a sense of history was beginning to introduce a further great change. Petrarch's *Letters to the Ancient Dead* revealed an awareness of their author's position in time. Addressing Livy, Petrarch dated one of his letters, "in the thirteen hundred and forty-eighth year of Him whom you would have known or of whom you would have heard had you lived a little longer." Combined with the perception of the ineluctable passage of time there was sentimental nostalgia for the civilization to which he looked back. This historical-mindedness was one of the factors in bringing about a reintegration of classical form and content. Humanist commentators on Roman law began to emphasize the fact that the texts which they were studying and explaining belonged to a past civilization and that technical terms were to be understood in the light of the whole knowledge about that civilization. Roman literature was inspected for the meaning it could provide for legal terminology. The same attitude characterized the approach to ancient art. It now became more usual to dress gods and goddesses in the garb which they were supposed to have worn in antiquity, and to keep the figures of Christian iconography free of classical ornament. It may thus be maintained that the development of a sense of historical distance was one of the most distinguishing marks of the cultural movement in Renaissance Italy, and this sense of distance paralleled the growth of a sense of perspective in painting and the general interest in archeology. In spite of the greater remoteness in which antiquity now appeared, there was nevertheless a determination to reach back into the past to re-create those forms of thought and expression which had been most characteristic of it. There began to be a highly self-conscious emphasis on the original sources. For example, the traditional literature on the interpretation of the ancient gods and goddesses as developed in the medieval period, explaining the allegorical significance and appropriate attitudes to be assigned to each divinity, now receded in

[3] *Ibid.*

importance in favor of a direct return to ancient authorities on the representation of the gods.[4]

In some cases this attempt to imitate and recreate the forms of classical antiquity was undeflected by any concern to relate the results to the Christian tradition. Brilliant humanists displayed their ability by writing poems and plays which might be represented as newly discovered texts of ancient authors. Thus Alberti passed off for a whole generation one of his youthful plays as a work of Plautus. Michelangelo's first work of sculpture was a statue sold as a recovered Roman marble. Such attempts were of course encouraged by the constant discovery of more examples of ancient sculpture and other remains. Among the most famous of these recoveries were the products of excavations in Rome. During the pontificate of Alexander VI the *Apollo Belvedere* was discovered, and during that of Julius II, the *Laocoön*. Michelangelo himself was present on the latter occasion and Sadoleto, the brilliant young humanist, afterward secretary to Leo X, composed a widely admired ode on the event.

Even in those cases where the imitation of antiquity was not thus direct and complete, artists and writers were supplied with themes by the humanists. The program for Botticelli's *Primavera* and the *Birth of Venus* was probably directly suggested by the neo-Platonic allegories of Ficino and his circle. These paintings, as well as others of Botticelli's works, appear to have been commissioned for the young Lorenzo di Pierfrancesco de' Medici, to whom Ficino had written a letter describing the significance of *Venus* as embodying the ideal of *humanitas*. Here was the transformation of a symbol whose meaning as now elaborated was very different from what it had been in the classical period.[5] Here again the recent studies on Botticelli's mythologies provide additional evidence against the "pagan" interpretation of many of the classical themes in the art of the *quattrocento*.

At the court of Mantua Isabella d'Este, the most celebrated patroness of her generation, gave exacting commissions to a whole succession of artists for the adornment of her grotto with paintings depicting classical mythological subjects. Mantegna was thus employed by her to do his *Parnassus* and the *Minerva Expelling the Vices*. Giovanni Bellini executed for her the *Feast of the Gods,* now in the National Gallery in Washington. In works like these, antique themes were imitated and adapted

---

[4] J. Seznec, *La survivance des dieux antiques* (London, 1940).

[5] E. H. Gombrich, "Botticelli's Mythologies," *Journal of the Warburg Institute,* VIII (1945), 7–60.

to contemporary interests. The classical framework provided an opportunity for both satire and realistic portraiture, where the classical themes
and forms served primarily as a decor.[6]

Much of the literature and art of the Italian *quattrocento* was characterized by the introduction of the classic in this decorative way. Yet
even where the influence of the classic appears most direct, it was interpreted in ways that were governed by contemporary thought and feeling.
Just as the "classicism" of the *quattrocento* differed from that of the
Middle Ages, so also did it differ from that of the beginning of the
cinquecento. It might be said that each generation looked at the world of
antiquity and found what it sought, in very much the same way that the
sixteenth-century travelers and missionaries were already producing
reports on distant lands and peoples which were entirely conditioned by
the attitudes and prejudices they carried with them. Thus, in the *quattrocento* style, as Wölfflin has described it, the artist sought in his classical
models movement, narrative detail and color, whereas in the sixteenth
century the emphasis was all on dignity, seriousness and the elimination
of the nonessential. In describing this difference the eminent historian of
art has directed attention to such a contrast as that between Benozzo
Gozzoli's treatment of the *Drunkenness of Noah* in the Campo Santo at
Pisa and the representation of the same subject by Michelangelo on the
Sistine ceiling. Though the subject was one derived from biblical rather
than classical legend, it makes equally clear the different ways of perceiving which governed the handling of the traditional material. In Gozzoli's
fresco the story was represented with a maximum of narrative detail. The
various stages in the process of making wine were depicted, together with
many aspects of the life of the people, while the central narrative was
submerged in the variety and realism of incident. In Michelangelo's
fresco, on the other hand, the interest was shifted from the extensive
narrative to an intensive concentration on the essentials of Noah's story,
intended to illustrate the human situation with all its implications. Only
the main figures appeared against a vague background, and by this process of elimination a "classic" effect of seriousness and serenity was
achieved. In similar ways the whole body of antique, biblical and Christian legends inherited from the past was subjected to interpretations
which varied in accordance with the situation and taste of the artist.[7]

It is in examining these differences between the most characteristic
monuments of the "classic" style of the *cinquecento* and those of the

[6] E. Wind, *Bellini's Feast of the Gods* (Harvard, 1948).
[7] H. Wölfflin, *The Art of the Italian Renaissance* (New York, 1903).

previous period that the relationship between artistic creation and the great innovations in intellectual history can best be studied. The sudden appearance of the style of the High Renaissance in the Rome of Julius II cannot be understood without relating it to some of the dynamic changes in modes of thought which have been discussed in earlier chapters of this book. Seen in this way the works of Michelangelo, Bramante and Raphael become in a certain way the most concrete illustrations of profound and widespread spiritual changes.

The more important creative effects of the classical inheritance are not, however, to be found in artistic themes and forms in the narrower sense, that is, in the vocabulary of the artist, but rather in the influence on general ideas, philosophical, religious, and aesthetic, which in turn conditioned the various types of plastic expression. Beyond the mere direct imitation of classical art and beyond the use of classical styles as decoration, there were aspects of the revival of antiquity, particularly the interest in the Platonic and neo-Platonic philosophy, which gave new suggestions and emphases for the interpretation of the Christian view of man and the world. New modes of religious thought and feeling underlay new styles in architecture, sculpture and painting.

The development of fifteenth-century ecclesiastical architecture provides one of the best examples of the interplay between the history of ideas and the history of the plastic arts. In the middle of the century Alberti was already experimenting with symmetrical circular churches. Behind this innovation in architectural forms lay, in all probability, the increasing popularity of Platonic and neo-Platonic ideas, with their emphasis on the perfection of the circle and the possibility of expressing all relationships in terms of mathematical harmonies. In the elaboration of these conceptions the works of Nicholas of Cusa were particularly important; here were expounded not only Pythagorean and neo-Platonic traditions, but also a whole philosophy built on the concept of the manifold ways in which the microcosm reflected the macrocosm. If the generation of Alberti took the first steps in linking metaphysical to architectural expression, many greater architects continued the tradition, and the circular church became an ideal Renaissance form. The sketches of Leonardo da Vinci testify to the importance he gave to approaching as nearly as possible to the circular form. Octagons and polygons, with chapels symmetrically added to the sides, were all forms which could be inscribed in a circle, or at least a geometrical construction of circles. The climax was reached in the original plans by Bramante, Michelangelo and San Gallo for St. Peter's. Here was the greatest church of the Christian world, the architectural monument of the greatest of Renaissance artists, which it was intended should be built on the same symmetrical principles. Contemporary religious attitudes found in this form their appropriate architectural expression. In a circular church the altar was at the center, equidistant from all parts of the circumference, corresponding to the position of an almost pantheistic God in a symmetrical and mathematically ordered universe. In the development of this conception the medieval notion of an intimate contact between human and divine had receded into the background, but at the same time the extent of possible achievement by the human will in the process of salvation was emphasized. St. Peter's was a church built to magnify not only the glory of God, but also the dignity of man. It has been well said that in the age when St. Peter's was building—at a cost which occasioned the indulgence controversy in Germany—a theocentric had been substituted for a Christocentric interest; God the Father, the Pantocrator, had replaced the Man of Sorrows as the religious center of the Renaissance.[8]

The same fusion of Platonism with the Christian tradition is apparent also in the frescoes that stand beside St. Peter's as the most comprehensive and impressive creation of the whole period—the Sistine ceiling. This had first been proposed to Michelangelo in 1506, when he was already engaged on the gigantic funeral monument planned by Julius II. Plans for the frescoes were interrupted by the quarrel between Michelangelo and the pope, but were resumed when Michelangelo returned to Rome after the reconciliation at Bologna. Working alone, in conditions of incredible difficulty and discomfort, the artist finished his task in a little over four years. The ceiling was unveiled in 1512, in time for the aged pope to view and enjoy, before he died, the work he had commanded.

The iconography of Michelangelo's frescoes was in part dictated by the scheme of decoration already adopted for the walls of the Sistine Chapel. On the right wall were the *quattrocento* paintings representing the history of man under the Mosaic law, and on the left the history of man under the Christian dispensation. To these historical themes Michelangelo now added on the ceiling a representation of the Creation and the history of the world before the establishment of the old law. At the first level of meaning, therefore, these Old Testament scenes are simply the completion of the historical scheme of decoration planned for the chapel as a whole. At the same time the scenes were arranged and executed in such a way as to convey a profound allegorical significance. The divisions

[8] R. Wittkower, *Architectural Principles in the Age of Humanism* (London, 1949), 1–28.

of the ceiling are made to appear as a trellis through which the spectator can behold an archetypical world. In this ideal world, far removed from the daily preoccupations of struggling humanity, the successive scenes present the human soul in its progress to identification with the divine. Whether one begins at the altar or at the entrance to the chapel these scenes are not arranged in a chronological order, and the argument that they were intended to be read as a symbolic sequence in reverse chronological order, beginning with the entrance, seems entirely convincing. According to this interpretation the first panel, the *Drunkenness of Noah*, may be taken to represent the imprisonment of the soul in the material condition of the body and of life on earth. The next scene, with its terrible and moving presentation of the *Deluge*, symbolizes the helplessness of primitive humanity before the light of grace has shone upon it. The *Sacrifice of Noah*, which follows, shows man awakening to a sense of his divine soul and the beginning of the contact through a sacrifice between man and God. Then follow in succession the *Fall*, with expulsion from Eden and its consciousness of sin, the *Creation of Eve*, the *Creation of Adam*, and finally the great representation of God the Father brooding over the sea, creating the sun and moon and separating the light from the darkness. The progress of the ascent, reading the successions of panels in this way, is one from materiality to the highest spirituality. It can be argued that these scenes are intended to reflect—and texts can be found which confirm this interpretation—the ascent of the soul in the hierarchy of being as it was outlined by Ficino and Pico. These theories had a pervasive influence on the art and literature of the period, and Michelangelo had grown up in the Florentine circle where neo-Platonic ideas of the soul and of love and of the relationship between man and the divine were most developed and most widely circulated. Conceptions the same as appear on the Sistine ceiling dominated also Michelangelo's designs for the mausoleum of Julius II and at a later date the funeral chapel of the Medici in Florence, where again the successive levels and aspects of the statues represent the freeing of the soul from its material connection and the ascent to the realm of pure form. In such syntheses the classic and particularly the Platonic tradition had been fused with Christian eschatology to present a confident and serene view of man and his position in the universe.[9]

[9] Ch. De Tolnay, *The Sistine Ceiling, Michelangelo* II (Princeton, 1945). The account of the Sistine ceiling given here is summarized from this work. For an alternative interpretation, stressing the anagogical interpretation of the Old Testament, see the article by Hartt cited above p. 163.

In the same years in which Michelangelo began work on the Sistine ceiling, Raphael was given the commission to decorate the chambers of Julius II in the Vatican. The son of a painter at the court of Urbino, Raphael had been brought up in the atmosphere created by the intellectual and artistic interests of the dukes. After a period of apprenticeship to Perugino he came to Florence, where he had an opportunity to learn from all the great figures of the generation immediately preceding his own. From Florence he was called to Rome to the service of Julius II at the instance of Bramante. The first and most famous of the stanzas, the so-called *Camera della Segnatura,* was completed by 1511, while the adjacent rooms were finished much later, with increasing participation by Raphael's pupils, some of whom painted the final frescoes of the series after the master's death.

The *Camera della Segnatura* is elaborate synthesis intended to symbolize the philosophic and religious truths of the age in ways that would provide plenty of scope for the display of the artist's skill in the composition and management of classical forms, as well as an opportunity for the introduction of contemporary portraiture. The iconography of these frescoes was the product of a collective effort, since it is probable that many of the humanists and literary figures at the court of Julius II made contributions and suggestions on the themes and on the design as a whole. On one wall, in the fresco now called *La Disputa,* is the representation of the church triumphant in the Heavens, with the whole company of the saints and the blessed, while below is the church militant, the two groups united in the adoration of the sacrament. Around the sacrament are grouped the four great doctors of the Latin Church and in the surrounding throng popes, cardinals, emperors and kings, indeed all humanity united in the ecclesiastical organization of western Christendom. Included among the individuals in this group are many contemporary personages such as Bramante and Raphael himself. Although more sophisticated in form and composition than traditional representations of this, the essential theme of the presentation of the church visible had been a common subject of medieval painting.

On the wall opposite the *Disputa* was presented the *School of Athens,* and the triumph of theology was thus confronted by the triumph of philosophy. This fresco, considered the most perfect exemplar of the classical style of the Renaissance, has been for generations celebrated as the archetype of academic painting, which successfully applied all the rules prescribed in the theoretical treatises. In a lofty and magnificent architectural setting the great philosophers and scientists of antiquity are arranged around the central figures of Plato and Aristotle. The whole conception proclaimed the harmony of reason and faith and was in fact a *cinquecento* classical version of the same themes as had been represented in the Spanish Chapel of Santa Maria Novella more than a hundred and fifty years before. The grouping of the philosophers indeed follows the description in Dante's *Inferno*.

On the remaining walls appear the representation of the cardinal virtues, with jurisprudence and the law on one side and Parnassus and the muses on the other. Among the great lawgivers are Justinian issuing the Pandects, and Gregory IX, with the features of Julius II, promulgating the decretals of the canon law. Among the attendants of the latter are the cardinals Medici and Farnese, who as Leo X and Paul III were to confront the age of religious revolution. On the opposite wall the contemporary figures of literature discourse with the great spirits of antiquity on a Mount Parnassus presided over by the muses. Thus within the walls of a single room an effort was made to summarize the intellectual and religious interests of the age and its idea of its own position with respect to both classic and Christian traditions.

In literature some of the products of the same age reflected even more self-conscious efforts to combine the antique with the Christian. Those who wrote in Latin frequently continued the process of mere imitation of classical examples, but the best of them, Politian, Pontano, Sannazaro, Bembo, combined some originality with their devotion to the world of the Greco-Roman inheritance. Sannazaro's widely admired *De partu virginis* may serve as an example. The story of the Incarnation was here told with grandiose solemnity and echoes of epic description. One of the shepherds standing at the cradle of the Christ child recites large parts of the Fourth Eclogue of Virgil. The same author's so-called *Piscatory Eclogues* attempted also to recapture a Virgilian mood, but substituted for shepherds the Neapolitan fishermen. This was the poet who together with Pontano was regarded as among the literary glories of the age and worthy of comparison with the greatest figures of classical antiquity.

The vernacular writings of some of the same poets have had a more enduring reputation than these imitations of classical models. Sannazaro's *Arcadia* had a pervasive influence and established the Arcadian scene in Renaissance literature. Politian's *Orfeo* and the stanzas called *La Giostra,* which were written for the victory of Giuliano de' Medici in a tournament, have had a far wider appeal than his Latin verses. Like the songs of Lorenzo de' Medici, at whose court they were written, they seem the bright and hopeful manifesto of creative expression in the vernacular. After the exaggerations and limitations of much humanist rhetoric and poetry, a return to the native tradition and to the language of Dante represented an enlargement of freedom, even though the dictates of classical taste were often still applied in a somewhat mechanical fashion.

Much of the greatest vernacular literature of the period rested ostensibly on the interpretation and continuation of medieval legend. In Florence Luigi Pulci finished in 1483 his *Morgante Maggiore*, which recast for a more sophisticated audience some of the materials of chivalric romance as they had been presented by the wandering minstrels to the people. At about the same time at the court of Ferrara the legends of the court of Charlemagne received an even more elaborate reinterpretation in the work of Boiardo, the *Orlando inamorato*. The elaborate chivalric romance, presented in a partly serious, partly satiric manner, found its appropriate audience in courts like that of the Este, where there flourished a kind of self-conscious cult of medieval ideals of nobility. In certain ways this phenomenon can be compared with the elaborate rituals of chivalry at the Burgundian court. In both cases ceremonial substitutes had been provided for real social functions which had either disappeared altogether or were being rapidly undermined. As the Knights of the Golden Fleece thought of themselves as the heirs of a real crusading tradition, so the circle at Ferrara and at other Italian courts identified themselves half seriously, half playfully with the paladins of the court of Charlemagne.

The literary form which Boiardo had made so popular was continued with greater success by Ariosto, who began to write his *Orlando Furioso* in 1503. Forty cantos were published in 1516, but the poet continued to rework and add to his epic until his death in 1533. Here the effect of the classic tradition was more apparent; the forms derived from the classic epic were imposed on the material of the medieval romance and the tale of the madness of Roland was also designed to contain episodes describing the foundation of the house of Este and magnifying its historical role. Thus the poem illustrates the incorporation of classical forms with medieval and contemporary themes.

These examples reveal the wide range of expression in literature and the plastic arts which can be considered under the rubric of classical influence. At one end of the scale was the simplest repetitive imitation of the art and poetry of the ancient world, while at the other classical philosophy provided the basis for the creation of new artistic forms. This freedom in the use of the heritage of classical antiquity indicates the essential independence of the Italian artists and writers of the fifteenth and sixteenth centuries. If there were a few who were exclusively dominated by Greek or Roman models, there were more who were able to transcend such models or discard them altogether. Innovation and tradition are always relative terms. The classic tradition must be described as a source of inspiration rather than by itself a creative force, and the view that the artist shaped the body of materials inherited by him is to be preferred to the view that his creations were entirely molded by the classical revival. Stated more generally this is what Burckhardt meant by declaring of the civilization of the Renaissance in Italy that it was not the revival of antiquity alone but its union with the genius of the Italian people that achieved the conquest of the western world.[10]

III. GOTHIC AND RENAISSANCE IN NORTHERN EUROPE: DÜRER

By the end of the fifteenth century Italian arts and letters were beginning to exercise their unprecedented influence over the cultural life of the western world. Already this influence was being felt in almost all the northern capitals, and artists and scholars regarded their education as incomplete if they had not made the Italian journey. Italian forms and fashions were carried to faraway Moscow, where architects from Bologna were employed in the rebuilding of the Kremlin, and to Poland, where the Sforza wife of a Jagellon king brought with her scholars, courtiers and artists who created for themselves a center of Renaissance culture. Likewise in Hungary the Italian marriage of Mathias Corvinus produced a court modeled on the Italian example. From France, Germany, the Netherlands, England and Spain an increasing succession of artists and scholars went to Italy and returned to their native countries with new ideas. In the Netherlands and Germany painting was increasingly affected by Italian influences and in France, among the architects and artists imported by the court in the wake of the Italian wars, Leonardo da Vinci was installed at Amboise by Francis I. Italian became and continued, at least till the time of Milton, to be the second modern language of educated men.

Even in the areas of greatest popularity, however, the new fashions in arts and letters were far from superseding the older traditions. In the national vernacular literatures there was no considerable effect of Italian

[10] Burckhardt, *Civilization of the Renaissance in Italy* (London, 1945), 104.

humanism until the turn of the century, though in many cases the forms which had been created by an earlier inspiration now seemed outworn, repetitive, exhausted. Neither in Germany, France, Spain nor England was the period from the middle of the fifteenth century to the eve of the Reformation an age of greatness in literary history. There were some individual masterpieces still read and cherished, the poems of Villon in France, the couplets of Jorge Manrique in Spain, and the *Morte d'Arthur* of Malory in England. Other productions, like the *Amadis de Gaul* and the *Celestina* in Spain and the French comedy, *Pathelin,* owe their importance to their great influence in literary history.

Beside these innovations, however, the great mass of the literature of these decades consisted of repetition, imitation or translation of medieval devotional and chivalric literature. Examples of work of this kind at its best are to be found in Caxton's translations of the *Four Last Things* and the *Legends of Troy.* The opposite end of the scale may be illustrated by the *Teurdank,* the fake chivalric poem composed in part by the Emperor Maximilian and describing his courtship of Mary of Burgundy. A more direct and unself-conscious expression of the age, of far greater value to the historian, were the satires. These again continued a medieval tradition, but one which developed and responded to contemporary conditions. The greatest satiric text of the late fifteenth century and one which enjoyed enormous circulation and imitation—it was translated and enlarged by Barclay in England—was the *Narrenschiff* (*Ship of Fools*) of Sebastian Brant. Here the follies of the whole range of human activity were exposed, but in a way which lacked the humanist touch of Erasmus' masterpiece of a decade later. The growth in the popularity of satire may not always be symptomatic of coming revolution, but the *Narrenschiff* and its imitators supplied ammunition against priests and monks to those whose belief in the old order had begun to fail. Here imaginative expression reflected the disillusionment and pessimism of the waning Middle Ages.

On the whole, then, in literature there was a hiatus between the greatest creations of the medieval genius and those of the sixteenth century. It was a period of preparation, at the end of which the reception of the classics under the leadership of Erasmian humanism provided the foundations on which the presiding geniuses of Renaissance literature, Rabelais, Montaigne, Cervantes and Shakespeare, were later to build.

In contrast with the scene in literature the plastic arts and particularly painting showed a continuing vitality, which was most apparent in the

Low Countries and in Germany. Although the work of the Van Eycks and most of that of Vander Weyden was over by the middle of the fifteenth century, the great tradition of Flemish painting continued in the work of Petrus Christus, Bouts, Memling, Van der Goes and Gerard David. Their portraits, madonnas and representations of the lives of the saints, like the Memling *Legend of St. Ursula* at Bruges, were triumphs of richly detailed observation presented with exquisite coloring.

The general impression of serenity produced by most of the works of this school was interrupted by the strangely fascinating and puzzling pictures of Hieronymus Bosch, who was able to combine with his grasp of realistic detail the power to represent esoteric religious visions and complicated allegories. His most impressive creations were filled with a symbolism which is not yet entirely explained. Sometimes, as in the case of the triptych called the *Hay Wagon,* he worked in part from biblical texts. The central panel of this picture shows the load of hay, symbolizing the desires of the flesh, drawn toward hell by the seven deadly sins. There follow in its wake a great crowd of people, among whom can be discerned an emperor and a pope. On top of the hay wagon a youth plays music to a maiden, while a third figure sounds a trumpet made of its own distorted nose. Love and Fame thus occupy the central place in the panorama of man's earthly desires, seducing him away from his true spiritual direction. In the foreground the distractions of human passion are further illustrated by a variety of figures engaged in trying to seize, bale and carry away as much hay as they can. To the left of the central panel is the representation of the fall of man, which occasioned the panorama of the center, and to the right is hell, whither the crowd following the hay wagon is bound. Here then is an allegory entirely medieval in spirit, filled probably with allusions to contemporary Flemish sayings as well as to the text of Isaiah. It emphasizes the corruption of man's condition and is untouched by any of those humanist ideals which in Italy proclaimed the dignity of man. It is perhaps no matter for surprise that the works of this artist in general and this picture in particular should have appealed to the taste of Philip II at the height of the Counter Reformation.

Even more extravagantly symbolic is the so-called *Garden of Earthly Lusts,* another of Bosch's great triptychs in the Madrid collection. It has been suggested that although the outward form of these creations is traditional, Bosch was using a luxuriant imagination to express sentiments which were far from orthodox, and that behind an obvious satire on contemporary abuses lurks an important assertion of fifteenth-century heresy, perhaps a survival of Adamite cults and the condemned doctrines of the Brethren of the Free Spirit. In accordance with this theory Bosch has been represented as foreshadowing the rejection of the formal channels of salvation through the visible church, and making an appeal to the sect mentality soon to reach revolutionary manifestations in the course of the next generation in the Anabaptist movement.[11] Attractive as it would be to find the varieties of religious belief of the age of the Reformation already depicted in the art of the end of the fifteenth century, credulity is strained by making Bosch the fervent apostle of a secret cult. The techniques of the Inquisition in the Netherlands were not what they were in contemporary Spain or what they were later to become in an age of religious persecution, but the Brethren of the Free Spirit had been condemned for over one hundred years when Bosch was painting and the town in which he spent most of his life was not a large place. The greater probability appears to be that the unexplained symbols and allegories in these powerful paintings are due not to esoteric religious beliefs but rather to an attempt to represent vividly contemporary folklore and habits of speech. As such, Bosch's devils and hell remain perfectly orthodox.

A less complicated orthodoxy was to be found in the German artistic tradition, which insisted on representations of Christian themes reflecting the spirit of the contemporary *Imitatio Christi*. A general characteristic of religious thought and expression in northern Europe during the fourteenth and fifteenth centuries was the increasing concentration on the life and passion of Christ. The transition from a theocentric to a Christocentric emphasis was manifest in a variety of ways. There was the institution of the Feast of Corpus Christi and its subsequent popularity, the adoration of the precious blood and wounds of Christ, the treatises on the importance of frequent communion, of which the last book of the *Imitatio Christi* is an example. This general direction of religious thought in the north contrasted, as we have seen, with the emergence in Italy under the influence of neo-Platonism of a theocentric and pantheistic belief centering worship and doctrine on the role of God the Father.

This contrast may be illustrated by referring to a celebrated example of late medieval German art, untouched by any classical or Italian influence. The *Eisenheim altarpiece* was painted for the abbey of the Knights Hos-

---

[11] W. Fraenger, *The "Millennium" of Hieronymus Bosch* (University of Chicago, 1952).

pitalers in Eisenheim by Mathias Grünewald, who finished it in 1516, only four years after the completion of the Sistine ceiling by Michelangelo. The altarpiece consists of nine panels folded together so that different scenes could be shown on different occasions. When the outer wings are closed they present a massive and somber crucifixion. The whole scene is executed with great realism, including an emphasis on the details of torture and death which is by itself revolting in its effect. The intention, however, was clearly not only to remind the spectator forcefully of the suffering upon the cross, but also to proclaim the growing triumph of Christ in the world. On two side panels were represented the patron saints of the monastery, St. Anthony and St. Sebastian. When the wings were opened, as they were on special occasion, the crucifixion was replaced by the scenes of the Annunciation, Incarnation and Resurrection. Finally, the shrine of St. Anthony, carved in wood, was revealed behind the second pair of wings, while on the backs were painted other scenes from the lives of the saints.

It is interesting to remember that this work was produced in the territories of the archbishop of Mainz, where the indulgences which Luther protested were already being preached. Grünewald was in fact court painter to Albert of Brandenburg, but the humanistic interests of this prince found no reflection in such a work as the *Eisenheim altarpiece*. The contrast between this altarpiece and the Sistine ceiling is a measure of the distance that divided the religious conceptions of the medieval world from those of the Renaissance. The most traditional representation of the Incarnation and Redemption, with its emphasis on the role of Christ, confronted the pantheistic God whose form had emerged from the attempt to synthesize Platonism and other antique philosophies with Christianity.[12]

The great genius who did most to bridge the gap between two styles and two modes of thought was Albrecht Dürer. Trained in the German workshops, his subsequent experience of Italian art and artists made a profound impression on him and, more than any other single individual, he enriched his native inheritance with the theoretical as well as the practical knowledge of the Renaissance.

Dürer was born in 1471, the son of a goldsmith of Nürnberg. He was originally trained to follow his father's profession, but gave it up for the attractions of a career in painting. His apprenticeship in the workshop of Wohlgemut was followed by two years of traveling in Germany. He was

[12] Arthur Burkhard, *Mathias Grünewald, Personality and Accomplishment* (Cambridge, 1936).

particularly responsive to such classical influences as were already present in German humanism and was interested in the copies of Italian drawings which circulated in Germany even before the date of his first Italian journey in 1494. This journey, however, made an enormously significant impression on the young artist, and the year has been often suggested as the beginning of the northern Renaissance because it marked so definite a stage in Dürer's development. He adapted classical themes and forms from Mantegna, Bellini, Pollaiuolo and others. Still more important, he derived from the Italian masters his interest in artistic theory and the relation between practical and theoretical knowledge.

By the time of the second Italian journey, eleven years later, Dürer was already a recognized master in painting, woodcarving and engraving. In all three of these arts his work revealed new and varied potentialities. He occupied in Nürnberg a great position as the artist who was the friend and companion of the most celebrated of German humanists, the portrait painter of such scholars as Erasmus and of such rulers as Frederick the Wise, and the particular protégé of Emperor Maximilian.

One of the most characteristic enterprises in which Dürer became engaged because of his connection with Maximilian was the emperor's project for a representation of a triumphal arch and a triumphal procession in woodcuts which should celebrate his glory and confirm his position in the eyes of posterity. The Triumphal Arch was a collaborative work, for which Maximilian himself and Pirckheimer, the humanist friend of Dürer, supplied much of the iconography. Dürer labored on selected woodcuts which were a part of the larger scheme and was himself responsible for bringing the enterprise which, when assembled, involved a woodcut yards in dimensions, to a successful conclusion. The arch contains an elaborate representation of the members of the imperial family stretching back through the whole fantastic genealogy which was one of the characteristic claims of sixteenth century royalty. It was complicated by a luxuriant symbolism, derived in large part from the *Hieroglyphs* of Horus Apollo, a fourth-century treatise, purporting to give the significance of hieroglyphic writing. This work had enjoyed great popularity in Italy; its claims to provide an esoteric universal language accorded well with the religious and linguistic interests of many humanists. Pirckheimer had been engaged on a translation of the *Hieroglyphs* and the emperor was personally interested in suggesting appropriate symbols from this source. He had himself represented as surrounded with so many allegorical animals and carrying so much allegorical regalia that the result could only be 'an artistic and iconographic failure.

The Triumphal Arch was completed, but the procession which was to pass under it was never finished according to the original specifications. The woodcuts for the procession were published posthumously by order of Maximilian's grandson Ferdinand in 1525. Dürer's contribution to these projects was of course far from his greatest work and far also from appealing to modern taste. The whole enterprise is, however, illustrative of many of the conditions and interests that had a determinative influence on his career. There was the relationship between artist and patron, the role played by Maximilian as the inspirer of this official panegyric, the emphasis upon an esoteric symbolism, and the interweaving of classical and medieval traditions.[13]

If the projects for Maximilian represent the extreme of that aspect of Dürer's work which looked to the past and depended on scholastic and humanist erudition, in the service of a feudal imperialism, the other extreme is to be found in his scientific and theoretical work, in which he makes a clear break with inherited modes of thought and presages a time which in many ways anticipates the characteristics which scientific thought was to assume in the future. As a theorist of art Dürer's two principal contributions were the *Instruction in Measurement* and the *Four Books on Human Proportions,* both intended as parts of a larger whole, but in the form in which we have them both extended beyond the scope they would have occupied in the completed plan.

In both these works the emphasis was upon the attainment of general rules, universally valid, as opposed to pragmatic rules of practice. On the subject of perspective Dürer took over what had been achieved by the Italians of the fifteenth century and added to the application of the theory by inventing a device to guide the artist. In analyzing the proportions of the human figure Dürer worked with the tradition inherited from Vitruvius on the mathematical determination of the perfect figure. Both these subjects were part of the more general problem of the representation of the world of nature in art. This theory of the artist's function involved the analysis of the object in nature itself, anatomy, the structure of rocks, etc., and it also involved the theoretical discussion of how to represent the three-dimensional, natural object in a two-dimensional medium in painting, drawing or engraving.[14] Hence Dürer's work on

[13] Panofsky, *Albrecht Dürer,* Vol. I (Princeton, 1943), 172–182.
[14] *Ibid.,* 244.

this subject, like that of Leonardo, reveals the closeness of the connection existing in the first decades of the sixteenth century between science, understood in something like its modern sense, and the world of art. The claim has in fact been made that the artists of the Renaissance were the first men of science. Not the artist alone, however, but the philosopher and the artisan as well contributed to the complex development that lay behind the appearance of an autonomous realm described as scientific activity. The contribution of the artist to this evolution, critically important as it was, must be viewed in a larger context of both intellectual and practical activity.

IV. TOWARD THE SCIENTIFIC REVOLUTION: LEONARDO

Every generation either constructs a new periodization of the past or puts a different emphasis upon the periodization it has inherited. In the middle of the twentieth century we have come to speak of a "scientific revolution," dated roughly between 1550 and 1700, and we commonly regard this revolution as the greatest change of direction in the history of western civilization since the birth of Christianity. In spite of the persistence of cultural patterns stemming ultimately from the Greeks and the Hebrews, we realize that the society which emerged from the scientific revolution was profoundly different from what had gone before; the work of Copernicus and Kepler, of Galileo, Descartes and Newton created a new world. For this reason increasing effort has been directed to the understanding of the immediate background of this revolution, that is, the history of scientific thought in the period of the later Middle Ages and the Renaissance.[15] How shall we analyze the combination of factors in the institutions and ideas of the western European world that brought about the development of the particular body of knowledge which we call "scientific," and the control of the physical world which followed? The question is one which our present techniques of investigation do not permit us to answer satisfactorily, but it is nevertheless most important that it be asked. This question indeed must take its place along with the problems of the emergence of nationalism and capitalism as one of the central themes on which not only our understanding of the history of Europe but also of our present situation is based.

The period with which we are concerned here is that between the lives of Nicholas of Cusa and Leonardo da Vinci, including the time when Copernicus was developing his revolutionary ideas, although they were

[15] Herbert Butterfield, *Origins of Modern Science, 1300–1800* (New York, 1950).

to see the light only in 1543, after his death. Attempts to summarize the contribution made by this period to the whole long story of the growth of scientific thought have distinguished three kinds of activity as particularly significant. In the first place, there was the scholastic tradition, founded on the Aristotelian philosophy. In this tradition the continuing critical discussion of Aristotle's physics was of the greatest importance. Secondly, there were the innovations of humanism, which supplied new attitudes toward the classics, new standards of accuracy in the interpretation of texts, and philosophical ideas derived from the Platonic and neo-Platonic traditions. Finally, in contrast to these essentially intellectual and theoretical sources, there was the contribution of those whose activity was purely empirical, such as cartographers who labored on sailing charts without benefit of theoretical formulas, or engineers who were solving problems in ballistics without reference to learned treatises. The union of these three different types of activity was perhaps first of all effectively realized by the great artist and this is why a Dürer or a Leonardo da Vinci has a great and justified place in the history of science as well as in the history of art. The achievement of Leonardo, however, would have been impossible without the previous separate contributions of the scholastic, the humanist and the artisan, and in the gradual construction of the framework within which the scientific revolution began, the scholastic tradition was initially the most important.[16]

During the course of the fourteenth century there had been elaborated at the Paris school an attack on the Aristotelian theory of motion. Aristotle's physics had assumed that bodies in their natural state were at rest and that what required explanation was motion. Consequently there had been the conception of the prime mover and, where the agent of motion was not obvious, this had to be invoked. In the case of projectiles the assumption was that they were carried along by the push of air. Now the critics of this theory among the fourteenth-century scholastics, chiefly Buridan, Oresme and Albert of Saxony, had developed an analysis of what they called impetus, a quality supposed to have been assumed by the projectile which carried it along in its flight. This was a stage on the way toward the modern theory of inertia, not finally developed until the seventeenth century.

This work of the Paris school was assimilated and developed particularly at Padua in the fifteenth and sixteenth centuries. The University of Padua was celebrated as the center of medical studies, and the home of

---

[16] See J. B. Conant, *Science and Common Sense* (Yale, 1951), 12–13.

a most persistent Aristotelian tradition. In particular the doctrines of Averroes, the celebrated Arabic commentator of Aristotle, attained there an enormous influence, reflected in many ways in the science and philosophy of the whole Italian Renaissance. Working on these materials, the scholars of Padua made important contributions to the evolution of scientific method by applying themselves to the constant and rigid critique of the traditional scholastic problems. This work of the Paduan school was eclipsed and misunderstood because of the attacks of the humanists in the fifteenth and sixteenth centuries. The philological and grammatical interests of the humanists, and their eagerness to attain a greater place in education for their discipline, led them to despise the traditional subjects of university instruction. Humanistic literature contains a long series of diatribes against science and scholastic logic. In spite of these attacks, however, the current of Aristotelian thinking persisted and made indispensable contributions to the development of scientific ideas, particularly on the subject of the theory of motion. The recognition of the historical importance of the school of Padua has thus finally provided an effective answer to those who condemned the sterility of the traditional debates in the name of a higher educational interest.[17]

The humanist contribution to the emergence of new scientific thinking may be summarized under two heads. It was in part a contribution to methods and in part an addition to a specific body of knowledge, chiefly about ancient science.

The critical scholarship of the humanists, although devoted almost exclusively to the elucidation of classical texts, must clearly have had an effect on other areas of thought. The painstaking research into the history of a text, the insistence on accuracy, the ideals of critical scholarship, connected as they were with a growing sense of history, could not but produce an alteration in the general intellectual climate. Furthermore, the interests of the humanist in a set of simple general ideas, derived from research into the meaning of a particular author, offered a striking contrast to the typical scholastic commentary cluttered with an infinity of detail. The broad lines, for example, of Erasmus' interpretation of the meaning of the Pauline Epistles, as contrasted with the *Sentences* of Peter Lombard, might have suggested a similar simplicity and directness of approach in dealing with problems in quite a different area. Although it is very difficult to document the humanist influence in this respect, it

[17] J. H. Randall, "The Development of Scientific Method in the School of Padua," *Journal of the History of Ideals,* I (April 1940).

is clearly not possible to neglect it altogether.

Far more obviously and directly important was the provision by the humanists of a body of texts and translations of Greek science and philosophy. The translations into Latin of Ptolemy, Archimedes, Galen, and others were landmarks in the history of western scientific thought. Those Greek works which were strictly scientific stimulated a new insight into the possibility of the investigation of the physical world. The Platonic revival, on the other hand, disposed men to think about the universe in terms of simple mathematical harmonies, and the combining of these two parts of the Greek inheritance had effects in both the arts and sciences, in the development of perspective, as well as the theories of human proportion, in architecture and in astronomy and cosmography.

The influence of Pythagorean and Platonic thought may be clearly discerned, for example, in the background of the ideas of Copernicus. Although his early training had been received at Cracow, he had studied at Bologna, where one of his teachers was Domenico Maria de Novara, who had been associated with the neo-Platonic circle in Florence. It is a commonplace that Copernicus was attracted to his hypothesis not by any new evidence about the motions of the heavenly bodies, but by the fact that his assumption offered a simpler mathematical explanation than Ptolemy's elaborate construction of orbits and epicycles. In effect, Copernicus' system reduced the number of circles from over eighty to thirty-four, but in spite of this radical change there were many elements of conservatism in the Copernican cosmology and the effects of his great innovation were not widely felt for nearly a century.[18]

The purely empirical tradition in the sciences and its interrelations with theory are perhaps best illustrated in the history of cartography. The Portolan charts developed in Italy in the late medieval period as a guide to Mediterranean navigation were elaborated and extended in the fifteenth century to include a representation of what was known about the rest of the world and some indications of the recent Portuguese voyages. On Fra Mauro's map of 1457, for example, not only did the representation of Asia take account of the data contained in Marco Polo, but also of the contributions of very recent travelers like Nicholas de Conti. On the Genoese Portolan of the same year the results of Prince Henry's voyages were indicated. These maps may be said to mark the culmination of the empirical tradition. At the same time that Fra Mauro and the Genoese cartographer were working on their maps, the revival of Ptolemy had stimu-

[18] E. A. Burtt, *Metaphysical Foundations of Modern Science* (London, 1932), ch. II.

lated the production of a great number of globes and charts based on his *Geography*. The famous Behaim globe, for example, produced in Nürnberg in the year in which Columbus sailed for America, was almost entirely based on Ptolemy, although its author had lived in Portugal for some years and professed to have taken part in Portuguese expeditions. The history of advance in geographical knowledge in the first decades of the sixteenth century is largely the story of the bridging of the gap between the separate traditions represented by Mauro and Behaim. By the time the famous Waldseemüller maps of the world were produced not twenty years after the first voyage of Columbus, empirical data had been welded together with the available theoretical knowledge.[19]

The harmonious combination of theory and practice in creative activity was one of the themes of Renaissance speculation and it is perhaps not surprising that the greatest advances were made in astronomy, geography and physics, all sciences which were closely related to the most intensive practical efforts which the European world was then making. This relationship is still more apparent in considering a single man than in analyzing the development of a subject. In the greatest scientific genius of the age it is clear that the effects of tradition were closely interrelated with the challenges derived from the attempt to solve practical problems. The work of Leonardo da Vinci is a single whole, but there can be distinguished in it the influence of scholasticism, of humanism, and of practical empirical activity.

The preponderance of one or another of these influences on the formation of Leonardo's genius has been debated. It has been maintained, for example, that Leonardo was saved by his ignorance and that his achievements in practical and theoretical science were possible only because he was spared subjection to the dogmatism of the formal scholastic tradition in the university.[20] It is true that he was apprenticed to the studio of Verrocchio at an early age, when he had only the minimum of a formal education, and he was therefore perhaps left more free to follow the bent of his curiosity unhampered by the learning which fashioned so many of his contemporaries.

On the other hand, however little formal education Leonardo had received, by the time he entered Verrocchio's studio he was already acquainted with Toscanelli, the famous Florentine scientist and presumed

---

[19] On fifteenth-century cartography see the important monograph of D. Durand, *The Vienna-Klosterneuburg Map Corpus* (Leiden, 1952).

[20] G. Sarton, *The Life of Science, Essays in the History of Civilization* (New York, 1949), 77.

correspondent of Columbus. Toscanelli undoubtedly fostered his interest in physics. Leonardo also attended the lectures of the Greek exile, Argyropoulos, who introduced him to the humanistic texts and especially to the Greek philosophic and scientific traditions. Clearly, even if we are to attempt to "explain" Leonardo on the grounds of his fortunate escape from a university education, the importance of both humanist and scholastic learning cannot be minimized.

With these beginnings Leonardo continued throughout his life to display an enormous range of interest in scientific and philosophical problems, although there were very few subjects either of theoretical or practical character the investigation of which he carried to a logical conclusion. The product of these interests consisted of the famous hundred and twenty notebooks which he bequeathed to his friend, Francesco de Melzi. Of these hundred and twenty notebooks only a part now remains, dispersed in various museums and libraries in Europe. From these fragments it is extraordinarily difficult to derive any coherent idea of what Leonardo's purpose was and what shape these volumes were ultimately to assume in his mind. Was this mass of notes intended to be ordered in a series of treatises on separate important subjects, or was it intended as a basis for a kind of *summa* on the current state of human knowledge about the universe? From the scanty indications we have it is impossible to tell. Clearly these notes as they exist were not intended for publication. Leonardo did not write in Latin but in a difficult Italian, complicated further by the fact that he used mirror-writing and wrote in reverse from right to left. Most of the manuscripts that survive date from the beginning of the sixteenth century and do not include any of his notes before 1500.[21]

A great deal has been made of the few remarks in Leonardo's manuscripts about the importance of following experience as opposed to theory. Clearly there were areas in which Leonardo followed this precept constantly and some of his insights, built on actual observation, do in fact anticipate the interests and achievements of a much later generation. This is particularly true of the problem of fossil shells found in the mountains far from the sea. It has been claimed that with his theoretical analysis of this subject Leonardo founded the science of paleontology. All his work on anatomy was also clearly founded on daily and painstaking observation. Some of the notes comprise a careful record of dissections, which were the basis of his accounts of human anatomy. Furthermore, in the

[21] E. MacCurdy, *Leonardo's Notebooks* (New York, 1939), 41–54.

practical engineering problems in which he interested himself, particularly his strange and long-continued absorption in the problem of constructing a flying machine and his investigation of the possibility of supporting underneath the water a submarine diver who would be constantly supplied with air, we have examples of the application of scientific observation of the sort that have been familiar to us since the period when the achievements of natural science began to dominate European intellectual history.

On the other hand, against these examples of the use of observation and the practical application of theory it must be recorded that large amounts of material in the notebooks are nothing more than digests of medieval scientific treatises, many of the conclusions of which were accepted by Leonardo in a completely uncritical and unscientific manner. His anatomical work led him to the very threshold of discovering the circulation of the blood, which he would have done except for his acceptance of Galen's theory of the invisible pores in the inner walls of the heart.[22] Here then is no example of the results of observation, but instead a case of the obstructive action of authority. Altogether we must conclude that Leonardo's scientific work, remarkable as it is in many ways, was not quite so unique as it has sometimes been represented to be. With Leonardo we are only partly on the way to the divorce between magic and the experimental method and the connection of the latter with natural science which was to be achieved in the seventeenth century, when the modern era in fact began.

In that progress it may perhaps be maintained that Leonardo's practical achievements were more important than his theoretical innovations. His preoccupation with feats of engineering like the flying machine, the control of the water supply, the construction of engines of war, represent the exploration of sources of power which became the central characteristic of western technology. Such practical applications were a constant stimulus to the formulation of new theoretical problems.[23]

The very multiplicity of the interests which Leonardo represented is a commentary on how little either his thought or his action was compartmentalized into those divisions which have become so characteristic of the modern world. The man who more than any other single figure has seemed to successive generations to be a microcosm of the creative forces of his age, the archetype of universal man, was at once scientist and artist,

[22] Butterfield, op. cit., 38–39.
[23] Sarton, op. cit., 79–82.

theorist and practitioner. He stood at a critical point when the great lines of division were beginning. The arts were ceasing to be crafts and were becoming "fine arts." The opposition between the world of science and the world of art was becoming discernible. The theorist was coming to be separated from the practical worker. Yet for Leonardo these dichotomies did not exist. The highest achievements of art could be determined by scientific rules, on the proportions of the human body, on perspective, on effects of light and shadow. Like those of his contemporaries who were concerned with harmonizing the historical religions and philosophic traditions, Leonardo perceived behind the apparent multiplicity of the universe a single truth.

Chapter Ten

CONCLUSION

ERASMUS dedicated his *Novum instrumentum* to Leo X on February 1, 1516. In the letter of presentation to the pope he celebrated the virtue and learning which had flourished under Leo's pontificate. He proclaimed that Leo X had restored morality even in Rome, but that his greatest virtue, commending him to heaven as well as to mortal admiration, was the zeal with which he had restored Christian piety. Even piety, Erasmus confessed, like all human things, had a tendency to relapse and degenerate under the impact of time and war unless sustained by constant effort. But to have restored was in his opinion a finer achievement than to have founded. It was therefore necessary for every Christian man to aid Leo's restoration to the best of his abilities. Men of great genius and wealth were contributing marble, ivory, gems and gold to the building of St. Peter's. Erasmus' own contribution was modestly offered as the restoration of the fundamental texts of the Christian tradition.[1]

The hopeful view for the future of Christian society announced in this document remained with Erasmus in the following months and was indeed sustained and encouraged by the developments of the succeeding year. After the conclusion of the concordat of Bologna, Erasmus' confidence was still more generalized. He wrote to his friend Wolfgang Capito on February 26, 1517:

It is not part of my nature, most learned Wolfgang, to be excessively fond of life; whether it is, that I have, to my own mind, lived long enough, having entered my fifty-first year or that I see nothing in this life so splendid or delightful that it should be desired by one who is convinced by the Christian faith that a happier life awaits those who in this world earnestly attach themselves to piety. But at the present moment I could almost wish to be young again, for no other reason but this, that I anticipate the approach of a golden age: so clearly do we see the minds of princes, as if changed by inspiration, devoting all their energies to the pursuit of peace. In this effort Pope Leo X and Francis the King of the French have been the principal leaders. . . .

[1] P. S. Allen, *Opus epistolarum Des. Erasmi Roterodami,* Vol. II (Oxford, 1910), No. 384.

Therefore when I see that the highest sovereigns of Europe, Francis of France, Charles, the Catholic King, Henry of England and the Emperor Maximilian have set all their war-like preparations aside and established peace upon solid and as I hope adamantine foundations, I am led to a confident hope that not only morality and Christian piety but also a genuine and purer literature may come to renewed life or greater splendor; especially as this object is pursued with equal zeal in various parts of the world,—at Rome by Pope Leo, in Spain by the Cardinal of Toledo, in England by Henry VIII, himself not unskilled in letters, and among ourselves by our young King Charles who seems to have something almost divine in his character. In France King Francis who seems as it were born for this object invites and entices from all countries men that excel in merit and learning. Among the Germans the same aim is pursued by many of their excellent princes and bishops and especially by Emperor Maximilian whose old age wearied of so many wars has decided to seek rest in the arts of peace, a resolution as suited to his years as it is fortunate for the Christian world. To the piety of these princes it is due that we see everywhere arising as if upon a given signal men of genius who conspire together to restore the best literature. . . . Polite letters which were almost extinct are now cultivated and embraced even by Scots, Danes and Irishmen. Medicine has a host of champions. . . . Roman law is restored and mathematics. In the theological sphere we are especially devoted to the exertions of Jacques Lefèvre d'Etaples.[2]

In April of the same year in another letter sent to Leo X while Erasmus was on the way to England to receive the dispensation and absolution granted by the pope, he reiterated the same great expectations:

. . . as a matter of public concern I congratulate this age of ours which promises to be an age of gold if ever there was one wherein I see under your happy auspices and by your holy counsels three of the chief blessings of humanity are about to be restored to her, I mean first that truly Christian piety which has in many ways fallen into decay, second learning of the best sort hitherto partly neglected and partly corrupted and third the public and lasting concord of Christendom, the source and parent of piety and erudition. These will be the undying trophies of Leo X, which, consecrated to eternal memory by the writings of learned men, will forever render your pontificate and your family illustrious.[3]

The hopes Erasmus cherished on the eve of the Reformation may be juxtaposed with the forebodings of Aeneas Sylvius some seventy years

---

[2] F. M. Nichols, *The Epistles of Erasmus from His Earliest Letters to His Fifty-First Year Arranged in Order of Time*, Vol. II (New York, 1904), pp. 505–508.

[3] *Ibid.*, p. 521.

before. The contrast is a measure of the changes in the civilization of Europe during those years. Erasmus was very explicit in basing his views on the imminent restoration of peace, learning and piety. On the first of these benefits it is difficult to see in retrospect how Erasmus could have had a greater expectation than Aeneas Sylvius that the perennial conflicts between the European states would be solved. There had certainly been no cessation of such conflicts; on the contrary, warfare had been intensified, waged on a larger scale and with improved military organization and equipment. The armies that fought the campaigns of Francis I in Lombardy and the famous Spanish infantry of Ferdinand were far more formidable forces than those which had been at the disposal of the dukes of Burgundy at the height of their power. Furthermore, the relationships among the European states had been to some extent regularized and systematized with the result that it might have been maintained there was less chance than ever of European unity. In spite of the great collection of territories which Maximilian had brought together and which he was about to hand on to his grandson Charles, it had long been clear that the political life of the European community would not crystallize into a single monolithic structure. Attempts to dominate there were and would be in the future, but the pattern already established indicated that such attempts would be checked or defeated. The French monarchy had in many ways an institutional strength which compared favorably with that of its Spanish and Hapsburg rivals. Charles V might still dream of a unified and peaceful Christendom subject to a historic central authority; at one time his chancellor even tried to persuade Erasmus to edit the *De monarchia* of Dante in the interests of the imperial propaganda. But these hopes bore little relation to contemporary realities and by the time of the battle of Marignano in 1515 there was an impressive body of evidence that competition among European states for such prizes as control of the Italian peninsula would grow more intense, that it would be waged between larger and more efficiently organized political units and that its effects would be correspondingly more severe.

A parallel intensification of conflict was to be observed in the history of the relations between church and state. After centuries of struggle, in which the rival theories had failed to bring about an enduring practical solution, the balance was now definitely shifting toward an increase of control by the secular state. In all the long history of concordats and treaties with the governments of Europe no popes had ever really surrendered more than did Sixtus IV in establishing the Spanish Inquisition and

Leo X in signing the concordat of Bologna. It may indeed be maintained that short-term gains for the papacy resulted from both of these acts and especially from the concordat of Bologna, but on balance they both constituted abdications by Rome. Relying on the authority derived from their control of the Inquisition the Spanish sovereigns in effect assumed the direction of the ecclesiastical life of their kingdoms, and in France, although the papacy retained financial benefits, the most Christian king nominated to all consistorial benefices. In a sense the creation of churches on a national or territorial basis, which was to be dramatically realized in England and Germany in the coming years, had already occurred without open revolution in Spain and France. The existence of both the Inquisition and the concordat must enter largely into our understanding of the subsequent limits attained by the spread of Protestantism.

The conflicts between state and state and between state and church were both aggravated by the issues of control of property. The accumulation of capital in private hands proceeded rapidly with the expansion of the trade routes and the rise in productivity of the European economy as a whole. The sanctions of private property became increasingly secure as the theoretical distinction between property and government was more sharply drawn. Economic power or property was one thing and political power or governmental authority another. The great merchant bankers like the Fugger and the Chigi financed the courts of Charles V and Leo X, and if it appeared to contemporary eyes and even to some subsequent historians that the finance capitalists were entirely the servants of the state, used and broken as soon as they had served their purposes, yet their very existence and their relationship to the rulers revealed certain limits in the power of political authority. The governments of the early sixteenth century did indeed extend their control over economic life in all phases and endeavored to extend it still further. But there remained an area, not yet autonomous as it later became, but sufficiently independent to ensure that within the typical western state political control should not be monolithic and, as we should say today, "totalitarian." The conflict between government, whether ecclesiastical or secular, and the property of the individual subject was a permanent part of the European institutional inheritance. In this field, perhaps more significantly than in other areas, the characteristic pluralism of that inheritance was maintained and strengthened. As the church began to lose its power as a rival of secular government, the claims of property, as a makeweight against secular power, grew in significance.

The extent and character of these institutional relationships were only partly apparent to the contemporary observer; in the area of intellectual history, however, there were tensions which produced an unavoidable and conscious sense of conflict. The most distinctive characteristic of the period was an effort to assimilate a wider knowledge of classical antiquity and fit it to the categories of Christian dogma. The hopes of humanist intellectuals centered on the Socratic belief that knowledge was virtue, that by taking thought man could increase his understanding of Christian revelation and so enhance his piety. The opposition maintained that the new learning would corrode traditional theology and eventually the social structure as well. This conflict was waged all over Europe in the universities, in the printing establishments, which were the research centers of scholarship, and even in the cabinets of kings. No one could yet foresee that the choice facing the next generation would be between the predestination of Calvinism and the submission to authority of the Jesuits and the council of Trent. Looking back from a period when the permanence of the ideological split has been almost taken for granted as a necessary stage in the development of the European mind, it is difficult to realize the hopes aroused by the prospect of an Erasmian reformation. Yet a whole generation shared with Erasmus the belief that the greater knowledge of the classical world and even of comparative religion could be fitted to the existing framework very much as the discovery of new lands and new peoples was regarded as only a further opportunity for the extension of the horizon of Christian thought. The tension between traditional Christianity and the classical world could be made real and its consequences were to be apparent in the history of the sixteenth century, but it was imperfectly realized by the generation which still felt that it was not innovating but only restoring an inheritance corrupted by centuries of accretions.

Thus in major fields of human activity the sixty-odd years between the middle of the fifteenth century and the eve of the religious revolution were filled with conflicts, some of which loomed large in the contemporary mind while the existence of others was hardly perceived. Study of the nature of these conflicts and some understanding, however partial, of their relationship with each other helps us to fix the significance of this epoch in the wider perspective of European history. The story of the rise of modern Europe is in one sense the story of the rise of nationalism, capitalism and science. We shall probably never be able to explain, as we explain certain phenomena of the natural world, why the small group of European peoples produced those institutions, ideas and techniques which ultimately transformed not only their own but also all other civilizations. Yet the very necessity of a deeper understanding of our own position today drives us to comparative study in an effort to determine how it was that sentiments of political identification extended as far but no further than the national state, why a middle class emerged in so much stronger a position in the European world, and why a learned and a practical tradition were able to work together to produce a mastery of nature. Although these questions are not of the kind to which our present knowledge and methods permit us to give specific answers, it is illuminating to bear them in mind in examining any particular time span in European history. The Renaissance was an age when the results of the expansion of the horizon in both the literal and the figurative sense were becoming visible. The immediate effect was often to produce a sense of disorder and chaos and it is precisely because the elements of conflict were enhanced that we can study better the relationship of the political, economic and intellectual achievements to the pluralistic background. Although no one can claim that nationalism, capitalism or modern science "began" in this period, we can nevertheless study the evolution of these institutions and ideas through an early phase in which the creative effect of competition and conflict can be analyzed.

The existence of these tensions also provides a background for understanding the fact that professional knowledge and areas of scholarly and creative activity were becoming increasingly compartmentalized. Where there was less cohesion in the social order and in the intellectual world as a whole, it became more satisfying and indeed necessary to seek for that more limited but more intensive unity which could be obtained by isolating and defining a given subject matter. Hence Machiavelli in political theory, Leonardo and Dürer in the theory of the arts, Erasmus in classical scholarship found autonomous areas in which they could pursue their investigations and draw their conclusions without reference to revealed truth or inherited knowledge about the universe as a whole. The age which we commonly think of as characterized by versatility and the universal man was in fact the period when the walls between art and science, between politics and ethics began to be built. Indeed the very concept of versatility implies that there are distinct "subjects" or "fields" in which a man can prove his capacity.

Yet this very specialization, if it may be called that—understood as a differentiation of subject matter rather than as a personal specialization in the modern sense—was still predicated on a conviction of the unity of truth and the ultimate harmony of all knowledge. Reaction to the pressure of contemporary events, judgments on the outlook for the future varied as they always have and always will so long as a civilization with any degree of organization remains. Hopes for a golden age, such as those expressed by Erasmus, could be matched by expressions of despair over the evils of the time. The *Speculum humanae salvationis* and the works of St. Antoninus of Florence were printed more often than most humanist literature. The dance of death attained its greatest literary and iconographic popularity in these years. Yet it is possible to maintain that the dominant note was sounded by those who believed in the secular future of European Christian civilization. If the optimists had not had behind them inherited unities of ideas and institutions, they could not have been so convinced of the creative possibilities of the future. There have been plenty of ages in which the sense of conflict was so intense that it produced only spiritual despair. The balance was a delicate one and those who had the deepest insight were more aware of the conditions necessary to maintain it. Hence the insistence of Erasmus on the necessity of the establishment of harmony among the Christian princes, the plea of More for the recognition of the harmony between classical thought and Christianity, and the search by Leonardo for the laws of harmony governing artistic creation. As the medieval world order was disappearing there was sought, with many false starts and changes of direction, a new kind of order, an order based upon the reconciliation of opposites, on the creative energy of conflict accepted and harmonized.

The hopes expressed by Erasmus during these years were shared by others. Lefèvre d'Etaples, writing a little later his introduction to the *Commentary on the Four Gospels,* published in 1521, described the increase in the knowledge of the Gospel and compared it with the contemporary discovery of the physical world.

The light of the Gospel is again entering the world at a time in which great numbers of people have been illuminated by divine light so that since the time of Constantine there has not been a greater knowledge of languages, nor a more extensive discovery of the globe nor a wider propagation of the name of Christ to the farthest corners of the earth than in these times of ours.[4]

Knowledge of languages came, he says, at the very time the Portuguese in the east and the Spanish in the west were discovering new lands. It

---

[4] Jacques Lefèvre d'Etaples (Faber Stapulessis), *Commentarii initiatorii in quatuor evangelia* (Basle, 1521), Introduction.

might therefore be hoped that the gospel of Christ would be announced purely and sincerely to all these previously unknown people.

In the thought of both Erasmus and Lefèvre ideas of purification, reform, rebirth were interestingly intertwined with ideas of novelty and development. Among their contemporaries were some who consciously attempted to measure the degree of innovation and to draw up as it were a balance sheet of change. During the pontificate of Leo X the famous Italian doctor, Fracastoro, wrote and dedicated to Pietro Bembo his epic poem on syphilis, the dread disease which had first appeared in Europe in virulent epidemic form at the end of the fifteenth century. This subject naturally led to concentration on the evils of the age and in his second book Fracastoro considered the wider question of the proportion of good and evil in the cultural situation of his age in comparison with former times:

Although a cruel tempest rages and the conjunction of the stars has been wicked yet not wholly has the clemency of the gods been removed from us. If this century has seen a new disease, the ravages of war, the sack of cities, floods and drouth, yet it has also been able to navigate oceans denied to antiquity, and has reached beyond the bounds of the previously known term of the world. We have attained a whole world different from ours both in its peoples and even in its heavens where there shine new stars. Our age also has seen a famous poet (Sannazaro) whom even the sacred shade of Vergil has applauded; it has seen Bembo and, above all, the precious gift of the rule of Leo X who has brought back to Latium the rule of justice and law and who shelters all the arts.[5]

Fracastoro thus expressed a kind of doctrine of compensation in which the great gains of the enlargement of the physical horizon and the achievements in literature and art balanced the increasing ravages of disease and war.

Such attitudes as this appeared against the traditional Christian strains of temporal pessimism and eternal hope. Christian pessimism about this world was perhaps most effectively expressed in a secularized form by Machiavelli. History, he held, is a pattern which repeats itself. There is only a certain amount of *virtù* in the world. What is *virtù* in one man may be another's evil fortune. Even if a mighty effort of intelligence and will should succeed in creating such conditions as those of the Roman republic, eventual decay could not be prevented. Yet even Machiavelli was an activist. The French and Spanish must be resisted; conditions

[5] J. Fracastoro, *Opera omnia* (Venice, 1555), 241–242.

which had been better in the time of Lorenzo de' Medici could be made so again by a heroic effort.

The various forms of a belief in the possibility of a restoration of a golden age, in the improvement of the temporal condition of humanity, however briefly sustained, the conviction that at least for some men higher levels would be reached and new horizons opened, all this flowered against a background of conflict when the diverse elements entering into the European intellectual and cultural inheritance were subjected to strains more manifest, more consciously felt, than they had been before. These conflicts, however, were on the whole more creative than destructive, in spite of what had been anticipated by a mind as acute as that of Aeneas Sylvius scarcely more than half a century before. The pessimism which was the dominant note of the waning Middle Ages passed by one of those sudden transitions which have marked the dynamism of western culture into a kind of confidence in the creative powers of European civilization to build a secular future.

Man was still a microcosm occupying a special place in the universe but the emphasis was shifting from his relation to God and eternity to his control of the social and temporal environment here and now on this earth. That such control was by almost all envisaged as simply one more manifestation of the divine spark in man indicates how slowly the humanist gospel separated itself from its theistic traditions. It is doubtful that Erasmus was aware how much his emphasis differed from that of St. Thomas Aquinas. And it was to be many centuries before the logical consequences of a belief in man's power to rule his own destiny became apparent in a doctrine of progress and the full tide of humanist atheism. In modern times the great distinguishing characteristic of western civilization, marking it off from most other historic societies and underlying the triumphs and defeats of nationalism, capitalism and modern science, has been the belief in the possibility of increasing the sum of temporal well-being on this earth. We are or have been until recently the heirs of the Enlightenment and the eighteenth century looms as the period in which these hopes received their classic formulations. Yet the eighteenth century looked back to the Renaissance and it was in the generation of the early sixteenth century, before the religious revolution, that we find clearly that note of optimism, still uncertain, still surrounded with statements of an older resignation, but nevertheless clearly sounded.

The creative possibilities of the future were thus clearly glimpsed, but at the same time the most sensitive and penetrating intelligences realized how precarious were the conditions on which those possibilities rested. If the appropriate conditions could not be realized then there would be no restoration of a golden age, but only decay and despair. If a single document were to be selected from all the richness of this period as most profoundly characteristic of this intellectual and spiritual attitude in Renaissance Europe the choice of Dürer's *Melancolia* might be defended.

This celebrated engraving was done in 1514. It represents a personification of melancholy as a heavy despondent female figure. She sits surrounded by a collection of instruments, which include various geometrical figures, hourglass, magic square, balance, compass and rule, all strewn about in confusion. On a grindstone a child scrawls on a slate. Professor Panofsky has pointed out that Dürer has here combined the popular tradition which represented the melancholic temperament as a lazy housewife with the personification of geometry among the seven liberal arts. Behind this merger lay the influence of Renaissance Platonism, which had developed a new conception of melancholy. In the works of Ficino in particular appeared an identification of the artistic genius and melancholy. Dürer's picture is accordingly to be interpreted as an analysis of the frustration of the creative impulse and it implies a contrast with those conditions in which productive activity can be realized. This contrast is presented by the engraving of St. Jerome in his study, which belongs to the same year and is in many ways a companion piece. In the study of St. Jerome every object is in its ordered place and the saint is engaged in the happiest contemplative and creative work. Even the animals, the lion and the little dog, are sleeping with expressions of content. In the *Melancholy*, on the other hand, the animals, this time a dog and a cat, appear as dismal as the figure of Melancholy herself, and everything is calculated to express the general chaos of the scene. The little boy is perched on top of a stone scribbling away without direction and without result. The impulse toward creative activity is frustrated by the divorce between theory and practice.

The mature and learned Melancholia typifies Theoretical Insight which thinks but cannot act. The ignorant infant making meaningless scrawls on his slate and almost conveying the impression of blindness, typifies practical skill which acts but cannot think. . . . Theory and practice are thus not "together" as Dürer demands and the result is impotence and gloom.[6]

If this interpretation of the engraving be accepted, it may be taken as a

[6] E. Panofsky, *Albrecht Dürer*, Vol. I (Princeton, 1943), 164.

symbol of the hopes and fears of a generation. Knowledge of the conditions of disharmony, awareness of the inner tensions in the European intellectual inheritance implied also the belief that these conflicts could be surmounted and harmonized to produce the golden age of achievement of which Erasmus dreamed. The promise of creativity was more than fulfilled, but underneath there persisted the danger of impotence, sterility, despair. It is as if a genius of the greatest insight had stood on the borderline between two worlds and prefigured the triumphant course of European civilization as it moved on toward the conquest of the world, while at the same time recognizing the delicacy of the balance between creation and destruction and the possibility that in the end the outcome might belie all the greatest hopes of his generation.

BIBLIOGRAPHY

(Revised as of August, 1958)

The publication of Wallace Ferguson's *The Renaissance in Historical Thought; Five Centuries of Interpretation* (Boston, 1948) makes superfluous any attempt to recapitulate the vast literature on the "problem of the Renaissance" and the evolution of this concept in historical writing. The following bibliographies are arranged to correspond in a general way with the organization of the chapters in the present volume. The most recent suggestive survey of the literature on the problem of the Italian Renaissance is Federico Chabod, *Machiavelli and the Renaissance* (London, 1958), pp. 201–247. The most recent general survey of the period is in volume one of the new Cambridge Modern History, *The Age of the Renaissance* (Cambridge, 1957), but this is without bibliography.

I. BIBLIOGRAPHIES

There are excellent bibliographical notices in Vols. VII and VIII of the French series, *Peuples et civilisations*. More comprehensive and analytical surveys of various topics are to be found in *Surveys of Recent Scholarship in the Period of Renaissance*, compiled for the Committee on Renaissance Studies of the American Council of Learned Societies, 1st ed. (1945). For additional current bibliographical information see also the annual April issue of *Studies of Philology*, which contains a very complete listing of all the year's publications in all fields of Renaissance scholarship. Additional bibliographical aids for items of current interest are to be found in the French periodical *Humanisme et Renaissance* and the Italian *La Rinascita* (1938–1943) and *Rinascimento* (1950–   ) (reviews of the Istituto nazionale di studi sul rinascimento). Also consult *Archiv für Reformationsgeschichte* and the *Renaissance News* (the quarterly of the Renaissance Society of America). There are extensive annual bibliographies published in the *Revue d'histoire ecclesiastique*. These bibliographical aids by period should be supplemented by those organized on a national basis, many of which are still more complete. For Germany, Dahlmann-Waitz, *Quellenkunde der deutschen Geschichte,* 9th ed. (Leipzig, 1931), and Bruno Gebhardt, ed., *Gebhardts Handbuch der deutschen Geschichte,* 2 vols., 7th ed. (Stuttgart, Berlin and Leipzig, 1930–1931), are the standard works. Max Jansen and Ludwig Schmitz-Kallenberg, *Historiographie und Quellen der deutschen Geschichte bis 1500,* 2nd ed. (Leipzig, 1914), is a discussion of the sources and literature of German medieval history. Franz Schnabel, *Deutschlands geschichtliche Quellen und Darstellungen in der Neuzeit,* Vol. I (Leipzig and Berlin, 1931), is a brilliant discussion of the sources of the Reformation period by one of the most distinguished of contemporary German historians. Gustav Wolf, *Quellenkunde der deutschen Reformationsgeschichte,* 3 vols. (Gotha, 1915–1923), is the older but still valuable handbook for the sources of the Reformation. Karl Schottenloher, ed., *Bibliographie zur deutschen Geschichte im Zeitalter der Glaubensspaltung, 1517–1585,* 6 vols. (Leipzig, 1933–1940), is the most comprehensive bibliography of sixteenth-century Germany, containing many references of value for the study also of the preceding decades.

In England the two standard manuals for the medieval and Tudor periods are Charles Gross, *The Sources and Literature of English History from the Earliest Times to about 1485,* 2nd rev. ed. (London and New York, 1915), and Conyers Read, *Bibliography of British History, Tudor Period, 1485–1603* (Oxford, 1933). The very complete information contained in these works may be supplemented by the following special bibliographies: On law: Joseph Henry Beale, *A Bibliography of Early English Law Books* (Cambridge, Mass., 1926); on historical literature: Charles L. Kingsford, *English Historical Literature in the Fifteenth Century* (Oxford, 1913); on literature: Rosemond Tuve, "A Critical Survey of Scholarship in the Field of English Literature of the Renaissance," *Studies in Philology,* XL (1943).

The parallel works covering the same period in French history are Auguste Molinier, *Les Sources de l'histoire de France des origines aux guerres d'Italie (1494),* 6 vols. (Paris, 1901–1906), and Henri Hauser, *Les Sources de l'histoire de France XVIᵉ siècle (1494–1610),* 4 vols. (Paris, 1906–1915). Gabriel Monod, *Bibliographie de l'histoire de France* (Paris, 1888), is an older catalogue of sources and literature now in many ways outdated, but still useful in its lists of the great publications of the nineteenth century. In Pierre Caron and Henri Stein, *Répertoire bibliographique de l'histoire de France,* 6 vols. (Paris,

1923–1938), there is information on recent publications arranged on a continuing basis.

For Spain, Raphael Ballester y Castell, *Bibliografía de la historia España; catálogo metódico y cronológica de las fuentes y obras principales relativas a la historia de España desde los orienes hasta nuestros dias* . . . (Gerona and Barcelona, 1921), and Benito Sánchez-Alonso, *Fuentes de la historia española e hispano-Americana; ensayo de bibliografía sistemática de impresos y manuscritos que illustran la historia política de España y sus antiguas provincias de ultramar,* 2 vols., 2nd ed. (Madrid, 1927), are extremely useful bibliographies covering both sources and literature. Raymond Foulché-Delbosc and L. Barrau-Dihigo, *Manuel de l'hispanisant,* 2 vols. (New York, 1920–1925), is an excellent guide to specialized topics in the study of Spanish civilization. Nicolás Antonio, *Bibliotheca hispana nova sive hispanorum scriptorum qui ab anno MD ad MDCLXXXIV,* 2 vols. (Madrid, 1788), is the work of a seventeenth-century scholar still, however, useful for identifying many works in the fifteenth and sixteenth centuries. For recent literature on Spain consult the *Indice histórico español* (from 1953).

In the case of Italy there is no national bibliographical work comparable to those which have been cited for France, England and Germany. Emilio Calvi, *Biblioteca di bibliografia storica italiana* (Rome, 1903), is not a particularly useful work, and the student in search of more helpful bibliographical guides should turn to those works which are recommended for particular Italian states. In particular see the bibliographies in Valeri, *L'Italia nell'eta dei principati 1343–1516* (Milan, 1949).

On Belgium and on the Netherlands consult Henri Pirenne, *Bibliographie de l'histoire de Belgique, catalogue méthodique et chronologique des sources et des ouvrages principaux relatifs à l'histoire de tous les Pays-Bas jusqu'en 1598* . . ., 3rd rev. ed. (Brussels, 1931).

II. THE TURKISH THREAT AND EXPANSION OF CHRISTENDOM

THE TURKISH THREAT

The most valuable work for the questions discussed in this section is that of Franz Babinger, *Mehmed der Eroberer und seine Zeit* (Munich, 1953; French translation, Paris, 1954). Of the three standard treatises N. Iorga, *Geschichte des osmanischen Reiches,* 5 vols. (Gotha, 1908–1913), is best for a general survey of Turkish foreign affairs, but is fairly incomplete on Ottoman institutions; J. von Hammer-Purgstall, *Geschichte des osmanischen Reiches,* 10 vols. (Budapest, 1827–1835), is exceedingly lengthy, with many irrelevant details, and somewhat out of date; while J. W. Zinkeisen, *Geschichte des osmanischen Reiches in Europa,* 7 vols. (Hamburg, 1840–1863), is good on the relations between the Ottoman Empire and western Europe but insufficient on domestic affairs. The briefer monographs by E. Driault, *La Question d'Orient depuis ses origines jusqu'à nos jours,* 6th ed. (Paris, 1914); J. A. R. Marriott, *The Eastern Question,* 4th ed. (Oxford, 1940); or W. S. Davis, *A Short History of the Near East from the Founding of Constantinople* (New York, 1922), are unsatisfactory for this period.

The best surveys of Ottoman foreign relations from Mohammed II to Suleiman I are J. W. Zinkeisen, "Die orientalische Frage," *Historisches Taschenbuch,* Dritte Folge, VI (1855) and VII (1856), and S. N. Fisher, *The Foreign Relations of Turkey, 1481-1512* (Urbana, 1948). These may be supplemented by L. Thuasne, *Djem-sultan, fils de Mohammed II, frère de Bayezid II (1459-1495)* (Paris, 1892); N. Susa, *The Capitulatory Régime of Turkey* (Baltimore, 1933); and G. Pélissié du Rausas, *Le Régime des capitulations dans l'Empire Ottoman,* 2 vols. (Paris, 1902-1905).

On Turkish relations with the Balkan states consult for Bulgaria the excellent study by A. Hajek, *Bulgarien unter der Türkenherrschaft* (Stuttgart, 1925); for Rumania the relevant parts of N. Iorga, *Geschichte des rumänischen Volkes im Rahmen seiner Staatsbildungen,* 2 vols. (Gotha, 1905), and A. D. Xenopol, *Histoire des roumains de la Dacie Trajane,* 2 vols. (Paris, 1896), may be supplemented by J. Ursu's excellent *Stefan cel Mare si Turcii* (Bucharest, 1914); for Serbia, Bosnia and Herzegovina, É. Haumant, *La Formation de la Yougoslavie (XVe-XXe siècles)* (Paris, 1930); for the Greek Peninsula and islands, G. Finlay, *A History of Greece,* ed. H. F. Tozer, 7 vols. (Oxford, 1877), and G. F. Hertzberg, *Geschichte Griechenlands, seit dem Absterben des antiken Lebens bis zur Gegenwart,* 4 vols. (Gotha, 1876-1879). Two recent monographs, F. S. Noli, *George Castrioti Scanderbeg (1405-1468)* (New York, 1947), and A. Gegaj, *L'Albanie et l'invasion turque au XVe siècle* (Louvain, 1937), adequately cover the conflicts between the Turks and Albania both before and after the death of Skanderbeg.

For Russo-Turkish relations in this period see H. Uebersberger, *Russlands Orientpolitik in den letzen zwei Jahrhunderten* (Stuttgart, 1913), which touches very briefly on this period in the opening chapter and is preferable to the out-of-date D. N. Bucharov, *La Russie et la Turque depuis le commencement de leurs relations politiques jusqu'à nos jours* (Amsterdam, 1877). T. Gasztowtt, *La Pologne et l'Islam* (Paris, 1907), is extremely factual and occasionally inaccurate. Equally factual but more reliable is L. Kupelwieser, *Die Kämpfe Ungarns mit den Osmanen bis zur Schlacht bei Mohács, 1526,* 2nd ed. (Vienna, 1899), the only complete survey of Turkish-Hungarian relations. V. Fraknói, *Mathias Corvinus, König von Ungarn (1458-1490)* (Freiburg im Breisgau, 1891), contains much material on Corvinus' Turkish policy.

There is no adequate study of Turkish activities in the Mediterranean. J. P. E. Jurien de la Gravière, *Doria et Barberousse* (Paris, 1886), will suffice, however, as a brief survey. Equally insufficient is the literature on the very important relations between the Ottoman Empire and the Venetian republic. Only H. Kretschmayr, *Geschichte von Venedig,* 3 vols. (Gotha, 1905-1934), and S. N. Fisher, *The Foreign Relations of Turkey, 1481-1512* (Urbana, 1948), give brief accounts for the period. Much information on the relations of the papacy and the Turks can be found in H. Pfeffermann, *Die Zusammenarbeit der Renaissancepäpste mit den Türken* (Winterthür, 1946). At least equally informative is E. Charrière, *Négociations de la France dans le Levant,* 4 vols. (Paris, 1848-1860), with much documentary material. A. Bruneau, *Traditions et politique de la France au Levant* (Paris, 1931) is brief but concise. There is, unfortunately, nothing comparable for the Empire. In the absence of any specialized study one may profitably consult relevant parts of H. Ulmann's masterly biography. *Maximilian I,* 2 vols. (Stuttgart, 1884-1891).

T. G. Djuvara, *Cent projets de partage de la Turquie (1281-1913)* (Paris, 1914), A. E. Krymskii, *Istoria Turechinii,* 2 vols. (Kiev, 1924-1927), S. C. Chew, *The Crescent and the Rose* (New York, 1937), F. L. V. Baumer, "England, the Turk, and the Common Corps of Christendom," *American Historical Review,* I (1944), and A. Scholtze, *Die orientalische Frage in der öffentlichen Meinung des sechzehnten Jahrhunderts* (Frankenberg, 1880), give us some insight into European reaction to the fall of Constantinople and later Turkish advances in Europe.

For the study of Ottoman institutions the reader is referred to A. H. Lybyer's detailed *The Government of the Ottoman Empire in the time of Suleiman the Magnificent* (Cambridge, Mass., 1913). B. Miller, *The Palace School of Muhammad the Conqueror* (Cambridge, Mass., 1941), is an excellent monograph. A. Djevad, *Etat militaire ottoman depuis la fondation de l'empire jusqu'à nos jours* (Constantinople, 1882), and N. Weissmann, *Les Janissaires* (Paris, 1938), add little to the history of the Janizaries.

THE PROGRESS OF EUROPEAN DISCOVERY

Despite its age, C. R. Beazley, *The Dawn of Modern Geography,* 3 vols. (London, 1897-1906), is still the best general treatment of the vast subject of geographical exploration. A shorter study is J. N. L. Baker's somewhat textbookish *A History of Geographical Discovery and Exploration* (London, 1931). A. Rein, *Die europäische Ausbreitung über die Erde* (Wildpark-Potsdam, 1931), is beautifuly illustrated and contains an excellent bibliography. Orjan Olsen, *La Conquête de la terre; histoire des découvertes et des explorations depuis les origines jusqu'à nos jours,* 6 vols. (Paris, 1933-1937), and P. M. Sykes, *A History of Exploration from the Earliest Times to the Present Day,* 3rd ed. (London, 1950), are too popular to be of much value. Alfred Martineau, *Tableau de l'expansion européenne à travers le monde de la fin du XIIe au début du XIXe siècle* (Paris, 1935), is an excellent collection, in tabular form, of events and dates relating to the expansion of Europe.

The most recent general account of Renaissance travel and discovery is that of Boies Penrose, *Travel and Discovery in the Renaissance, 1420-1620* (Harvard, 1952). An earlier general study is by A. P. Newton, ed., *The Great*

Age of Discovery (London, 1932). S. Ruge, *Geschichte des Zeitalters der Entdeckungen* (Berlin, 1881), C. de Lannoy and H. van der Linden, *Histoire de l'expansion coloniale des peuples européens*, 3 vols. (Brussels, 1907-1921), I, and J. A. Williamson, *Maritime Enterprise, 1485-1558* (Oxford, 1913), are all scholarly and informative. E. Zechlin, *Maritime Weltgeschichte* (Hamburg, 1947), covers the medieval period and provides a competent analysis of the background of the great discoveries.

On Portuguese expansion during this period consult D. Peres, *História dos descobrimentos portugueses* (Porto, 1943-1946). E. Prestage, *The Portuguese Pioneers* (London, 1933), and C. de Lannoy and H. van der Linden, *Histoire de l'expansion coloniale des peuples européens,* Vol. I, Part 1, are entirely adequate for those who do not read Portuguese. S. E. Morison, *Portuguese Voyages to America in the Fifteenth Century* (Cambridge, Mass., 1940), is an admirable study of the subject. Much additional information on Portuguese enterprises and colonial policy may be found in F. C. Danvers, *The Portuguese in India,* 2 vols. (London, 1894), R. S. Whiteway, *The Rise of Portuguese Power in India, 1497-1550* (Westminster, 1899), George McCall Theal, *The Portuguese in South Africa* (London, 1896), J. W. Blake, *European Beginnings in West Africa 1454-1578* (New York, 1937), J. Saintoyant, *La Colonisation européenne du XVe au XIXe siècle* (Paris, 1947), and C. F. Rey's very popular *The Romance of the Portuguese in Abyssinia* (London, 1929). A. Kammerer, *La Découverte de la Chine par les portugais au XVIème siècle et la cartographie des portulans* (Leiden, 1944), H. Cordier, *Relations de l'Europe et de l'Asie avant et après le voyage de Vasco de Gama* (Paris, 1898), and "L'arrivée des Portugais en Chine," *T'oung Pao,* Ser. II, XII (1911), A. Jann, *Die katholischen Missionen in Indien, China und Japan* (Paderborn, 1915), W. Zechlin, "Die Ankunft der Portugesen in Indien, China und Japan *als* Problem der Universalsgeschichte," *Historische Zeitschrift,* CLVII (1937), and T'ien-Tsê-Chang, *Sino-Portuguese Trade from 1514 to 1664* (Leyden, 1934), are important studies on Portuguese relations with China and Japan. From among the numerous monographs on individual Portuguese explorers and *conquistadores* one may profitably read C. R. Beazley, *Prince Henry the Navigator* (New York, 1894), and J. P. Oliveira Martins, *The Golden Age of Prince Henry the Navigator* (London, 1914), F. Hümmerich's scholarly *Vasco da Gama und die Entdeckung des Seewegs nach Ostindien* (München, 1898), J. Cortesão, *A Expediçao de Pedro Alvarez Cabral e o descobrimento do Brasil* (Lisbon, 1922), and, finally, Henry Morse Stephens, *Albuqerque* (London, 1892) and A. Baião, *Alfonso de Albuquerque* (Lisbon, 1914).

On Spanish expansion overseas, in addition to the previously cited Saintoyant, *La Colonisation européenne du XVe au XIXe siècle* (Paris, 1947), J. W. Blake, *European Beginnings in West Africa 1454-1578* (New York, 1937), and C. de Lannoy and H. van der Linden, *Histoire de l'expansion coloniale des peuples européens,* Vol. I, Part 2, consult F. Braudel, "Les Espagnols et l'Afrique du

Nord de 1492 à 1577," *Revue africaine*, LXIX (1928), and especially J. H. Parry, *The Spanish Theory of Empire in the Sixteenth Century* (Cambridge, England, 1940). A. de Altolaguirrery Duvale, *Vasco Nuñez de Balboa* (Madrid, 1914), is also valuable.

No attempt will be made to give anything like a complete bibliography of the complex subject of Columbus and the discovery of America. The reader is referred to the extensive bibliography of S. E. Morison's outstanding *Admiral of the Ocean Sea*, 2 vols. (Boston, 1942), C. E. Nowell, "The Columbus Question. A Survey of Recent Literature and Present Opinion," *American Historical Review*, XLIV (1939), and Comité International des Sciences Historiques, "Bibliographie (1912–1931)," *Travaux de la commission pour l'histoire des grands voyages et des grandes découvertes* (Paris, 1936). The best individual studies are by S. E. Morison, *Admiral of the Ocean Sea*, 2 vols. (Boston, 1942), H. Vignaud, *Études critiques sur la vie de Colomb* (Paris, 1905), and *Histoire critique de la grande entreprise de Christophe Colomb . . .*, 2 vols. (Paris, 1911), and H. Harrisse, *Christophe Colomb*, 2 vols. (Paris, 1884). Among the more recent monographs those by A. Ballesteros y Beretta, *Cristóbal Colón y el descubrimiento de América*, 2 vols. (Buenos Aires, 1945), and E. de Gandia, *Historia de Cristóbal Colón* (Buenos Aires, 1942), are the most valuable. G. Friederici, *Der Charakter der Entdeckung und Eroberung Amerikas durch die Europäer*, 3 vols. (Stuttgart, and Gotha, 1925–1936), Vol. I, E. G. Bourne, *Spain in America* (New York, 1904), and again C. de Lannoy and H. van der Linden, *Histoire de l'expansion coloniale des peuples européens*, Vol. I, Part 2, are essential for the study of Spanish colonial policy in America. Additional information may be obtained by consulting the scholarly A. Magnaghi, *Amerigo Vespucci*, 2nd ed. (Rome, 1926), and F. H. Pohl, *Amerigo Vespucci, Pilot Major* (New York, 1944). The most recent book on Vespucci is by Germán Arciniegas, *Amerigo and the New World* (New York, 1955).

On the explorations of other European nations before 1517 consult C. de La Roncière, *Histoire de la marine française*, 6 vols. (Paris, 1899–1932), Vol. III, F. Hümmerich, *Die erste deutsche Handelsfahrt nach Indien 1505–06* (Munich and Berlin, 1922), and the excellent studies of H. Harrisse, *John Cabot, the discoverer of North America . . .* (London, 1895), and J. A. Williamson, *The Voyages of the Cabots and the English Discovery of North America under Henry VII and Henry VIII* (London, 1929).

On the most interesting voyages of the Chinese in the fifteenth century read P. Pelliot, "Les grands voyages maritimes Chinois au début du XVe siècle," *T'oung Pao*, Ser. II, XXX (1933), and "Notes additionelles sur Tcheng Houo et sur ses voyages," *T'oung Pao*, Ser. II, XXXI (1935).

For recent bibliographies on early cartography see the periodical *Imago Mundi* (edited at Leyden from 1951). Older works are O. F. Peschel, *Geschichte der Erdkunde bis auf A. von Humboldt und Carl Ritter*, 2nd ed.

(Munich, 1877), and S. de Ispizúa, *Historia de la geografía y de la cosmografía en las edades antigua y media con relación a los grandes descubrimientos marítimos realizados en los siglos XV y XVI por Españoles y Portugueses,* 2 vols. (Madrid, 1922–1926). These may be supplemented by J. Bensaude, *L'Astronomie nautique au Portugal à l'époque des découverts* (Berne, 1912) and *Historie de la science nautique des découvertes portugaises* (Lisbon, 1921), A. Barbosa, *Novos subsidios para a história da ciência náutica portuguesa da época dos descobrimentos* (Porto, 1948), and E. G. R. Taylor, *Tudor Geography, 1485–1583* (London, 1930). C. de La Roncière's more popular *A la conquête des mers* (Paris, 1938) forms, nevertheless, an adequate introduction to the scientific aspects of geographical exploration. There are several important studies on Renaissance geography. Among these the learned monographs by François de Dainville, *La Géographie des humanistes* (Paris, 1940), and L. Gallois, *Les Géographes allemands de la Renaissance* (Paris, 1890), are outstanding.

THE TITLE TO DOMINION AND THE UNITY OF CHRISTENDOM

The excellent studies by W. Fritzemeyer, *Christenheit und Europa, Beiheft XXIII der historischen Zeitschrift* (Munich, 1931), G. Zeller, "Les relations internationales au temps de la Renaissance: I. L'unitarisme médiéval: son déclin," *Revue des cours et conférences,* XXXVII (1935), and F. L. V. Baumer, "The Church of England and the Common Corps of Christendom," *Journal of Modern History,* XVI (1944) and "The Conception of Christendom in Renaissance England," *Journal of the History of Ideas,* VI (1945), should be added to the pertinent bibliographical references given in this chapter. Also consult Lewis Hanke, *Colonisation et conscience chrétienne au XVIe siècle* (Paris, 1957), and J. B. Aquarone, "L'Humanisme européen et les civilisations d'Extrême-Asie: La Découverte spirituelle de l'Extrême-Asie par l'humanisme européen. L'aventure portugaise dans les mers de l'Inde," *Bull. de l'Asso. G. Budé* (October, 1953).

III. ECONOMIC HISTORY

GENERAL ECONOMIC HISTORIES

Of textbooks covering the economic history of Europe in moderate compass, Herbert Heaton, *Economic History of Europe,* rev. ed. (New York, 1948), is probably the best. More comprehensive and detailed but particularly valuable for its bibliographies is Iosif M. Kulisher, *Allgemeine Wirtschaftgeschichte des Mittelalters und der Neuzeit,* 2 vols. (Munich and Berlin, 1928). An older work, William Cunningham's *An Essay on Western Civilization in its*

Economic Aspects, 2 vols. (Cambridge, England, 1910), still contains much valuable generalization.

THE COMMERCIAL REVOLUTION

On the discovery of new sea routes by the Portuguese, see R. S. Whiteway, *The Rise of Portuguese Power in India, 1497–1550* (Westminster, 1899), and Frederick Charles Danvers, *The Portuguese in India: Being a History of the Rise and Decline of their Eastern Empire*, 2 vols. (London, 1894), which, although old, have a very detailed account of the spice trade. On the Spanish trade with the New World, the indispensable monographs are Earl J. Hamilton, *American Treasure and the Price Revolution in Spain, 1501–1660* (Cambridge, Mass., 1934), and C. H. Haring, *Trade and Navigation between Spain and the Indies in the Time of the Hapsburgs* (Cambridge, Mass., 1918). Henri Hauser, *Recherches et documents sur l'histoire des prix en France de 1500 à 1800* (Paris, 1936), and Liautey, *La Hausse des prix et la lutte contre la cherté en France au XVIe siècle* (Paris, 1921), contain material on the price rise especially in France. André E. Sayous, "Les débuts du commerce de l'Espagne avec l'Amérique (1503–1518) d'après des actes inédits de notaires de Séville," *Revue Historique*, CLXXIV (1934), the same author's "Le rôle d'Amsterdam dans l'histoire du capitalisme commercial et financier," *op. cit.*, CLXXXIII (1938), and his "Le rôle des Génois, lors des premiers mouvements réguliers d'affaires entre l'Espagne et le Nouveau-Monde (1505–1520), d'après des actes inédits des archives notariales de Séville," *Académie des Inscriptions et Belles-Lettres. Comptes rendus des séances de l'année 1932* (July-September, 1932), are recent monographs and articles illustrating various aspects of European commerce both external and internal at the beginning of the sixteenth century. Frederick Chapin Lane, "Venetian Shipping during the Commercial Revolution," *American Historical Review*, XXXVIII (1933), is of particular value for understanding the role of Venetian shipping, and Dorothy Burwash, *English Merchant Shipping, 1460–1540* (Toronto, 1947), contains material of the same kind on the English. Albert Girard, *Le Commerce français à Séville et Cadix au temps des Hapsburg; contribution à l'étude du commerce étranger en Espagne aux XVIe et XVIIe siècles* (Paris, 1932); Jan Goris, *Étude sur les colonies marchandes méridionales (portugais, espagnols, italiens) à Anvers de 1488 à 1567; contribution à l'histoire des débuts du capitalisme moderne* (Louvain, 1925); and F. Simiand, *Recherches anciennes et nouvelles sur le mouvement général des prix du XVIe au XIXe siècle* (Paris, 1932), are useful monographs on more special aspects of the subject.

For the Hanseatic league and Baltic commerce, see J. A. Gade, *The Hanseatic Control of Norwegian Commerce during the Late Middle Ages* (Leyden, 1952).

The best general survey of both trade and industry of late Medieval Europe is provided by Volume I of *The Cambridge Economic History of Modern Europe*, edited by M. M. Postan and E. E. Rich (Cambridge, 1952).

The industrial development of Europe has been the subject of an enormous output of historical literature, some of which is more controversial than historical. The essays of Max Weber, *Gesammelte Aufsätze zur Religionssoziologie*, 3 vols. (Tübingen, 1922–1923), and Ernst Troeltsch, *Die Bedeutung des Protestantismus für die Entstehung der modernen Welt*, 3rd ed. (Munich and Berlin, 1924), contain insights which illuminate our understanding of the period as a whole. Werner Sombart's *Der moderne Kapitalismus*, 3 vols. in 5 (Munich and Leipzig, 1916–1927), was a great pioneering work, which in many ways established the basis for future discussion of the subject. See also the same author's *Die Juden und das Wirtschaftsleben* (Leipzig, 1911) and "Capitalism" in *Encyclopedia of the Social Sciences*, ed. by Edwin R. A. Seligman, III (New York, 1930), 195–208. A criticism of Sombart's views is contained in Lujo Brentano, *Die Anfänge des modernen Kapitalismus* (Munich, 1916), and also in Robert Davidsohn, "Über die Entstehung des Kapitalismus," *Forschungen zur Geschichte von Florenz*, IV (Berlin, 1908); Alfred Doren, *Storia economica dell'Italia nel medio evo (Wirtschaftsgeschichte Italiens in Mittelalter)* (Padua, 1937); Amintore Fanfani, *Catholicism, Protestantism, and Capitalism* (New York, 1939); and Fanfani's *Le origini dello spirito capitalistico in Italia* (Milan, 1935). The debate on the origins of capitalism is continued in Henri Hauser, *Les Débuts du capitalisme* (Paris, 1927); Hector M. Robertson, *Aspects of the Rise of Economic Individualism; a Criticism of Max Weber and His School* (Cambridge, England, 1933); and Henri Sée, *Modern Capitalism, its Origin and Evolution* (London and New York, 1928). A useful summary in English of Sombart's views is presented by F. L. Nussbaum, *A History of the Economic Institutions of Modern Europe: an Introduction to "Der Moderne Kapitalismus" of Werner Sombart* (New York, 1933). See also the analysis of the meaning of capitalism in Talcott Parsons, "Capitalism in Recent German Literature: Sombart and Weber," *Journal of Political Economy*, XXXVI (1928) and XXXVII (1929). The outstanding recent Marxist account is Maurice H. Dobb, *Modern Capitalism: its Origin and Growth* (London, 1928). See also his *Studies in the Development of Capitalism* (London, 1946).

On particular industries, Ephraim Lipson, *History of the Woollen and Worsted Industries* (London, 1921); J. Nef, "Industrial Europe at the Time of the Reformation," *Journal of Political Economy*, XLIX (1941); and Charles Singer, *The Earliest Chemical Industry; an Essay in the Historical Relations of Economics and Technology Illustrated from the Alum Trade* (London,

1948), are outstanding monographs, and the general work by George Unwin, *Industrial Organization in the Sixteenth and Seventeenth Centuries* (Oxford, 1904), although old, is still a good comprehensive picture of the situation, particularly in England.

BANKING

On Renaissance banking, the best work is still Richard Ehrenberg's *Das Zeitalter der Fugger. Geldkapital und Creditverkehr im 16. Jahrhundert* (Jena, 1896), although modified by Henri Hauser, "Réflexions sur l'histoire des banques à l'époque moderne de la fin du XVe à la fin du XVIIIe siècle," *Annales d'histoire économique et sociale*, I (1929); Raymond de Roover, *The Medici Bank, Its Organization, Management, Operations, and Decline* (New York, 1948); and his *Money, Banking, and Credit in Medieval Bruges; Italian Merchant-Bankers; Lombards and Money-Changers, a Study in the Origins of Banking* (Cambridge, Mass., 1948), the latter two of which are particularly brilliant and thorough investigations of their subjects. On particular countries, Bernardino Barbadoro, *Le finanze della repubblica fiorentina, imposta diretta e debita pubblico fino all'instituzione del monte* (Florence, 1929), is good on Florence; and H. Sieveking, "Die kapitalistische Entwicklung in den italienischen Städten des Mittelalters," *Vierteljahrschrift für Sozial- und Wirtschaftsgeschichte*, VII (1909), and Armando Sapori, *Studi di storia economica medievale*, 2nd ed. (Florence, 1947), are good on Italy in general. For France, see the general work by Henri Sée, *Histoire économique de la France* (Paris, 1939–1942), and the discussion of public credit in Paul Harsin, *Crédit public et Banque d'État en France du XVIe au XVIIIe siècle* (Paris, 1933). The activities of the Fugger are studied in Jacob Strieder, *Jacob Fugger der Reiche* (Leipzig, 1926), and other publications of the Fugger Foundation. See also R. De Roover, *L'Évolution de la lettre de change, XIVe-XVIIe siècles* (Paris, 1953), and B. N. Nelson, *The Idea of Usury* (Princeton, 1949).

THE LAND

Volume I of the uncompleted *Cambridge Economic History of Europe from the Decline of the Roman Empire* (Cambridge, England, 1941; New York, 1944), deals with the history of European agriculture through the medieval period. It is the work of a group of specialists and has both the virtues and the faults of a collaborative enterprise. The best general history of textbook size is Norman Gras, *A History of Agriculture in Europe and America*, 2nd ed. (New York, 1940). See also the other works of the same author: *The Evolution of the English Corn Market from the Twelfth to the Eighteenth Century* (Cambridge, Mass., 1915); and (with Ethel C. Gras) *The Economic and Social History of an English Village (Crawley, Hampshire)* A.D. *909–1928* (Cambridge, Mass., 1930). Marc Bloch's *Les Caractères originaux de l'histoire rurale française* (Cambridge, Mass., and Oslo, 1931), is one of the most brilliant monographs of a very great historian, and although its scope far exceeds the period of interest in this volume, many of its conclusions are of the highest relevance.

On England, where the discussion of enclosures has been particularly important, Edwin F. Gay, "Inclosures in England in the Sixteenth Century," *Quarterly Journal of Economics,* XVII (1903), remains the fundamental monograph, supplemented by W. H. R. Curtler, *The Enclosure and Redistribution of our Land* (Oxford, 1920); Baron R. E. P. Ernle, *English Farming, Past and Present,* 5th ed., Sir A. D. Hall, ed. (London and New York, 1936); and Russell M. Garnier, *History of the English Landed Interest; Its Customs, Laws, and Agriculture,* 2 vols. (London and New York, 1892–1893). Broader economic and social implications are brilliantly analyzed in R. H. Tawney, *The Agrarian Problem in the Sixteenth Century* (London, 1912). For France, in addition to the general economic histories mentioned above, see Gaston Roupnel, *Histoire de la campagne française* (Paris, 1932); Roger Dion, *Essai sur la formation du paysage rural français* (Tours, 1934); and Paul Raveau, *L'agriculture et les classes paysannes, la transformation de la propriété dans le Haut Poitou au XVIᵉ siècle, précédé d'une étude sur le pouvoir d'achat de la livre tournois du règne de Louis VI à celui de Louis XIII* (Paris, 1926). In the absence of a general history of Spanish agriculture, Julius Klein, *The Mesta: A Study in Spanish Economic History* (Cambridge, Mass., 1920), although devoted to a particular subject, is more enlightening than any other work.

SOCIAL CLASSES

In spite of the interest in social history which has been characteristic of recent years, there remain comparatively few works on this important aspect of the history of the Renaissance. The analysis of the bourgeois spirit was first presented by Werner Sombart in his great work *Der Bourgeois; zur Geistesgeschichte des modernen Wirtschaftsmenschen* (Munich and Leipzig, 1913; English edition: London, 1915). The same problem was treated by Franz Borkenau in a general interpretation, *Der Übergang vom feudalen zum bürgerlichen Weltbild; Studien zur Geschichte der Philosophie der Manufakturperiode* (Paris, 1934). A good brief summary of the character and condition of all social classes is contained in Georges Renard and Georges Weulersse, *Life and Work in Modern Europe (Fifteenth to Eighteenth Centuries)* (London and New York, 1926). A recent article by J. H. Hexter, "Education of the Aristocracy in the Renaissance," *Journal of Modern History,* XXII (1950), raises the question of reinterpreting the role of the nobility in the early sixteenth century.

For England, in addition to the brilliant recent survey by G. M. Trevelyan,

English Social History, 2nd ed. (London, 1946), there is the older comprehensive collection of data in Henry Duff Traill and J. S. Mann, eds., *Social
England; a record of the progress of the people in religion, laws, learning, arts,
industry, commerce, science, literature and manners, from the earliest times to
the present day*, 6 vols. (London and New York, 1901–1904). More limited
in scope and including also cultural history is J. H. Harvey, *Gothic England;
a Survey of National Culture, 1300–1550* (London, 1947); consult also Annie
Abram, *Social England in the Fifteenth Century, a Study of the Effects of
Economic Conditions* (London and New York, 1909), which is particularly
concerned with the effects of economic changes. A noteworthy recent monograph on the importance of the merchant class is Sylvia Thrupp, *The Merchant Class of Medieval London, 1300–1500* (Chicago, 1948).

A comparatively greater amount of work has been devoted to the analysis
of social conditions in Germany because of the interest in the origins of the
religious revolution. A recent interpretation, heavily Marxist in tone, is Roy
Pascal, *Social Basis of the German Reformation; Martin Luther and His
Times* (London, 1933). Reginald R. Betts, "La société dans l'Europe centrale
et dans l'Europe orientale; son développement vers la fin du moyen âge,"
Revue d'histoire comparée, N. S., VII (1948), offers a brief general survey of
the evolution of society not only in Germany but in Central Europe as a whole.
Among many analyses of the peasantry, Sidney B. Fay, "The Roman Law and
the German Peasant," *American Historical Review*, XVI (1911), and Hans
Nabholz, "Zur Frage nach den Ursachen des Bauernkrieges 1525," *Aus
Sozial- und Wirtschaftsgeschichte; Gedächtnisschrift für Georg von Below*
(Stuttgart, 1928), deserve special mention. On the nobility, the best discussion
is to be found in Robert Fellner, *Die fränkische Ritterschaft von 1495–1524*
(Berlin, 1905). The recent work of Erich Fromm, *Escape from Freedom* (New
York, 1941), contains in the opening chapters a significant attempt to apply
to sixteenth-century Germany some of the recent findings of psychology.

In France, Bernhard Groethuysen, *Origines de l'esprit bourgeois en
France, I, L'Église et la bourgeoisie* (Paris, 1927), represents an ambitious
attempt to apply to French society the concepts developed by Sombart. Alfred
Franklin, *La Vie privée d'autrefois. Arts et métiers, modes, moeurs, usages des
parisiens du XIIe au XIIIe siècle, d'après des documents originaux ou inédits*
(Paris, 1887–1902), is an elaborate compilation designed to give a vivid picture
of the occupations and daily lives of the inhabitants of Paris. A more analytical and comprehensive treatment of the same subject is to be found in Abel
Lefranc, *La vie quotidienne au temps de la Renaissance* (Paris, 1938). The
role of the urban proletariat is studied in the important work of Henri Hauser,
Travailleurs et marchands dans l'ancienne France (Paris, 1920).

One of the most interesting studies of society in Italy in the fourteenth and
fifteenth centuries is Alfred von Martin, *Sociology of the Renaissance* (Oxford,

1944). For the ambiguities of the social position of the humanists, see the work of Trinkhaus, *Adversity's Noblemen* (New York and London, 1940).

IV. THE STATE IN THEORY AND PRACTICE

COMPARATIVE INSTITUTIONAL DEVELOPMENT

The comparative analysis of European political institutions has only recently been the subject of interpretative study. Besides the older work of Gierke, one of the earliest important statements of the problem was Hans Spangenberg, *Vom Lehnstaat zum Ständestaat; ein Beitrag zur Entstehung der landständischen Verfassung* (Munich and Berlin, 1912). See also the same author's bibliographical discussion, "Territorialverfassung und Ständestaat" in *Jahresberichte für deutsche Geschichte,* 1926 (Leipzig, 1928) and 1928 (Leipzig, 1930). These works attempted to provide a typology for European political development from feudalism to absolutism. In 1928 the great French historian Marc Bloch made a plea for the development of the comparative method in his "Pour une histoire comparée des sociétés médiévales," *Resumés des communications présentées au VI⁰ Congrès International des Sciences Historiques* (Oslo, 1928). Attention was called to the importance of the evolution of representative institutions by Otto Hintze, "Weltgeschichtliche Bedingungen der Repräsentativverfassung," *Historische Zeitschrift,* CXLIII (1930). On this subject see also Robert H. Lord, "The Parliaments of the Middle Ages and the Early Modern Period," *Catholic Historical Review,* XVI (1930), and especially Alexander Marcuse, *Die Repräsentativverfassung in Europa bis zum Durchbruch des Absolutismus* (Berlin, 1935), which summarizes the history of representative bodies up to the Enlightenment. To these should be added the important publications of Emil Lousse: "La Formation des états dans la société européene du moyen âge et l'apparition des assemblées d'états, questions de fait et de méthodes," *Bulletin of the International Committee of Historical Sciences* (1933); "Les caractères essentiels de l'état corporatif médiéval," *Études classiques,* VI (1937); "Les facteurs de civilisation à l'époque moderne. I. Le Facteur politique: de l'état corporatif à la monarchie constitutionelle," *Études classiques* IV (1935); "Parliamentarisme ou corporatisme? Les origines des assemblées d'états," *Revue historique de droit français et étranger,* 4th series, XIV (1935). Professor Lousse has also been the permanent secretary of the Commission on the History of Assemblies of Estates established by the Historical Congress at Warsaw in 1933. This commission has published a series of monographs and articles on assemblies in the Medieval period and the *Ancien Régime,* many of which are relevant to the problems discussed in this chapter.

THE THEORY AND PRACTICE OF GOVERNMENT—THE NATIONAL STATES

The following is a selection from the literature on the internal history of the European states.

ENGLAND: The most recent general account is that in the Oxford History of England, J. D. Mackie, *The Earlier Tudors, 1485–1558* (Oxford, 1952). Wilhelm Busch, *England unter den Tudors, I, König Heinrich VII, 1485–1509* (Stuttgart, 1892), is a general account of Tudor England by a German scholar who was one of the great authorities in the field. Its approach is now somewhat outdated. Gilbert W. Child, *Church and State under the Tudors* (London, 1890), discusses the relationship between the civil and the ecclesiastical powers and is especially good on the importance of Wolsey's legatine jurisdiction. Albert Venn Dicey, *The Privy Council;, the Arnold Prize Essay, 1860* (London and New York, 1887), was one of the earlier works of its famous author and traces the history of the council from the end of the Middle Ages. Frederick C. Dietz, *English Government Finance, 1485–1558* (Urbana, 1921), is a more recent monograph by an American scholar on the resources available to early Tudor governments. Corrado Fatta, *Il regno di Enrico VII d'Inghilterra; secondo i documenti contemporanei* (Florence, 1938), is another general account by an Italian scholar, incorporating the results of the latest continental as well as English research. Herbert A. L. Fisher, *The History of England from the Accession of Henry VII to the Death of Henry VIII, 1485–1547* (London, 1906), is the volume devoted to the period in the *Political History of England* series. A standard short biography of Henry VII is James Gairdner, *Henry the Seventh* (London and New York, 1889). The above-mentioned work by Dicey should be supplemented by Dorothy M. Gladish, *The Tudor Privy Council* (Retford, 1915). Norman S. B. Gras, *The Early English Customs System; a Documentary Study of the Institutional and Economic History of the Customs from the Thirteenth to the Sixteenth Century* (Cambridge, Mass., 1918), is a valuable addition to our knowledge of Tudor finance. F. Hackett, *Henry the Eighth* (New York, 1929), is a superficial attempt to describe the psychology of Henry VIII. Sir William Searle Holdsworth, *A History of English Law,* 12 vols. (London, 1922–1938), is the present standard history of English law. F. W. Maitland's *The Constitutional History of England* (Cambridge, England, 1908) and Charles H. McIlwain, *The High Court of Parliament and Its Supremacy; an Historical Essay on the Boundaries between Legislation and Adjudication in England* (New Haven, 1910), are both classic works on constitutional history to which we owe most of our understanding of the evolution of parliament. Arthur Percival Newton, "The King's Chamber under the Early Tudors," *English Historical Review,* XXXII (1917), and "Tudor Reforms in the Royal Household," *Tudor Studies Presented to Albert Frederick Pollard,* ed. by R. W. Seton-Watson (London, 1924), are useful articles also on constitutional subjects. Kenneth Pickthorn, *Early Tudor Government: Henry VII* and *Early Tudor Government: Henry VIII* (Cambridge, England, 1934), are comprehensive descriptions of the governmental system under both Henry VII and Henry VIII. A. F. Pollard, "Council, Star Chamber and Privy Council under the Tudors," *English His-*

torical Review, XXXVII (1922) and XXXVIII (1923): "The Council," July, 1922, pp. 337–60; "The Star Chamber," October, 1922, pp. 516–39; "The Privy Council," January, 1923, pp. 42–60; Pollard's *The Evolution of Parliament,* 2nd ed. (London and New York, 1926); his *Henry VIII* (London, 1902); and also his *The Reign of Henry VII from Contemporary Sources,* 3 vols. (London and New York, 1913–1914), are standard works by the greatest of authorities on the Tudor period. Particularly important is the three-volume collection of documents from contemporary sources illustrating the reign of Henry VII. Gladys Temperley, *Henry VII* (Boston and New York, 1914), is a brief, competent biography. Charles H. Williams, *The Making of the Tudor Despotism* (New York, 1935), is an attempt to explain how Tudor despotism got its start and Fritz Caspari, *Humanism and the Social Order in Tudor England* (Chicago, 1954), is a stimulating discussion of the relationship between intellectual and institutional life.

FRANCE: Gaston du Fresne Beaucourt, *Histoire de Charles VII* (Paris, 1881–1891) and *Charles VII et Louis XI d'aprés Thomas Basin* (Paris, 1860), are the massive and unrelieved histories of Charles VII done in the best style of nineteenth-century French historiography. Albert Buisson, *Le Chancelier Antoine Duprat* (Paris, 1935), is an excellent biography of the chancellor of Francis I, the man who played so prominent a part in the negotiations leading to the concordat of Bologna. Pierre Champion, *Louis XI* (Paris, 1927), is a life of Louis XI somewhat popular in tone but based upon a real knowledge of the sources in literature of the fifteenth century. Claude de Cherrier, *Histoire de Charles VIII, roi de France, d'après des documents diplomatiques inédits ou nouvellement publiés,* 2 vols., 2nd ed. (Paris, 1870), is a good biography of Charles VIII. Pierre Clement, *Jacques Coeur et Charles VII, ou la France au XVᵉ siècle* (Paris, 1853), is the older standard account of the career of Jacques Coeur and his relationship to the French monarchy. Gaston Dodu, *Les Valois; histoire d'une maison royale (1328–1589)* (Paris, 1934), is a sensational and popular description of the Valois kings.

One of the best recent histories of French institutions is that by R. Doucet, *Les Institutions de la France au XVIᵉ siècle* (Paris, 1948). Among histories of institutions, Gustave Dupont-Ferrier's *La Formation de l'état français et l'unité française (des origines au milieu du XVIᵉ siècle),* 2nd ed. (Paris, 1934) and *Les Officiers royaux des bailliages et sénéchaussées et les institutions monarchiques locales en France à la fin du moyen âge* (Paris, 1902) are invaluable. They rest upon an enormous amount of research and incorporate the best traditions of French historical scholarship. Armand d'Herbomez, "Le 'fonctionarisme' en France à la fin du moyen âge," *Revue des questions historiques,* LXXIV (1903), is a useful article on the growth of bureaucracy. French royal finances and the development of the taxing power are the subjects of R. Eberstadt, *Das französische Gewerberecht und die Schaffung staatlicher Gesetzgebung und Verwaltung in Frankreich vom dreizehnten Jahrhundert bis 1581; ein Beitrag zur Entstehungsgeschichte der vollkommenen Staats-gewalt* (Leipzig, 1899). R. Gandilhon, *Politique économique de Louis XI* (Paris, 1941), is a recent work on the economic policies of Louis XI. Charles Hirschauer, *Les États d'Artois de leurs origines à l'occupation française, 1340–1640* (Paris, 1923), is one of the many useful monographs on the provincial estates in France. E. J. Hoffman, *Alain Chartier, His Work and Reputation* (New York, 1942), and Gabriel Joret-Desclosières, *Un écrivain national au XVᵉ siècle, Alain Chartier,* 4th ed. (Paris, 1899), are biographies and critical studies of the poet whose work has many interesting implications for the development of a national sentiment. Similar studies devoted to the satirist of Louis XI are E. L. Kerdaniel, *Un soldat-poète du XVᵉ siècle, Jehan Meschinot* (Paris, 1915), and Arthur de La Broderie, *Jean Meschinot, sa vie et ses oeuvres, ses satires contre Louis XI* (Paris, 1896). René de Maulde La Clavière, *Histoire de Louis XII,* 6 vols. (Paris, 1889–1893), is the big standard account of the reign of Louis XII. Like Beaucourt's *Histoire de Charles VII,* it omits nothing and is today almost impossible to read. D. Neuville, "Le parlement royal à Poitiers, 1418–1436," *Revue historique,* VI (1878), is one of those useful local studies of institutions with which French scholars have abundantly provided us. P. L. Pechenard, *Jean Juvénal des Ursins, historien de Charles VI* (Paris, 1876), is an analysis of the principal contemporary historian of Charles VI. The best monograph on the regency of the Beaujeu is still Paul Pélicier, *Essai sur le gouvernement de la dame de Beaujeu, 1483–1491* (Chartres, 1882). The chapters on the reigns of Charles VII, Louis XI, and Charles VIII for Lavisse's great history of France were written by Charles Petit-Dutaillis (Vol. IV, Pt. II of Ernest Lavisse, *Histoire de France, depuis les origines jusqu'à la révolution,* 9 vols. [Paris, 1900–1911]). Although in many ways inadequate and outdated, Georges Picot, *Histoire des états généraux, considérés au point de vue de leur influence sur le gouvernement de la France de 1355 à 1614* (Paris, 1872), is still the only consecutive history of the estates-general. H. Prentout, *Les Etats provinciaux de Normandie,* 3 vols. (Caen, 1925–1927), and "Les états provinciaux en France," *Bulletin of the International Committee of Historical Sciences,* I, No. 5 (1928), are again model studies on the provincial estates. Jules Quicherat, *Rodrigue de Villandrando, l'un des combattants pour l'indépendance française au quinzième siècle* (Paris, 1879), is a biographical study illuminating conditions during the closing years of the Hundred Years' War, N. Valois, *Le Conseil du roi aux XIVᵉ, XVᵉ, et XVIᵉ, siècles; nouvelles recherches suivies d'arrêts et de procès-verbaux du conseil* (Paris, 1888), is the authoritative work on the evolution of the royal council from the fourteenth to the sixteenth century.

GERMANY: Willy Andreas, *Deutschland vor der Reformation; eine Zeitenwende,* 5th ed. (Stuttgart, 1948), is one of the best recent surveys of German society in the period just before the Reformation. It contains some brilliant interpretations of the cultural history of the period. Adolph Bachmann, *Deutsche*

Reichsgeschichte im Zeitalter Friedrich III und Maximilian I. Mit besonderer Berücksichtigung der österreichischen Staatengeschichte, 2 vols. (Leipzig, 1884–1894), is a constitutional history of the Empire in the age of Frederick III and Maximilian. The fifteenth-century diets are analyzed in Rudolph Bemmann, *Zur Geschichte des deutschen Reichstages im XV. Jahrhundert* (Leipzig, 1907), while Wilhelm Becker, *Uber die Teilnahme der Städte an den Reichsversammlungen unter Friedrich III, 1440–1493* (Bonn, 1891), deals with the role of the cities in the diets of Frederick III. Gottlob Egelhaaf, *Deutsche Geschichte im sechzehnten Jahrhundert bis zum Augsburger Religionsfrieden; Zeitalter der Reformation,* 2 vols. (Stuttgart, 1889–1892), is one of the older general histories of Germany in the sixteenth century. *The Peasant War in Germany* (London, 1927) is Friedrich Engels' famous essay on the Peasant War. Although beyond the scope of this volume, his conclusions have important implications for the early history of the sixteenth century. A good short account is to be found in Bruno Gebhardt, ed., *Gebhardts Handbuch der deutschen Geschichte,* 2 vols., 7th ed. (Stuttgart, Berlin, and Leipzig, 1930–1931). Otto von Gierke, *Das deutsche Genossenschaftsrecht* (Berlin, 1868–1913), is the great work on corporations and groups in the Middle Ages and early modern times. It has had a diverse and continuing influence. Fritz Hartung, *Deutsche Verfassungsgeschichte vom 15. Jahrhundert bis zur Gegenwart,* 5th rev. ed. (Stuttgart, 1950), is one of the best of the constitutional histories and "Die Reichsreform von 1485 bis 1495, ihr Verlauf und ihr Wesen," a short article by the same author in *Historische Vierteljahrschrift,* XVI (1913), is also valuable. Johannes Janssen, *Geschichte des deutschen Volkes seit dem Ausgang des Mittelalters,* 3 vols., 19th and 20th ed. (Freiburg im Breisgau, 1913–1917, 1st ed., 8 vols. 1879–1894), is one of the classic histories of the nineteenth century which attempted to prove the disastrous effects of the Reformation on the development of German life. Victor von Kraus and Kurt Kaser, *Deutsche Geschichte am Ausgange des Mittelalters, 1438–1519,* 2 vols. (Stuttgart, 1905–1912), is another detailed general history in one of the twentieth-century series. Still another general account covering the period through the Thirty Years' War is given by G. Mentz, *Deutsche Geschichte im Zeitalter der Reformation, der Gegenreformation und des dreissigjährigen Krieges, 1493–1648* (Tübingen, 1913). Johann Joachim Müller, *Das Heil. Römischen Reichs, teutscher Nation, Reichs-tags Theatrum, wie selbiges, unter Këyser Maximilians I, allerhöchsten Regierung gestanden . . .,* 2 vols. (Jena, 1718–1719), is an eighteenth-century analysis of the Empire under Maximilian; Johann Stephan Pütter, *Historische Entwickelung der heutigen Staatsverfassung des Teutschen Reichs* (Göttingen, 1786–1787), is also an eighteenth-century account of the development of the constitution. Rudolf Smend, *Das Reichskammergericht. Erster Teil: Geschichte und Verfassung* (Weimar, 1911), deals with the beginnings of the imperial jurisdiction. Heinrich Ulmann, *Kaiser Maximilian I,* 2 vols. (Stuttgart, 1884–1891), is the best modern biography of Maximilian. Glenn Elwood Waas, *The Legendary Character of Kaiser Maximilian* (New York, 1941), is an interesting monograph on the myths that have accumulated around the figure of Maximilian. Will Winker, *Kaiser Maximilian I. Zwischen Wirklichkeit und Traum,* I (Munich, 1950), likewise attempts to dispel the legends and reveal Maximilian as he truly was. Andreas Walther, *Die Anfänge Karls V* (Leipzig, 1911), is a good description of the youth of Charles V. Karl Brandi; *Kaiser Karl V; Werden und Schicksal einer Persönlichkeit und eines Weltreiches* (Munich, 1937; English ed., London, 1939) is by all odds the best life of Charles V. It represents the results of years of careful scholarship and a command of the sources matched by no other authority.

SPAIN: For bibliography, consult E. Allison Peers (ed.), *Spain. A Companion to Spanish Studies* (New York, 1956). Rafael Altamira y Crevea, *Historia de España y de la civilización española,* 4 vols., 3rd ed. (Barcelona, 1900–1930; English ed., London, 1930), is the general history of Spanish civilization by one of the most brilliant historians of modern times. It is beautifully illustrated and contains elaborate bibliographies. Antonio Ballesteros y Beretta, *Historia de España y su influencia en la historia universal,* 9 vols., 2nd ed. (Barcelona, 1918–1941), is another great work of Spanish historiography, still more philosophic than Altamira's. See also the stimulating essay by Américo Castro, *The Structure of Spanish History* (Princeton, 1954). The best study of the formation of Spanish unity is the recent work by Joseph Calmette, *La Formation de l'unité espagnole* (Paris, 1946). A good short account in English is contained in Charles Edward Chapman, *A History of Spain, Founded on the Historia de España y de la civilización españole* (New York, 1927), which is summarized from Altamira. The most extensive as well as the best book in English is R. B. Merriman, *The Rise of the Spanish Empire, in the Old World and the New,* 4 vols. (New York, 1918–1934). Jerónimo Lopez de Ayala y Alvárez de Toledo, *El cardenal Cisneros, gobernador del reino; estudio histórico* (Madrid, 1921), is one of the best recent biographies of Ximenes, and Jean Hippolyte Mariéjol, *L'Espagne sous Ferdinand et Isabelle; le gouvernement, les institutions et les moeurs* (Paris, 1892), although old, is still perhaps the best study of governmental institutions under the Catholic kings. The most recent work on Isabella the Catholic is Manuel Ballesteros Gaibrois, *La obra de Isabel la Católica* (Segovia, 1953).

ITALY: The best general survey of Italian history in this period is now provided by Nino Valeri, *L'Italia nell'eta dei principati 1343–1516* (Milan, 1949). Carlo Cipolla, *Storia delle signorie italiane dal 1313 al 1530,* 2 vols. (Milan, 1881), in the *Storia generale d'Italia,* Pasquale Villari, ed., 8 vols. (Milan, 1874–1882), is the older standard history of Italy for this period. Luigi Simeoni, *Storia politica d'Italia,* I and II, *Le Signorie, 1313–1559* (Milan, 1950), is the most recent work of this kind. Eduard Fueter, *Geschichte des europäischen Staatensystems von 1492 bis 1559* (Munich and Berlin, 1919), includes the

Italian states in his survey. In English there is Henry B. Cotterill, *Italy from Dante to Tasso, 1300–1600; Its Political History as Viewed from the Standpoint of the Chief Cities* . . . (London, 1919), which does not compare with the other works in scholarship. Piero Pieri, *La crisi militare italiana nel rinascimento nelle sue relazioni con la crisi politica ed economica* (Naples, 1934), presents an analysis of the economic and social structure, the evolution of the art of war, and the national crisis, 1494–1530. For historical reasons reference may also be made to J. C. L. Simonde de Sismondi, *Histoire des républiques italiennes du moyen âge*, 16 vols. (Paris, 1809–1818), and to John Addington Symonds, *Renaissance in Italy*, I, *The Age of Despots*, 7 vols. (London, 1875–1886).

On Venice, the two major works are still Pompeo Gherardo Molmenti, *Venice, Its Individual Growth from the Earliest Beginnings to the Fall of the Republic*, 6 vols. (London, 1906–1908), and Heinrich Kretschmayr, *Geschichte von Venedig*, 3 vols, (Gotha, 1905–1934). A more recent, very brief history of Venice is Auguste Bailly, *La Sérénissime république de Venise* (Paris, 1946). An indispensable source for the years 1496 to 1533 is Marino Sanuto, *I diarii di Marino Sanuto*, 58 vols. in 59 (Venice, 1879–1903), since Sanuto had access to many state documents and was a tireless observer and compiler.

On Florence, both Gino Capponi, *Storia della Repubblica di Firenze*, 2 vols. (Florence, 1875), and François T. Perrens, *Histoire de Florence depuis la domination des Médicis jusqu'à la chute de la République (1434–1531)*, 6 vols. (Paris, 1883–1886), are already largely obsolete, indicating the rapid advances of scholarship in this field. The most masterful history of Florence, which unfortunately does not cover the Medicean period, is that of Robert Davidsohn, *Geschichte von Florenz*, 4 vols. (Berlin, 1896–1927), together with his *Forschungen zur Geschichte von Florenz*, 4 vols. (Berlin, 1896–1908). Many later histories have been dependent on Davidsohn's work, but of the more independent studies that by Romolo Caggese, *Firenze dalla decadenza di Roma al Risorgimento d'Italia*, 3 vols. (Florence, 1912–1921), is the best in its modern approach and critical spirit. Ferdinand Schevill, *History of Florence from the Founding of the City through the Renaissance* (New York, 1936), is a fine synthesis showing an awareness of the great amount of specialized scholarship on individual phases of Florentine history. The Medici have attracted the attention of many biographers. Biographies of Cosimo in English are K. D. Ewart, *Cosimo de' Medici* (London, 1889), and C. S. Gutkind, *Cosimo d'Medici* (Oxford, 1938). Among the useful works on Lorenzo are A. Fabroni, *Laurentii Magnifici vita*, 2 vols. (Pisa, 1784); A. von Reumont, *Lorenzo de' Medici*, 2 vols. (Leipzig, 1874); B. Buser, *Lorenzo de' Medici als italienischer Staatsmann* (Leipzig, 1879) and his *Die Beziehungen der Mediceer zu Frankreich während der Jahre 1434–1491, in ihrem Zusammanhang mit den allgemeinen Verhältmissen Italiens* (Leipzig, 1879); Eduard Heyck, *Florenz und die Mediceer*, 2nd ed. (Bielefeld and Leipzig, 1902); W. Roscoe, *The Life of*

Lorenzo de' Medici, 10th ed. (London, 1895); E. Armstrong, *Lorenzo de' Medici* (London, 1927); and, emphasizing cultural developments, E. L. S. Horsburgh, *Lorenzo the Magnificent and Florence in Her Golden Age* (London, 1909), and Emilio Santini, *Il rinascimento a Firenze nell' età di Lorenzo de' Medici* . . . (Rome, 1943). It should be noted that the popular work of Colonel G. F. Young, *The Medici,* 2 vols. (London, 1909), and many subsequent editions, is defective in both technical scholarship and historical perspective. A recent provocative discussion of Lorenzo the Magnificent is Warman Welliver, *L'Impero Fiorentino* (Firenze, 1957). For literature on Machiavelli see the bibliographical suggestions under "Formal Political Theory."

On Milan, Gino Barbieri, *Economia e politica nel ducato di Milano, 1386–1535* (Milan, 1947), is the most recent study of the period. D. Noyes, *The Story of Milan* (London, 1908), is a general history useful as an introduction. Useful for background to the half-century of the Sforzas are Dorothy Muir, *A History of Milan under the Visconti* (London, 1924), and Giorgio Nicodemi, *La signoria dei Visconti* (Milan, 1950). Cecilia Ady, *A History of Milan under the Sforza* (London, 1907), may be supplemented by a number of scholarly studies: E. Rubieri, *Francesco I Sforza* (Florence, 1879); P. Ghinzoni, "Galeazzo Maria Sforza e Luigi XI," *Archivio storico lombardo,* 2nd series, II (1885), and "Galeazzo Maria Sforza e il regno di Cipro," *op. cit.,* 1st series, VI (1879); E. Dürr, "Galeazzo Maria Sforza und seine Stellung zu den Burgunderkriegen," *Basler Zeitschrift für Geschichte und Altertumskunde,* X (1911); E. Casanova, "L'uccisione di Galeazzo Maria Sforza," *Archivio storico lombardo,* 3rd series, XII (1899); Francesco Malaguzzi-Valeri, *La corte di Lodovico il Moro,* 4 vols. (Milan, 1913–1923); L. G. Pélissier, *Louis XII et Ludovic Sforza,* 2 vols. (Paris, 1896); and as an excellent sequel, Mussi Cazzamini, *Milano durante la dominazione spagnola, 1526–1706* (Milan, 1947).

On Rome, Ferdinand Gregorovius, *Geschichte der Stadt Rom im Mittelalter,* 8 vols., 5th ed. (Stuttgart, 1903–1908), is the outstanding work. W. Miller, *Mediaeval Rome from Hildebrand to Clement VIII, 1073–1600* (London, 1904), presents a general view. On the internal tensions of the city, Emmanuel Rodocanachi, *Histoire de Rome de 1354 à 1471; l'antagonisme entre les romains et la Saint-Siège* (Paris, 1922) and his *Les Institutions communales de Rome sous la papauté* (Paris, 1901) are of interest. A general history of the papal states is Moritz Brosch, *Geschichte des Kirchenstaates,* 2 vols. (Gotha, 1880–1882). Jean Guiraud, *L'État pontifical après le grand schisme. Étude de géographie politique* (Paris, 1896), is a study of each locality in the papal states in politico-geographic terms in the first half of the fifteenth century. An older monograph, still of value, is M. Brosch, *Julius II und die Gründung des Kirchenstaats* (Gotha, 1878). See also W. von Hofmann, *Forschungen zur Geschichte der kurialen Behörden von Schisma bis zur Reformation* (Rome, 1914).

On Naples, Gennaro Maria Monti, *Dal duecento al settecento; studi storico-giuridici* (Naples, 1925), treats specific topics such as the work of the Inquisition and the like. Giuseppe Coniglio, *Il regno di Napoli al tempo di Carlo V, amministrazione e vita economica-sociale* (Naples, 1951), describes the absorption of Naples into the Hapsburg system. On Genoa, James T. Bent, *Genoa: How the Republic Rose and Fell* (London, 1881), and the as yet incomplete *Storia di Genova dalle origini al tempo nostro,* 3 vols. (Milan, 1941–   ). On Ferrara, Casimir Chledowski, *Der Hof von Ferrara* (Munich, 1919). On Mantua and Urbino, Alessandro Luzio and Rodolfo Renier, *Mantua e Urbino: Isabella d'Este ed Elisabetta Gonzaga nelle relazioni famigliarie e nelle vicende politiche* (Turin and Rome, 1893), and S. Brinton, *The Gonzaga Lords of Mantua* (London, 1927). On Bologna, E. James, *Bologna, Its History, Antiquities, and Art* (London, 1909). Finally, on Savoy, F. Gabotto, *Lo stato sabaudo da Amedeo VIII ad Emanuele Filiberto, 1467–1496,* 3 vols. (Turin and Rome, 1892–1895).

EASTERN EUROPE: A basic history of Poland to be recommended for this period is Ezechiel Zivier, *Neuere Geschichte Polens,* I, *Die zwei letzten Jagellonen (1506–1572),* Vol. I (Gotha, 1915). Two brief manuals of Polish history are Oskar Halecki, *A History of Poland* (New York, 1943), and W. Sobieski, *Histoire de Pologne des origines à nos jours,* A. de Pennache, trans. (Paris, 1934). Above all, the *Cambridge History of Poland,* I, *From the Origins to Sobieski (to 1696)* (Cambridge, England, 1950; Vol. II, 1941) is the most recent and complete general history. A third volume yet to appear will furnish a complete bibliography. P. Simson, *Geschichte der Stadt Danzig,* 4 vols. (Danzig, 1913–1918), contains material relevant to this period. Jan Rutkowski, *Histoire économique de la Pologne avant les partages* (Paris, 1927), is the best on economic history. T. Schiemann, *Russland, Polen und Livland bis ins 17. Jahrhundert,* 2 vols. (Berlin, 1886–1887), is still a very useful work. F. Papée, *Polsai Litwa na przelomie wieków średnich,* I (Cracow, 1904–   ), treats Poland and Lithuania at the end of the Middle Ages. See also Constantine Jurgela, *History of the Lithuanian Nation* (New York, 1948), L. Kolankowski, *Polska Jagiellonów* (Warsaw, 1937), and E. Seraphim, *Geschichte Liv-Esth-und Kurlands,* 2 vols. (Reval, 1897–1903). Ernest Denis, *Fin de l'indépendance bohême,* 2 vols. (Paris, 1890), relates the history of Bohemia to that of Poland and Hungary with a special treatment of Podiebrad and the Jagellons.

Useful general histories of Hungary are: A. Domanovski, *Die Geschichte Ungarns* (Munich, 1923); F. Eckhart, *Introduction à l'histoire hongroise* (Paris, 1928; English ed.: London, 1931); and Otto Zarek, *The History of Hungary,* P. Wolkonsky, trans. (London, 1939). Vilmos Fraknói, *Mathias Corvinus, König von Ungarn, 1458–1490* (Freiburg im Breisgau, 1891), presents a broad picture of events during the reign of Corvinus.

For Russia the basic work is still that of Vasily Kliuchevskii, *A History of Russia,* C. J. Hogarth, trans., 5 vols. (New York, 1911–1926). A. Rambaud, *Histoire de Russie,* 7th ed. (Paris, 1918), and K. Stählin, *Geschichte Russlands,* 4 vols. (Stuttgart, 1923–1939), are both useful general histories. More recent is Valentin Gitermann, *Geschichte Russlands,* 2 vols. (Zurich, 1944–1945). See also Robert Nisbet Bain, *Slavonic Europe; a Political History of Poland and Russia from 1447 to 1796* (Cambridge, England, 1908), for the relations of the two countries. S. von Herberstein, *Notes upon Russia, 1516–1527,* 2 vols. (London, 1851–1852), contains the interesting observations of a foreign visitor in this early period.

DIPLOMACY OF THE EUROPEAN STATE SYSTEM

ITALIAN DIPLOMACY TO 1494:

For a general analysis of Renaissance diplomacy see Garrett Mattingly, *Renaissance Diplomacy* (Boston, 1955). The best account of the relations between the Italian states in the period before the French invasion is given in Nino Valeri, *L'Italia nell'eta dei Principati, 1343–1516* (Milan, 1949), which contains excellent bibliographies. A very valuable analysis of the political relations between the Italian city-states is given in Hans Baron, "Die politische Entwicklung der italienischen Renaissance," *Historische Zeitschrift,* June, 1952. See also the same author, "A Struggle for Liberty in the Renaissance. Florence, Venice and Milan in the Early Quattrocento," *American Historical Review,* 1953, and "The Anti-Florentine Discourses of the Doge Tommaso Mocenigo (1414–1423): Their Date and Partial Forgery," *Speculum,* Autumn 1952. Among more special studies, Armand Baschet, *La Diplomatie vénitienne. Les princes de l'Europe au XVIe siècle . . . d'après les rapports des ambassadeurs vénétiens* (Paris, 1862), is devoted to Venetian diplomacy with an analysis of many of the reports of the Venetian ambassadors. Willy Andreas, *Staatskunst und Diplomatie der Venezianer im Spiegel ihrer Gesandtenberichte* (Leipzig, 1943), is a collection of studies worth mention. P. Egidi, "La politica del regno di Napoli negli ultimi mesi dell' anno 1480," *Archivio storico per la provincie napoletane,* XXXV (1910), is on the problem of the Neapolitan baronage in the pontificate of Sixtus IV. Enrico Fiumi, *L'impresa di Lorenzo de' Medici contro Volterra (1472)* (Florence, 1948), is an excellent discussion of the Florentine attack on Volterra in 1472 and the diplomacy that lay behind it. The relations between Galeazzo Maria Sforza and Louis XI are discussed in Pietro Ghinzoni, "Galeazzo Maria Sforza e Luigi XI," *Archivio storico lombardo,* XII (1885). Eugène Sol, *Les rapports de la France avec l'Italie du VIIe siècle à la fin du Ier empire, d'après la série K. des Archives nationales* (Paris, 1905), is an extended account of the relations of France and Italy from the twelfth century to the Napoleonic period.

DIPLOMATIC RELATIONS OF THE NORTHERN POWERS TO 1494:

David Jayne Hill, *A History of Diplomacy in the International Develop-*

ment of Europe, 3 vols. (New York, 1905–1914), is a good general account of European diplomacy in this period. It may be supplemented by the following monographs: Prosper Boissonade, *Histoire de la réunion de la Navarre à la Castile; essai sur les relations des princes Foix-Albret avec la France et l'Espagne (1479–1521)* (Paris, 1893), is an essay on the problem of the kingdom of Navarre. The works of Joseph Calmette, *Le Grande règne de Louis XI* (Paris, 1938); "La fin de la domination française en Rousillon au XV° siècle; étude d'histoire diplomatique," *Bulletin de la société agricole, scientifique et littéraire des Pyrénées-Orientales,* XLIII (1902); *Louis XI et l'Angleterre 1461–1483* (with G. Perinelle) (Paris, 1930); *Louis XI, Jean II et la révolution catalane (1461–1473)* (Toulouse and Paris, 1903); "La politique espagnole dans la crise de l'indépendance bretonne (1489–1492)," *Revue historique,* CXVII (1914); "La politique espagnole dans la guerre de Ferrare (1482–1484)," *Revue historique,* XCII (1906); and "La politique espagnole dans l'affaire des barons napolitains (1485–1492)," *Revue historique,* CX (1912), deal with various aspects of the relations between Louis XI and his contemporaries. Charles Cestre, *France, England and European Democracy, 1215–1915; a Historical Survey of the Principles Underlying the Entente Cordiale* (New York and London, 1918), is a popular account of the relations between France and England. Ian D. Colvin, *The Germans in England, 1066–1598* (London, 1915), discusses the Germans in England with special reference to the Hanseatic League. J. Combet, *Louis XI et le Saint-Siège (1461–1483)* (Paris, 1903), analyzes the relationship between Louis XI and the papacy. Pierre Corbin, *Histoire de la politique extérieure de la France* (Paris, 1912), was begun as a general history of French foreign policy but the only volume published takes the account to 1483. Georges Daumet, *Étude sur l'alliance de la France et de la Castille aux XVI° et au XV° siècles* (Paris, 1898), is another study of the alliances between France and the kingdom of Castile. The Franco-German question is dealt with in a somewhat popular fashion in Johannes Haller, *France and Germany, the History of One Thousand Years* (London, 1932). Alfred Hoffman, *Kaiser Friedrichs III. (IV) Beziehungen zu Ungarn in den Jahren 1458–1464* (Breslau, 1887), is a treatment of the Hapsburg policy in the east. Louis XI's occupation of Cerdagne is discussed in F. Pasquier, "La domination française en Cerdagne sous Louis XI d'après les documents inédits des archives municipales de Puycerda, Espagne," *Bulletin historique et philologique du comité des travaux historiques et scientifiques* (1895). Diplomatic negotiations between France and Switzerland in the last years of the fifteenth and the beginning of the sixteenth centuries are well handled in Edouard Rott, *Histoire de la représentation diplomatique de la France après des cantons suisses, de leurs alliés et de leurs confédérés,* I, *1430–1559,* 9 vols. (Berne and Paris, 1900–1926). Georg von Schoch, *Die politischen Beziehungen zwischen Deutschland und England vom Ausgang des Mittelalters bis zum Jahre 1815* (Bonn, 1921), is another and sounder general discussion of political relations between Germany and England. The Burgundian problem is analyzed in two of its aspects in Louis Stouff, *Les origines de l'annexion de la Haute-Alsace à la Bourgogne en 1469. Étude sur les terres engagées par l'Autriche en Alsace depuis le XVIe siècle, specialement la seigneurie de Florimont* (Paris, 1901), and Émile Paul Toutey, *Charles le Téméraire et la ligue de Constance* (Paris, 1902); and there are also valuable brief remarks in Gaston Zeller, *La France et l'Allemagne depuis dix siècles* (Paris, 1932), written by one of the best students of French institutions in the sixteenth century.

THE INVASION OF ITALY AND THE EUROPEAN STATE SYSTEM TO 1517:

The best manual analyzing the evolution of the European state system from 1492 is Eduard Fueter, *Geschichte des europäischen Staatensystems von 1492 bis 1559* (Munich and Berlin, 1919). It contains brilliant descriptions of the resources of the great powers and of the diplomatic and military combinations that emerged from the period of the Italian wars. The most recent treatment of European diplomatic alliances in this period is Gerhard Ritter, *Die Neugestaltung Europas im 16. Jahrhundert* (Berlin, 1950). An older French work, *Réné de Maulde La Clavière, La diplomatie au temps de Machiavel,* 3 vols. (Paris, 1892–1893), analyzes the diplomacy of the period at exhaustive length. Francesco Ercole, *Da Carlo VIII a Carlo V; la crisi della libertà italiana* (Florence, 1932), is a valuable study of the situation in Italy from Charles VIII to Charles V. On the League of Cambrai, see Antonio Bonardi, "Venezia e la lega di Cambrai," *Nuovo archivio veneto,* n.s., VII (1904). Joseph Calmette, "La France et l'Espagne à la fin du quinzième siècle; du rôle joué par leur premier grand conflit dans l'élaboration du système politique moderne," *Revue des Pyrénées,* XVI (1904), discusses the role of France and Spain at the time of the first Italian invasions. Eugène Cavaignac, *Politique mondiale, 1492–1757* (Paris, 1934), is another general account of international policy in the same period. The role of the Swiss under Cardinal Schiner is treated in Ernst Gagliardi, *Der Anteil der Schweizer an den italienischen Kriegen, 1494–1516* (Zurich, 1919). André Joseph Ghislain Le Glay, *Négociations diplomatiques entre la France et l'Autriche durant les trente premières années du XVIe siècle,* 2 vols. (Paris, 1845), contains documents on the negotiations between France and the Empire during the first thirty years of the sixteenth century. The works of Léon G. Pélissier, *Recherches dans les archives italiennes; Louis XII et Ludovic Sforza (8 Avril 1498–23 Juillet 1500),* 2 vols. in 3 (Paris, 1896–1897); *L'Alliance milano-allemande à la fin du XVe siècle; l'ambassade d'Herasmo Brasca à la cour de l'empereur Maximilien, Avril-Décembre 1498* (Turin, 1897); and *Documents pour l'histoire de la domination française dans le Milanais, 1499–1513* (Toulouse, 1891), are detailed investigations which were a product of his studies preparatory to the publication of his large-scale general account. Charles Kohler, *Les Suisses dans les guerres d'Italie de 1506 à 1512* (Geneva, 1897), is another discussion of the Swiss in the period of Julius II.

Wolfgang Windelband, *Die auswärtige Politik der Grossmächte in der Neuzeit, von 1494 bis zur Gegenwart,* 5th ed. (Essen, 1942), is an attempt to bring up to date certain aspects of Fueter's book, although the emphasis is much more on foreign policy alone than on the internal dynamic by which the great powers were motivated.

FORMAL POLITICAL THEORY:

There are a number of excellent general histories of the political thought of the sixteenth century. Among them may be mentioned particularly John William Allen, *A History of Political Thought in the Sixteenth Century,* 2nd ed. (New York, 1928); A. J. and R. W. Carlyle, *A History of Medieval Political Theory in the West,* 6 vols. (Edinburgh and London, 1909–1936), of which the sixth volume is on the sixteenth century, but far less adequately treated than the earlier period; John Neville Figgis, *Studies of Political Thought from Gerson to Grotius, 1414–1625,* 2nd ed. (Cambridge, England, 1916); Pierre Mesnard, *L'Essor de la philosophie politique au XVIᵉ siècle* (Paris, 1936), which is probably the best of recent comprehensive surveys of the subject; Ernest Barker, *Natural Law and the Theory of Society, 1500 to 1800, with a lecture on the ideas of natural law and humanity, by Ernest Troeltsch* (Cambridge, England, 1934), is a translation of Otto von Gierke's great work on law and society, with a valuable introduction and commentary. Similar topics are analyzed in the works of G. de Lagarde, *Recherches sur l'esprit politique de la réforme* (Paris, 1926) and the six-volume work *La Naissance de l'esprit laique au déclin du moyen âge* (Paris, 1942–1948). The fundamental concepts inherited by sixteenth-century theorists are best presented in C. H. McIlwain, *The Growth of Political Thought in the West* (New York, 1932).

On the reception of Roman law in Germany, the older work by Karl Adolf Schmidt, *Die Rezeption des römischen Rechts in Deutschland* (Rostock, 1868), has been superseded by the works of Roderich Stintzing, *Geschichte der deutschen Rechtswissenschaft,* 3 vols. (Munich and Leipzig, 1880–1910); *Geschichte der populären Literatur des römisch-kanonischen Rechts in Deutschland am Ende des fünfzehnten und am Anfang des sechszehnten Jahrhunderts* (Leipzig, 1867); "Zur Geschichte des römischen Rechts in Deutschland," *Historische Zeitschrift,* XXIX (1873); and by those of Joseph Hürbin, ed., "Der 'Libellus de Cesarea Monarchia' von Hermann Peter aus Andlau," *Zeitschrift der Savigny-Stiftung für Rechtsgeschichte,* XII (1891); "Der 'Libellus de Cesarea monarchia' von Hermann Peter aus Andlau, Liber Secundus," *op. cit.,* XIII (1892); "Eine Ergänzung des 'Libellus de Cesarea Monarchia' Peters von Andlau," *op. cit.,* XVI (1895). The great work by Friedrich Karl von Savigny, *Geschichte des römischen Rechts im Mittelalter,* 7 vols., 2nd ed. (Heidelberg, 1834–1851; English edition: Edinburgh, 1829), is still valuable for the earlier period on the biographical side. A recent authoritative work on the whole problem of the survival and importance of Roman law in western Europe is P.

Koschaker, *Europa und das römische Recht* (Munich, 1947). Among many monographs, those of Hürbin already cited as well as his *Peter von Andlau, der Verfasser des ersten deutschen Reichsstaatsrechts; ein Beitrag zur Geschichte des Humanismus am Oberrhein im XV. Jahrhundert* (Strassburg, 1897) are the best treatment of Peter von Andlau, and Walter Köhler, "Die deutsche Kaiseridee am Anfang des 16. Jahrhunderts," *Historische Zeitschrift,* CXLIX (1933), presents a thorough analysis of the meaning of the imperial idea at the beginning of the sixteenth century. In this connection also Alois Dempf in *Sacrum Imperium; Geschichts- und Staatsphilosophie des Mittelalters und der politischen Renaissance* (Munich and Berlin, 1929), has contributed an analysis distinguished for its far-reaching implications.

On the political theory of Commynes, see W. J. Bouwsma, "The Politics of Commynes." *Journal of Modern History,* XXIII (1951).

The best survey of English political theory in the fifteenth century is to be found in Stanley Bertram Chrimes, *English Constitutional Ideas in the Fifteenth Century* (Cambridge, England, 1936). There are also interesting general remarks on popular attitudes in Charles L. Kingsford, *Prejudice and Promise in Fifteenth Century England* (Oxford, 1925). On the work of Sir John Fortescue, in addition to the work of Chrimes, the best recent analysis is in Felix Gilbert's "Sir John Fortescue's *Dominium Regale et Politicum,*" *Medievalia et Humanistica,* II (1944). For the more legal and constitutional topics, F. W. Maitland, *English Law and the Renaissance* (Cambridge, England, 1901), and the more recent Franklin Le Van Baumer, *The Early Tudor Theory of Kingship* (New Heaven, 1940), are the most useful. The best biography of Sir Thomas More is that of R. W. Chambers, *Thomas More* (London, 1935). Interesting and opposed points of view are to be found in Karl Kautsky, *Thomas More and his Utopia* (London and New York, 1927), which emphasizes the view that More anticipated the development of modern socialism. A recent work by Russell Ames, *Citizen Thomas More and His Utopia* (Princeton, 1949), attempts to develop a compromise between the views of Kautsky and Chambers.

The political thought of Erasmus is most comprehensively dealt with by L. K. Born, "Erasmus on Political Ethics: The *Institutio Principis Christiani,*" *Political Science Quarterly,* XLIII (1928). See also the section already cited in Pierre Mesnard. Although Augustin Renaudet's *Erasme, sa pensée religieuse et son action d'après sa correspondance (1518–1521)* (Paris, 1926) is primarily devoted to an analysis of Erasmus' religious thought and action, its detailed account gives us valuable insights into the development of his political ideas as well.

The general story of political thought in Italy in the age of Machiavelli and the immediately preceding decades has been the subject of an enormous amount of writing. Recent works on the political thought of the humanists are: Felice Battaglia, *Enea Silvio Piccolomini e Francesco Patrizi, due politici Senesi del quattrocento* (Siena, 1936); the same author's *Lineamenti di storia delle dottrine politiche con appendici bibliografiche* (Rome, 1936); Valeria Benetti-Brunelli, *Il rinnovamento della politica nel pensiero del secolo XV in Italia* (Turin, 1927); and Friedrich Meinecke, *Die Idee der Staatsräson in der neueren Geschichte,* 3rd ed. (Munich and Berlin, 1929). By these a great deal of light has been cast on the background of Machiavelli and the relation of his work to the preceding humanist tradition. On Machiavelli himself, Federico Chabod, "Sulla composizione de Il Principe di Niccolò Machiavelli," *Archivum romanicum,* XI (1927), was one of the first to work out a comprehensive theory of the composition of *The Prince.* On this subject, see also the monographs by Herbert Butterfield, *The Statecraft of Machiavelli* (London, 1940); Federico Chabod, *Del "Principe" di Niccolò Machiavelli* (Milan and Rome, 1926); Francesco Ercole, *La Politica di Machiavelli* (Rome, 1926); Leonhard von Muralt, *Machiavellis Staatsgendanke* (Basle, 1945); and J. H. Whitfield, *Machiavelli* (Oxford, 1947) are important general treatments of the meaning of Machiavelli and his significance in the history of political thought. The polar extremes are represented by Butterfield and Whitfield. While for Mr. Butterfield Machiavelli remains almost the Machiavelli of the Elizabethans, Mr. Whitfield has presented him as a misunderstood Christian moralist. The older comprehensive lives are Pasquale Villari, *Niccolò Machiavelli and His Times,* 4 vols. (London, 1878–1883), and Tommasini, *La vita e gli scritti di Niccolò Machiavelli nella loro relazione col machiavellismo,* 2 vols. (Rome, 1883–1911). The articles of Felix Gilbert call for particular mention, especially his "Machiavelli and Guiccardini," *Journal of the Warburg Institute,* II (1939), and "The Humanist Concept of the Prince and *The Prince* of Machiavelli," *Journal of Modern History,* XI (1939). The latter has a particularly important summary of present data on the composition of *The Prince.* See also Roberto Ridolfi, *Opuscoli di storia letteraria e di erudizione; Savonarola, Machiavelli, Guiccardini, Giannotti* (Florence, 1942), which contains new data not only on Machiavelli but also on Savonarola and Guiccardini, and the excellent review by Hans Baron, "New Light on the Political Writers of the Florentine Renaissance," *Journal of the History of Ideas,* VIII (1947). The edition of *The Discourses* translated and edited by Leslie Walker, S.J., 2 vols. (London and New York, 1950), is the most careful and comprehensive. Interpretations of particular interest are to be found in M. Praz, *Machiavelli e gli Inglesi dell'epoca elisabettiana* (Florence, 1928); Gerhard Ritter, *Machtstaat und Utopie; vom Streit um die Dämonie der Macht seit Machiavelli und Morus* (Munich and Berlin, 1940), which contains a stimulating comparison of Machiavelli and More; E. W. Mayer, *Machiavellis Geschichtsauffassung und sein Begriff "Virtù,"* (Munich, 1912), which is the most detailed analysis of the concept of *virtù;* and Ernst Cassirer, *The Myth of the State* (New Haven, 1946), which attempts to place Machiavelli's reputation in the general line of evolution of western political thought. A most stimulating and thorough treatment of Florentine political thought in the age of Machiavelli is contained in the important work by Rudolf von Albertini, *Das Florentinische Staatsbewusstsein im Übergang von der Republik zum Principat* (Bern, 1955). The most recent general study in Gennaro Sasso, *Niccolò Machiavelli* (Turin, 1958).

V. THE CHURCH

Of the general histories of the church in this period the most recent is R. Aubenas and R. Ricard, *Histoire de l'église depuis les origines jusqu'à nos jours*, XV, *L'Église et la Renaissance*, A. Fliche and V. Martin, eds., 24 vols. (Paris, 1934–   ), which contains valuable bibliographical notes. See also Daniel-Rops, *L'Église de la Renaissance et de la Réforme* (Paris, 1955). The first volume of Hubert Jedin, *A History of the Council of Trent* (London, 1957), contains a noteworthy analysis of the conciliar idea in the fifteenth century. The older F. Mourret, *Histoire générale de l'église*, V, *La Renaissance et la réforme*, 7 vols. (Paris, 1914–1916; English trans.: St. Louis and London, 1930–1946), is still a useful work. The new *Kirchengeschichte*, Johann Peter Kirsch, ed., 4 vols. in several parts (Freiburg in Breisgau, 1930–   ) is supplanting Cardinal Joseph Hergenröther, *Handbuch der Kirchengeschichte*, 4 vols., 6th ed. (Freiburg im Breisgau, 1925). A particularly useful manual because of its carefully outlined organization and detailed bibliographical materials is that of the Protestant scholar Gustav Krüger, ed., *Handbuch der Kirchengeschichte für Studierende*, 4 vols., 2nd ed. (Tübingen, 1923–1931). The volume on the Renaissance and Reformation is written by Heinrich Hermelink. Johannes von Walter, *Die Geschichte des Christentums*, 2 vols. in 4 (Gütersloh, 1932–1938), provides a brief and direct treatment of the period. L. Todesco, *Corsa di storia della chiesa*, 5 vols., 4th ed. (Turin and Rome, 1944–1948), is by far the best Italian church history, superior, for example, to Ernesto Buonaiuti, *Storia del cristianesimo*, 3 vols., 2nd ed. (Milan, 1943–1944). A. Dufourcq, *L'Avenir du christianisme*, VII, *Le Christianisme et la désorganisation individualiste, 1294–1527*, 9 vols. (Paris, 1908–1936), was written from a pronounced Catholic point of view but with interesting philosophical implications. The same is true of Gustav Schnürer, *Kirche und Kultur im Mittelalter*, 3 vols. (Paderborn, 1924–1929). Philip Hughes in his *A History of the Church*, III, Part 1, *The Revolt Against the Church: Aquinas to Luther*, 3 vols. (New York, 1934–   ) candidly acknowledges ecclesiastical weaknesses, much as Joseph Lortz and other contemporary Catholic historians have reversed Janssen's glowing picture of conditions in the fifteenth century. Nevertheless, on Luther he follows Grisar without revision.

On the history of the popes, besides the older works of Von Ranke and Creighton, see the classic work, Ludwig von Pastor, *Geschichte der Päpste seit dem Ausgang des Mittelalters*, 16 vols. (Freiburg im Breisgau, 1886–1933), which exists also in English, French, and Italian translations. Franz Seppelt, *Das Papsttum im Spätmittelalter und in der Zeit der Renaissance, 1295–1534*

(Leipzig, 1941), is an excellent recent study of the papacy in the period from Boniface VIII to Clement VII. J. Guiraud, *L'Église romaine et les origines de la renaissance,* 5th ed. (Paris, 1921), discusses papal patronage of Renaissance learning from Boniface VIII to Nicholas V and the interaction of the ecclesiastical and classic cultures. An interesting contrast is provided by the juxtaposition of the apologetic Orestes Ferrara, *The Borgia Pope, Alexander VI,* English translation by F. J. Sheed (New York, 1940), with Ludwig Geiger, *Alexander VI und sein Hof,* 10th ed. (Strassburg, 1920). For the church councils and doctrinal developments see the standard references, Heinrich Denzinger, *Enchiridion symbolorum, definitionum et declarationum de rebus fidei et morum,* 21st–23rd eds. (Freiburg im Breisgau, 1937), and C. J. von Hefele, *Conciliengeschichte,* 9 vols. (Freiburg im Breisgau, 1855–1887). H. J. Schroeder, O.P., *Disciplinary Decrees of the General Councils* (St. Louis, 1937), contains in translation selections from the decrees of the fifth Lateran council (1512–1517). In H. Jedin, *Geschichte des Konzils von Trient,* Vol. I (Freiburg im Breisgau, 1949), we have the first volume of what will undoubtedly be the definitive modern history of the council of Trent; it filled with a wealth of detail and new information on the background of the conciliar movement.

There are numerous good histories of the church on a national basis. For England, see W. Capes, *A History of the English Church in the Fourteenth and Fifteenth Centuries* (London, 1900). To F. A. Gasquet, *The Eve of the Reformation, Studies in the Religious Life and Thought of the English People* . . . (London, 1900), may be added P. Janelle, *Angleterre catholique à la veille du schisme* (Paris, 1935), and Herbert Maynard Smith, *Pre-Reformation England* (London, 1938), an excellent study of the religious life and thought of clergy and laity. For France there is P. Imbart de la Tour, *Les Origines de la réforme,* 4 vols. (Paris, 1905–1935), a work of massive scope, now somewhat outdated, and A. Renaudet, *Préréforme et humanisme à Paris pendant les premières guerres d'Italie 1494–1517* (Paris, 1916), a classic monograph on the relationship between humanism and reform in France. Marcel Godet, *La Congrégation de Montaigu (1490–1580)* (Paris, 1912), contains a study of a particular order important in the French reform movement; and Jules Thomas, *Le Concordat de 1516, ses origines, son histoire au XVIᵉ siècle,* 3 parts (Paris, 1910), is the most complete work on the concordat of Bologna. These special studies may be supplemented by Charles Poulet, *Histoire de l'église de France,* 3 vols. (Paris, 1946–1949), which is one of the most recent general histories. Germany has the old classic work, Johannes Janssen, *Geschichte des deutschen Volkes beim Ausgang des Mittelalters,* 3 vols., 19th and 20th eds. rev. by Pastor (Freiburg im Breisgau, 1913–1917), full of obvious bias, but also containing unrivaled documentation about all aspects of German life in the later medieval period. The standard church history is Albert Hauck, *Kirchengeschichte Deutschlands,* 5 vols., 2nd ed. (Leipzig, 1898–1920). Part I of the previously cited Willy Andreas, *Deutschland vor der Reformation,* 5th ed. (Stuttgart, 1948), describes the church and popular religion on the eve of the Reformation. Albert Werminghoff, *Nationalkirchliche Bestrebungen im deutschen Mittelalter* (Stuttgart, 1910), is a study of the Gallican tendencies in the north, carried through the reign of Maximilian. P. Kirn, *Friedrich der Weise und die Kirche* (Leipzig, 1926), is an interesting study of the church on the territorial level, presenting the policy of the prince both before and after Luther. For Spain, the two older general church histories are Pius Bonifacius Gams, *Die Kirchengeschichte von Spanien,* 3 vols. in 5 (Regensburg, 1862–1879), and Vicente de la Fuente, *Historia eclesiástica de España,* 6 vols., 2nd ed. (Madrid, 1873–1875). These may be supplemented for this period by C. J. von Hefele, *Der Cardinal Ximenes und die kirchlichen Zustände Spaniens am Ende des 15. und Anfange des 16. Jahrhunderts* (Tübingen, 1851), and Fernandez de Retana, *Cisneros y su siglo,* 2 vols. (Madrid, 1929–1930). The work of M. Bataillon, *Erasme et l'Espagne: recherches sur l'histoire spirituelle du XVIᵉ siècle* (Paris, 1937), contains in its opening chapters a brilliant account of the early reform movement in Spain. E. de Moreau, *Histoire de l'église en Belgique,* 4 vols., 2nd ed. (Brussels, 1945–), is a recent comprehensive history of the church in Belgium. On Poland there is Karl Völker, *Kirchengeschichte Polens* (Berlin and Leipzig, 1930).

The most recent complete biography on Savonarola is Roberto Ridolfi, *Vita di Girolamo Savonarola* (Rome, 1952). An older complete narrative is that of Pasquale Villari, *La Storia di Girolamo Savonarola e de suoi tempi,* 2 vols., 2nd ed. (Florence, 1910). It should be supplemented by R. Ridolfi, *Studi savonaroliani* (Florence, 1935), and G. Schnitzer, *Savonarola,* 2 vols. (Munich, 1924), which contains a comprehensive bibliographical essay on earlier works on Savonarola. Pier Misciatelli, *Savonarola* (Milan, 1925; English ed., 1929), deserves special mention. See also the article, Joseph Urban Bergkamp, O.P., "Savonarola in the Light of Modern Research," *Catholic Historical Review,* XI (1925).

On the problem of the origins of the Reformation older works still of interest are Felix Rocquain, *La Cour de Rome et l'esprit de réforme avant Luther,* 3 vols. (Paris, 1893–1897); Johannes Haller, *Papsttum und Kirchenreform,* I (Berlin, 1903–); and Friedrich Thudichum, *Papsttum und Reformation im Mittelalter, 1143–1517* (Leipzig, 1903). A recent book in the same tradition is Leonard Elliott-Binns, *The History of the Decline and Fall of the Medieval Papacy* (London, 1934). A. C. Flick, *The Decline of the Medieval Church,* 2 vols. (London, 1930), is extensive in scope but a somewhat uneven study of the abuses in the medieval church. An important contribution to the subject is L. Febvre, "Une question mal posée: les origines de la réforme française et le problème général des causes de la réforme," *Revue historique,* CLXI (1929). James MacKinnon, *The Origins of the Reformation* (London, 1939), is a relatively recent attempt to summarize the problem. There are valuable reflections in Wilhelm Pauck, *The Heritage of the Reformation* (Boston, 1950).

On the young Luther one of the most satisfactory comprehensive accounts is still Otto Scheel, *Martin Luther. Vom Katholizismus zur Reformation,* 2 vols., 3rd ed. (Tübingen, 1921–1930). His *Dokumente zur Luthers Entwicklung,* 2nd ed. (Tübingen, 1929), is a useful compend of relevant sources. Heinrich Böhmer, *Der junge Luther* (Gotha, 1925), translated as *Road to Reformation* (Philadelphia, 1946), is a straightforward narration by a leading Protestant scholar. James Mackinnon, *Luther and the Reformation,* I, *Early Life and Religious Development to 1517,* 4 vols. (London and New York, 1925–1930), remains an important study. Roland H. Bainton, *Here I Stand: a Life of Martin Luther* (New York and Nashville, 1951), and E. G. Schwiebert, *Luther and His Times* (St. Louis, 1951), the most recent excellent biographies by two American scholars, take into account the findings of modern Luther research. On the specifically religious development of Luther to 1517, see A. V. Müller, *Luthers Werdegang bis zum Turmerlebnis* (Gotha, 1920); Henri Strohl, *L'Evolution religieuse de Luther jusqu'en 1515* (Strassburg and Paris, 1922); Ernst Wolf, *Staupitz und Luther* (Leipzig, 1927); and Robert H. Fife, *Young Luther. The Intellectual and Religious Development of Martin Luther to 1518* (New York, 1928). To these must be added a number of theological studies which have contributed much to our understanding of Luther's development: Adolf Hamel, *Der junge Luther und Augustin,* 2 vols. (Gütersloh, 1934–1935); Erich Vogelsang, *Die Anfänge von Luthers Christologie ...* (Berlin and Leipzig, 1929); Hans Iwand, *Rechtfertigungslehre und Christusglaube* (Leipzig, 1930); Erich Seeberg, *Luthers Theologie,* 2 vols. (Göttingen, 1929–1937); and Edgar M. Carlson, *The Reinterpretation of Luther* (Philadelphia, 1948). The latest studies are Gordon Rupp, *Luther's Progress to the Diet of Worms 1521* (London, 1951), and tracing the development of Luther's conception of justification, Uuras Saarnivaara, *Luther Discovers the Gospel* (St. Louis, 1951).

VI. SCHOLARSHIP AND PHILOSOPHY
THE HEBREW REVIVAL

A very valuable general discussion of scholarship in this period is provided by E. H. Harbison, *The Christian Scholar in the Age of the Reformation* (New York, 1956). Biographical studies of the Christian Hebraists are contained in the series of articles by Moritz Steinschneider, "Christliche Hebräisten," *Zeitschrift für hebräische Bibliographie,* I–IV (1896–1901). See also Frank Rosenthal, "Christian Hebraists of Western Europe: the Hebrew Scriptures in Christian Learning from the time of the *Vulgate* of Jerome to the *Opus Grammaticum* of Münster" in *The University of Pittsburgh Bulletin. The Graduate School,* XLII (1946); Charles Singer, "Hebrew Scholarship in the Middle Ages among Latin Christians," *Legacy of Israel,* ed. by. E. R. Bevan and Charles Singer, (Oxford, 1927) and G. H. Box, "Hebrew Studies in the Reformation Period and After: Their Place and Influence," *Legacy of Israel*. William Gesenius, *Geschichte der hebräischen Sprache und Schrift* (Leipzig, 1815), is a more general history of the Jewish language and literature. S. A. Hirsch, "Early English Hebraists: Roger Bacon and his Predecessors," *Jewish Quarterly Review*, XII (1899), contains valuable background material, and M. Kayserling, "Les Hébraisants chrétiens du XVIIe siècle," *Revue des études juives*, XX (1890), carries the story forward into the seventeenth century. Dean P. Lockwood and Roland H. Bainton, "Classical and Biblical Scholarship in the Age of the Renaissance and Reformation," *Church History*, X (1941), established the place of Hebraic studies in the wider picture of Renaissance scholarship. A book of the greatest importance is Joseph L. Blau, *The Christian Interpretation of the Cabala in the Renaissance* (New York, 1944), which analyzes the many-sided influence of the Cabala in the sixteenth century. See also the important articles of François Secret, "Les debuts du kabbalisme chrétien en Espagne et son histoire à la Renaissance," *Sefarad*, XVII (1957), and "L'Interpretazione della Kabbala nel Rinascimento," *Convivium*, XXIV (1956). Hans Rost, *Die Bibel im Mittelalter; Beiträge zur Geschichte und Bibliographie der Bibel* (Augsburg, 1939); Samuel Berger, *La Bible au seizième siècle* (Paris, 1879); and Henry Guppy, "William Tindale and the Earlier Translators of the Bible into English," *Bulletin of the John Rylands Library*, IX (1925), are works dealing with problems encountered by the earliest translators of the Bible.

PRINTING

On the origin and development of printing, two recent works summarize European contributions: Pierce Butler, *The Origin of Printing in Europe* (Chicago, 1940), and Douglas C. McMurtrie, *The Book, the Story of Printing and Bookmaking* . . . , 3rd rev. ed. (New York and London, 1943). Other works are: André Blum, *The Origins of Printing and Engraving*, trans. by Harry M. Lydenberg (New York, 1940); Henri Bouchet, *The Book: Its Printers, Illustrators and Binders from Gutenberg to the Present Time* (London, 1890); John M. Lenhart, *Pre-Reformation Printed Books: a Study in Statistical and Applied Bibliography, Franciscan Studies*, XIV (New York, 1935); Robert A. Peddie, *Fifteenth-Century Books: a Guide to Their Identification* (London, 1913); John C. Oswald, *A History of Printing; Its Development through Five Hundred Years* (New York and London, 1928); and Robert A. Peddie, ed., *Printing, a Short History of the Art* (London, 1927). An important monograph which discusses the relation between the printed book and Renaissance culture is E. P. Goldschmidt, *The Printed Book of the Renaissance* (Cambridge, Mass., 1950).

For the history of printing in England, see Henry R. Plomer, *A Short History of English Printing, 1476–1898* (London, 1900); George Parker Winship, *William Caxton and His Work* (Berkeley, Cal., 1937); and Nellie Slayton

Aurner, *Caxton, Mirrour of Fifteenth-century Letters: a Study of the Literature of the First English Press* (Boston, 1926). On France, a mass of valuable detailed information is to be found in Anatole Claudin, *Histoire de l'imprimerie en France au XVe et au XVIe siècle,* 4 vols. (Paris, 1900–1914), and, by the same author, *Documents sur la typographie et la gravure en France, aux XVe et XVIe siècles* (London, 1926). Italian printing is discussed in William Dana Orcutt, *The Book in Italy during the Fifteenth and Sixteenth Centuries* (New York and London, 1928); Theodore Low De Vinne, *Notable Printers of Italy during the Fifteenth Century* (New York, 1910); and Horatio F. Brown, *The Venetian Printing Press* (New York and London, 1891). German printing, in Konrad Haebler, *Die deutschen Buchdrucker des XV. Jahrhunderts in Auslande* (Munich, 1924), and Ernst von Voulliéme, *Die deutschen Drucker des fünfzehnten Jahrhunderts,* 2nd ed. (Berlin, 1922). Josef Benzing, *Buchdruckerlexikon des 16. Jahrhunderts* (Frankfurt, 1952), on the development of printing in German-speaking countries, contains concise notes on the life and work of the old masters. Spanish and Portuguese, in Konrad Haebler, *The Early Printers of Spain and Portugal* (London, 1897).

PHILOSOPHY

Of general works on the history of philosophy in the period of the Renaissance, one of the most important is Ernst Cassirer, *Individuum und Kosmos in der Philosophie der Renaissance* (Leipzig and Berlin, 1927), which analyzes the philosophy of Nicholas of Cusa in relationship to the Florentine neo-Platonists and maintains the thesis that a specific Renaissance philosophy emerged among these thinkers. The same problems are further discussed in the same author's *Das Erkenntnisproblem in der Philosophie und Wissenschaft der neueren Zeit,* 3 vols. (Berlin, 1906–23). Other general works on the philosophy of the fifteenth century as a whole are: Adolph Dyroff, *Renaissance und Philosophie,* 13 vols. (Bonn, 1908–1920); Eugenio Garin, "Aristotelismo e Platonismo del Rinascimento," *La Rinascita,* II (1939); Richard Hönigswald, *Denker der italienischen Renaissance; Gestalten und Probleme* (Basle, 1938); Francesco Olgiati, *L'anima dell'umanesimo e del rinascimento; saggio filosofico* (Milan, 1924); F. Schultze, *Geschichte der Philosophie der Renaissance* (Jena, 1874). Among these, the work of Garin is particularly important and should be considered together with that of Kristeller cited in the section on humanism. On particular thinkers, see the article on Valla by Jakob Freudenthal, "Lorenzo Valla als Philosoph," *Neue Jahrbücher für das klassische Altertum Geschichte und deutsche Literatur und für Pädogogik,* XXIII (1909); on Bessarion, Ludwig Mohler, *Kardinal Bessarion als Theologe, Humanist und Staatsmann,* 3 vols. (Paderborn, 1923–1942), and Henri Vast, *Le cardinal Bessarion (1403–1472), étude sur la chrétienté et la renaissance vers le milieu du XVe siècle* (Paris, 1878); and on Cusa, in addition to the above-mentioned work of Cassirer, Paolo Rotta, *Il cardinale Nicolò di Cusa, la vita ed il pensiero*

(Milan, 1928), and Edmond Vansteenberghe, *Le cardinal Nicolas de Cues (1401-1464); l'action—la pensée* (Paris, 1920).

On the Florentine neo-Platonists there is an enormous literature. The best of the older books are: Nesca Adeline Robb, *Neoplatonism of the Italian Renaissance* (London, 1935); and Arnaldo della Torre, *Storia dell'accademia platonica di Firenze* (Florence, 1902). More recently an important contribution has been made by Giuseppe Saitta in *Filosofia italiana e umanesimo* (Venice, 1928) and *La filosofia di Marsilio Ficino* (Messina, 1923). On Ficino, the works of A. J. Festugière, "Studia Mirandulana," *Archives d'histoire doctrinale et littéraire du moyen âge,* VII (1932), and *La philosophie de l'amour de Marsile Ficin et son influence sur la littérature française au XVI⁰ siècle* (Coimbra, 1923) and *La révélation d'Hermès Trismégiste,* 2 vols. (Paris, 1944–), are of great importance, particularly in emphasizing the connection between Florentine philosophy in this period and the esoteric and magical literature. For a discussion of the problem of the freedom of the will in Ficino see Marian Heitzman, "La libertà e il fato nella filosofia di Marsilio Ficino," *Rivista di filosofia neo-scolastica,* XXVIII (1936) and XXIX (1937). The most comprehensive and authoritative treatment of the whole of Ficino's philosophy is to be found in the work of P. O. Kristeller, *The Philosophy of Marsilio Ficino* (New York, 1943). On Pico there are ample introductory remarks in the selected translations by Arthur Liebert, *Giovanni Pico della Mirandola; Ausgewählte Schriften* (Jena, 1905), and by Victor M. Hamm, *Pico della Mirandola; . . . Of Being and Unity (De ente et uno)* (Milwaukee, 1943). The most complete of recent studies are Giovanni Semprini, *Giovanni Pico della Mirandola, la fenice degli ingegni* (Todi, 1921), and *La filosofia di Pico della Mirandola* (Milan, 1936), although they may be supplemented by Ivan Pusino, "Ficinos und Picos religiös-philosophische Anschauungen," *Zeitschrift für Kirchengeschichte,* XLIV (1925), and by the same author, "Zur Quellenkritik für eine Biographie Picos," *Zeitschrift für Kirchengeschichte,* XLV (1926), which both make important contributions to our biographical knowledge of Pico. Léon Dorez and Louis Thuasne, *Pic de la Mirandole en France (1485–1488)* (Paris, 1897), is an older but still valuable study of the career of Pico in France.

John Wilson Taylor, *Georgius Gemistus Pletho's Criticism of Plato and Aristotle* (Menasha, Wis., 1921), and B. Koeszkowski, *Studi sul platonismo del rinascimento in Italia* (Florence, 1936), contain some account of the controversy between the supporters of Plato and those of Aristotle in the fifteenth century.

On the influence of the neo-Platonists on literature in Italy and other countries: Vittorio Rossi, *Il Quattrocento,* 3rd ed. (Milan, 1933), a standard manual of Italian literature, discusses its connections with the great literary figures of the *quattrocento.* D. Cantimori in "Anabattismo e neoplatonismo nel XVI secolo in Italia," *Rendiconti della R. Accademia de Lincei. Classe di scienze morali, storiche e filologiche,* XII (1936), explores the connection between neo-Platonism and Italian heretics in the sixteenth century. For the influence on French literature see: A. J. Festugière, "La philosophie de l'amour de Marsile Ficin et son influence sur la littérature française au XVIième siècle," *Revista de Universidade de Coimbra,* VIII (1922); Abel Lefranc, "Le platonisme et la littérature en France à l'époque de la renaissance (1500–1550)," *Revue d'histoire littéraire de la France,* III (1896); and Walter Mönch, *Die italienische Platonrenaissance und ihre Bedeutung für Frankreichs Literatur- und Geistesgeschichte (1450–1550)* (Berlin, 1936). Kurt Schroeder, *Platonismus in der englischen Renaissance vor und bei Thomas Eliot, nebst Neudruck von Eliot's 'Disputacion Platonike,' 1533* (Berlin, 1920), discusses Platonism in the English Renaissance, and Roy Wesley Battenhouse, "Doctrine of Man in Calvin and in Renaissance Platonism," *Journal of the History of Ideas,* IX (1948), and August Wilhelm Hunzinger, *Luthers Neuplatonismus in der Psalmen-Vorlesung von 1513–1516* (Rostock, 1905), maintain the neo-Platonic influence on even the two leading figures of the Reformation.

On the skeptics and so-called Averroists, most recent investigation has turned on the analysis of the philosophy of Pomponazzi, the study of whom is being renewed by the work of Kristeller. See also the following older works: Ernest Renan, *Averroès et l'averroïsme; essai historique* (Paris, 1852), which has long remained the classic discussion of this subject, but which now appears to require considerable modification; Andrew Halliday Douglas, *The Philosophy and Psychology of Pietro Pomponazzi* (Cambridge, England, 1910), and John Owen, *The Skeptics of the Italian Renaissance* (London, 1893), are older and less useful works; Erich Weil, "Die Philosophie des Pietro Pomponazzi," *Archiv für Geschichte der Philosophie,* XLI (1932), is a more recent German study; and Delio Cantimori, *Eretici italiani de cinquecento; richerche storiche* (Florence, 1939), is the best study of Italian heretical movements in the sixteenth century, although the emphasis is placed rather on the spread of the reform than on the philosophical heretics in the early period of the sixteenth century.

VII. CHRISTIAN HUMANISM AND ERASMUS

CHRISTIAN HUMANISM

The classic books on the significance of humanism from which all modern discussion has started are Jacob Burckhardt, *Die Cultur der Renaissance in Italien: Ein Versuch* (Basle, 1860), and Georg Voigt, *Die Wiederbelebung des classischen Althertums oder das erste Jahrhundert des Humanismus* (Berlin, 1859). L. Geiger, *Renaissance und Humanismus in Italien und Deutschland* (Berlin, 1882), is a more detailed treatment of the same subject covering Europe as a whole, by a pupil of Burckhardt. The same tradition is exemplified in English by J. A. Symonds, *Renaissance in Italy,* 7 vols. (London, 1875–1886). The standard manual of the history of classical scholarship in English is J. E. Sandys, *A History of Classical Scholarship from the Sixth Century B. C. to the End of the Middle Ages,* 3 vols. (Cambridge, England, 1903–1908). It must be supplemented by Remigio Sabbadini, *Le Scoperte dei codici Latini e Greci ne' secoli XIV e XV,* 2 vols. (Florence, 1905–1914), and his *Storia del ciceronianisimo e di altre questioni letterarie nell' età della rinascenza* (Turin, 1885), which give the detailed picture of the recovery of classical manuscripts in the fifteenth century. For a general discussion of the classical heritage, see R. Bolgar, *The Classical Heritage and its Beneficiaries* (Cambridge, 1954), and Paul Kristeller, *The Classics and Renaissance Thought* (Cambridge, 1955). Among many modern works of reinterpretation, Konrad Burdach, *Reformation, Renaissance, Humanismus; zwei Abhandlungen über die Grundlage moderner Bildung und Sprachkunst,* 2nd. ed. (Berlin and Leipzig, 1926), is particularly important in maintaining the continuity between medieval and Renaissance thought. Giuseppe Toffanin in *Chè cosa fu l'umanesimo; il risorgimento dell' antichità classica nella coscienza degli Italiani fra i tempi di Dante e la riforma* (Florence, 1929), and *Storia del'umanesimo (dal XIII al XVI secolo),* 3rd ed. (Bologna, 1947), attempted to establish the orthodox religious character of humanism. Paul Joachimsen, "Aus der Entwicklung des italienischen Humanismus," *Historische Zeitschrift,* CXXI (1920), and "Renaissance, Humanismus, und Reformation," *Zeitwende,* II (1925), and Karl Brandi, "Renaissance und Reformation, Wertungen und Umwertungen," *Preuszische Jahrbücher,* CC (1925), are attempts by German scholars to summarize their positions. One of the most valuable recent articles discussing the whole program is by Paul Kristeller, "The Place of Classical Humanism in Renaissance Thought," *Journal of the History of Ideas,* IV (1943). Various aspects of the history of humanism in Italy are treated in the following: Delio Cantimori, "Rhetoric and Politics in Italian Humanism," *Journal of the Warburg and Courtauld Institutes,* I (1937); E. Gothein, *Schriften zur Kulturgeschichte der Renaissance, Reformation, und Gegenreformation;* Vol. I: *Die Renaissance in Süditalien,* 2 vols. (Munich and Leipzig, 1924); Vittoria Rossi, *Il Quattrocento,* 3rd ed. (Milan, 1933); Giuseppe Saitta, *L'educazione dell'umanesimo in Italia* (Venice, 1928); and Giuseppe Toffanin, *Storia dell'umanesimo* (Bologna, 1943). The most stimulating treatment of the subject is contained in the works of Eugenio Garin, especially *L'Umanesimo Italiano: Filosofia e vita civile nel Rinascimento* (Bari, 1952); *Medioevo e Rinascimento* (Bari, 1954); and the recent *L'educazione in Europa (1400–1600)* (Bari, 1957). See also B. L. Ullman, *Studies in the Italian Renaissance* (Rome, 1955).

The history of humanism in Germany has been complicated by the controversy over its Italian versus its indigenous origin as well as by the debate over the relation between humanism and religious reformation. On these questions, the following works should be consulted: Karl Brandi, *Mittelalterliche Weltanschauung, Humanismus und nationale Bildung* (Berlin, 1925); Paul Kalkoff,

"Die Stellung der deutschen Humanisten zur Reformation," *Zeitschrift für Kirchengeschichte*, XLVI (1927), N.F. IX; Hans Baron, "Zur Frage des Ursprungs des deutschen Humanismus und seiner religiösen Reformbestrebungen," *Historische Zeitschrift*, CXXXII (1925); Hermann Langerbeck, "Deutschland und der Humanismus," *Deutsche Beiträge. Eine Zweimonatsschrift*, II (1948); H. Hermelink, *Die religiösen Reformbestrebungen des deutschen Humanismus* (Tübingen, 1907); Gerhard Ritter, *Die Heidelberger Universität: Ein Stück deutscher Geschichte, I Das Mittelalter, 1386–1508* (Heidelberg, 1936–   ) and his "Die geschichtliche Bedeutung des deutschen Humanismus," *Historische Zeitschrift*, CXXVII (1923); and Hans Rupprich, ed., *Humanismus und Renaissance in den deutschen Städten und an den Universitäten* (Leipzig, 1935), containing representative selections of humanist writings. Among these the best synthesis is provided by the works of Gerhard Ritter. For France, there is no good work on one of the central figures of French humanism, Lefèvre d'Etaples. See, however, the elaborate and detailed study of A. Renaudet, *Préréforme et humanisme à Paris pendant les premières guerres d'Italie, 1494–1517* (Paris, 1916); see also Arthur Tilley, *The Literature of the French Renaissance*, 2 vols. (Cambridge, England, 1904), and Verdun L. Saulnier, *La Littérature française de la renaissance, 1500–1610*, 2nd rev. ed. (Paris, 1948), which are primarily devoted to vernacular literature. Recent articles are H. Bédarida (ed.), "Pensée humaniste et tradition chrétienne aux XVᵉ et XVIᵉ siècles," *Revue des études italiennes*, Supp. vol. (1950); A. Abel, "La Religion des humanistes," *Rev. de l'Univ. de Bruxelles* (mars-mai 1956); and A. Renaudet, "Un Problème historique: la pensée religieuse de Jacques Lefèvre d'Etaples," *Medioevo e Rinascimento. Studi in onore di B. Nardi* (Firenze, 1955).

For the Low Countries, A. Hyma, *The Christian Renaissance; A History of the "Devotio Moderna"* (New York, 1924), remains a work of great importance. Alphonse Roersch, *L'Humanisme belge à l'époque de la renaissance, études et portraits*, 2nd series (Louvain, 1933), studies primarily the group of humanist scholars associated with the University of Louvain. Rudolf Wackernagel, *Humanismus und Reformation in Basel* (Basle, 1907–1924), is a detailed monograph on the humanistic circle in Basle, the conclusions of which are of interest to the general student. Humanism in Spain is best treated for the sixteenth century in the great work of Marcel Bataillon, *Erasme et l'Espagne; recherches sur l'histoire spirituelle du XVIᵉ siècle* (Paris, 1937). See also the extensive discussion in the older Marcelino Menédez y Pelayo, *Historia de los heterodoxos Españoles* (Madrid, 1911–1932), and the more recent biographical study by Aubrey F. G. Bell, *Luis de Leon; a Study of the Spanish Renaissance* (Oxford, 1925). For England we have the classic account in Frederick Seebohm, *The Oxford Reformers: John Colet, Erasmus and Thomas More*, 2nd rev. ed. (London, 1869), and the more recent discussions of the fifteenth-century background in Walter F. Schirmer, *Der englische*

Frühhumanismus; ein Beitrag zur englischen Literaturgeschichte des 15. Jahrhunderts (Leipzig, 1931), and Roberto Weiss, *Humanism in England during the Fifteenth Century* (Oxford, 1941). By far the best brief account of the significance of English humanism as a whole is Douglas Bush, *The Renaissance and English Humanism* (Toronto, 1939). Various special topics are treated by Howard L. Gray, "Greek Visitors to England in 1455–1456" in *Anniversary essays in medieval history, by students of Charles Homer Haskins . . .* (Boston, 1929); in Franck L. Schoell, *Études sur l'humanisme continental en Angleterre à la fin de la Renaissance: M. Ficinus, L. Gyraldus, N. Comes et alii* (Paris, 1926), who analyzes the relationship between English and continental humanism; and in George Truett Buckley, *Atheism in the English Renaissance* (Chicago, 1932). On eastern Europe, see Ivan Pusino, "Die Kultur der Renaissance in Italien und in Russland. (Versuch einer vergleichenden Analyse)," *Historische Zeitschrift,* CXL (1929), and the relevant parts of *The Cambridge History of Poland,* I, *from the Origins to Sobieski (to 1696),* 2 vols. (Cambridge, England, 1950, Vol. II, 1941).

ERASMUS

The foundation for modern studies of Erasmus was provided by P. S. and H. S. Allen in their great edition of the letters, *Opus epistolarum Des. Erasmi Roterodami; denuo recognitum et auctum* (Oxford, 1906–1947). Dr. Allen is also responsible for two short but illuminating discussions, *The Age of Erasmus* (Oxford, 1914) and *Erasmus; Lectures and Wayfaring Sketches* (Oxford, 1934). Of the older biographies that by Preserved Smith, *Erasmus* (New York and London, 1923), is the most sympathetic. J. Huizinga in *Erasmus* (New York, 1924), emphasizes Erasmus as a Dutch figure and has many reservations on his character. The best discussion of Erasmus' youth is found in P. Mestwerdt, *Die Anfänge des Erasmus; Humanismus und "Devotio Moderna." Mit einer Lebenskizze von C. H. Becker,* ed. (Leipzig, 1917). The significance of his Italian experiences is treated in Pierre de Nolhac, *Érasme en Italie; étude sur un épisode de la renaissance avec douze lettres inédites d'Érasme* (Paris, 1888). Jean Hoyoux, "Les Moyens d'existence d'Érasme," *Bibliothèque d'humanisme et Renaissance,* V (1944), is an interesting article on how Erasmus made his living. Relations between Erasmus and Luther are analyzed in Robert Henry Murray, *Erasmus and Luther: Their Attitude to Toleration* (London, 1920); André Meyer, *Étude critique sur les relations d'Érasme et de Luther* (Paris, 1909); and Paul Kalkoff, *Erasmus, Luther, und Freidrich der Weise. Eine reformationsgeschichtliche Studie* (Leipzig, 1919). The evolution of Erasmus' religious thought has been discussed by Ivan Pusino, "Der Einfluss Picos auf Erasmus," *Zeitschrift für Kirchengeschichte,* XLVI (1927); by Margaret Mann, *Érasme et les débuts de la Réforme française (1517–1536)* (Paris, 1933); and by Jean-Baptiste Pineau, *Érasme, sa pensée religieuse* (Paris, 1924), which is a general summary. See also the following recent works: S. Nulli, *Erasmo e il Rinascimento* (Torino, 1955); Karl Schätti, *Erasmus von Rotterdam und die Römische Kurie* (Basel, 1954); and Émile Telle, *Érasme de Rotterdam et le Septième Sacrement* (Geneva, 1954). However, on this subject the most valuable work has been done by Augustin Renaudet, "Érasme, sa vie et son oeuvre jusqu'en 1517, d'après sa correspondance," *Revue historique,* CXI (1912) and CXII (1913); *Érasme, sa pensée religieuse et son action d'après sa correspondance (1518–1521)* (Paris, 1926); and *Études érasmiennes, 1521–1529* (Paris, 1939). These volumes contain a study of the development of Erasmian thought almost day by day as it is derived from a close analysis of his correspondence. They are indispensable to the serious student of the subject. To these the author has added a subsequent volume, *Erasme et l'Italie* (Geneva, 1954).

VIII. ARTS AND SCIENCES

THE ARTS

Of general histories of the plastic arts the best is probably André Michel, ed., *Histoire de l'art depuis les premiers temps chrétiens jusqu'à nos jours,* 8 vols. (Paris, 1905–1929), of which Vol. 4 is particularly relevant to this period. Louis Réau, ed., *Histoire universelle des arts des temps primitifs jusqu'à nos jours,* 4 vols. (Paris, 1930–1936), and René Schneider and Gustave Cohen, *La formation du génie moderne dans l'art de l'Occident; arts plastiques, art littéraire* (Paris, 1936), are more recent attempts, likewise by French authors, to summarize the universal history of the arts.

Study of the classic tradition in all the arts has been greatly stimulated by the publications of the Warburg Institute. *The Journal of the Warburg and Courtauld Institutes* should be consulted for many articles of fundamental importance. The best and most recent summary of the classical tradition in western literature is Gilbert Highet, *The Classical Tradition; Greek and Roman Influences on Western Literature* (Oxford and New York, 1949). On the survival of the antique mythologies, see J. Seznec, *La Survivance des dieux antiques* (London, 1940). K. Borinski, *Die Antike in Poetik und Kunsttheorie vom Ausgang des klassischen Altertums bis auf Goethe und Wilhelm von Humboldt,* 2 vols. (Leipzig, 1914–1924), and, by the same author, *Die Poetik der Renaissance und die Anfänge der litterarischen Kritik in Deutschland* (Berlin, 1886), are also valuable studies on the relationship of the antique to Renaissance literature. Sir Richard Winn Livingstone, ed., *The Legacy of Greece* (Oxford, 1921), contains a useful chapter on literature, and Otto Gruppe, *Geschichte der klassischen Mythologie und Religionsgeschichte während des Mittelalters im Abendland und während der Neuzeit* (Leipzig, 1921), may be cited with the work of Seznec noticed above.

Of the enormous literature on Italian art in this period Bernard Berenson, *The Italian Painters of the Renaissance,* rev. ed. (Oxford, 1930), occupies a fundamental position. Heinrich Wölfflin, *Die klassische Kunst; eine Einführ-*

ung in die italienische Renaissance, 4th ed. (Munich, 1908), is the famous analysis of the classical style of the High Renaissance. Max Dvořák, *Geschichte der italienischen Kunst im Zeitalter der Renaissance,* 2 vols. (Munich, 1927–1929), is a more recent and stimulating discussion of the same subject. Frederick Antal, *Florentine Painting and Its Social Background* (London, 1948), is an interesting attempt to relate the history of Florentine painting to the economic and social background. For the relationship between *quattrocento* art and humanism, Erwin Panofsky, *Studies in Iconology; Humanistic Themes in the Art of the Renaissance* (New York, 1939), is essential. Aby Warburg, *Die Erneuerung der heidnischen Antike,* 2 vols. (Leipzig, 1932), and, by the same author, *Sandro Botticelli's "Geburt der Venus" und "Frühling"* (Frankfurt a M., 1892), are older studies on the same theme. R. Wittkower, *Architectural Principles in the Age of Humanism* (London, 1949), is a particularly stimulating recent discussion of the relationship between architectural and philosophical ideas. Edgar Wind, *Bellini's Feast of the Gods; a Study in Venetian Humanism* (Cambridge, Mass., 1948), is an interesting monograph on Bellini. Anthony Blunt, *Artistic Theory in Italy, 1450–1600* (Oxford, 1940), discusses the history of artistic theories throughout the period of the Renaissance. A stimulating monograph is that of André Chastel, *Marsile Ficin et l'art* (Geneva, 1954). On Rome in the High Renaissance, see Julian Klaczko, *Rome and the Renaissance, the Pontificate of Julius II,* trans. from the French by John Dennie (New York, 1903); Emmanuel Rodocanachi, *Histoire de Rome; le pontificat de Léon X, 1513–1521* (Paris, 1931) and *Histoire de Rome; le pontificat de Jules II, 1503–1513* (Paris, 1928). On Michelangelo, the older works of Henry Thode, *Michelangelo und das Ende der Renaissance,* 4 vols. (Berlin, 1902–1912) and *Michelangelo, kritische Untersuchungen über seine Werke,* 3 vols. (Berlin, 1908), are still important. The most recent and comprehensive study is Charles de Tolnay, *Michelangelo,* 3 vols. to date (Princeton, 1943–1948). See also the recent article, F. Hartt, *"Lignum Vitae in Medio Paradisi:* the Stanza d'Eliodoro and the Sistine Ceiling," *Art Bulletin,* XXXII (1950), which presents a radically different interpretation of the Sistine ceiling.

On Leonardo da Vinci, the most stimulating works are: Sir Kenneth M. Clark, *Leonardo da Vinci; an Account of his Development as an Artist* (Cambridge, England, 1939); Edward McCurdy, *The Mind of Leonardo da Vinci* (New York, 1928); Jean Paul Richter, *Leonardo* (London and New York, 1880); Adolfo Venturi, *Leonardo da Vinci, pittore* (Bologna, 1920); and Antonina Vallentin, *Léonard de Vinci* (Paris, 1939). The latter is the best brief biography. A highly literary and imaginative interpretation is contained in R. A. Taylor, *Leonardo the Florentine, a Study in Personality* (London, 1927). In addition, the following works may be cited: Fred Bérence, *Léonard de Vinci ouvrier de l'intelligence,* rev. ed. (Paris, 1947); F. M. Bongioanni, *Leonardo pensatore* (Piacenza, 1935); Langton Douglas, *Leonardo da Vinci* (Chicago, 1944); Georg Gronau, *Leonardo da Vinci,* Eng. trans. (London and

New York, 1903); Ridolfo Mazzucconi, *Leonardo da Vinci* (Florence, 1943); Eugène Müntz, *Leonard de Vinci, Artist, Thinker and Man of Science,* Eng. trans., 2 vols. (London and New York, 1898); Gabriel Séailles, *Léonard de Vinci, l'artiste et le savant,* 2nd ed. (Paris, 1907); Woldemar von Seidlitz, *Leonardo da Vinci, der Wendepunkt der Renaissance,* 2 vols. (Berlin, 1909); Edmondo Solmi, *Leonardo, 1452-1519,* 3rd ed. (Florence, 1913); Adolpho Venturi, *Leonardo e la sua scuola* (Novara, 1942, and French trans. Paris, 1948).

One of the best studies of Renaissance art in northern Europe is contained in Otto Benesch, *The Art of the Renaissance in Northern Europe; Its Relation to the Contemporary Spiritual and Intellectual Movements* (Cambridge, Mass., 1945), originally delivered as Lowell Lectures in Boston. Ernest Lotthé, *La Pensée, Chrétienne dans la peinture flamande et hollandaise de Van Eyck à Rembrandt (1432 à 1669) Le Christ et la Vièrge Marie,* 2 vols. (Lille, 1947), studies the Christian tradition in Flemish painting. Erwin Panofsky, *Albrecht Dürer,* 2 vols., 3rd ed. (Princeton, 1948), is the fundamental work on Dürer, which may be described as more informative and valuable about Renaissance art than all the manuals of synthesis. The same may be said of the same author's *Early Netherlandish Painting* (Harvard, 1953). See also Max Friedländer, *From Van Eyck to Bruegel. An Introduction to Early Netherlandish Painting* (London, 1956). W. Fraenger, *Hieronymus Bosch. Das tausendjährige Reich* (Coburg, 1947), is a special study of the work of Bosch, with an attempt to relate it to the religious history of the period. For the younger Holbein, Ulrich Christoffel, *Hans Holbein d. J.* (Berlin, 1950), is to be recommended as a concise introduction with beautiful illustrations. Arthur Burkhard, *Matthias Grünewald; Personality and Accomplishment* (Cambridge, Mass., 1936), written for nonspecialists and provided with excellent illustrations, serves as a good introduction to this artist of the north.

The best synthesis on the history of art in France in this period is in the Penguin volume, Anthony Blunt, *Art and Architecture in France, 1500 to 1700* (Baltimore, 1953).

The various national literatures have been the subject of many manuals and monographs. For England, the standard works are: C. S. Lewis, *English Literature in the Sixteenth Century* (Oxford, 1954), and Sir Edmund K. Chambers, *English Literature at the Close of the Middle Ages* (Oxford, 1945). Lewis Einstein, *The Italian Renaissance in England* (New York and London, 1902), is a discussion of Italian influences in England. On the same subject, see also Walter F. Schirmer, *Der englische Frühhumanismus* (Leipzig, 1931), and *Antike, Renaissance und Puritanismus,* 2nd ed. (Munich, 1933). Laurie Magnus, *English Literature in its Foreign Relations, 1300 to 1800* (London, 1927), summarizes English literature in relation to foreign countries in general, while Sidney Lee, *The French Renaissance in England* (New York and Oxford, 1910), is particularly devoted to England and France, and C. H. Herford,

Studies in the Literary Relations of England and Germany in the 16th Century (Cambridge, England, 1886), is concerned with England and Germany. C. L. Kingsford, *English Historical Literature in the Fifteenth Century* (Oxford, 1913), contains the best discussion of historical literature; J. M. Berdan, *Early Tudor Poetry, 1485–1547* (New York, 1920), and Douglas Bush, *Mythology and the Renaissance Tradition in English Poetry* (Minneapolis, 1932), the best discussions of poetry; J. A. K. Thomson, *The Classical Background of English Literature* (London, 1948), and Huntington Brown, *The Classical Tradition in English Literature* (Cambridge, Mass., 1935), provide information on the classical background; and H. B. Lathrop, *Translations from the Classics into English from Caxton to Chapman, 1477–1620* (Madison, 1933), and Aurelius Pompen, *The English Versions of the Ship of Fools* (London, New York, 1925), are on the many translations which were done in this period.

In France, the older standard histories are Joseph Bédier and Paul Hazard, *Histoire de la littérature française, illustrée*, 1st ed. (Paris, 1923–1924), title of rev. ed., *Littérature française*, 2 vols. (Paris, 1948–1949), and Gustave Lanson, *Histoire de la littérature française*, 18th ed. (Paris, 1924). They may be supplemented by W. A. Nitze and E. P. Dargan, *A History of French Literature from the Earliest Times to the Present*, 3rd ed. (New York, 1938). Ferdinand Brunetière, *Histoire de la littérature française classique (1515–1830)*, Vols. I and II, 4th ed., Vols. III and IV, 3rd ed. (Paris, 1921–1927), and Émile Faguet, *Histoire de la littérature française*, 2 vols., 6th ed. (Paris, 1900–1901), are important analyses in the nineteenth-century tradition. J. Plattard, *La Renaissance des lettres en France de Louis XII à Henri IV*, 3rd ed. (Paris, 1925), is a special discussion of the French Renaissance by a great author. An older and now outmoded work is L. Palustre, *La Renaissance en France*, 3 vols. (Paris, 1879–1885). The poetic tradition is discussed in Henri Gambier, *Italie et renaissance poétique en France* (Padua, 1936); Henry Guy, *Histoire de la poésie française au XVIᵉ siècle*, 2 vols. (Paris, 1910–1924); and A. Hulubei, "Virgile en France au XVIᵉ siècle," *Revue du seizième siècle*, XVIII (1931). Walter Mönch, *Die italienische Platonrenaissance und ihre Bedeutung für Frankreichs Literatur- und Geistesgeschichte (1450–1550)* (Berlin, 1936), is one of the best studies on the significance of neo-Platonism in French literature. For Italy, the standard works on the history of literature are Vittorio Rossi, *Il quattrocento*, 3rd ed. (Milan, 1949), and Giuseppe Toffanin, *Il cinquecento*, 3rd rev. ed. (Milan, 1929). Francesco de Sanctis, *Storia della letteratura italiana*, 2 vols., 2nd ed. (Bari, 1912), has attained the status of a classic. Berthold Wiese and Erasmo Pèrcopo, *Geschichte der italienischen Litteratur von den ältesten Zeiten bis zur Gegenwart* (Leipzig, 1899) is an older study. Joel E. Spingarn, *A History of Literary Criticism in the Renaissance; with Special Reference to the Influence of Italy in the Formation and Development of Modern Classicism*, 2nd ed. (New York, 1908), is the most influential monograph on the history of Renaissance literary criticism. For Germany, see the general histories on German literature, Adolf Bartels, *Geschichte der deutschen Literatur,* 19th ed. (Braunschweig, 1943), and F. Vogt and M. Koch, *Geschichte der deutschen Literatur von den ältesten Zeiten bis zur Gegenwart,* 3 vols., 5th ed. (Leipzig, 1934–1938), Kuno Francke, *A History of German Literature as Determined by Social Forces* (New York, 1901). Hans Rupprich, *Die Frühzeit des Humanismus und der Renaissance in Deutschland* (Leipzig, 1938), is a particular discussion of humanism in the Renaissance in Germany. L. S. Thompson, "German Translations of the Classics between 1450 and 1550," *Journal of English and Germanic Philology,* XLII (1943), is an important article, and Günther Müller, *Deutsche Dichtung von der Renaissance bis zum Ausgang des Barocks,* 8 parts (Wildpark-Potsdam, 1927), basic on German poetry. For Spain see Guillermo Diáz-Plaja (ed.), *Historia general de las literaturas hispánicas.* Vol. II: *Pre-renacimiento y renacimiento* (Barcelona, 1951); and Gerald Brenan, *The Literature of the Spanish People* (Cambridge, 1953). See also J. Hurtado y Jiménez de la Serna, *Historia de la literatura española,* 6th ed. (Madrid, 1949), and J. Fitzmaurice-Kelley, *A New History of Spanish Literature* (London, 1926). The most valuable bibliographical discussions are contained in O. H. Green, "A Critical Survey of Scholarship in the Field of Spanish Renaissance Literature, 1914–1944," *Studies in Philology,* XLIV (1947).

Of the recent summaries of Renaissance music the most successful is Heinrich Besseler, *Die Musik des Mittelalters und der Renaissance* (Potsdam, 1931). See also André Pirro, *Histoire de la musique de la fin du XIVe siècle à la fin du XVIe* (Paris, 1940). Nesta de Robeck, *Music of the Italian Renaissance* (London, 1928), is an appreciative though somewhat rose-colored essay. E. J. Dent, *Music of the Renaissance in Italy* (London, 1934), the annual Italian lecture of the British Academy in 1933, stresses the importance of Italian secular music prior to 1600 and particularly the achievement of the Renaissance in the creation of modern harmony. Of the older general histories of music devoting special attention to this period, August Wilhelm Ambros, *Geschichte der Musik,* 5 vols. (Leipzig, 1878–1891), is the most profound and comprehensive. *The Oxford History of Music,* 6 vols. (Oxford, 1901–1905; 2nd ed., 1929–1938), contains the work of H. E. Wooldridge on "The Polyphonic Period," which, however, has been in part superseded by later research. Hugo Riemann, *Handbuch der Musikgeschichte,* 2 vols. in 5 (Leipzig, 1904–1913), in Vol. 2, Part 1, "Das Zeitalter der Renaissance bis 1600," stresses the significance of the *ars nova* for modern music and is still useful. A stimulating and unorthodox account by Cecil Gray, *The History of Music* (London and New York, 1928), describes Renaissance music as a momentary digression, having no connection with anything that preceded or followed it. Of the numerous attempts to integrate music and history, the most successful perhaps is that of Paul H. Lang, *Music in Western Civilization* (New York, 1941).

Hugo Leichtentritt, *Music, History, and Ideas* (Cambridge, Mass., 1938), attempts to relate music to its physical setting, to political events, and to the world of the spirit. His article "The Renaissance Attitude toward Music," *The Musical Quarterly,* I (1915), presents a critical discussion of modern theories revising the traditional estimate of Renaissance music. Dagobert Frey, *Gotik und Renaissance* (Augsburg, 1929), utilizes Italian musical treatises in his penetrating cultural analysis.

There is an extensive monographic and periodical literature on sacred music and court music, on musical forms and instruments, as well as numerous biographies of musicians of the period. Three contributions by leading scholars in the field to the excellent and up-to-date compendium on musicology, Guido Adler, ed., *Handbuch der Musikgeschichte,* 2nd ed. (Berlin, 1930), deserve special notice: Alfred Orel, "Die mehrstimmige geistliche (Katholische) Musik von 1430–1600"; Alfred Einstein, "Die mehrstimmige weltliche Musik 1450–1600"; and Wilhelm Fischer, "Instrumentalmusik von 1450–1600." An antiquated and not altogether reliable but interesting monograph on St. Marks is Francesco Caffi, *Storia della musica sacra nella già cappella ducale di San Marco in Venezia dal 1318–1797,* 2 vols. (Milan, 1931; 1st ed., Venice, 1854). Similar studies of sacred music are G. Tebaldini, *L'archivio musicale della cappella musicale del duomo di Milano dalle origini al presente* (Milan, 1930), and P. Guerrini, "La cappella musicale del duomo di Salò," *Rivista musicale italiana,* XXIX (1922). Representative of studies of the court music are Alfonso Lazzari, *La musica alla corte dei duchi di Ferrara* (Ferrara, 1928); Emilio Motta, "Musici alla corte degli Sforza," *Archivio storico lombardo,* IV (1887), covering the years 1450 to 1498 with good bibliographical references; and Nestore Pelicelli, "Musicisti in Parma nei secoli XV–XVI," *Note d'archivio per la storia musicale,* VIII (1931) and IX (1932), the best study of music at the Farnese court.

On musical form the standard work by Hugo Leichtentritt, *Musical Form* (Cambridge, Mass., 1951), is most realiable. Manfred Bukofzer, *Studies in Medieval and Renaissance Music* (New York, 1950), contains an essay on the beginners of choral polyphony. Willi Apel, *The Notation of Polyphonic Music, 900–1600,* 4th rev. ed. (Cambridge, Mass., 1949), is an accurate presentation of this technical subject. Karl Geiringer, *Musical Instruments, Their History in Western Culture* (New York, 1946), is a recent general history. There are a number of good studies on the organ and the lute, the leading sacred and secular instruments of the Renaissance. Otto Kinkeldey, *Orgel und Klavier in der Musik des 16. Jahrhunderts* (Leipzig, 1910), is still the basic work, to which may be added Y. Rokseth, *La musique d'orgue au XV\^{e\} siècle* (Paris, 1930), and Knud Jeppesen, *Die italienische Orgelmusik am Anfang des Cinquecento* (Copenhagen, 1943). On the lute, see E. Engel, *Die Instrumental-Formen in der Lauten-Musik des 16. Jahrhunderts* (Berlin, 1915). Studies of individual musicians in this period may be represented by O. Gombosi, *Jacob Obrecht;*

eine stilkritische Studie (Leipzig, 1925), on that master of the motet form and H. Moser, *Paul Hofhaimer, ein Lied-und Orgelmeister des deutschen Humanismus* (Stuttgart and Berlin, 1929). Archibald Davison and Willi Apel, *Historical Anthology of Music* (Cambridge, Mass., 1946), contains two chapters of selected music of the late fifteenth and early sixteenth centuries.

SCIENCE

The two most recent publications summarizing present-day knowledge of the origins of modern science are James B. Conant, *Science and Common Sense* (New Haven, 1951), and Herbert Butterfield, *The Origins of Modern Science, 1300–1800* (London, 1949). See also A. C. Crombie, *Augustine to Galileo: The History of Science A.D. 400–1650* (London, 1953); and George Sarton, *The Appreciation of Ancient and Medieval Science during the Renaissance (1450–1600)* (Philadelphia, 1955). Among the more philosophical works on the relationship between philosophy and science, the following may be mentioned particularly: Edwin A. Burtt, *Metaphysical Foundations of Modern Physical Science,* rev. ed. (London, 1932), emphasizes the Platonic contribution to the background of Copernicus; Pierre M. M. Duhem, *Le Système du monde; histoire des doctrines cosmologiques de Platon à Copernic,* 5 vols. (Paris, 1913–1917), is a work of fundamental importance which opened new directions in intellectual history and is indispensable for any student of Renaissance science; Arthur O. Lovejoy, *The Great Chain of Being* (Cambridge, Mass., 1936); Dampier-Whetham, *A History of Science and Its Relations with Philosophy and Religion,* 4th rev. ed. (Cambridge, England, 1948), is an ambitious attempt to relate the history of science and religion; Kurd Lasswitz, *Geschichte de Atomistik vom Mittelalter bis Newton,* 2 vols. (Hamburg and Leipzig, 1890), is the best analysis of the Greek atomists in the Renaissance; George de Santillana and Edgar Zilsel, "The Development of Rationalism and Empiricism," *International Encyclopedia of Unified Science,* II, 8 (Chicago, 1941), is a brief but stimulating discussion of the origin of a scientific attitude; Abraham Wolf, *A History of Science, Technology and Philosophy in the Sixteenth and Seventeenth Centuries,* rev. ed. (London, 1950), a standard manual; Friedrich Dannemann, *Die Naturwissenschaften in ihrer Entwicklung und in ihrem Zusammenhange,* 2nd ed., 4 vols. (Leipzig, 1920–1923), a large-scale attempt to relate the developments between the several sciences; F. R. Johnson, "Preparation and Innovation in the Progress of Science," *Journal of the History of Ideas,* IV (1943), a stimulating article on the progress of scientific discovery.

The standard history of technology is Franz Marie Feldhaus, *Kulturgeschichte der Technik,* 2 vols. (Berlin, 1928). It should be read with Leonardo Olschki, *Geschichte der neusprachlichen Wissenschaftlichen Literatur,* 3 vols. (Heidelberg, 1919–1927), which discusses not only applied knowledge but also the theoretical background. An exhaustive history of the experimental method in Italy is provided in Raffaello Caverni, *Storia del metodo sperimentale in Italia,* 6 vols. (Florence, 1891-1900). See also the important article by John Hermann Randall, "The Development of Scientific Method in the School of Padua," *Journal of the History of Ideas,* I (1940), which was a pioneer study of the Paduan school. In Lynn Thorndike, *A History of Magic and Experimental Science,* 6 vols. (New York, 1923-1941), and, by the same author, *Science and Thought in the Fifteenth Century* (New York, 1929), we have in many ways the most complete discussion of the relationship between magic and experimental science. There are stimulating essays in M. F. Ashley Montagu, ed., *Studies and Essays in the History of Science and Learning Offered in Homage to George Sarton . . .* (New York, 1947), and the periodical, *Isis,* edited for many years by Sarton, should also be mentioned. The distinguished English historian of science, Charles Singer, has discussed the origins of scientific method in *Studies in the History and Method of Science,* 2 vols. (Oxford, 1917-1921). Pierre Duhem, *Études sur Léonard de Vinci,* 3 vols. (Paris, 1906-1913), is the most comprehensive of all studies on the scientific background of Leonardo da Vinci. A more recent work on Leonardo's mechanics is Ivor Blashka Hart, *The Mechanical Investigations of Leonardo da Vinci* (London, 1925). Edgar Zilsel, "The Sociological Roots of Science," *American Journal of Sociology,* XLVII (1942), contains a provocative discussion of that topic. The recent fourth centenary of Leonardo da Vinci's birth produced a series of studies on his work, of which the most valuable are *Léonard da Vinci et l'expérience scientifique au XVIe siècle* (Paris, 1953); *Atti del convegno di studi vinciani* (Firenze, 1953); and Ludwig Heydenreich, *Leonardo da Vinci,* 2 vols. (New York, 1955).

On particular branches of the sciences there are many good works. For mathematics in general see Walter W. R. Ball, *A Short Account of the History of Mathematics,* 4th ed. (London, 1908), and Florian Cajori, *A History of Mathematics,* 2nd ed. (New York, 1919). For mathematics in Italy, Guillaume Libri, *Histoire des sciences mathématiques en Italie, depuis la renaissance des lettres jusqu'à la fin du 17e siècle,* 4 vols. (Paris, 1838-41); for Germany, Siegmund Günther, *Geschichte des mathematischen Unterrichts im deutschen Mittelalter bis zum Jahre 1525* (Berlin, 1887). In physics, two recent studies are: Edward William Strong, *Procedures and Metaphysics; a Study in the Philosophy of Mathematical-physical Science in the 16th and 17th Centuries* (Berkeley, 1936), and Marshall Clagett, *Giovanni Marliani and Late Medieval Physics* (New York and London, 1941)—the latter particularly important. For astronomy, in addition to the major works of Duhem cited above, there are the general histories: John L. E. Dreyer, *History of the Planetary Systems from Thales to Kepler* (Cambridge, England, 1906), and Ernst Zinner, *Die Geschichte der Sternkunde von den ersten Anfängen bis zur Gegenwart* (Berlin, 1931). See also his *Geschichte und Bibliographie der astronomischen Literatur in Deutschland zur Zeit der Renaissance* (Leipzig, 1941). More special studies on Copernicus are: Edgar Zilsel, "Copernicus and Mechanics," *Journal of the History of Ideas,* I (1940), and Aleksander Birkenmajer, *Le premier système héliocentrique imaginé par Nicolas Copernic* (Warsaw, 1933); and Philip Paul Wiener, "The Tradition behind Galileo's Methodology," *Osiris,* I (1936), examines the tradition behind Galileo. Francis Rarick Johnson, *Astronomical Thought in Renaissance England* (Baltimore, 1937), is a special study of great interest. The two best general histories of chemistry are: John Maxson Stillman, *The Story of Early Chemistry* (New York, 1924), and James Riddick Partington, *A Short History of Chemistry* (London, 1937). For biology and medicine, see especially Arturo Castiglioni, *A History of Medicine,* translated from the Italian and edited by E. B. Krumbhaar, 2nd ed. (New York, 1947), and Charles Singer, *The Story of Living Things* (New York, 1931). Charles Singer, *A Short History of Medicine* (New York, 1928) is a good summary; Douglas Guthrie, *A History of Medicine* (London, 1945) is one of the most recent studies; and Arturo Castiglioni, *The Renaissance of Medicine in Italy* (Baltimore, 1934), is a special study by a great authority. On astrology and magic, in addition to the fundamental work by Thorndike cited above, see Franz Boll, *Sternglaube und Sterndeutung, die Geschichte und das Wesen der Astrologie,* 4th ed. (Leipzig, 1931), and Will Erich Peuckert, *Pansophie; ein Versuch zur Geschichte der weissen und schwarzen Magie* (Stuttgart, 1936).

INDEX

Acton, Lord, xiii
Aden, 44
Adolph of Veere, 206
Adrianople, 9
Africa, 11, 16, 32, 33
Age of Enlightenment, 266
Agnadello, 158
Agricola, Rudolph, 220
Agriculture, 61 ff.
Albania, 10
Albert of Brandenburg, 65, 249
Albert of Hapsburg, 93
Albert of Hohenzollern, 173 f.
Albert of Saxony, 253
Alberti, 147, 237
   Della famiglia, 231
Albertus Magnus, 197
Albuquerque, 27
Alcala, University of, 199, 209, 210, 211
Aldine press, 188, 190
Aldus Manutius, 188, 190
Aleander, 184
Alemanno, Johann, 197
Aleppo, 43
Alexander VI, 17, 18, 41, 76, 77, 157, 162, 180, 232, 237
Alexandria, 44, 147
Alfonso V, 40
Alfonso the Magnanimous, 233
Alliances, system of, 140
Almeida, Francisco de, 27
Alsace, 79
Alum, 53 f.
Amadis de Gaul, 246
Amboise, 233
America, discovery of, 31
Ancona, 17
Andlau, Peter von, *Monarchy of Caesar,* 129
Anjou, 82
Anne, Duchess, 82
Anti-Semitism, 198
Antwerp, 46, 121, 213
Apollo Belvedere, 237
Apollo, Horus, *Hieroglyphs,* 250
Appenzell, 118
Appian, 190
Aquinas, St. Thomas, 3, 184, 193, 197, 268
Arabs, 20, 34, 43
Aragon, 38, 73, 85 ff., 97, 98, 101
Archimedes, 255
Argonauts, 16

Argyropoulos, 257
Ariosto, 233
   Orlando Furioso, 244
Aristotle, 138, 184, 190, 193, 216, **253**
Art, 229 ff.
Artist and patron, 229 ff.
Asia, 22, 23, 27, 31
Asia Minor, 11, 17, 22
Asti, 83, 84
Atlantic, 28
Atlantis, 35
Augustan Rome, 230
Aurispa, Giovanni, 191
Ausonius, 183, 184
Austria, 93, 97
Averroes, 254
Avignon, 76
Azores, 24, 28
Aztec Empire, 31

Bacon, Roger, 34
Balance of power, 139 ff.
Balkans, 9, 13, 21, 22
Banks, 56 ff., 153 f.
Barbaro, Ermalao, 216
Barclay, *Ship of Fools,* 246
Bardi, 56
Basra, 43
Bayazid, 11, 17
Behaim globe, 256
Belgium, 80
Belgrade, 12
Bellini, Giovanni, 13, 250
   Feast of the Gods, 237
Bembo, Pietro, 267
Bentivogli, 117
Bessarion, Cardinal, 183, 184, 190
Biblical scholarship, 199 ff.
Biel, Gabriel, 2
Block-printing, 187 f.
Bobbio, 182
Boccaccio, 236
Bohemia, 55, 74, 93, 95, 96, 220
Boiardo, 233
   Orlando inamorato, 244
Bojeador, C., 33, 40
Bologna, 77, 117, 178, 255
   concordat of, 159, 170, 260, 263
Borgia, Caesar, 76 f., 158
   Lucrezia, 233
   Roderigo, 162

319

Revised January, 1970

hARpER ✦ torchbooks

PERRY MILLER: Errand Into the Wilderness
TB/1139
PERRY MILLER & T. H. JOHNSON, Eds.: The Puritans: *A Sourcebook of Their Writings*
Vol. I TB/1093; Vol. II TB/1094
EDMUND S. MORGAN: The Puritan Family: *Religion and Domestic Relations in Seventeenth Century New England* TB/1227
RICHARD B. MORRIS: Government and Labor in Early America TB/1244
WALLACE NOTESTEIN: The English People on the Eve of Colonization: 1603-1630. † *Illus.*
TB/3006
FRANCIS PARKMAN: The Seven Years War: *A Narrative Taken from Montcalm and Wolfe, The Conspiracy of Pontiac, and A Half-Century of Conflict. Edited by John H. McCallum* TB/3083
LOUIS B. WRIGHT: The Cultural Life of the American Colonies: 1607-1763. † *Illus.*
TB/3005
YVES F. ZOLTVANY, Ed.: The French Tradition in America + HR/1425

American Studies: The Revolution to 1860

JOHN R. ALDEN: The American Revolution: 1775-1783. † *Illus.* TB/3011
MAX BELOFF, Ed.: The Debate on the American Revolution, 1761-1783: *A Sourcebook*
TB/1225
RAY A. BILLINGTON: The Far Western Frontier: 1830-1860. † *Illus.* TB/3012
STUART BRUCHEY: The Roots of American Economic Growth, 1607-1861: *An Essay in Social Causation. New Introduction by the Author.*
TB/1350
WHITNEY R. CROSS: The Burned-Over District: *The Social and Intellectual History of Enthusiastic Religion in Western New York, 1800-1850* TB/1242
NOBLE E. CUNNINGHAM, JR., Ed.: The Early Republic, 1789-1828 + HR/1394
GEORGE DANGERFIELD: The Awakening of American Nationalism, 1815-1828. † *Illus.*
TB/3061
CLEMENT EATON: The Freedom-of-Thought Struggle in the Old South. *Revised and Enlarged. Illus.* TB/1150
CLEMENT EATON: The Growth of Southern Civilization, 1790-1860. † *Illus.* TB/3040
ROBERT H. FERRELL, Ed.: Foundations of American Diplomacy, 1775-1872 + HR/1393
LOUIS FILLER: The Crusade against Slavery: 1830-1860. † *Illus.* TB/3029
DAVID H. FISCHER: The Revolution of American Conservatism: *The Federalist Party in the Era of Jeffersonian Democracy* TB/1449
WILLIAM W. FREEHLING, Ed.: The Nullification Era: *A Documentary Record* ‡ TB/3079
WILLIM W. FREEHLING: Prelude to Civil War: *The Nullification Controversy in South Carolina, 1816-1836* TB/1359
PAUL W. GATES: The Farmer's Age: *Agriculture, 1815-1860* Δ TB/1398
FELIX GILBERT: The Beginnings of American Foreign Policy: *To the Farewell Address*
TB/1200
ALEXANDER HAMILTON: The Reports of Alexander Hamilton. ‡ *Edited by Jacob E. Cooke*
TB/3060
THOMAS JEFFERSON: Notes on the State of Virginia. ‡ *Edited by Thomas P. Abernethy*
TB/3052
FORREST MCDONALD, Ed.: Confederation and Constitution, 1781-1789 + HR/1396

BERNARD MAYO: Myths and Men: *Patrick Henry, George Washington, Thomas Jefferson*
TB/1108
JOHN C. MILLER: Alexander Hamilton and the Growth of the New Nation TB/3057
JOHN C. MILLER: The Federalist Era: 1789-1801. † *Illus.* TB/3027
RICHARD B. MORRIS, Ed.: Alexander Hamilton and the Founding of the Nation. *New Introduction by the Editor* TB/1448
RICHARD B. MORRIS: The American Revolution Reconsidered TB/1363
CURTIS P. NETTELS: The Emergence of a National Economy, 1775-1815 Δ TB/1438
DOUGLASS C. NORTH & ROBERT PAUL THOMAS, Eds.: *The Growth of the American Economy to 1860* + HR/1352
R. B. NYE: The Cultural Life of the New Nation: 1776-1830. † *Illus.* TB/3026
GILBERT OSOFSKY, Ed.: Puttin' On Ole Massa: *The Slave Narratives of Henry Bibb, William Wells Brown, and Solomon Northup* ‡
TB/1432
JAMES PARTON: The Presidency of Andrew Jackson. *From Volume III of the* Life of Andrew Jackson. *Ed. with Intro. by Robert V. Remini* TB/3080
FRANCIS S. PHILBRICK: The Rise of the West, 1754-1830. † *Illus.* TB/3067
MARSHALL SMELSER: The Democratic Republic, 1801-1815 † TB/1406
TIMOTHY L. SMITH: Revivalism and Social Reform: *American Protestantism on the Eve of the Civil War* TB/1229
JACK M. SOSIN, Ed.: The Opening of the West + HR/1424
GEORGE ROGERS TAYLOR: The Transportation Revolution, 1815-1860 Δ TB/1347
A. F. TYLER: Freedom's Ferment: *Phases of American Social History from the Revolution to the Outbreak of the Civil War. Illus.*
TB/1074
GLYNDON G. VAN DEUSEN: The Jacksonian Era: 1828-1848. † *Illus.* TB/3028
LOUIS B. WRIGHT: Culture on the Moving Frontier TB/1053

American Studies: The Civil War to 1900

W. R. BROCK: An American Crisis: *Congress and Reconstruction, 1865-67* ° TB/1283
T. C. COCHRAN & WILLIAM MILLER: The Age of Enterprise: *A Social History of Industrial America* TB/1054
W. A. DUNNING: Reconstruction, Political and Economic: 1865-1877 TB/1073
HAROLD U. FAULKNER: Politics, Reform and Expansion: 1890-1900. † *Illus.* TB/3020
GEORGE M. FREDRICKSON: The Inner Civil War: *Northern Intellectuals and the Crisis of the Union* TB/1358
JOHN A. GARRATY: The New Commonwealth, 1877-1890 † TB/1410
JOHN A. GARRATY, Ed.: The Transformation of American Society, 1870-1890 + HR/1395
WILLIAM R. HUTCHISON, Ed.: American Protestant Thought: *The Liberal Era* ‡ TB/1385
HELEN HUNT JACKSON: A Century of Dishonor: *The Early Crusade for Indian Reform.* † *Edited by Andrew F. Rolle* TB/3063
ALBERT D. KIRWAN: Revolt of the Rednecks: *Mississippi Politics, 1876-1925* TB/1199
WILLIAM G. MCLOUGHLIN, Ed.: The American Evangelicals, 1800-1900: An Anthology ‡
TB/1382
ARTHUR MANN: Yankee Reforms in the Urban Age: *Social Reform in Boston, 1800-1900*
TB/1247

ARNOLD M. PAUL: Conservative Crisis and the Rule of Law: *Attitudes of Bar and Bench, 1887-1895. New Introduction by Author*
TB/1415

JAMES S. PIKE: The Prostrate State: *South Carolina under Negro Government.* ‡ *Intro. by Robert F. Durden*
TB/3085

WHITELAW REID: After the War: *A Tour of the Southern States, 1865-1866.* ‡ *Edited by C. Vann Woodward*
TB/3066

FRED A. SHANNON: The Farmer's Last Frontier: ....*Agriculture, 1860-1897*
TB/1348

VERNON LANE WHARTON: The Negro in Mississippi, 1865-1890
TB/1178

American Studies: The Twentieth Century

RICHARD M. ABRAMS, Ed.: The Issues of the Populist and Progressive Eras, 1892-1912 +
HR/1428

RAY STANNARD BAKER: Following the Color Line: *American Negro Citizenship in Progressive Era.* ‡ *Edited by Dewey W. Grantham, Jr. Illus.*
TB/3053

RANDOLPH S. BOURNE: War and the Intellectuals: *Collected Essays, 1915-1919.* ‡ *Edited by Carl Resek*
TB/3043

A. RUSSELL BUCHANAN: The United States and World War II. † *Illus.*
Vol. I TB/3044; Vol. II TB/3045

THOMAS C. COCHRAN: The American Business System: *A Historical Perspective, 1900-1955*
TB/1080

FOSTER RHEA DULLES: America's Rise to World Power: 1898-1954. † *Illus.*
TB/3021

JEAN-BAPTISTE DUROSELLE: From Wilson to Roosevelt: *Foreign Policy of the United States, 1913-1945. Trans. by Nancy Lyman Roelker*
TB/1370

HAROLD U. FAULKNER: The Decline of Laissez Faire, 1897-1917
TB/1397

JOHN D. HICKS: Republican Ascendancy: 1921-1933. † *Illus.*
TB/3041

ROBERT HUNTER: Poverty: *Social Conscience in the Progressive Era.* ‡ *Edited by Peter d'A. Jones*
TB/3065

WILLIAM E. LEUCHTENBURG: Franklin D. Roosevelt and the New Deal: 1932-1940. † *Illus.*
TB/3025

WILLIAM E. LEUCHTENBURG, Ed.: The New Deal: *A Documentary History* +
HR/1354

ARTHUR S. LINK: Woodrow Wilson and the Progressive Era: 1910-1917. † *Illus.* TB/3023

BROADUS MITCHELL: Depression Decade: *From New Era through New Deal, 1929-1941* ∧
TB/1439

GEORGE E. MOWRY: The Era of Theodore Roosevelt and the Birth of Modern America: 1900-1912. † *Illus.*
TB/3022

WILLIAM PRESTON, JR.: Aliens and Dissenters: *Federal Suppression of Radicals, 1903-1933*
TB/1287

WALTER RAUSCHENBUSCH: Christianity and the Social Crisis. ‡ *Edited by Robert D. Cross*
TB/3059

GEORGE SOULE: Prosperity Decade: *From War to Depression, 1917-1929* ∆
TB/1349

GEORGE B. TINDALL, Ed.: A Populist Reader: *Selections from the Works of American Populist Leaders*
TB/3069

TWELVE SOUTHERNERS: I'll Take My Stand: *The South and the Agrarian Tradition. Intro. by Louis D. Rubin, Jr.; Biographical Essays by Virginia Rock*
TB/1072

Art, Art History, Aesthetics

CREIGHTON GILBERT, Ed.: Renaissance Art **
Illus.
TB/1465

EMILE MALE: The Gothic Image: *Religious Art in France of the Thirteenth Century.* § *190 illus.*
TB/344

MILLARD MEISS: Painting in Florence and Siena After the Black Death: *The Arts, Religion and Society in the Mid-Fourteenth Century. 169 illus.*
TB/1148

ERWIN PANOFSKY: Renaissance and Renascences in Western Art. *Illus.*
TB/1447

ERWIN PANOFSKY: Studies in Iconology: *Humanistic Themes in the Art of the Renaissance. 180 illus.*
TB/1077

JEAN SEZNEC: The Survival of the Pagan Gods: *The Mythological Tradition and Its Place in Renaissance Humanism and Art. 108 illus.*
TB/2004

OTTO VON SIMSON: The Gothic Cathedral: *Origins of Gothic Architecture and the Medieval Concept of Order. 58 illus.*
TB/2018

HEINRICH ZIMMER: Myths and Symbols in Indian Art and Civilization. *70 illus.* TB/2005

Asian Studies

WOLFGANG FRANKE: China and the West: *The Cultural Encounter, 13th to 20th Centuries. Trans. by R. A. Wilson*
TB/1326

L. CARRINGTON GOODRICH: A Short History of the Chinese People. *Illus.*
TB/3015

DAN N. JACOBS, Ed.: The New Communist Manifesto and Related Documents. *3rd revised edn.*
TB/1078

DAN N. JACOBS & HANS H. BAERWALD, Eds.: Chinese Communism: *Selected Documents*
TB/3031

BENJAMIN I. SCHWARTZ: Chinese Communism and the Rise of Mao
TB/1308

BENJAMIN I. SCHWARTZ: In Search of Wealth and Power: *Yen Fu and the West* TB/1422

Economics & Economic History

C. E. BLACK: The Dynamics of Modernization: *A Study in Comparative History* TB/1321

STUART BRUCHEY: The Roots of American Economic Growth, 1607-1861: *An Essay in Social Causation. New Introduction by the Author.*
TB/1350

GILBERT BURCK & EDITORS OF *Fortune:* The Computer Age: *And its Potential for Management*
TB/1179

JOHN ELLIOTT CAIRNES: The Slave Power. ‡ *Edited with Introduction by Harold D. Woodman*
TB/1433

SHEPARD B. CLOUGH, THOMAS MOODIE & CAROL MOODIE, Eds.: Economic History of Europe: *Twentieth Century* #
HR/1388

THOMAS C.COCHRAN: The American Business System: *A Historical Perspective, 1900-1955*
TB/1180

ROBERT A. DAHL & CHARLES E. LINDBLOM: Politics, Economics, and Welfare: *Planning and Politico-Economic Systems Resolved into Basic Social Processes*
TB/3037

PETER F. DRUCKER: The New Society: *The Anatomy of Industrial Order* TB/1082

HAROLD U. FAULKNER: The Decline of Laissez Faire, 1897-1917 ∆
TB/1397

PAUL W. GATES: The Farmer's Age: *Agriculture, 1815-1860* ∧
TB/1398

WILLIAM GREENLEAF, Ed.: American Economic Development Since 1860 +
HR/1353

J. L. & BARBARA HAMMOND: The Rise of Modern Industry. ‖ *Introduction by R. M. Hartwell*
TB/1417

3

ROBERT L. HEILBRONER: The Future as History: *The Historic Currents of Our Time and the Direction in Which They Are Taking America* TB/1386
ROBERT L. HEILBRONER: The Great Ascent: *The Struggle for Economic Development in Our Time* TB/3030
FRANK H. KNIGHT: The Economic Organization TB/1214
DAVID S. LANDES: Bankers and Pashas: *International Finance and Economic Imperialism in Egypt. New Preface by the Author* TB/1412
ROBERT LATOUCHE: The Birth of Western Economy: *Economic Aspects of the Dark Ages* TB/1290
ABBA P. LERNER: Everybody's Business: *A Reexamination of Current Assumptions in Economics and Public Policy* TB/3051
W. ARTHUR LEWIS: Economic Survey, 1919-1939 TB/1446
W. ARTHUR LEWIS: The Principles of Economic Planning. *New Introduction by the Author°* TB/1436
ROBERT GREEN MC CLOSKEY: American Conservatism in the Age of Enterprise TB/1137
PAUL MANTOUX: The Industrial Revolution in the Eighteenth Century: *An Outline of the Beginnings of the Modern Factory System in England°* TB/1079
WILLIAM MILLER, Ed.: Men in Business: *Essays on the Historical Role of the Entrepreneur* TB/1081
GUNNAR MYRDAL: An International Economy. *New Introduction by the Author* TB/1445
HERBERT A. SIMON: The Shape of Automation: *For Men and Management* TB/1245
PERRIN STRYER: The Character of the Executive: *Eleven Studies in Managerial Qualities* TB/1041
RICHARD S. WECKSTEIN, Ed.: Expansion of World Trade and the Growth of National Economies ** TB/1373

Education

JACQUES BARZUN: The House of Intellect TB/1051
RICHARD M. JONES, Ed.: Contemporary Educational Psychology: *Selected Readings* ** TB/1292
CLARK KERR: The Uses of the University TB/1264

Historiography and History of Ideas

HERSCHEL BAKER: The Image of Man: *A Study of the Idea of Human Dignity in Classical Antiquity, the Middle Ages, and the Renaissance* TB/1047
J. BRONOWSKI & BRUCE MAZLISH: The Western Intellectual Tradition: *From Leonardo to Hegel* TB/3001
EDMUND BURKE: On Revolution. Ed. by Robert A. Smith TB/1401
WILHELM DILTHEY: Pattern and Meaning in History: *Thoughts on History and Society.° Edited with an Intro. by H. P. Rickman* TB/1075
ALEXANDER GRAY: The Socialist Tradition: *Moses to Lenin °* TB/1375
J. H. HEXTER: More's Utopia: *The Biography of an Idea. Epilogue by the Author* TB/1195
H. STUART HUGHES: History as Art and as Science: *Twin Vistas on the Past* TB/1207
ARTHUR O. LOVEJOY: The Great Chain of Being: *A Study of the History of an Idea* TB/1009
JOSE ORTEGA Y GASSET: The Modern Theme. *Introduction by Jose Ferrater Mora* TB/1038

RICHARD H. POPKIN: The History of Scepticism from Erasmus to Descartes. *Revised Edition* TB/1391
G. J. RENIER: History: *Its Purpose and Method* TB/1209
MASSIMO SALVADORI, Ed.: Modern Socialism # HR/1374
GEORG SIMMEL et al.: Essays on Sociology, Philosophy and Aesthetics. *Edited by Kurt H. Wolff* TB/1234
BRUNO SNELL: The Discovery of the Mind: *The Greek Origins of European Thought* TB/1018
W. WARREN WAGER, ed.: European Intellectual History Since Darwin and Marx TB/1297
W. H. WALSH: Philosophy of History: In Introduction TB/1020

History: General

HANS KOHN: The Age of Nationalism: *The First Era of Global History* TB/1380
BERNARD LEWIS: The Arabs in History TB/1029
BERNARD LEWIS: The Middle East and the West ° TB/1274

History: Ancient

A. ANDREWS: The Greek Tyrants TB/1103
ERNST LUDWIG EHRLICH: A Concise History of Israel: *From the Earliest Times to the Destruction of the Temple in A.D. 70 °* TB/128
ADOLF ERMAN, Ed.: The Ancient Egyptians: *A Sourcebook of their Writings. New Introduction by William Kelly Simpson* TB/1233
THEODOR H. GASTER: Thespis: *Ritual Myth and Drama in the Ancient Near East* TB/1281
MICHAEL GRANT: Ancient History ° TB/1190
A. H. M. JONES, Ed.: A History of Rome through the Fifgth Century # *Vol. I: The Republic* HR/1364
Vol. II The Empire: HR/1460
SAMUEL NOAH KRAMER: Sumerian Mythology TB/1055
NAPHTALI LEWIS & MEYER REINHOLD, Eds.: Roman Civilization *Vol. I: The Republic* TB/1231
Vol. II: The Empire TB/1232

History: Medieval

MARSHALL W. BALDWIN, Ed.: Christianity Through the 13th Century # HR/1468
MARC BLOCH: Land and Work in Medieval Europe. *Translated by J. E. Anderson* TB/1452
HELEN CAM: England Before Elizabeth TB/1026
NORMAN COHN: The Pursuit of the Millennium: *Revolutionary Messianism in Medieval and Reformation Europe* TB/1037
G. G. COULTON: Medieval Village, Manor, and Monastery HR/1022
HEINRICH FICHTENAU: The Carolingian Empire: *The Age of Charlemagne. Translated with an Introduction by Peter Munz* TB/1142
GALBERT OF BRUGES: The Murder of Charles the Good: *A Contemporary Record of Revolutionary Change in 12th Century Flanders. Translated with an Introduction by James Bruce Ross* TB/1311
F. L. GANSHOF: Feudalism TB/1058
F. L. GANSHOF: The Middle Ages: *A History of International Relations. Translated by Rémy Hall* TB/1411
W. O. HASSALL, Ed.: Medieval England: *As Viewed by Contemporaries* TB/1205
DENYS HAY: The Medieval Centuries ° TB/1192
DAVID HERLIHY, Ed.: Medieval Culture and Society # HR/1340

J. M. HUSSEY: The Byzantine World   TB/1057
ROBERT LATOUCHE: The Birth of Western Economy: *Economic Aspects of the Dark Ages* °   TB/1290
HENRY CHARLES LEA: The Inquisition of the Middle Ages. || *Introduction by Walter Ullmann*   TB/1456
FERDINAND LOT: The End of the Ancient World and the Beginnings of the Middle Ages. *Introduction by Glanville Downey*   TB/1044
H. R. LOYN: The Norman Conquest   TB/1457
ACHILLE LUCHAIRE: Social France at the time of Philip Augustus. *Intro. by John W. Baldwin*   TB/1314
GUIBERT DE NOGENT: Self and Society in Medieval France: *The Memoirs of Guibert de Nogent*. || Edited by John F. Benton TB/1471
MARSILIUS OF PADUA: The Defender of Peace. *The Defensor Pacis. Translated with an Introduction by Alan Gewirth*   TB/1310
CHARLES PETET-DUTAILLIS: The Feudal Monarchy in France and England: *From the Tenth to the Thirteenth Century* °   TB/1165
STEVEN RUNCIMAN: A History of the Crusades Vol. I: *The First Crusade and the Foundation of the Kingdom of Jerusalem. Illus.*   TB/1143
Vol. II: *The Kingdom of Jerusalem and the Frankish East 1100-1187. Illus.*   TB/1243
Vol. III: *The Kingdom of Acre and the Later Crusades. Illus.*   TB/1298
J. M. WALLACE-HADRILL: The Barbarian West: *The Early Middle Ages, A.D. 400-1000*   TB/1061

History: Renaissance & Reformation

JACOB BURCKHARDT: The Civilization of the Renaissance in Italy. *Introduction by Benjamin Nelson and Charles Trinkaus. Illus.*   Vol. I TB/40;   Vol. II TB/41
JOHN CALVIN & JACOPO SADOLETO: A Reformation Debate. *Edited by John C. Olin*   TB/1239
FEDERICO CHABOD: Machiavelli and the Renaissance   TB/1193
THOMAS CROMWELL: Thomas Cromwell on Church and Commonwealth,: *Selected Letters 1523-1540.* ¶ *Ed. with an Intro. by Arthur J. Slavin*   TB/1462
R. TREVOR DAVIES: The Golden Century of Spain, 1501-1621 °   TB/1194
J. H. ELLIOTT: Europe Divided, 1559-1598 *a* °   TB/1414
G. R. ELTON: Reformation Europe, 1517-1559 ° *a*   TB/1270
DESIDERIUS ERASMUS: Christian Humanism and the Reformation: *Selected Writings. Edited and Translated by John C. Olin*   TB/1166
DESIDERIUS ERASMUS: Erasmus and His Age: *Selected Letters. Edited with an Introduction by Hans J. Hillerbrand. Translated by Marcus A. Haworth*   TB/1461
WALLACE K. FERGUSON et al.: Facets of the Renaissance   TB/1098
WALLACE K. FERGUSON et al.: The Renaissance: *Six Essays. Illus.*   TB/1084
FRANCESCO GUICCIARDINI: History of Florence. *Translated with an Introduction and Notes by Mario Domandi*   TB/1470
WERNER L. GUNDERSHEIMER, Ed.: French Humanism, 1470-1600. * *Illus.*   TB/1473
MARIE BOAS HALL, Ed.: Nature and Nature's Laws: *Documents of the Scientific Revolution* #   HR/1420
HANS J. HILLERBRAND, Ed., The Protestant Reformation #   HR/1342
JOHAN HUIZINGA: Erasmus and the Age of Reformation. *Illus.*   TB/19

JOEL HURSTFIELD: The Elizabethan Nation   TB/1312
JOEL HURSTFIELD, Ed.: The Reformation Crisis   TB/1267
PAUL OSKAR KRISTELLER: Renaissance Thought: *The Classic, Scholastic, and Humanist Strains*   TB/1048
PAUL OSKAR KRISTELLER: Renaissance Thought II: *Papers on Humanism and the Arts*   TB/1163
PAUL O. KRISTELLER & PHILIP P. WIENER, Eds.: Renaissance Essays   TB/1392
DAVID LITTLE: Religion, Order and Law: *A Study in Pre-Revolutionary England.* § *Preface by R. Bellah*   TB/1418
NICCOLO MACHIAVELLI: History of Florence and of the Affairs of Italy: *From the Earliest Times to the Death of Lorenzo the Magnificent. Introduction by Felix Gilbert*   TB/1027
ALFRED VON MARTIN: Sociology of the Renaissance. ° *Introduction by W. K. Ferguson*   TB/1099
GARRETT MATTINGLY et al.: Renaissance Profiles. *Edited by J. H. Plumb*   TB/1162
J. E. NEALE: The Age of Catherine de Medici °   TB/1085
J. H. PARRY: The Establishment of the European Hegemony: 1415-1715: *Trade and Exploration in the Age of the Renaissance* TB/1045
J. H. PARRY, Ed.: The European Reconnaissance: *Selected Documents* #   HR/1345
BUONACCORSO PITTI & GREGORIO DATI: Two Memoirs of Renaissance Florence: *The Diaries of Buonaccorso Pitti and Gregorio Dati. Edited with Intro. by Gene Brucker. Trans. by Julia Martines*   TB/1333
J. H. PLUMB: The Italian Renaissance: *A Concise Survey of Its History and Culture*   TB/1161
A. F. POLLARD: Henry VIII. *Introduction by A. G. Dickens.* °   TB/1249
RICHARD H. POPKIN: The History of Scepticism from Erasmus to Descartes   TB/139
PAOLO ROSSI: Philosophy, Technology, and the Arts, in the Early Modern Era 1400-1700. || *Edited by Benjamin Nelson. Translated by Salvator Attanasio*   TB/1458
FERDINAND SCHEVILL: The Medici. *Illus.*   TB/1010
FERDINAND SCHEVILL: Medieval and Renaissance Florence. *Illus.* Vol. I: *Medieval Florence*   TB/1090
Vol. II: *The Coming of Humanism and the Age of the Medici*   TB/1091
R. H. TAWNEY: The Agrarian Problem in the Sixteenth Century. *Intro. by Lawrence Stone*   TB/1315
H. R. TREVOR-ROPER: The European Witch-craze of the Sixteenth and Seventeenth Centuries and Other Essays °   TB/1416
VESPASIANO: Rennaissance Princes, Popes, and *XVth Century: The Vespasiano Memoirs. Introduction by Myron P. Gilmore. Illus.*   TB/1111

History: Modern European

RENE ALBRECHT-CARRIE, Ed.: The Concert of Europe #   HR/1341
MAX BELOFF: The Age of Absolutism, 1660-1815   TB/1062
OTTO VON BISMARCK: Reflections and Reminiscences. *Ed. with Intro. by Theodore S. Hamerow* ¶   TB/1357
EUGENE C. BLACK, Ed.: British Politics in the Nineteenth Century #   HR/1427

5

EUGENE C. BLACK, Ed.: European Political History, 1815-1870: *Aspects of Liberalism* ¶ TB/1331

ASA BRIGGS: The Making of Modern England, 1783-1867: *The Age of Improvement* ° TB/1203

D. W. BROGAN: The Development of Modern France ° Vol. I: *From the Fall of the Empire to the Dreyfus Affair* TB/1184
Vol. II: *The Shadow of War, World War I, Between the Two Wars* TB/1185

ALAN BULLOCK: Hitler, A Study in Tyranny. ° *Revised Edition. Illus.* TB/1123

EDMUND BURKE: On Revolution. *Ed. by Robert A. Smith* TB/1401

E. R. CARR: International Relations Between the Two World Wars. 1919-1939 ° TB/1279

E. H. CARR: The Twenty Years' Crisis, 1919-1939: *An Introduction to the Study of International Relations* ° TB/1122

GORDON A. CRAIG: From Bismarck to Adenauer: *Aspects of German Statecraft. Revised Edition* TB/1171

LESTER G. CROCKER, Ed.: The Age of Enlightenment # HR/1423

DENIS DIDEROT: The Encyclopedia: *Selections. Edited and Translated with Introduction by Stephen Gendzier* TB/1299

JACQUES DROZ: Europe between Revolutions, 1815-1848. ° *a Trans. by Robert Baldick* TB/1346

JOHANN GOTTLIEB FICHTE: Addresses to the German Nation. *Ed. with Intro. by George A. Kelly* ¶ TB/1366

FRANKLIN L. FORD: Robe and Sword: *The Re-Louis XIV* TB/1217

ROBERT & ELBORG FORSTER, Eds.: European Society in the Eighteenth Century # HR/1404

C. C. GILLISPIE: Genesis and Geology: *The Decades before Darwin* § TB/51

ALBERT GOODWIN, Ed.: The European Nobility in the Enghteenth Century TB/1313

ALBERT GOODWIN: The French Revolution TB/1064

ALBERT GUERARD: France in the Classical Age: *The Life and Death of an Ideal* TB/1183

JOHN B. HALSTED, Ed.: Romanticism # HR/1387

J. H. HEXTER: Reappraisals in History: *New Views on History and Society in Early Modern Europe* ° TB/1100

STANLEY HOFFMANN et al.: In Search of France: *The Economy, Society and Political System In the Twentieth Century* TB/1219

H. STUART HUGHES: The Obstructed Path: *French Social Thought in the Years of Desperation* TB/1451

JOHAN HUIZINGA: Dutch Civilisation in the 17th Century and Other Essays TB/1453

LIONAL KOCHAN: The Struggle for Germany: 1914-45 TB/1304

HANS KOHN: The Mind of Germany: *The Education of a Nation* TB/1204

HANS KOHN, Ed.: The Mind of Modern Russia: *Historical and Political Thought of Russia's Great Age* TB/1065

WALTER LAQUEUR & GEORGE L. MOSSE, Eds.: Education and Social Structure in the 20th Century. ° *Volume 6 of the Journal of Contemporary History* TB/1339

WALTER LAQUEUR & GEORGE L. MOSSE, Eds.: International Fascism, 1920-1945. ° *Volume 1 of the Journal of Contemporary History* TB/1276

WALTER LAQUEUR & GEORGE L. MOSSE, Eds.: Literature and Politics in the 20th Century. ° *Volume 5 of the Journal of Contemporary History.* TB/1328

WALTER LAQUEUR & GEORGE L. MOSSE, Eds.: The New History: *Trends in Historical Research and Writing Since World War II.* ° *Volume 4 of the Journal of Contemporary History* TB/1327

WALTER LAQUEUR & GEORGE L. MOSSE, Eds.: 1914: *The Coming of the First World War.* ° *Volume3 of the Journal of Contemporary History* TB/1306

C. A. MACARTNEY, Ed.: The Habsburg and Hohenzollern Dynasties in the Seventeenth and Eighteenth Centuries # HR/1400

JOHN MCMANNERS: European History, 1789-1914: *Men, Machines and Freedom* TB/1419

PAUL MANTOUX: The Industrial Revolution in the Eighteenth Century: *An Outline of the Beginnings of the Modern Factory System in England* TB/1079

FRANK E. MANUEL: The Prophets of Paris: *Turgot, Condorcet, Saint-Simon, Fourier, and Comte* TB/1218

KINGSLEY MARTIN: French Liberal Thought in the Eighteenth Century: *A Study of Political Ideas from Bayle to Condorcet* TB/1114

NAPOLEON III: Napoleonic Ideas: *Des Idées Napoléoniennes, par le Prince Napoléon-Louis Bonaparte. Ed. by Brison D. Gooch* ¶ TB/1336

FRANZ NEUMANN: Behemoth: *The Structure and Practice of National Socialism, 1933-1944* TB/1289

DAVID OGG: Europe of the Ancien Régime, 1715-1783 ° *a* TB/1271

GEORGE RUDE: Revolutionary Europe, 1783-1815 ° *a* TB/1272

MASSIMO SALVADORI, Ed.: Modern Socialism # TB/1374

HUGH SETON-WATSON: Eastern Europe Between the Wars, 1918-1941 TB/1330

DENIS MACK SMITH, Ed.: The Making of Italy, 1796-1870 # HR/1356

ALBERT SOREL: Europe Under the Old Regime. *Translated by Francis H. Herrick* TB/1121

ROLAND N. STROMBERG, Ed.: Realism, Naturalism, and Symbolism: *Modes of Thought and Expression in Europe, 1848-1914 #* HR/1355

A. J. P. TAYLOR: From Napoleon to Lenin: *Historical Essays* ° TB/1268

A. J. P. TAYLOR: The Habsburg Monarchy, 1809-1918: *A History of the Austrian Empire and Austria-Hungary* ° TB/1187

J. M. THOMPSON: European History, 1494-1789 TB/1431

DAVID THOMSON, Ed.: France: Empire and Republic, 1850-1940 # HR/1387

ALEXIS DE TOCQUEVILLE & GUSTAVE DE BEAUMONT: Tocqueville and Beaumont on Social Reform. *Ed. and trans. with Intro. by Seymour Drescher* TB/1343

G. M. TREVELYAN: British History in the Nineteenth Century and After: 1792-1919 ° TB/1251

H. R. TREVOR-ROPER: Historical Essays TB/1269

W. WARREN WAGAR, Ed.: Science, Faith, and MAN: *European Thought Since 1914 #* HR/1362

MACK WALKER, Ed.: Metternich's Europe, 1813-1848 # HR/1361

ELIZABETH WISKEMANN: Europe of the Dictators, 1919-1945 ° *a* TB/1273

JOHN B. WOLF: France: 1814-1919: *The Rise of a Liberal-Democratic Society* TB/3019

Literature & Literary Criticism

JACQUES BARZUN: The House of Intellect TB/1051

w. J. BATE: From Classic to Romantic: *Premises of Taste in Eighteenth Century England* TB/1036

VAN WYCK BROOKS: Van Wyck Brooks: The Early Years: *A Selection from his Works, 1908-1921* Ed. with Intro. by Claire Sprague TB/3082

ERNST R. CURTIUS: European Literature and the Latin Middle Ages. *Trans. by Willard Trask* TB/2015

RICHMOND LATTIMORE, Translator: The Odyssey of Homer TB/1389

JOHN STUART MILL: On Bentham and Coleridge. *Introduction by F. R. Leavis* TB/1070

SAMUEL PEPYS: The Diary of Samual Pepys. ° *Edited by O. F. Morshead. 60 illus. by Ernest Shepard* TB/1007

ROBERT PREYER, Ed.: Victorian Literature ** TB/1302

ALBION W. TOURGEE: A Fool's Errand: *A Novel of the South during Reconstruction. Intro. by George Fredrickson* TB/3074

BASIL WILEY: Nineteenth Century Studies: *Coleridge to Matthew Arnold* ° TB/1261

RAYMOND WILLIAMS: Culture and Society, 1780-1950 ° TB/1252

Philosophy

HENRI BERGSON: Time and Free Will: *An Essay on the Immediate Data of Consciousness* ° TB/1021

LUDWIG BINSWANGER: Being-in-the-World: *Selected Papers. Trans. with Intro. by Jacob Needleman* TB/1365

H. J. BLACKHAM: Six Existentialist Thinkers: *Kierkegaard, Nietzsche, Jaspers, Marcel, Heidegger, Sartre* ° TB/1002

J. M. BOCHENSKI: The Methods of Contemporary Thought. *Trans. by Peter Caws* TB/1377

CRANE BRINTON: Nietzsche. *Preface, Bibliography, and Epilogue by the Author* TB/1197

ERNST CASSIRER: Rousseau, Kant and Goethe. *Intro. by Peter Gay* TB/1092

FREDERICK COPLESTON, S. J.: Medieval Philosophy TB/376

F. M. CORNFORD: From Religion to Philosophy: *A Study in the Origins of Western Speculation* § TB/20

WILFRID DESAN: The Tragic Finale: *An Essay on the Philosophy of Jean-Paul Sartre* TB/1030

MARVIN FARBER: The Aims of Phenomenology: *The Motives, Methods, and Impact of Husserl's Thought* TB/1291

MARVIN FARBER: Basic Issues of Philosophy: *Experience, Reality, and Human Values* TB/1344

MARVIN FARBER: Phenomenology and Existence: *Towards a Philosophy within Nature* TB/1295

PAUL FRIEDLANDER: Plato: *An Introduction* TB/2017

MICHAEL GELVEN: A Commentary on Heidegger's "Being and Time" TB/1464

J. GLENN GRAY: Hegel and Greek Thought TB/1409

W. K. C. GUTHRIE: The Greek Philosophers: *From Thales to Aristotle* ° TB/1008

G. W. F. HEGEL: On Art, Religion Philosophy: *Introductory Lectures to the Realm of Absolute Spirit. || Edited with an Introduction by J. Glenn Gray* TB/1463

G. W. F. HEGEL: Phenomenology of Mind. ° || *Introduction by George Lichtheim* TB/1303

MARTIN HEIDEGGER: Discourse on Thinking. *Translated with a Preface by John M. Anderson and E. Hans Freund. Introduction by John M. Anderson* TB/1459

F. H. HEINEMANN: Existentialism and the Modern Predicament TB/28

WERER HEISENBERG: Physics and Philosophy: *The Revolution in Modern Science. Intro. by F. S. C. Northrop* TB/549

EDMUND HUSSERL: Phenomenology and the Crisis of Philosophy. § *Translated with an Introduction by Quentin Lauer* TB/1170

IMMANUEL KANT: Groundwork of the Metaphysic of Morals. *Translated and Analyzed by H. J. Paton* TB/1159

IMMANUEL KANT: Lectures on Ethics. § *Introduction by Lewis White Beck* TB/105

WALTER KAUFMANN, Ed.: Religion From Tolstoy to Camus: *Basic Writings on Religious Truth and Morals* TB/123

QUENTIN LAUER: Phenomenology: *Its Genesis and Prospect. Preface by Aron Gurwitsch* TB/1169

MAURICE MANDELBAUM: The Problem of Historical Knowledge: *An Answer to Relativism* TB/1338

GEORGE A. MORGAN: What Nietzsche Means TB/1198

H. J. PATON: The Categorical Imperative: *A Study in Kant's Moral Philosophy* TB/1325

MICHAEL POLANYI: Personal Knowledge: *Towards a Post-Critical Philosophy* TB/1158

KARL R. POPPER: Conjectures and Refutations: *The Growth of Scientific Knowledge* TB/1376

WILLARD VAN ORMAN QUINE: Elementary Logic *Revised Edition* TB/577

WILLARD VAN ORMAN QUINE: From a Logical Point of View: *Logico-Philosophical Essays* ° TB/566

JOHN E. SMITH: Themes in American Philosophy: *Purpose, Experience and Community* TB/1466

MORTON WHITE: Foundations of Historical Knowledge TB/1440

WILHELM WINDELBAND: A History of Philosophy *Vol. I: Greek, Roman, Medieval* TB/38 *Vol. II: Renaissance, Enlightenment, Modern* TB/39

LUDWIG WITTGENSTEIN: The Blue and Brown Books ° TB/1211

LUDWIG WITTGENSTEIN: Notebooks, 1914-1916 TB/1441

Political Science & Government

C. E. BLACK: The Dynamics of Modernization: *A Study in Comparative History* TB/1321

KENNETH E. BOULDING: Conflict and Defense: *A General Theory of Action* TB/3024

DENIS W. BROGAN: Politics in America. *New Introduction by the Author* TB/1469

CRANE BRINTON: English Political Thought in the Nineteenth Century TB/1071

ROBERT CONQUEST: Power and Policy in the USSR: *The Study of Soviet Dynastics* ° TB/1307

ROBERT A. DAHL & CHARLES E. LINDBLOM: Politics, Economics, and Welfare: *Planning and Politico-Economic Systems Resolved into Basic Social Processes* TB/1277

HANS KOHN: Political Ideologies of the 20th Century TB/1277

ROY C. MACRIDIS, Ed.: Political Parties: *Contemporary Trends and Ideas* ** TB/1322

ROBERT GREEN MC CLOSKEY: American Conservatism in the Age of Enterprise, 1865-1910 TB/1137

MARSILIUS OF PADUA: The Defender of Peace. *The Defensor Pacis. Translated with an Introduction by Alan Gewirth* TB/1310

KINGSLEY MARTIN: French Liberal Thought in the Eighteenth Century: *A Study of Political Ideas from Bayle to Condorcet* TB/1114

7

Religion: Early Christianity Through Reformation

ANSELM OF CANTERBURY: Truth, Freedom, and Evil: *Three Philosophical Dialogues*. *Edited and Translated by Jasper Hopkins and Herbert Richardson*   TB/317

MARSHALL W. BALDWIN, Ed.: Christianity through the 13th Century #   HR/1468

W. D. DAVIES: Paul and Rabbinic Judaism: *Some Rabbinic Elements in Pauline Theology. Revised Edition* °   TB/146

ADOLF DEISSMAN: Paul: *A Study in Social and Religious History*   TB/15

JOHANNES ECKHART: Meister Eckhart: *A Modern Translation by R. Blakney*   TB/8

EDGAR J. GOODSPEED: A Life of Jesus   TB/1

ROBERT M. GRANT: Gnosticism and Early Christianity   TB/136

WILLIAM HALLER: The Rise of Puritanism   TB/22

GERHART B. LADNER: The Idea of Reform: *Its Impact on the Christian Thought and Action in the Age of the Fathers*   TB/149

ARTHUR DARBY NOCK: Early Gentile Christianity and Its Hellenistic Background   TB/111

ARTHUR DARBY NOCK: St. Paul °   TB/104

ORIGEN: On First Principles. *Edited by G. W. Butterworth. Introduction by Henri de Lubac*   TB/311

GORDON RUPP: Luther's Progress to the Diet of Worms °   TB/120

Religion: The Protestant Tradition

KARL BARTH: Church Dogmatics: *A Selection. Intro. by H. Gollwitzer. Ed. by G. W. Bromiley*   TB/95

KARL BARTH: Dogmatics in Outline   TB/56

KARL BARTH: The Word of God and the Word of Man   TB/13

HERBERT BRAUN, et al.: God and Christ: *Existence and Province. Volume 5 of* Journal for Theology and the Church, *edited by Robert W. Funk and Gerhard Ebeling*   TB/255

WHITNEY R. CROSS: The Burned-Over District: *The Social and Intellectual History of Enthusiastic Religion in Western New York, 1800-1850*   TB/1242

NELS F. S. FERRE: Swedish Contributions to Modern Theology. *New Chapter by William A. Johnson*   TB/147

WILLIAM R. HUTCHISON, Ed.: American Protestant Thought: *The Liberal Era* ‡ TB/1385

ERNST KASEMANN, et al.: Distinctive Protestant and Catholic Themes Reconsidered. *Volume 3 of* Journal for Theology and the Church, *edited by Robert W. Funk and Gerhard Ebeling*   TB/253

SOREN KIERKEGAARD: On Authority and Revelation: *The Book on Adler, or a Cycle of Ethico-Religious Essays. Introduction by F. Sontag*   TB/139

SOREN KIERKEGAARD: Crisis in the Life of an Actress, *and Other Essays on Drama. Translated with an Introduction by Stephen Crites*   TB/145

SOREN KIERKEGAARD: Edifying Discourses. *Edited with an Intro. by Paul Holmer*   TB/32

SOREN KIERKEGAARD: The Journals of Kierkegaard. ° *Edited with an Intro. by Alexander Dru*   TB/52

SOREN KIERKEGAARD: The Point of View for My Work as an Author: *A Report to History.* § *Preface by Benjamin Nelson*   TB/88

SOREN KIERKEGAARD: The Present Age. § *Translated and edited by Alexander Dru. Introduction by Walter Kaufmann*   TB/94

SOREN KIERKEGAARD: Purity of Heart. *Trans. by Douglas Steere*   TB/4

SOREN KIERKEGAARD: Repetition: *An Essay in Experimental Psychology* §   TB/117

SOREN KIERKEGAARD: Works of Love: *Some Christian Reflections in the Form of Discourses*   TB/122

WILLIAM G. MCLOUGHLIN, Ed.: The American Evangelicals: 1800-1900: *An Anthology*   TB/1382

WOLFHART PANNENBERG, et al.: History and Hermeneutic. *Volume 4 of* Journal for Theology and the Church, *edited by Robert W. Funk and Gerhard Ebeling*   TB/254

JAMES M. ROBINSON, et al.: The Bultmann School of Biblical Interpretation: New Directions? *Volume 1 of* Journal for Theology and the Church, *edited by Robert W. Funk and Gerhard Ebeling*   TB/251

F. SCHLEIERMACHER: The Christian Faith. *Introduction by Richard R. Niebuhr.*
    Vol. I TB/108;   Vol. II TB/109

F. SCHLEIERMACHER: On Religion: *Speeches to Its Cultured Despisers. Intro. by Rudolf Otto*   TB/36

TIMOTHY L. SMITH: Revivalism and Social Reform: *American Protestantism on the Eve of the Civil War*   TB/1229

PAUL TILLICH: Dynamics of Faith   TB/42

PAUL TILLICH: Morality and Beyond   TB/142

EVELYN UNDERHILL: Worship   TB/10

Religion: The Roman & Eastern Christian Traditions

A. ROBERT CAPONIGRI, Ed.: Modern Catholic Thinkers II: *The Church and the Political Order*   TB/307

G. P. FEDOTOV: The Russian Religious Mind: *Kievan Christianity, the tenth to the thirteenth Centuries*   TB/370

GABRIEL MARCEL: Being and Having: *An Existential Diary. Introduction by James Collins*   TB/310

GABRIEL MARCEL: Homo Viator: *Introduction to a Metaphysic of Hope*   TB/397

Religion: Oriental Religions

TOR ANDRAE: Mohammed: *The Man and His Faith* §   TB/62

EDWARD CONZE: Buddhism: *Its Essence and Development.* ° *Foreword by Arthur Waley*   TB/58

EDWARD CONZE: Buddhist Meditation   TB/1442

EDWARD CONZE et al, Editors: Buddhist Texts through the Ages   TB/113

ANANDA COOMARASWAMY: Buddha and the Gospel of Buddhism   TB/119

H. G. CREEL: Confucius and the Chinese Way   TB/63

FRANKLIN EDGERTON, Trans. & Ed.: The Bhagavad Gita   TB/115

SWAMI NIKHILANANDA, Trans. & Ed.: The Upanishads   TB/114

D. T. SUZUKI: On Indian Mahayana Buddhism. ° *Ed. with Intro. by Edward Conze.* TB/1403

Religion: Philosophy, Culture, and Society

NICOLAS BERDYAEV: The Destiny of Man TB/61

RUDOLF BULTMANN: History and Eschatology: *The Presence of Eternity* °   TB/91

RUDOLF BULTMANN AND FIVE CRITICS: Kerygma and Myth: *A Theological Debate*   TB/80

9

RUDOLF BULTMANN and KARL KUNDSIN: Form
Criticism: *Two Essays on New Testament Re-
search. Trans. by F. C. Grant*　　TB/96
WILLIAM A. CLEBSCH & CHARLES R. JAEKLE: Pas-
toral Care in Historical Perspective: *An
Essay with Exhibits*　　TB/148
FREDERICK FERRE: Language, Logic and God.
New Preface by the Author　　TB/1407
LUDWIG FEUERBACH: The Essence of Christianity.
§ *Introduction by Karl Barth. Foreword by
H. Richard Niebuhr*　　TB/11
C. C. GILLISPIE: Genesis and Geology: *The
Decades before Darwin* §　　TB/51
ADOLF HARNACK: What Is Christianity? § *Intro-
duction by Rudolf Bultmann*　　TB/17
KYLE HASELDEN: The Racial Problem in Chris-
tian Perspective　　TB/116
MARTIN HEIDEGGER: Discourse on Thinking.
*Translated with a Preface by John M. Ander-
son and E. Hans Freund. Introduction by
John M. Anderson*　　TB/1459
IMMANUEL KANT: Religion Within the Limits of
Reason Alone. § *Introduction by Theodore
M. Greene and John Silber*　　TB/FG
WALTER KAUFMANN, Ed.: Religion from Tol-
stoy to Camus: *Basic Writings on Religious
Truth and Morals. Enlarged Edition*　　TB/123
JOHN MACQUARRIE: An Existentialist Theology:
A Comparison of Heidegger and Bultmann. °
Foreword by Rudolf Bultmann　　TB/125
H. RICHARD NIERUHR: Christ and Culture　　TB/3
H. RICHARD NIEBUHR: The Kingdom of God in
America　　TB/49
ANDERS NYGREN: Agape and Eros. *Translated by
Philip S. Watson* °　　TB/1430
JOHN H. RANDALL, JR.: The Meaning of Reli-
gion for Man. *Revised with New Intro. by
the Author*　　TB/1379
WALTER RAUSCHENBUSCHS Christianity and the
Social Crisis. ‡ *Edited by Robert D. Cross*
　　TB/3059
JOACHIM WACH: Understanding and Believing.
Ed. with Intro. by Joseph M. Kitagawa
　　TB/1399

Science and Mathematics

JOHN TYLER BONNER: The Ideas of Biology. Σ
Illus.　　TB/570
W. E. LE GROS CLARK: The Antecedents of
Man: *An Introduction to the Evolution of
the Primates.* ° *Illus.*　　TB/559
ROBERT E. COKER: Streams, Lakes, Ponds. *Illus.*
　　TB/586
ROBERT E. COKER: This Great and Wide Sea: *An
Introduction to Oceanography and Marine
Biology. Illus.*　　TB/551
W. H. DOWDESWELL: Animal Ecology. *61 illus.*
　　TB/543
C. V. DURELL: Readable Relativity. *Foreword by
Freeman J. Dyson*　　TB/530
GEORGE GAMOW: Biography of Physics. Σ *Illus.*
　　TB/567
F. K. HARE: The Restless Atmosphere　　TB/560
S. KORNER: The Philosophy of Mathematics: *An
Introduction*　　TB/547
J. R. PIERCE: Symbols, Signals and Noise: *The
Nature and Process of Communication* Σ
　　TB/574
WILLARD VAN ORMAN QUINE: Mathematical Logic
　　TB/558

Science: History

MARIE BOAS: The Scientific Renaissance, 1450-
1630 °　　TB/583
W. DAMPIER, Ed.: Readings in the Literature of
Science. *Illus.*　　TB/512

STEPHEN TOULMIN & JUNE GOODFIELD: The Architecture of Matter: *The Physics, Chemistry
and Physiology of Matter, Both Animate and
Inanimate, as it has Evolved since the Beginnings of Science*　　TB/584
STEPHEN TOULMIN & JUNE GOODFIELD: The Discovery of Time　　TB/585
STEPHEN TOULMIN & JUNE GOODFIELD: The Fab-
ric of the Heavens: *The Development of
Astronomy and Dynamics*　　TB/579

Science: Philosophy

J. M. BOCHENSKI: The Methods of Contempor-
ary Thought. *Tr. by Peter Caws*　　TB/1377
J. BRONOWSKI: Science and Human Values. *Re-
vised and Enlarged. Illus.*　　TB/505
WERNER HEISENBERG: Physics and Philosophy:
*The Revolution in Modern Science. Introduc-
tion by F. S. C. Northrop*　　TB/549
KARL R. POPPER: Conjectures and Refutations:
The Growth of Scientific Knowledge　　TB/1376
KARL R. POPPER: The Logic of Scientific Dis-
covery　　TB/576
STEPHEN TOULMIN: Foresight and Understand-
ing: *An Enquiry into the Aims of Science.
Foreword by Jacques Barzun*　　TB/564
STEPHEN TOULMIN: The Philosophy of Science:
An Introduction　　TB/513

Sociology and Anthropology

REINHARD BENDIX: Work and Authority in In-
dustry: *Ideologies of Management in the
Course of Industrialization*　　TB/3035
BERNARD BERELSON, Ed., The Behavioral Sci-
ences Today　　TB/1127
JOSEPH B. CASAGRANDE, Ed.: In the Company of
Man: *Twenty Portraits of Anthropological
Informants. Illus.*　　TB/3047
KENNETH B. CLARK: Dark Ghetto: *Dilemmas of
Social Power. Foreword by Gunnar Myrdal*
　　TB/1317
KENNETH CLARK & JEANNETTE HOPKINS: A Rele-
vant War Against Poverty: *A Study of Com-
munity Action Programs and Observable So-
cial Change*　　TB/1480
W. E. LE GROS CLARK: The Antecedents of Man:
*An Introduction to the Evolution of the
Primates.* ° *Illus.*　　TB/559
LEWIS COSER, Ed.: Political Sociology　　TB/1293
ROSE L. COSER, Ed.: Life Cycle and Achieve-
ment in America **　　TB/1434
ALLISON DAVIS & JOHN DOLLARD: Children of
Bondage: *The Personality Development of
Negro Youth in the Urban South* ‖
　　TB/3049
ST. CLAIR DRAKE & HORACE R. CAYTON: Black
Metropolis: *A Study of Negro Life in a
Northern City. Introduction by Everett C.
Hughes. Tables, maps, charts, and graphs*
　　Vol. I TB/1086; Vol. II TB/1087
PETER E. DRUCKER: The New Society: *The Anat-
omy of Industrial Order*　　TB/1082
CORA DU BOIS: The People of Alor. *With a
Preface by the Author*
　　Vol. I *Illus.* TB/1042; Vol. II TB/1043
EMILE DURKHEIM et al.: Essays on Sociology
and Philosophy: *with Appraisals of Durk-
heim's Life and Thought.* ‖ *Edited by Kurt
H. Wolff*　　TB/1151
LEON FESTINGER, HENRY W. RIECKEN, STANLEY
SCHACHTER: When Prophecy Fails: *A Social
and Psychological Study of a Modern Group
that Predicted the Destruction of the World* ‖
　　TB/1132

11